THE
CABINET

THE
CABINET

GEORGE WASHINGTON AND THE

CREATION OF AN AMERICAN

INSTITUTION

LINDSAY M. CHERVINSKY

THE BELKNAP PRESS OF
HARVARD UNIVERSITY PRESS

CAMBRIDGE, MASSACHUSETTS
LONDON, ENGLAND   2020

First printing

Cataloging-in-Publication Data available from the Library of Congress

ISBN: 978-0-674-98648-0

To Jake and JQDA

Contents

THE
CABINET

Introduction

At ELEVEN THIRTY in the morning on August 22, 1789, a large cream-colored coach pulled up to the front door of Federal Hall at 26 Wall Street in New York City. Six matching, perfectly groomed horses pulled the elegant carriage with sparkling gold trim. The coachman, outfitted in crisp white- and red-trimmed livery, jumped down from the back of the carriage and opened the door. An elegantly dressed man with powdered hair stepped down with a portfolio of papers under his arm. He towered over his companion, Henry Knox, the acting secretary of war, and his slaves tending to his horses. His ornate coach and his imposing presence drew curious stares from strangers passing by on the street. He walked up to the front door of Federal Hall and was immediately announced to the Senate. George Washington, the first president of the United States, had arrived for his first visit to the United States Senate.

This was no ordinary meeting. Two years earlier, the delegates at the Constitutional Convention in Philadelphia had agreed that the Senate would "advise and consent" on treaties and other questions of foreign policy. But in practice, how the president and the Senate would interact remained for the first officeholders to work out.

Washington's relationship with the Senate was just one of countless governing details that he had to establish as the first president. Establishing precedent for every presidential action consumed his thoughts in the first few years of his administration.[1] Not only would the American public and an international audience judge his every action, but his successors would be guided by his choices. The stakes could not have been higher; the future of the Republic rested on Washington making the right decisions. He approached every new situation with caution and took action only after consulting with his advisors. His first visit to the Senate was no different.

The tense relationship between Native American nations and the United States posed an immediate challenge after Washington's inauguration on April 30, 1789. Most Native American nations had sided with the British during the Revolutionary War, recognizing the threat that American settlers posed to native land.[2] On September 15, 1789, representatives from the national government, North and South Carolina, the Creeks, and the Cherokees planned to meet to discuss the controversial treaties signed between 1783 and 1789, and to negotiate a new treaty. Washington had to select the representatives to send on behalf of the federal government—another important first for the new president.

At his August 22 meeting with the Senate, Washington planned to seek advice about what instructions he should give to the commissioners. Because he considered Native American relations to fall under the heading of "foreign policy," he followed the constitutional guidelines calling for him to meet with the Senate. On May 25, 1789, less than one month after his inauguration, Washington sent to the Senate all of the United States' previous treaties with Indian nations, along with a number of supporting documents.[3] After a brief discussion, the Senate postponed its consideration of these papers. At the beginning of August, the Senate created a committee to meet with Washington. The committee planned the minute details of the upcoming meeting, down to where Washington would sit and how he would enter the chamber. On August 20 and 21, Washington nominated commissioners to negotiate with the "Southern Indians." On August 21, he sent an official note to the Senate announcing his visit the next day to discuss the terms of the proposed treaty.[4]

When Washington and Knox arrived at Federal Hall at 11:30 A.M., the doorkeeper announced their arrival. Washington sat at the front of the chamber, and Knox took the chair to his right. Washington handed his remarks to Knox, who in turn handed them to Vice President John Adams. Adams read the statement, but as Senator William Maclay from Pennsylvania recalled, the senators could "not master . . . one Sentence of it."[5] Adams wasn't known for his public speaking skills, but the senators' struggles weren't entirely his fault. The Senate gathered for their work in the large chamber that occupied the first floor of Federal Hall. Because of the August heat in New York City, the doorkeeper had opened the windows in search of a cooling breeze. But along with fresh air, noise from Wall Street's pedestrians, carriages, peddlers, and horses flowed into the Senate chamber. The clamor overpowered Adams's voice, so few senators could make out the words that Washington had carefully crafted. After a few complaints, Adams repeated the speech from the beginning. Washington's remarks offered a brief synopsis of the current diplomatic state between the United States and the Southern Indians, and posed seven questions for the Senate to answer with an aye or a no.[6]

Adams finished his recitation and sat. The seconds ticked by as the senators remained in awkward silence. A few shuffled papers or cleared their throats. Maclay speculated in his diary that his colleagues were so intimidated by Washington's presence in the Senate chamber that they cowered in shameful silence. Eager to show that they could be active participants in the creation of foreign policy, Maclay stood up and suggested referring Washington's seven questions to committee for discussion in detail. Washington lost his temper, stood up, and shouted, "This defeats every purpose of my coming here!" The senators fell into a stunned hush before Washington acquiesced to Maclay's suggestion and offered to return to the Senate a few days later.[7] Although he did return the following Monday, his first visit to the Senate was an inauspicious start to the executive-legislative relationship. As he returned to his carriage, Washington muttered under his breath that he would never return for advice. He kept his word—August 22, 1789, was the first and last time he visited the Senate to request guidance on foreign affairs.[8] Unfortunately, the diplomatic challenges facing the United States during the Washington presidency were just beginning.

More than two years later, on November 26, 1791, Washington invited the department secretaries and the attorney general to the first cabinet meeting. Secretary of War Henry Knox, Secretary of State Thomas Jefferson, Secretary of the Treasury Alexander Hamilton, and Attorney General Edmund Randolph convened in Washington's private study on the second floor of the President's House in Philadelphia.[9] The cabinet met a handful of times in 1791 and 1792 before the threat of international war with France and Great Britain forced the cabinet to meet fifty-one times in 1793. By mid-1793, the cabinet served as a visible, central part of the executive branch.

Despite the important role that the cabinet would come to play, the United States Constitution actually does not mention a cabinet at all. Article II permits the president to request advice from the department secretaries, but specifies that the secretaries must provide their opinions in writing. Nor did Congress pass any legislation to authorize the cabinet or regulate its meetings. On the contrary, in 1787, the delegates to the Constitutional Convention rejected several proposals for an executive council, including a proposal by Charles Cotesworth Pinckney that would have established a cabinet almost identical to the one that Washington eventually created.

So where did the cabinet come from? Washington designed the cabinet to provide advice and support during crucial diplomatic crises and constitutional conundrums. He did not enter the presidency intending to create the cabinet, and he explored many alternatives before establishing this new institution. In fact, Washington did not convene the first cabinet meeting until November 26, 1791—more than two and a half years into his administration. Yet as he grappled with the threat of international invasion, domestic insurrection, and challenges to presidential authority, Washington became convinced that the options outlined in the Constitution were insufficient to get the job done. The first cabinet developed organically in response to these governing challenges.

Washington selected experienced politicians and diplomats for his department secretary positions. But he also chose individuals whose advice he trusted: he intended to listen to their opinions, at first individually and then collectively in the cabinet. Washington selected Edmund Randolph as the first attorney general based on his lengthy legal career, his extensive state experience in Virginia, and their decades-long friendship. Washington chose Alexander Hamilton for secretary of the treasury and Henry Knox for secretary of war because of their loyal service to him in the Continental Army. He also valued Hamilton's state service and the expertise Knox acquired as secretary of war under the Confederation Congress. Washington picked Thomas Jefferson as the first secretary of state thanks to Jefferson's stint as the American minister to France and his expansive diplomatic knowledge. Washington placed great weight on his secretaries' opinions.

Washington and his secretaries were shaped by war, politics, cultural exchange, and foreign sojourns in the eighteenth century. They were products of an intertwined Atlantic world, just like the new nation they represented. As they created institutions and customs from scratch, they relied on their previous experiences to inform their decisions.

Washington did not design the cabinet in a vacuum. Once he determined that he needed a cabinet to govern the new nation, he drew on several existing institutions to shape his interactions with the department secretaries. As commander in chief of the Continental Army during the Revolutionary War, Washington had summoned councils of war with his officers and aides-de-camp. He relied on councils before entering major military engagements, selecting locations for winter quarters, or undertaking controversial retreats. As president of the United States, Washington used cabinet meetings for similar purposes. He called a cabinet meeting before establishing constitutional precedent, responding to a domestic rebellion, or signing a potentially unpopular treaty. Washington also employed many of the same strategies in both councils and cabinets. He often sent questions to the participants in advance and then used those questions as the meeting's agenda. If the attendees disagreed with each other, Washington requested written opinions after the end of the discussion. These opinions allowed him to consider everyone's position and make a final decision at his own pace.

Washington's secretaries also left their own stamp on the creation of the cabinet. The secretaries were well-regarded, elite, prideful gentlemen. They expected to be treated with respect and to have their advice considered by the president. They were also stubborn and opinionated. In short, they would not have engaged in frequent cabinet discussions unless they were willing to participate. Once gathered in

Washington's private study, their outsized personalities shaped the cabinet and its goals. While they all agreed that Washington had the final say, the secretaries brought their own unique perspectives to each cabinet debate.

Although Washington remained the unquestioned leader of the administration, his relationship with the cabinet developed in a symbiotic way. If the cabinet unanimously opposed an approach he wished to take, he would not adopt it. At the same time, the secretaries did not pursue initiatives without his consent. As Washington and the secretaries toiled in the cabinet, they pursued two shared goals. First, they strove to protect and assert executive jurisdiction over both foreign and domestic issues. To preserve and expand presidential authority, they sidelined Congress and the state governments. Even Jefferson, who later criticized Washington's expansion of executive power, initially opposed congressional attempts to interfere in diplomacy. Second, the president and the secretaries viewed the cabinet as a tool to bolster and defend executive power, not to limit or compete with the president. In the summer of 1794, when violence erupted in western Pennsylvania over excise taxes on whiskey, the secretaries persuaded, berated, and threatened state officials to ensure that Washington and the executive branch would lead the federal response against the rebellion. The department secretaries promoted the powers of the executive, but they did not seek to expand their own authority at the expense of the president.

Washington and the secretaries were committed to ensuring that the president had sufficient power to lead the nation, but they never expected the cabinet to serve as the giant administrative institution that we see in the twenty-first century. Instead, they expected cabinet meetings to provide private support and guidance for the president. The secretaries maintained their bureaucratic roles and consulted individually with the president on most department matters. When they gathered for a cabinet meeting, they provided Washington with support and guidance on larger, more complicated issues that defied categorization in one department. As a result, the cabinet was inherently idiosyncratic. Washington convened frequent meetings when it suited him and ignored the cabinet in favor of one-on-one consultations when he felt that approach would provide better advice.

Many of these characters and moments will be familiar to both historians and those reading about the Early Republic for the first time. Scholars have rightly covered Washington's inauguration, the feud between Thomas Jefferson and Alexander Hamilton, the Neutrality Crisis, the Whiskey Rebellion, and the Jay Treaty debates as defining moments in the Early Republic and the formation of the nation.[10] But these stories have all been told assuming that the cabinet existed from the very beginning of Washington's presidency and that it occupied an immutable position in the executive branch. It didn't. The institution's beginnings remain obscure and its relationship to the larger executive branch unexplored. Henry Barrett Learned wrote in 1912 about the legislative origins of the nine executive departments then in existence; amazingly, this was the last work published on the creation of the cabinet.[11]

I have built on the excellent scholarship exploring the political institutions and social life in the Early Republic. Scholars have examined the political culture of the Early Republic, emphasizing how honor and reputation provided strict guidelines for discourse and public behavior. With such high stakes for personal reputation and the future of the new nation, anxiety pervaded every social interaction.[12] Others have done innovative work on the Republican Court—the semi-private gatherings hosted by women to provide space for informal discourse on theater, culture, and above all politics.[13] Recent scholarship has also analyzed the formation of state institutions, including the custom houses under Treasury Department supervision and the fiscal-military complex that enabled the growth of the government and the nation during the Early Republic.[14]

I bring together these discussions of political culture and institutions to offer the first comprehensive study of the executive branch. The growing state institutions and the broader cultural themes in the Early Republic depended on a small group of people showing up to the office every day and engaging in social rituals. While the larger social and political developments are critical to understanding society in the Early Republic, so too are the personal stories that led the institutions and crafted the sociopolitical trends. The emergence of the cabinet is the story of a few individuals who operated under unique social pressures to build the beginnings of an influential new institution.

Many historians believe that federal governance took an "executive turn" late in the nineteenth century. Contrary to that narrative, the origins of the president's cabinet in Washington's administration demonstrate that the executive had developed significant authority long before the nineteenth century.[15] While the federal government and all of its bureaucracies certainly expanded after the Civil War and up through the New Deal, this book shows how George Washington and his cabinet asserted presidential prerogative, claimed authority over diplomatic and domestic issues, and rejected challenges from the states and Congress that aimed to diminish executive authority. The president was no mere figurehead during the Early Republic.

We will begin our story in the Revolutionary War, following the wartime experiences of Washington's cabinet members as patriots, reformers, state representatives, and finally federal officials. The chronological development of the cabinet is critical for three reasons. First, exploring the 1780s shows what Washington, the secretaries, and the nation faced during the Revolutionary War. Second, by tracing the gradual evolution of the presidency, we can see how events in the Early Republic shaped the national government's interpretation of its own power and Washington's creation of the cabinet within the new federal framework. The cabinet, the presidency, and the rest of the government emerged reactively in response to the challenges faced by the new nation. Finally, working our way through the first few years of Washington's presidency emphasizes how the cabinet emerged slowly in response to the pressures of governing, and only near the end of Washington's first term. Most people incorrectly assume that the cabinet existed from day one of Washington's presidency or that its development was inevitable—especially since the original cabinet members occupied their offices starting in the fall of 1789. On the contrary, Washington created the cabinet only after he had tried other options.

The book opens with Washington's experience as commander in chief of the Continental Army. Washington convened councils of war with his officers and aides-de-camp, where he learned how to manage the outsized personalities in his officer corps. He also established a social life in camp to boost morale for his soldiers, host visiting dignitaries, and foster relationships with civilian authorities. He drew on all these experiences as president.

The wartime experiences of the future department secretaries were equally important. All of Washington's appointees served in the military, in the state governments, or in the Confederation Congress. Their frustrations directly shaped their contributions to the president's cabinet a few years later.

We then explore the political culture in the 1780s leading up to the Constitutional Convention, including Americans' efforts to grapple with their Anglo-American heritage. The new nation struggled to define its character, especially in relation to the British Empire. We will consider how the delegates at the convention tried to respond to these concerns in the Constitution by providing elected advisors for the president, and will examine the expectations for the new executive leading up to Washington's inauguration on April 30, 1789.

Drawing on his previous military experience, Washington spent the first two years of his administration establishing a working atmosphere that befitted a virtuous republic and negotiating interactions with the other branches of government. In tracking the cabinet's eventual emergence as the president's advisory body, we will see Washington's preferred cabinet practices, how the secretaries interacted, and how the public responded to the emerging institution.

In the Neutrality Crisis of 1793, we will trace the cabinet's efforts to keep the new nation out of a dangerous international war. The cabinet fought to establish the president's control over the diplomatic process and ensure that foreign nations respected the president's authority. Faced with its first major diplomatic crisis, the cabinet gathered fifty-one times—the high-water mark for cabinet activity in Washington's presidency. In another moment of crisis, the Whiskey Rebellion in 1794 underlined the cabinet's central role in formulating the military response to the insurrection and ensuring that state and federal authorities complied with the president's orders. Finally, we will examine the debates over the Jay Treaty in 1795 and 1796, and the cabinet's further development, including the first major cabinet scandal and Washington's return to individual conferences with trusted advisors.

The book concludes with a consideration of the short- and long-term consequences of Washington's cabinet precedents. He intended for the cabinet to serve as a personal advisory body and for each president to craft his or her own relationships with their advisors. Washington's successor, John Adams, struggled with that flexibility, while Jefferson, the nation's third president, thrived with the opportunity to create his own cabinet practices. We will also explore how the power of Washington's precedents and the cabinet tradition continues to guide modern presidents.

By centering our exploration of Washington's administration on his cabinet, we will better understand several pivotal moments in the early years of the new nation. By 1793, Hamilton and Jefferson hated each other. Yet as fellow members of Washington's cabinet, they found themselves confined in a small room for hours on end, several days a week, stifling in the Philadelphia summer heat. Their participation in the cabinet exacerbated partisan tensions and accelerated the development of the first party system. The cabinet supported the growth of executive power and greatly expanded the role of the president in both domestic and diplomatic issues. Cabinet machinations also ensured that Congress and the state governments were kept out of these critical moments. Finally, Washington's relationship with the cabinet sheds new light on the precedents established by the first president. Washington tinkered with cabinet practices throughout his administration, summoning regular meetings at certain times and preferring written advice and individual conferences at others.

The cabinet stood at the center of almost every major development in the 1790s and reveals the power and importance of the executive branch in the Early Republic. It was the product of the first officeholders and reflected their backgrounds and governing experience. It emerged in response to the international challenges, domestic pressures, and pervasive anxieties about the future of the Republic. The formation of the cabinet thus embodies the emergence of the United States. And— like the United States—it might not have survived at all.

I

Forged in War

DURING THE REVOLUTIONARY WAR, the thirteen rebelling colonies experienced violence, disruption, and expansive change. Families lost loved ones, rummaging soldiers and cannon fire damaged farms, and naval warfare on the high seas destroyed businesses. Many individuals who survived the war found that their perspective on society and government had changed dramatically. Each state produced its own new constitution, and in 1781, the Continental Congress adopted the Articles of Confederation as its governing charter. George Washington's role during the war offered him a unique perspective on the nation's evolution—he experienced the loss and devastation firsthand, but the war also prepared him for future leadership.

Washington began his military career as a major in the Virginia militia. In 1753, he experienced his first grand adventure when he completed a 300-mile journey to report on French military movements in the Allegheny River Valley.[1] The next year, in his new rank as colonel, Washington led 300 men to attack the French at Fort Duquesne (now Pittsburgh). This mission was a complete disaster. On July 3, 1754, Washington signed articles of surrender and was forced to abandon the newly constructed Fort Necessity, and the skirmish accelerated the outbreak of the Seven Years' War between France, Great Britain, and their respective allies.[2] Despite the defeat, Washington was appointed as an aide-de-camp to General Edward Braddock. While serving with Braddock, Washington again faced battle, this time serving bravely to organize the British forces after Braddock's death on the battlefield. In recognition of his service, the Virginia House of Burgesses promoted Washington again, and at just twenty-three years old he became the commander of all Virginia troops. For the next few years, the Virginia forces under Washington's command fought admirably, including at a battle that captured Fort Duquesne from the French. In 1758, Washington resigned from the military out of disgust for politicians' lack of support for the war and the troops. But he did not discard his uniform.[3]

On May 10, 1775, Washington attended the first meeting of the Second Continental Congress in Philadelphia as one of the selected delegates from Virginia.[4] John Adams, a delegate from Massachusetts, noted to his wife, Abigail, "Coll. Washington appears at Congress in his Uniform and, by his great Experience and Abilities in military Matters, is of much service to Us."[5] A few weeks later, Adams spearheaded the effort to appoint Washington "GENERAL AND COMMANDER IN CHIEF of the army of the United Colonies and of all the forces raised."[6]

At the pinnacle of his military career, Washington understood the high stakes of the war better than anyone—if he failed, independence would fail. Furthermore, if Washington lost the war, he and all of the other rebel leaders would be executed. He observed firsthand the violence and destruction of the war. Washington gained invaluable leadership and managerial experience during the war. He developed leadership strategies to manage his officers, obtain advice, and navigate the sometimes conflicting political aims of the army, civilians, and Congress. When Congress struggled to supply the army or oversee the war

FIGURE 1.1 George Washington, Charles Willson Peale, 1776. White House Historical Association

effort, he urged government reform to meet the demands of the new nation. Washington witnessed Congress's attempts to professionalize the executive committee system, and he became convinced that the new nation needed a strong central government to survive.

Once Washington assumed leadership over the executive branch, he used his experience as commander in chief as a template for governing, creating social environments, and managing complex personalities. He faced similarly high stakes as he had during the Revolution— if he failed, the nation would fail. Washington drew inspiration from his leadership experience as commander in chief of the Continental Army during the Revolutionary War in four ways. First, he modeled cabinet meetings after his councils of war. Second, he developed an administrative system that allowed him to monitor important developments and correspondence, delegate the details to subordinates, and employ his department secretaries as ambassadors for the executive branch, just as his aides had represented his authority as commander in chief. Third, he recreated a social environment similar to the one he had enjoyed at headquarters. Fourth, he supported government reforms that produced independent executive departments in the Confederation Congress. The First Federal Congress adopted these departments in 1789, creating the positions that would become Washington's secretaries. His presidential leadership cannot be understood without first analyzing his military experience.

Washington's councils of war and their collaborative atmosphere were an integral part of his war command and the first leadership element that he replicated as president. As commander in chief, Washington convened councils of war when he wished to consult multiple officers before significant decisions.[7] These councils served several purposes:

they provided advice, helped Washington build consensus among his officers, and offered political cover for controversial decisions. Washington usually hosted the councils in his dining room at headquarters. If he summoned a council during a battle, the officers would gather at a local house or tavern. When the Continental Congress appointed him to the Continental Army, they instructed him to follow the British tradition of consulting with councils of war, but expected Washington to put his own spin on the institution.[8] Congress directed Washington to "use your best circumspection and (advising with your council of war) to order and dispose of the said army under your command."[9] Washington initially interpreted Congress's instructions as orders to secure the council's approval for all major measures.[10] After his defeat in New York in the summer of 1776, however, Congress encouraged him to follow his own judgment and noted that they intended councils simply to advise. John Adams explained that the instruction meant "only that Councils of War, should be called and their Opinions and Reasons demanded, but the General like all other Commanders of Armies, was to pursue his own Judgment after all."[11] Thereafter, Washington convened meetings less frequently and occasionally issued orders against his officers' advice. He never dictated policy at his councils, however, instead preferring to gather advice from his officers before making his own decision. Washington called councils before commencing almost every major engagement, establishing winter quarters, or adopting a controversial position throughout his tenure as commander in chief.

Washington employed a few strategies to manage his councils of war. Prior to summoning his officers, he almost always developed a series of questions. He often submitted these questions to his officers in advance of the council to give them time to consider the issues and offer thoughtful advice. For example, on October 8, 1775, Washington asked seven questions, including "What Number of Men are sufficient for Winters Campaign," "Can the pay of the privates be reduced & how much," and "What Regulations are further necessary for the Government of the Forces?"[12] He then used these questions to control the agenda of the meeting. If the officers failed to reach a unanimous decision, he requested written opinions from each officer at the completion of the meeting.

These written opinions served two purposes. First, some of the officers possessed big personalities and dominated council debates. Charles Lee, for example, usually entered a room flanked by a rowdy pack of hounds baying at his heels. As one of the most experienced officers, he was quick to assert his seniority and his opinions. He cared little for human companionship, so he rarely considered *how* he offered his wisdom or whether his words offended the other officers.[13] By requesting written opinions, Washington ensured that more reserved officers had the opportunity to share their positions, and he was able to gather as much advice and information as possible. Second, he preferred to consider all options and come to a final decision slowly, which he would then implement immediately and decisively. The written opinions gave Washington more time to consider each position in private.

Washington used councils of war for many purposes. From the beginning of his command, he employed councils to build consensus for an upcoming campaign. Washington found this strategy especially helpful during his first year as commander in chief, when he was building relationships with an officer corps that did not know him or have much reason to trust his leadership. In several councils of war held during the fall of 1775, he proposed an attack on the British troops in Boston. As the new commander in chief, Washington was eager to prove himself. The first round of army enlistments was about to expire and he believed a full frontal attack was necessary. Each time, his officers wisely opposed an attack, citing the British camp's strong defensive position and the American troops' inexperience. General Nathanael Greene agreed that an attack was not practicable unless "10,000 Men could be landed at Boston."[14] At a council of war in November 1775, Washington secured the officers' approval for a bit of decisive action. The officers agreed to bombard the British troops from Dorchester Heights, but regretfully informed Washington that the Continental Army lacked the necessary artillery for such an attack to succeed.[15] Not to be deterred, Washington instructed Henry Knox to travel to upstate New York to get more cannons. Knox departed almost immediately and spent the next several months transporting sixty tons of cannons and other artillery from Ticonderoga to Boston.[16]

After Knox returned, Washington called a council of war on February 16, 1776. He updated his officers on the recent reinforcements from Massachusetts, Connecticut, and New Hampshire, and shared intelligence regarding the depleted British forces. He suggested an all-out attack on Boston, taking advantage of the recent shift in weather. During a cold spell, Cambridge and Roxbury Bay (now filled in and part of Boston) had frozen over, so rather than rounding up thousands of vessels to transport his soldiers, Washington planned to march the army across the ice. Envisioning thousands of American troops slipping and sliding across the ice—easy targets for British sharpshooters—the officers politely rejected Washington's proposal: "Resolved that an Assault on the Town of Boston in the present circumstances of the Continental Army is . . . Judged Improper." Although Washington's discipline and training had improved the appearance of the army, most of the soldiers were still woefully inexperienced and could not be trusted to follow orders in the face of British fire. Furthermore, the war effort was less than a year old. Some states favored independence, while others were still on the fence. An overwhelming defeat might end the war before it had truly begun.

Washington then asked if the council would support "a Cannonade & Bombardment with the present stock of powder." The officers agreed to a bombardment as soon as "a proper Supply of powder" arrived. In the meantime, the council recommended taking immediate possession of Dorchester Hill with Knox's new cannons, which they thought would draw out the British from their encampment in Boston. Washington finally adjourned the council with a plan of action in hand.[17]

On the night of March 4, Washington deployed 1,500 men to drag the Ticonderoga cannons up to the top of Dorchester Hill. When the fog burned off the next morning, the British woke to formidable defensive works atop the hill and American artillery pointed at their navy. British general William Howe offered a temporary truce to Washington: If the British army was allowed to leave unmolested, he would leave the city of Boston intact. Otherwise, he would burn the city to the ground. At this point in the war, Washington was willing to trade the city for an army and accepted the deal.[18] At each council meeting leading up to this victory, Washington had yielded to the officers' judgment and found a compromise plan of action. Upon entering Boston after the British abandoned the city, he expressed gratitude for his officers' caution. It turned out that the British had installed barricades throughout the entire city, making the roads nearly impassable. Any attempt to recapture the city would have resulted in a bloodbath.[19]

Washington also convened councils of war to provide political cover before adopting a potentially controversial decision. For example, Washington sought support for a series of retreats from New York to New Jersey during the summer and fall of 1776. While the retreats were sound military decisions, he believed Congress expected him to defend the city, and he allowed pressure from congressional delegates to color his judgment. In May, John Hancock, president of the Continental Congress, had politely summoned Washington to "consult with Congress, upon such Measures as may be necessary for the carrying on the ensuing Campaign."[20] No record remains of Washington's conversation with Congress once he arrived on May 23, but he left fully persuaded that Congress wanted him to stand and fight for New York City.[21]

Later on in the war, Washington relied on his own judgment and the assessments of his officers rather than the political motivations of Congress. Allowing Congress to influence policy was one of many mistakes he made during the New York campaign. When he first arrived in New York in the summer of 1776, he immediately broke one of the cardinal rules of military command—he split his forces between Brooklyn and Manhattan. General Greene commanded the Brooklyn forces, entrenched on high ground on eastern Long Island, while Washington oversaw the Manhattan forces. General William Howe, the British commander, did not make the same mistake. Instead, he worked in concert with the enormous British navy. As a result, the British troops were highly mobile and could easily flank American positions. Although holding New York forever was likely impossible, Washington hoped that the defensive obstructions installed around the city would slow down the British.

On August 27, 1776, the British forces attacked the American position on Long Island and inflicted an overwhelming defeat.[22] The remaining American troops hunkered down behind fortifications on Brooklyn Heights. British forces blocked the escape on land to the north of Brooklyn, and the British navy controlled the East River, eliminating the escape on water. Washington knew an immediate retreat to the island of Manhattan was necessary before he lost half his army. He recognized, however, that the decision to retreat in the face of British victory would be controversial. A few days later, Washington convened a council to discuss next steps with his officers. As the sun went down, the officers straggled into Washington's headquarters. Most had not slept since before the battle on Long Island and were exhausted, wet from three days of torrential downpour, and covered with mud. As a thick fog settled over the harbor and crept over the American defenses on Brooklyn Heights, the officers debated their future and the future of the Continental Army. The ominous weather outside matched the mood of the council inside headquarters.[23] Very quickly the officers resolved unanimously in favor of a retreat because the "great Loss sustained in the death or Captivity of Several valuable Officers," had resulted in "great confusion and discouragement among the Troops."[24] After the council of war, Washington reported the decision and the retreat to Congress: "I have Inclosed a Copy of the Council of War held previous to the Retreat, to which I beg leave to refer Congress for the Reasons or many of them, that led to the adoption of that measure."[25]

After the council of war on the night of August 29, Washington issued immediate evacuation orders. Under the cover of the thick fog, the troops piled into ferries, boats, and any other floating device they could find. Over the next six hours, Washington and his aides supervised the retreat from the shoreline and followed in one of the last boats that escaped to Manhattan. When the British inspected the American lines the next morning, only five lonely cannons were left guarding the empty defensive works.[26]

The new American position provided scant haven from British might, however. Much like Long Island, Manhattan could easily be surrounded by British warships. If the British army landed on Manhattan Island north of the city and blocked the land escape, the army could be trapped. On September 15, Washington discovered this potential nightmare scenario when the British troops landed at Kip's Bay. He quickly pulled his troops back to Harlem Heights, abandoning New York City to the mercy of the British.[27] For a few weeks, the Americans

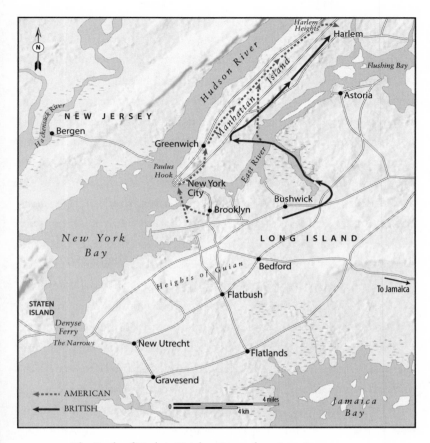

FIGURE 1.2 The Battle of Harlem Heights, September 16, 1776.

enjoyed a small reprieve. Washington established his headquarters in the elegant Morris Mansion, now the Morris-Jumel Mansion, on top of the bluff in Harlem Heights. From this site, the army had an excellent view of British movements in New York City and the harbor. The American troops also won a small victory in the Battle of Harlem Heights, in which they withstood an attack and drove back the British troops.[28]

Just a few weeks after the American victory at Harlem Heights, Washington and his officers received intelligence that the British planned to land north of Harlem and trap the Continental Army. On the night of October 16, Washington gathered the officers in the formal parlor at the Morris Mansion. Perhaps some of the officers stood around the ornate fireplace to warm their hands and feet after riding to headquarters. Others may have peeked out the windows to inspect fortifications or look for signs of an impending British attack. Washington opened the council on a somber note. He read aloud accounts by deserted British soldiers that revealed the British army's plans to circle behind American lines and surround the Continental Army. After much deliberation, Washington and the officers agreed to retreat further to White Plains to maintain an escape route.[29] After another defeat at White Plains, Washington finally led his troops to safety in New Jersey.[30]

While Washington's retreats in New York were technically sound decisions, they called his abilities into question. When the army retreated to New Jersey, it left New York City and the valuable harbor to the mercy of the British. Philadelphia remained the biggest city and port in the new world, but New York City was growing rapidly. The deep harbor provided an excellent stop for warships, and the city's importance as a trade hub increased daily. Additionally, the Americans abandoned valuable artillery and supplies to complete a hasty retreat out of the city.[31] Finally, losing the large and wealthy city of New York to the British inflicted an enormous psychological blow to the army and the country. Washington worried about public backlash and gathered the officers' opinions. On September 12, 1776, he called another council to make sure he retained the support of his officers before abandoning Manhattan entirely to the British.[32] Although Washington never faced a formal inquiry from Congress, he possessed the written support of his officers if he needed it.

Washington also convened councils of war to learn from the expertise and judgment of his officers. On December 25, 1776, Washington's forces famously crossed the Delaware River and inflicted an overwhelming defeat on Hessian forces hired by the British and stationed at Trenton, New Jersey. A few nights later, on January 2, 1777, Washington held a critical council of war. After his Trenton victory, Washington had planned to retreat quickly back across the Delaware River to safety from a British counterattack. However, he longed to strike again at the British while they were reeling from the Americans' surprise victory, so he postponed his retreat into Pennsylvania. Suddenly, British reinforcements under the command of General Charles Cornwallis advanced more rapidly and in larger numbers from Princeton to Trenton than Washington expected. On the morning of January 2, American forces had defended their position against initial British attacks. Washington's sources revealed that Cornwallis planned to attack the next morning: the British would try to ford Assupink Creek north of the American defenses, attack the right flank of the American position, and pin Washington against the Delaware River. The American army risked entrapment in a vulnerable position. The Delaware River hemmed in the rear of the American army, and the British forces blocked Washington's escape to the north.

Cornwallis had pursued Washington for months but had failed to inflict a fatal blow. At last, Cornwallis believed, he finally had the Americans cornered. Cornwallis had every reason to be confident, perhaps even arrogant: he was the most aristocratic of all the British commanders, he had succeeded to his family's title in his early twenties, and he came from a long line of distinguished military service. His military record spoke for itself; he had been awarded significant promotions by age twenty-three and served as a privy councilor to the king by age thirty. Cornwallis had received the finest education at Eton

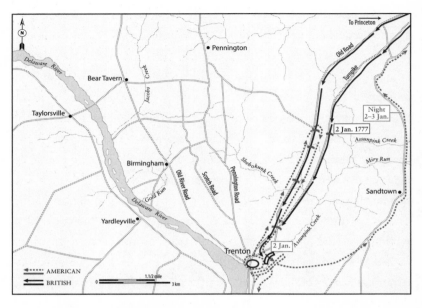

FIGURE 1.3 Trenton and vicinity, January 2–3, 1777.

College and Cambridge before serving with distinction in Frederick the Great's army during the Seven Years' War. Once in America, he had racked up victories in New York against the Continental forces, often capturing cannons, provisions, and—most embarrassingly—the personal baggage of Washington's officers.[33] Only Washington had eluded him. On January 2, Cornwallis confidently predicted a British victory and boasted that he would finally bag "the old fox."[34] The Continental Army appeared to be cornered.

Washington met the officers at General Arthur St. Clair's quarters, a modest two-and-a-half-story clapboard structure known as the Douglass House. The Douglass House sat on the outskirts of Trenton, just next to the army's camp. It was significantly smaller than the council's usual settings, but Washington had yet to establish a new headquarters in New Jersey. On the night of January 2, Washington hastily gathered his officers to address the British threat and the precarious American position. Just after dark, the officers stuffed into the living room on the first floor of the Douglass House and crowded around the small fireplace. They were followed by their aides-de-camp and local citizens Washington had invited.[35] The aides removed the chairs and much of the furniture to make space for the dozens of people in attendance. The participants were on edge as they considered the possibility of battle the next morning.

Washington opened the meeting by apprising the officers of their situation. He praised the army for its recent victory in Trenton and their stalwart defense against Cornwallis's troops that morning. He then turned to the current dilemma. As he saw it, the army had two options: attempt a dangerous and hasty retreat over the Delaware River in the middle of the night in freezing temperatures and high winds, or engage in a "hazardous general engagement" by directly attacking the British defenses.[36] The Continental forces had already tempted fate once by crossing the Delaware River at night in the middle of winter. He was not eager to repeat the experience. The winds had picked up, and Washington no longer had the element of surprise on his side. British forces were carefully watching the American lines. If American soldiers tried to cross back over the Delaware, they would be easy targets for British sharpshooters and artillery.

Directly attacking the British line seemed like a poor alternative. Cornwallis had entrenched his defensive position and lined up his artillery to face the Americans. At best, Washington knew, his forces would sustain devastating casualties. At worst, Cornwallis's troops would defeat the Continental Army once and for all. With retreat over the Delaware impossible, Washington would have to surrender—an unthinkable outcome.

Arthur St. Clair suggested a third alternative. St. Clair held the extreme right flank of the army, and his men had patrolled the country lanes just beyond camp. They discovered that the army could escape to Princeton if the troops swung southeastward around the British forces. A few of Washington's officers from New Jersey confirmed St. Clair's report of the country lanes. Adjutant Joseph Reed, who had been raised in Trenton, reported that he had patrolled the back roads earlier that day and they were clear of British soldiers. Encouraged by this new option, Washington asked his soldiers to consult with local civilians nearby to confirm that the path would take his army to Princeton. The locals offered their encouragement and even volunteered to guide the army through their farmland.[37] The civilian support convinced Washington to move forward with the plan, so he issued orders with unanimous approval from his officers.[38]

To disguise the American escape, Washington had work parties build giant fires and make a great show of improving their fortifications as if preparing for an attack. Behind the diversion, the other soldiers packed up camp, wrapped wagon wheels in rags to muffle any noise, and began marching silently toward Princeton. British soldiers on duty reported the troop movement, but Cornwallis mistakenly assumed the Americans were planning a frontal attack, just as Washington hoped. Instead, Washington evaded Cornwallis yet again.[39] The next morning, Cornwallis realized the Continental Army had escaped and gave chase to Princeton, but Washington's army had already surprised the British forces under Lt. Colonel Charles Mawhood and inflicted more than 450 casualties. The Battle of Princeton provided a numerical and ideological victory for the Americans.[40]

On the night of January 2, Cornwallis himself had held a council of war. Cornwallis's council was a much smaller, more intimate affair than the one Washington held. Most of the attending officers came from high aristocratic families, had attended prestigious boarding schools together, and served in Parliament. Cornwallis treated councils as his own personal court and ruled over them. The officers addressed him as "my lord," and he called the officers by their old nicknames from their boarding school days. At the council, Cornwallis presented his own plan and expected his subordinates to heartily agree. One subordinate, Sir William Erskine, did venture a contrary opinion. He suggested that if Cornwallis "trust[ed] those people tonight you will see nothing of them in the morning." Cornwallis dismissed Erskine's concerns and assured him that "he had the enemy safe enough, and could dispose of them next morning."[41] He was wrong.

The cultures fostered by Cornwallis and Washington differed greatly. The officers in Washington's councils of war deeply respected him, but deference did not restrain their conversations. Washington sometimes invited local citizens to attend—from the poorest farmer to elite plantation owners—which meant that the councils were much more representative of American society than the aristocratic enclave at Cornwallis's court. Observers also noticed that the officers spoke like civilians rather than well-educated military officers. They spoke with regional accents instead of in posh English, and they used colloquial phrases rather than military terminology. During the January 2, 1777, council, Knox described the American army as "'cooped up' like a flock of chickens."[42] While not always the case, the bluntness of American officers sometimes offered a sharp contrast with the behavior of the aristocratic officers in Cornwallis's army.

Not all British councils of war were dominated by aristocratic yesmen. During the Seven Years' War, Washington convened and attended many councils of war with the British army, each with its own practices and ethos. In the spring of 1754, Washington led 150 men to the forks of the Monongahela, Allegheny, and Ohio Rivers to protect the new British fort located on the bank of the rivers. While marching west, Washington received news that French forces had seized the fort with little resistance. On April 23, Washington convened a council of war with his officers and Indian allies. The council determined that attacking the French without additional reinforcements would be foolish and instead proposed that they march for a fortified store-house on Red Stone Creek. This location would make a good defensive position to wait for additional troops from the Carolinas and New York.[43] In this council, Washington proposed the plan and the attendants appeared to readily offer their approval.

The next year, Washington attended several councils as an aide-de-camp in Major General Edward Braddock's official family. Washington's records suggest a few of Braddock's strategies for governing his councils. On May 30, Braddock presented a dilemma for his officers' consideration: there were simply too many wagons and too much baggage for the army to march quickly. According to Washington, the officers agreed to send back as much "of their Baggage as they could do with[ou]t . . . with great chearfulness and zeal."[44] Apparently this cheerfulness evaporated rather quickly, because one month later Braddock summoned his officers again. He appealed to the officers' sense of duty and encouraged them to act "laudably" by further reducing their baggage. Washington wryly noted that the officers reduced the number of bags from 210 to 200, which "had no perceivable effect."[45] Compared to Cornwallis's council of January 2, 1777, Braddock's councils appear almost democratic and demonstrate the great variety of practices among British officers.

While not all Washington's councils were so successful, his January 2 council showcased his greatest strengths as commander in chief. Inheriting a vague British council of war practice, he modified his gatherings to reflect his circumstances and the talents of his subordinates. Washington received little formal book training and never authored political treatises, but he possessed rare social intelligence. He accepted his weaknesses and sought out advisors and subordinates who brought different skills and knowledge.

Finally, Washington used councils to protect his reputation when he avoided direct engagement with the British. Throughout the war, he often surveyed the state of the army and concluded that an attack would fail due to lack of artillery, supplies, and clothing. He understood that he had to preserve the army in the short term to win the war in the long term, and he relied on councils of war to support that strategy. For example, before the British forced Washington to abandon New York City, he proposed a counterattack on the British camp on Staten Island. At a council held on July 12, 1776, the officers unanimously opposed an attack, as he probably anticipated.[46] In his next report to Congress, Washington wished "to acquaint them that by the advice of Genl Mercer and the other Officers at Amboy, It will be impracticable to do anything upon a large Scale for want of Craft, and as the Enemy have the entire command of the Water all round the Island."[47] When congressmen desired action, Washington used the advice of his officers to deflect potential criticism.

Similarly, in the late fall of 1777, Washington contemplated attacking the British troops occupying Philadelphia. Greene described Washington's unenviable task of having to choose between two unpleasant alternatives: "To fight the Enemy without the least Prospect of Success . . . or remain inactive, & be subject to the Censure of an ignorant & impatient populace."[48] Over the next several weeks, Washington requested input from his officers.[49] On October 29, Washington summoned a council of war at headquarters in the Dawesfield Mansion (also known as Camp Morris) in Whitpain, Pennsylvania. In the council minutes, Hamilton noted sixteen generals present. Washington likely welcomed the officers into the parlor. The Dawesfield parlor was opulent, but considerably smaller than some of Washington's previous headquarters. With at least seventeen men in attendance, the room would have been a tight fit and chairs scarce. Once again, the officers found themselves huddled around a fireplace in a too-small room tasked with determining the army's future. American forces suffered embarrassing defeats at the Battles of Brandywine and Germantown on September 11 and October 4. These defeats left Philadelphia open to the British army and forced the Continental Congress to flee to avoid capture. The future seemed dire. At the conclusion of the meeting, Washington requested written opinions from the officers.

On November 24, Washington still felt compelled to attack Philadelphia. He convened another meeting and again requested written opinions after the conclusion of the meetings. A week later, Washington sent a circular to the officers requesting their opinions one last time on whether they should engage in a winter campaign or enter winter headquarters.[50] On all three occasions, most of the officers opposed a winter campaign and encouraged Washington instead to rest, supply, and train the troops. In his opinion, Greene wrote that to attack would

> make a bad matter worse and take a Measure, that if it proves unfortunate, you [Washington] may stand condemned for . . . [I]n pursuing the other [winter quarters] you have the Approbation of your own mind, you give your Country an opportunity to exert itself to supply the present Deficiency, & also act upon such military Principles as will justify you to the best Judges in the present day, & to all future Generations.[51]

Washington agreed, but not before securing written support from his officers—three separate times—for a choice that he knew might be unpopular.

Washington created a process to manage the business of commanding and administering an army, which he would go on to recreate a decade later as president. His command required the support of several brilliant and talented aides-de-camp whose abilities complemented his own. He held high expectations for his aides. In his mind, they ought to have been men from respectable middle-class or elite families so that they could comfortably mingle with the dignitaries at camp. He required them to have a solid education so that they could read and write effectively. And they needed to have a calm demeanor to withstand the pace and anxieties of war. In January 1777, Washington wrote to his former aide Robert Hanson Harrison and asked if Harrison's brother-in-law would be interested in serving as an aide. In the letter, Washington listed the qualities he valued: "A Man of Education. I believe him to be a Man of Sense—these are two very necessary qualifications; but how is his temper?" Washington went on to assure Harrison that he did not expect his aides to have military knowledge, but "if they can write a good Letter—write quick—are methodical, & deligent, it is all I expect to find in my Aids."[52]

Washington emphasized writing skills beyond all other factors because the aides spent the bulk of their time on paperwork. During the eight years of the Revolutionary War, Washington's headquarters produced more than fifty thousand documents.[53] Aides read incoming correspondence, drafted outgoing letters, compiled reports of manpower, and maintained expense accounts. They also kept these documents relatively organized while traveling thousands of miles across the American countryside, often lodging in different headquarters from one week to the next or sleeping in tents on the battlefield. The aides produced this voluminous correspondence on top of the social obligations of hosting dignitaries at headquarters and delivering Washington's orders on the battlefield under enemy fire. Washington kept a close eye on all correspondence, but the aides completed most of the writing: "The General's usual mode of giving notes to his secretaries or aids for letters of business. Having made out a letter from such notes, it was submitted to the General for his approbation and correction—afterwards copied fair, when it was again copied and signed by him."[54] This arrangement allowed Washington to monitor all developments at headquarters without getting bogged down in minutiae or wasting time writing thousands of letters himself. There were simply too many details to track, letters to write, orders to issue, reports to read, and defenses to inspect for Washington to take care of everything himself. Overseeing and administering the Continental Army required delegation.

Washington also deployed his subordinates as ambassadors for his agenda, cultivated their connections to curry favor, and assigned tasks to make the most of their abilities. He refined this strategy as commander in chief and took the same approach with his department secretaries as president.

During the Revolutionary War, Washington's aides were indispensable. He conducted most of the daily business in headquarters with his aides. They drafted and delivered instructions to the subordinate officers, and on any given day, a few officers would also stop by Washington's lodgings to discuss upcoming marches, fortifications, or battle plans. Washington also relied on his aides to survey territory and gather intelligence before battle. In the middle of the disastrous New York campaign, Washington used his aides to survey the damage inflicted by British attacks. On September 9, 1776, Tench Tilghman described to his father how he climbed up to the battery at Hell Gate, which had been attacked by two British ships: "The General set me up last Night to see what Situation things were in, when I found our Fortification but little damaged, not more than could be repaired in an hour."[55]

The Battle of Monmouth Court House on June 28, 1778, demonstrated the important trust that Washington placed in his aides during a battle. The previous fall, the Continental Army had suffered several embarrassing defeats before abandoning Philadelphia to the British. After a long winter, Washington was spoiling for a fight to redeem himself. As soon as the British Army left winter quarters in Philadelphia and marched north into New Jersey, he planned to order an attack at the back of the British troops. At 5:00 A.M. on June 28, Washington received reports that the British troops were on the move. He sent Richard Kidder Meade to instruct General Charles Lee to undertake an immediate attack on the rear of the British army.[56] While Lee led the initial attack, Washington planned to bring up the rest of the army from the camp in Penelopen and meet up with Lee in Monmouth. Meanwhile, he instructed John Laurens and James McHenry to inspect the terrain near the courthouse. As part of the plan, Lee expected backup from troops under Washington's command. Instead, Washington inexplicably delayed his march until later in the morning and left Lee without support. Faced with much larger British forces, Lee ordered an immediate retreat. Washington received the first reports of Lee's retreat at 12:35 P.M. and immediately dispatched Robert Harrison and John Fitzgerald to ride ahead of the troops and gather intelligence.[57]

When Washington finally met up with Lee at 12:45 P.M., they were both far west of the town. The commander in chief was irate. Despite his best efforts, Lee could offer no explanation that would excuse his

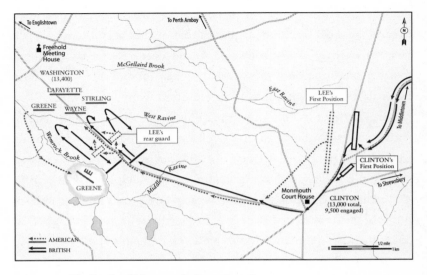

FIGURE 1.4 The Battle of Monmouth, June 28, 1778.

behavior in Washington's mind. Washington took control of the army himself and positioned Anthony Wayne's battalion in the woods to slow down the British march.[58] He also dispatched Tilghman to bring up Lieutenant Colonel David Rhea, who was from New Jersey and could provide information on the surrounding area.[59] The two armies clashed over the next several hours before darkness ended the battle on the night of June 28. British commander General Sir Henry Clinton had no intention of continuing the battle the next morning and organized a silent evacuation to New York overnight.

Washington shared some of the blame for Lee's retreat and the ambivalent outcome of the battle. He had approved a complex battle plan that required precise execution and constant contact between officers. Although the American forces had a rocky start to the battle, Washington, with his aides' assistance, salvaged a stalemate in the face of near-certain defeat.

Washington also used his aides as intermediaries between headquarters and Congress. Sometimes he asked the aides to send battlefield updates to Congress when he was too busy to write. While the Continental Army suffered several defeats in New York City during the summer of 1776, Washington had used his aides to keep Congress abreast of developments. On August 27, 1776, Robert Hanson Harrison provided a report of the Americans' defeat on Long Island to the president of Congress:

> This minute returned from our lines on Long Island where I left his Excellency the General. From him I have it in command to inform the Congress that yesterday he went there and continued till evening, where from the enemy's having landed a considerable part of their forces, and many of their movements, there was reason to apprehend they would make in a little time a general attack. . . . Early this morning a smart engagement ensued between the enemy and our detachments, which being unequal to the force they had to contend with, have sustained a considerable loss.[60]

These reports reminded congressmen, locked in a chamber debating policy measures far away from the battlefield, of the dangers of war and the high stakes of each battle. Perhaps by sending messages through his aides, Washington also wished to send the subtle message that he had his hands full and could not always correspond with Congress as quickly as it wished.

Other times, Washington used his aides to influence congressional decisions indirectly. On December 12, 1776, a British patrol had captured General Charles Lee while he enjoyed a beverage at White's Tavern in

Basking Ridge, New Jersey. After his capture, Lee had requested a meeting with a congressional delegation to discuss peace negotiations and prisoner of war exchanges, which Congress refused. Washington felt that the meeting would cause no harm because the request came from Lee and not the British generals. The next March, he encouraged Tilghman to write to Robert Morris, hoping that Morris would use his influence to change Congress's decision. In his letter, Tilghman confided in Morris, indicating that Washington often held his tongue to not disrespect the civilian power instilled in Congress:

> I should not have given you my Sentiments on these Subjects thus freely and confidentially, but I know I can say more to you than the General would wish to say to Congress, least they should construe a freedom of Expression into an abuse and ill use of those extensive powers with which they have lately vested in him. If my Sentiments and Reasons should happily coincide with yours upon the occasion, I hope the Influence which you possess in the House, may enable you to obtain such an Alteration in the Measures alluded to, as may be of more advantage to Genl. Lee, whom they are principally intended to serve, and of more essential good to the public.[61]

Tilghman, and many of Washington's other aides, served as effective ambassadors for his administration. Washington recognized his aides' elite connections and their effective lobbying on his behalf and did not hesitate to take advantage of these contacts.

While Washington commanded and administered the Continental Army, he also kept close tabs on the daily operations back home at his slave plantation at Mount Vernon using many of the same strategies.

When home, he preferred a hands-on approach to managing his property, enslaved workers and free employees, crops, and livestock. He visited all five of the farms that made up his plantation each day, riding more than twenty miles to inspect the 3,000 acres under cultivation, observe the 200 enslaved people laboring on the plantation, and review his agricultural experiments. On Saturdays, the farm managers visited Washington to report on the week's progress.[62]

When he was away, Washington required weekly reports on the plantation. Lund Washington, a distant cousin, cared for the plantation and Washington's family during the war. Meticulous and attentive to details, he carefully drafted lengthy updates at least once a week, sometimes up to six letters per month.[63] Lund agonized over Washington's financial accounts—eager to pay off the appropriate debts and ensure that Washington was paid what he was owed, but acutely aware that he was not always privy to Washington's conversations and did not always have all the information. As he explained in one of his letters, "I find my self equally anxious to discharge a Debt against you, as I am to pay one of my own, I sometimes am askd for small sums which they say you owe them, it may be true or false I cannot tell, but it destresses me, for I woud that you should owe no man." When directing the extensive mansion improvements, Lund followed Washington's instructions to a fault: "I have had a great Inclination to alter the Doors, but am unwilg to make an alteration in any thing that you have directed—it will not look well being different from the Kitchen."[64]

Although he was far from home, Washington did not relinquish control, even over the small details. He sent back ongoing instructions about the house renovations, where to plant specific trees, and countless other plantation details.[65] He evidently approved of Lund's handling of the estate and their communications, as he tried to recreate similar working relationships through contractual obligations with future managers. When Washington had to hire a new manager for the plantation during the presidency, he detailed his expectations in the contract. For example, in September 1793, Washington signed an agreement with William Pearce that outlined specific agricultural goals, including the introduction of "Clover & other Grasses" and the substitution of "live in place of dead fences." The agreement obligated Pearce to provide "regular weekly reports from each Farm & class of people," "an exact list" of "tools & implements of husbandry" from each farm, "regular accounts with each Farm, & with every separate branch of business."[66]

As with his aides-de-camp and military officers, Washington intended to be kept apprised of all plantation developments. Washington granted latitude to dependable subordinates and laid out specific expectations and demands for those who had yet to earn his trust. His experience supervising his plantation managers from afar served as a model for communication and delegation that Washington would consider in all of his leadership positions.

Washington embraced an active social life as commander in chief, and he recreated it as president. He established an official family by surrounding himself with his favorite officers and aides-de-camp. Washington inherited the concept of an official military family from when he served in the British army as a major. As far back as March 1755, Washington had shared with friends and family that General Braddock had "honour[ed me] by kindly inviting me to become one of his Family."[67] British military tradition allowed each commanding officer to select his own aides. The aides shared lodgings and meals, and traveled with the commanding officer, so the group was described as a family.[68] The Continental Army continued this tradition. All of the officers, including Washington, selected their own aides and formed their own families. Washington's aides provided company, processed daily correspondence at headquarters, served as intermediaries between headquarters and Congress, and scouted battlefields.

Washington fostered a social life in camp that endeared him to his aides. During each campaign, he often slept in a large tent on the field with the army. His aides joined him, pitching their own tents or sleeping in the outer compartments of Washington's larger tent. While each officer decided on his own sleeping location, many generals preferred to set up camp in a nearby house or tavern. The fact that Washington always slept on the field with his troops during a campaign did not go unnoticed by his troops. James McHenry described the lifestyle: "In sleeping in the open fields—under trees exposed to the night air and all changes of the weather I only followed the example of our General. . . . When I joined his Excellency's suite I gave up soft beds— undisturbed repose—and the habits of ease and indulgence which reign in some departments—for a single blanket—the hard floor—or the softer sods of the fields—early rising and almost perpetual duty."[69] Most of the troops loved Washington for not using his lofty position to escape the hardships of army life.

During the winter, Washington enjoyed a slightly more comfortable routine. Each winter, the Continental Army selected one location to set up longer-term quarters. Washington usually established his headquarters in a private home or inn. Lower-ranking officers shared a house, and the infantry built wood huts instead of using tents. Sometimes the homes were large and elegant, like the Vassall House (now the Longfellow House), which served as Washington's headquarters from June 1775 to April 1776. The Vassall family used their vast wealth from their Caribbean sugar plantations to construct the elegant, three-story yellow mansion, which still stands at 105 Brattle Street in Cambridge,

Massachusetts. The room featured ornate woodwork, marble fireplaces in each room, and extensive gardens. More often, however, only small, bare homes were available for Washington's headquarters.

During the 1777 winter season, Washington and his officers selected Valley Forge for its proximity to Philadelphia and the British Army. Washington's wife, Martha, soon joined her husband at headquarters, as she did every winter. The following March, she wrote to Mercy Otis Warren and described their lodgings: "The Genral is in camped in what is called the Great Valley on the Banks of the Schuykill . . . the Generals appartment is very small he has had a log cabben built to dine in which has made our quarter much more tolarable than they were at first."[70]

A few years later, the Marquis de Chastellux visited Washington at his new headquarters at Morehouse's Tavern in New Jersey. The Marquis was less than impressed with the General's surroundings:

> The headquarters at Newburgh consists of a single house, neither spacious nor convenient. . . . The largest room in it, which had served as the owner's family parlor and which General Washington has converted into his dining room, is in truth fairly spacious, but it has seven doors and only one window. The fireplace, or rather the fire back, is against the walls, so that there is in fact but one vent for smoke, and the fire is in the room itself. I found the company assembled in a rather small room which served as the "parlour."[71]

Winter quarters provided comforts beyond four solid walls and a roof. Martha's presence at camp encouraged the wives of other generals to join their husbands, and the women fostered a lively social scene, which often provided much-needed boosts to morale. The *New-York Journal* described a feast hosted at headquarters to celebrate the Franco-American alliance: "Mrs. Washington, the Countess of Stirling [Sarah Livingston Alexander], Lady Kitty her daughter, Mrs. Greene, and a number of other ladies favored the feast with their company, amongst whom good humour and the graces were contending for the pre-eminence."[72]

The officers' wives created a daily social scene, in addition to the special balls and feasts. Martha Dangerfield Bland described her visit to Washington's headquarters to her sister-in-law, Frances Bland Randolph. Bland detailed her regular interactions with the Washingtons and the busy social schedule at camp while visiting her husband, Theodorick: "We visit them twice or three times a week by particular invitation—Ev'ry day frequently from Inclination—he is generally busy in the forenoon—but from dinner till night he is free for all company." Bland expressed her approval of both the commander in chief and his wife: "*Our* Noble and Agreable Commander (for he commands both Sexes) one by his Excellent Skill in Military Matters, the other by his ability politeness and attention. His Worthy Lady seems to be in perfect felicity while she is by the side of her *Old Man* as she calls him." Bland also recounted their enjoyable outings with Washington's family: "We often make partys on Horse Back the Genl his lady Miss [Susan] Livingstone & his Aid de Camps. . . . These are the Genls family all polite sociable gentlemen who make the day pass with a great deal of satisfaction to the Visitors." At the end of her letter, Bland confided to her sister that Washington was far from reserved, as she had previously assumed: "[During the rides] General Washington throws off the Hero—and takes on the chatty agreeable companion—he can be down right impudent sometimes—such impudence, Fanny, as you and I like."[73]

While Washington may have been warm with Martha Bland, humor and engaging conversation did not always come easily to him. He recognized his social limitations and surrounded himself with people who offered skills that he lacked. As a result, he expected his aides to serve as unofficial hosts at his headquarters. He believed that as commander in chief, he needed to remain slightly aloof from company, which suited his more reserved nature anyway. His sociable and friendly aides allowed him to maintain this persona while still welcoming guests to camp.[74] John Trumbull, one of Washington's aides in 1775, struggled with the social responsibilities of the aides: "I now suddenly found myself in the family of one of the most distinguished and dignified men of the age; surrounded at his table, by the principal officers of the army, and in constant intercourse with them." Trumbull labored to fulfill his responsibilities, including his "duty to receive company [and] do the honors of the house to many of the first people of the country of both sexes. I soon felt myself unequal to the *elegant* duties of my situation." Trumbull expressed relief when new aides arrived and relieved his burden: "[I] was gratified when Mr. Edmund Randolph . . . and Mr. Baylor arrived from Virginia, and were named aids-du-camp, to succeed Mr. Mifflin and myself."[75]

Guests noticed how the aides-de-camp played a central role in the social life at headquarters. The Marquis de Chastellux described a dinner at Washington's table: "The Meal was in the English fashion, consisting of eight or ten large dishes of meat and poultry, with vegetables of several sorts, followed by a second course of pastry, comprised under the two denominations of 'pies' and 'puddings.'" After the end of the official meal, servants removed the tablecloth and brought out fruit and enormous bowls of nuts as after-dinner snacks. The servants also brought out "a few bottles of good Bordeaux and Madeira" for the table. Every evening a different aide sat at the head of the table. This aide "performed the honors of the table at dinner . . . seated . . . near the General, to serve all the dishes and distribute the bottles." While eating, Washington, the aides, officers, and guests participated in a round of toasts. Chastellux described the toasts as "a sort of refrain punctuating the conversation, as a reminder that each individual is part of the company and that the whole forms but one society." At first Washington suggested a few solemn toasts, which were then offered by the aides. The toasts later in the evening were proposed by the aides without order or formality.[76]

Social events at headquarters served several important purposes. Washington welcomed social elites, representatives from Congress, and state officials to headquarters to build important political networks. Visitors brought news and important personal correspondence. They brought firsthand accounts of the debates in Congress and the state of affairs elsewhere in the country. They also served as private carriers and brought letters and dispatches from friends, family, and colleagues.[77]

Congressional visits to headquarters were one of the most crucial social events Washington hosted. He invited representatives to witness the hardships suffered by his troops, adopt measures to improve the supply chain, and discuss strategy for upcoming engagements. For example, in the fall of 1777, Washington had consulted with his officers and decided against attacking the British army in Philadelphia. He knew Congress expected some sort of aggressive action, so he invited a committee of congressmen to tour the camp and provide counsel. He understood that the committee would see the army's weariness and low morale. Washington succeeded in his goal of subtly convincing the committee that an attack on the British army was unwise. After the visit, the committee concluded that "a general discontent in the army and especially among the Officers" rendered a successful winter campaign unlikely. The committee vowed to make several recommendations to Congress to reform the army and improve the condition of the troops.[78]

Washington also showcased the hospitality expected of genteel southern aristocrats, doing so in order to sway local elites. In 1775, he initially greeted civilians in Boston with "ceremonious Civility," but the New Englanders mistook his gravity for coldness. After learning of this mistake, he promised to "endeavor at reformation" of his approach and began working to win over his critics.[79] By the time he left Boston, the leading families reported on his charms. Mercy Warren found Washington to be "the most amiable and accomplished gentleman, both in person, mind, and manners" that she had ever met.[80] Abigail Adams agreed: "Dignity with ease, and complacency, the Gentleman and Soldier look agreeably blended in him. Modesty marks every line and feature of his face."[81]

Finally, dinners with officers and aides fostered an esprit de corps and offered an opportunity to discuss the day's events. He cultivated relationships with his officers and their families at daily meals. Washington frequently invited visiting dignitaries, as well as his officers, to large dinners served at headquarters every day at three o'clock in the afternoon. On July 5, 1776, Dr. James Clitherall of Charleston, South Carolina, noted, "We dined with [Washington] in company with Gen Wadsworth and Mercer, Col. Read, adjutant general of the army, Major ——, and the gentlemen of his household [Washington's aides-de-camp]." Clitherall observed that "the General seemed a little unbent at his table, was very affable and requested our company to King's Bridge the next morning."[82] Washington sometimes discussed strategy with attending officers, including on June 28, 1781, when he invited Colonel Alexander Scammel for dinner the next evening to discuss "an accurate state of the Troops under [Scammel's] command,

and also of Major Porter's Detachment."[83] Should Scammel not be able to attend dinner, Washington requested his presence at head-quarters at his earliest convenience.

Around seven thirty each night, Washington gathered again with his aides for a light supper, usually consisting of leftovers from the after-noon meal. On November 24, 1780, the Marquis de Chastellux de-scribed a supper "composed of three or four light dishes, some fruit, and above all, a great abundance of nuts, which were as well received in the evening as at dinner." Chastellux reluctantly joined the dining party, for he feared his presence would interfere with army business. Washington implored Chastellux to join his aides, and the visitor greatly enjoyed the evening, "for there were then no strangers, and no-body remained but the General's 'family.'"[84] These informal gather-ings were much more personal than the dinners served in the after-noon. Washington rarely invited additional guests, and the small group allowed for relaxed conversation about family and home. Washington's aides served as some of his closest advisors and helped execute his orders, so this private time included conversations about the adminis-tration of the army.[85]

The social life at camp demonstrated Washington's emotional in-telligence. He encouraged socialization to build relationships be-tween officers and foster trust between himself and his subordi-nates. He recognized the value of social bonds between his officers and the affection the troops felt for him, and he understood that these ties would sustain the army during difficult months and under tension in battle. Washington also grasped that deep-rooted rela-tionships would help officers overcome disagreements with each other and accept his orders even when they disagreed with the deci-sion. Such ties were critical to his command and administration of the army.

As president, Washington used many of the same strategies to create a similar social environment with his department secretaries.

The Continental and Confederation Congresses underwent several rounds of unsuccessful reform before the challenges of war prompted the initial development of the executive departments. In 1775 and 1776, many states adopted radical constitutions that severely limited executive power in favor of unicameral legislatures. These constitutions were a direct response to the British monarchy, in which the king was sovereign and parliament served as a mere expression of his sovereignty. In the unicameral legislatures of the new American states, the people were sovereign. After the initial burst of enthusiasm for independence waned, many representatives at the state and national levels lamented that the unicameral legislatures were woefully inefficient. By 1780, many leaders supported a gradual move to restore limited executive authority at both the state and federal levels. The evolution of executive departments in the national government followed this pattern— Congress initially abolished permanent departments and created temporary committees staffed by its members. The heavy turnover of congressmen convinced Congress to establish standing committees to manage foreign affairs and different components of the war effort. Governing by committee proved too inefficient, however, and Congress finally concentrated authority in single individuals under congressional supervision. Washington observed Congress's struggles to manage the war effort, encouraged this concentration of political power, and lamented that reform did not create even stronger central authority.

On September 6, 1774, the Continental Congress gathered for the first time, with Washington in attendance. Right away, Congress created temporary committees to manage correspondence between the colonies and to coordinate the boycott of imported British goods.[86] Early the next year, Congress dispersed executive power into standing committees to oversee the war effort, conduct diplomacy, manage interstate relationships, and draft legislation. These committees quickly spiraled out of control, with Congress creating dozens and dozens of committees, including committees to reform other committees.[87]

Although the Continental Congress managed the interstate collaboration in the early years of the Revolution, it did not have any governing authority from the states. To rectify this problem, Congress adopted the Articles of Confederation as its new governing charter in late 1777. Unfortunately, almost immediately the committee system under the new Confederation Congress bungled the herculean tasks of waging war, supplying an army, and coordinating thirteen new states.[88] By nature, committees required group participation and agreement, which produced a slow and conflicted decision-making process. Congress also suffered high rates of turnover, which sapped the body of institutional knowledge. Combined with a steep learning curve for new members, many crucial details slipped through the cracks during transitions. Furthermore, Congress rarely granted committees enough authority to acquire supplies from unwilling merchants or collect money from states that hoarded their meager funds to pay their own militias. As a result, the committees struggled to raise money, purchase supplies and ammunition, and get them to the army in a timely fashion. Food rotted, clothing languished in warehouses, and gunpowder spoiled. War required decisive leadership that could quickly enforce decisions. The committee system in Congress utterly failed at that task and left Washington to pick up the pieces.

As the war effort progressed, the inefficient system took a human toll. Continental Army officers, including Washington, blamed the system's inefficiency for the lack of pay, supplies, and clothing for the suffering army. On December 23, 1777, Washington explained that the want of provisions threatened to destroy the army over the winter. Washington concluded that the current system for supplying the army was failing: "The present commissaries are by no means equal to the execution of the office."[89]

In June 1776, the Continental Congress had created the Board of War, a standing committee, to oversee the administration and supply efforts for the Continental Army. Congress intended for the Board of War to solve many of the supply issues by staffing it with former officers and experienced congressmen. When the army still struggled to obtain the necessary supplies more than a year later, Washington suggested that the Board of War send members to his headquarters to discuss how to secure better aid.[90] On January 28, 1778, the committee gathered a few miles from Valley Forge. Washington and John Laurens, one of Washington's favorite subordinate officers and son of Henry Laurens, the president of Congress, attended the meeting. Washington shared a memorandum outlining proposed reforms for army organization and logistics and supply. The committee observed the perilously low food supplies, the cold and damp housing conditions, the poor health of the soldiers, and the tattered uniforms and shoes of the infantry. Witnessing the suffering of the army firsthand shocked the committee, and the delegates promised Washington they would pursue his recommended reforms.[91] A few years later, the army was still barely surviving, and the committee system continued to shoulder most of the blame. On May 23, 1780, General Greene, one of Washington's most talented officers, suggested that Washington "ask the decided opinion of the Committee (of War) in writing whether they think their powers are competent to the business expected of them."[92]

After years of Washington's encouragement and subtle nagging, Congress finally started committee reform that very same month.

James Duane proposed a new committee to report on the department of foreign affairs. A few months later, Robert Livingston proposed a committee of five to create a plan for new civil executive departments to be led by a single secretary for maximum efficiency.[93] Joseph Jones, a Virginia delegate to the Continental Congress, wrote to James Madison to reflect on the urgency of reforming the committee structure and selecting department heads:

> I was also of a Committee: to arrange or reform the civil departments of Congress and it was in contemplation to place at the head of the Foreign affairs the Admiralty and Treasury some respectable persons to conduct the Business and be responsible. Has any thing been done in these matters[?] [T]hey are important and should not be forgotten. We shall never have these great departments well managed untill something of this kind is done.[94]

The delegates recognized that the current committee system undermined the war effort, but they waited until December 15, *seven months later,* to review the report. In early 1781, Congress established the foreign affairs secretary position and placed the War, Marine, and Treasury Departments under the control of individual secretaries as well. Individual secretaries, instead of committees, would allow for decisive action and prevent committee delays. Yet the delegates delayed the reform effort once again. Beset by factional bickering over candidates, Congress took an additional *eight months* to fill these positions. Robert Morris, the candidate for superintendent of finance, also delayed the process by demanding complete control over his subordinates. After negotiating for a few months, Congress finally yielded to Morris's demands, and he assumed office on May 14, 1781.[95] That fall, Congress filled the final vacancy by appointing General Benjamin Lincoln as the secretary of the Department of War—a year and a half after commencing the committee reform process.[96]

As commander in chief of the Continental Army, Washington witnessed firsthand this slow crawl toward departments led by individual secretaries. Washington regularly corresponded with the president of Congress, various committees, and the Board of War once it was established in June 1776. He also hosted delegates at headquarters to facilitate communication between the army and Congress.[97] On November 20, 1780, Washington lamented to John Sullivan, one of his generals, that the unorganized committee system increased the army's expenditures unnecessarily: "The want of system in the execution of business and a proper timing of things, that our public expenditures are inconceivably greater than they ought to be." Washington believed the obvious solution was to place more power in the hands of individuals to streamline the decision-making process, noting "the evident necessity of committing more of the executive business to small boards, or responsible characters than is practiced at present."[98] When Congress adopted this reform, Washington naturally supported the concentration of power in individual secretaries as long as it promised to improve the supply and oversight of his army and the war effort.[99]

When Congress created the department secretary positions under the Articles of Confederation in 1781, it did not instruct the secretaries to gather for group meetings. As secretary of the Finance Department, Morris wielded the most power of all the secretaries and controlled the lion's share of financial resources doled out by Congress. But he still faced an uphill battle, as many congressmen distrusted both him and his office. He believed that the departments would be run more efficiently and could overcome Congress's intransigence if the secretaries coordinated their efforts, so he took it upon himself to organize meetings with the other secretaries: Secretary of War Benjamin Lincoln, Secretary of Foreign Affairs Robert Livingston, and Secretary of Congress Charles Thomson.

On November 26, 1781, Washington arrived in Philadelphia. He stayed with Robert Morris for a week before acquiring housing for the winter.[100] Morris seized the opportunity to work closely with Washington and ensure that the departments responded directly to the army's needs. A week later, Morris invited Washington, Gouverneur Morris (Robert Morris's secretary, but no relation), and the other department secretaries to meet in his office for the first time. Morris proposed that they "should meet every Monday Evening for the purpose of Communication to each other whatever may be necessary and for Consulting and Concerting Measures to promote the Service and Public Good."[101] Over the next several months, Washington gathered in Morris's office with the other secretaries almost every week until he left the city in March 1782. In these meetings, they discussed "various public measures necessary to be adopted" pertaining to the end of the war. For example, in February, the secretaries discussed the upcoming negotiations with British commissioners on the exchange of prisoners and the past treatment of captured soldiers.[102]

Washington never revealed exactly what he thought about these meetings or about his interactions with Morris and the other secretaries, but he probably found them to be a helpful way to exchange information and coordinate efforts among the different departments. Washington considered Gouverneur and Robert Morris to be good friends, and Benjamin Lincoln had served as a loyal and trusted officer under Washington's command.[103] Washington also seemed to find the meetings useful. On December 15, 1781, Washington wrote to Nathanael Greene and described the gatherings: "I am detained [in Philadelphia] by Congress to assist in the arrangements for the next year—and I shall not fail, in conjunction with the Financier, Minister of Foreign affairs and secretary at War, who are all most heartily well disposed, to impress upon Congress . . . the necessity of the most vigorous exertions."[104] This collaborative experience, though it only lasted for a few months, likely confirmed in Washington's mind the value of collective meetings.

Congress recognized that the individually led departments increased efficiency and continued the department system after the war. In 1787, delegates met once again to craft a new governing document, this time at the Constitutional Convention in Philadelphia. At the Convention, the delegates accepted the department model for the new national government. They devoted relatively little time to discussing the future departments, concluding that they would resemble those under the Confederation Congress.[105] On August 20, 1787, Charles Cotesworth Pinckney of South Carolina proposed five executive departments: domestic affairs, commerce and finance, foreign affairs, war, and marine, each headed by a single secretary appointed by the president.[106] The new Federal Congress, which gathered for the first time in 1789 under the new United States Constitution, finalized this process during its inaugural session. On May 20, Madison proposed three executive departments: Foreign Affairs, Treasury, and War, each headed by a secretary nominated by the president and approved by the Senate.[107] In the fall, Congress completed the process when it created the final department, the Department of the Treasury.[108]

The Revolutionary War transformed the lives of most Americans, but Washington experienced this change on a grand scale. In 1774, he attended the First Continental Congress as a well-known, wealthy plantation owner from Virginia. In 1783, he was the most famous

American in the world, with unparalleled military and leadership experience. In between, he campaigned for more centralized power in the executive departments to effectively manage the war effort, he developed strategies to command and administer the Continental Army, he refined council-of-war practices to provide crucial advice and support, and he developed relationships with his aides and officers that lasted long beyond the war. These experiences, and his conclusions about leadership and power, provided the perfect model to guide Washington's actions once in office. He fostered a social environment that replicated his official family, created the cabinet based on councils of war, and pursued the concentration of federal authority in the executive branch. For Washington, serving as commander in chief of the Continental Army was the perfect training ground to be the first president of the United States.

2

The Original Team of Rivals

WASHINGTON FIRST CONVENED the cabinet meeting on November 26, 1791. Just as he had surrounded himself with talented subordinates as commander in chief of the Continental Army, Washington selected department secretaries that brought extensive experience and knowledge to their positions. They were well-educated, opinionated, prideful men accustomed to sharing their beliefs openly, and they expected to be treated with respect. Washington depended on their advice in private consultations and invited them to cabinet meetings to share their expertise. Which was just as well, because they probably would have offered their opinions either way.

Much like Washington, they had been forged by the war. They had experienced administrative inefficiency that shaped their thinking about the executive: they had endured Congress's ineptitude in the face of danger; they had witnessed the obstacles to executive power imposed by the state legislatures; and their communities had suffered when the state militias could not offer sufficient protection. Their military and government experiences prior to serving in the federal government influenced their understanding of executive power, forged their shared commitment to expanding presidential authority, and informed their advice once in the cabinet.

In recent years, some cabinet secretaries have received more scholarly and popular attention than others. Scholars have devoted considerable attention to Alexander Hamilton's efforts to create a strong federal government, and for good reason—he created the nation's financial system, which yielded the funds that the government needed to keep its doors open.[1] But Hamilton was one of many trusted advisors. Thomas Jefferson has long been a scholarly favorite as well. Even Jefferson, who later protested the expansion of presidential power, supported increased executive authority after his tenure as the governor of Virginia. But the cabinet was not just Hamilton and Jefferson. Each of the secretaries played a critical role shaped by their war experience. Here I will offer a glimpse into the extraordinary lives of five of Washington's secretaries—Henry Knox, Edmund Randolph, Thomas Jefferson, Alexander Hamilton, and William Bradford. The first four served as the original cabinet and the core of Washington's administration. After Jefferson's retirement and Randolph's promotion to the State Department, Bradford became the second attorney general and played a central role in the cabinet during his year in office.

History has largely forgotten or dismissed Secretary of War Henry Knox's central role in the Washington administration. Perhaps this oversight occurs because Knox almost always supported Hamilton's agenda in the cabinet. But Knox endured his own hardships that convinced him of the need for a powerful, active president, and he made substantive contributions in the cabinet to achieve those goals. During the Revolutionary War, he witnessed firsthand the Continental

Congress's inability to provide for the army. As general of artillery, Knox was responsible for maintaining the army's field pieces, securing replacements for damaged or lost cannons, acquiring ammunition, and deploying artillery in battle. But he found these efforts continuously frustrated by congressional action. On February 11, 1778, Congress passed new regulations creating one commissary general in charge of all military stores. The commissary general would be responsible for acquiring and delivering all arms and ammunition, from rifles to cannons and everything in between.[2] In order to procure supplies for battle, Knox would have to request materials from the commissary general.

From the very beginning, he protested this new arrangement. In June 1778, he wrote to Washington, miserable about the new regulations. He pointed to several European armies as a more sensible model. All other successful models had the general of artillery overseeing his own "ordnance," meaning supplies and ammunitions. This chain of command ensured that the general of artillery could remedy any deficiencies in his supply. Knox could not suppress his outrage that Congress had adopted such an untested plan of action: "There cannot be an instance pointed out in any service where the Commissaries or Clerks are made independent, and unamenable to the Commanding Officer of Artillery, as in the Regulations of the Ordnance Department, Feby 12th."[3]

By the end of the 1778 campaign season, matters had not improved. As the army prepared to enter winter quarters in Middlebrook, New Jersey, Knox again wrote to Washington describing the problem: "During the course of the past Campaign I have repeatedly, on an emergency, found myself at a loss to know where to send for Stores, by reason of not having the Returns of all the Departments; the Commissaries not conceiving themselves obligated to send me Returns, even

FIGURE 2.1 Henry Knox, Charles Peale Polk, 1783. National Portrait Gallery, Smithsonian Institution

on my sending for them." Knox made clear that the deficiencies of the organizational structure were not just some new kinks that needed to be worked out: "I have a request for a Return to the principal Commissary uncomplied with at this moment, although I sent the Letter above two months ago; and at present I am totally ignorant of what is doing in the Ordnance Department in Pennsylvania."[4] Sympathetic to these concerns, Washington forwarded Knox's original letter to Henry Laurens, president of the Continental Congress. Yet Knox's continuing complaints indicate how slowly Congress moved to centralize the war administration or fix the problems with the command structure. In February 1779, Congress invited Knox to come to Philadelphia and brief them on the artillery. Based on Knox's testimony, it finally passed legislation to regulate the ordnance departments later that month.[5]

After the American victory at Yorktown in October 1781, the bulk of the Continental Army spent the next two years waiting for the results of peace negotiations between the United States and Great Britain. While Hamilton was gone from the army between April and October 1781, and again after the siege of Yorktown, Knox remained in the military until the very end of the war and served in many prestigious positions. In March 1782, Congress appointed Knox and Gouverneur Morris, the assistant superintendent of finance, to negotiate prisoner-of-war exchanges with the British.[6] Knox served as a major general of artillery until August 1782, when Washington honored him with command of West Point, a valuable defensive position.

In the meantime, the lull in action gave Knox and many other officers ample opportunity to consider the new American nation. Frustrated with limited central government during the war, Knox advocated for greater power for the Confederation government. On February 21, 1783, he wrote to Financier of the Treasury Robert Morris, "As the present Constitution is so defective, why do not you great men call the people together and tell them so; that is, to have a convention of the States to form a better Constitution. This appears to us, who have a superficial view only, to be the more efficacious remedy."[7]

With no plan to revise the Confederation government in sight, Knox and many other officers feared the nation would be left leaderless. Determined that their sacrifices during the war not go to waste, they created a new fraternal organization to fill the leadership vacuum.[8] On May 13, 1783, a meeting of officers adopted the first constitution of the Society of the Cincinnati at Verplanck House, near Fishkill, New York.[9] The society was founded to perpetuate wartime friendships between American, French, and German officers and would protect the virtues and republican morality of the fledgling nation. The society was also intended to step in when Congress failed to care for the widows and children of indigent veteran officers. If the civilian government would not offer strong leadership, the officers would. Knox carried this ethos with him into the federal government, always convinced that a corps of officers was best suited to lead the country.

On March 17, 1785, Knox accepted the appointment of secretary of war. He entered the office hopeful that the Confederation Congress, and his position under its authority, wielded enough power to address its responsibilities. Shortly after accepting his appointment, Knox explained to Washington that he agreed to hold the position because "Congress have rendered the powers, and duties of the Office respectable."[10] As the first secretary of war under the Continental Congress, Knox's responsibilities included overseeing the tiny Continental Army and Indian affairs. He also held an expansive view of his powers. As all troops were under his oversight, Knox considered himself commander in chief. He also believed all military issues should be under the purview of the national government. He repeatedly rejected Virginia's efforts to establish a military store in the Ohio territory. He was not trying to sabotage Virginia's self-defense; rather, he argued that national defense was a responsibility of Congress rather than of the states.[11] During the Whiskey Rebellion, an insurrection in western Pennsylvania over the whiskey excise tax, we will see Knox again argue that defense was a national responsibility, although this time he believed the responsibility lay with the executive, and he urged the president to put down the insurrection rather than leaving the issue to Pennsylvania.

Despite Knox's high hopes upon entering office, he quickly discovered that Congress and his position did not meet his expectations. Knox attempted to secure peace with Indian tribes both through negotiations and by deploying troops to protect western settlers. Both efforts were hamstrung by state interference, limited federal authority, and Congress's inability to raise adequate funds.

First, Congress had no real authority to restrict state action, and often pursued goals that conflicted with those of the states. For example, in December 1785, Congress granted Cherokee Indians exclusive rights to land west of North Carolina. Congress hoped that by granting Cherokees sovereignty over specific territory, the federal government could stop white settlers from encroaching on Native land and limit Native attacks on white families and settlements. However, after signing an agreement with the Cherokees, Congress learned that North Carolina had already parceled out the same land to its own settlers.[12] The next year, Kentucky and Virginia threatened Congress's Indian policy. In late summer 1786, Knox worked to keep various native nations from banding together in one united confederacy against the United States. He believed he could keep individual Indian tribes at peace if the states would temporarily ignore attacks by radical fringe groups. Much to Knox's frustration, General George Rogers Clark led an excursion that destroyed several Shawnee towns. The violence committed by Virginian troops undermined the federal policy of containment and diplomacy, but Congress had no authority to penalize the states for pursuing conflicting policies.[13]

Second, Congress commanded insufficient military forces to limit white settlement in western territories. In June 1786, Knox requested that Congress raise an additional 800 troops to establish posts in the western territories. Congress did not respond to his proposal.[14] Later that fall, Knox again encouraged Congress to raise more troops. This time Congress heeded his recommendations under the guise of protecting western settlements against Indian warfare. Shays' Rebellion, an insurrection in western Massachusetts over harsh tax policies led by army veteran Daniel Shays, struck closer to home and inspired congressional action. Despite Congress's best intentions, few states responded to the request for troops and only two companies of artillery were raised.[15] Recognizing that Congress was not able to supply the much-needed federal army, Knox also submitted a proposal to Congress titled "A Plan for the General Arrangement of the Militia of the United States." He proposed the creation of three corps based on age ranges, with the number of mandatory days of service to be determined by age. In his report, Knox argued in favor of compulsory militia service because "military education shall be an indispensable qualification of a free citizen." Congress could not even consider the proposal because not enough members showed up in New York City to reach a quorum.[16]

Third, Congress could raise no money to fund military action or to conduct effective negotiations with Native Americans. Most of Congress's problems could be attributed to lack of money. Congress established annual quotas for state taxation, but it depended on the states voluntarily complying with these requests. There was no enforcement mechanism. Compounding its lack of tax revenue, the nation owed significant debts to the French and Dutch, with looming due dates. One example of the states' power over Congress's finances took place in November 1785. Congressionally appointed peace commissioners signed a treaty with Cherokee representatives at Hopewell, on the Keowee River.[17] However, the peace commissioners had to clear the terms of the treaty with state governors before signing the final document. Additionally, Congress mandated that the states affected by the proposed treaty raise funds to cover the cost of the negotiations. When Georgia threw "every obstruction in the way to prevent the Commissioners from treating with the Creek Nation," there was nothing Congress could do except hope that the negotiations would continue.[18]

Knox witnessed Congress's fiscal limitations firsthand. No matter how compelling the reason, most of his requests for funding were turned down. On June 14, 1786, the Board of Treasury confessed that they wished to supply Knox with the support he requested, but "there are not sufficient sums in the treasury to defray the salaries of the public officers whose services are indispensably necessary for the support of the mere form of the civil government."[19] Put another way, Congress did not have money to pay federal officials, much less supply an army out west. In late October 1786, Knox wrote to Washington of the depressing state of the Confederation Congress: "The powers of Congress are utterly inadequate to preserve the balance between the respective States, and oblige them to do those things which are essential to their own welfare, and for the general good."[20]

Perhaps the most disheartening moment for Knox came in January 1787 during Shays' Rebellion. Knox, in his capacity as secretary of war, was responsible for overseeing Congress's response to the rebellion. Knox quickly traveled to Springfield, Massachusetts, to visit the federal arsenal and assess for himself the situation on the ground. His visit gave him little confidence that the Massachusetts militia would turn up to defend the arsenal against their friends and neighbors. He was devastated to see the change in his home state.[21] A decade earlier, he had pored over military texts in his Boston bookstore to teach himself the art of artillery. He had protested the British taxation policies in the streets of Boston and had enthusiastically joined the militia after the Battles of Lexington and Concord in April 1775.[22] Now Knox could not trust the militia to uphold the laws of the new government he had fought eight years to protect.

On October 18, 1787, Knox submitted a full report to Congress, sharing his "firm conviction, unless the present commotions are checked with a strong hand, that an armed tyranny may be established on the ruins of the present constitution."[23] Two days later, Congress resolved unanimously to raise 2,040 troops to prepare for future wars with Native Americans. But Congress secretly intended to send these troops to quell the domestic rebellion gaining steam in Massachusetts.[24] Yet when Knox returned to New York City to organize the troops, there was no money to pay the soldiers or buy supplies. Only Virginia had responded to Congress's plea for funds.[25] Knox was forced to tell Massachusetts officials that he had no ability to intervene—he had no armed force to send to protect the federal arsenal in Springfield.[26]

Knox took some comfort that his beloved Society of the Cincinnati contributed to the resolution of Shays' Rebellion. After Congress failed to provide resources for federal forces, the officers of the Society of the Cincinnati stepped forward. In early 1787, the network of officers gathered troops, and Benjamin Lincoln, the president of the Massachusetts chapter, established a subscription to pay for the army. Within twenty-four hours, wealthy merchants, government officials, and elites in Boston had raised the money to outfit the new army. Lincoln's army marched to Springfield and confronted the rebels. The rebellion crumbled and the leaders were captured and arrested. As a native Bostonian, an active member of the Society of the Cincinnati, and the secretary of war, Knox served as an important conduit for information and resources.[27]

Knox brought these experiences to his tenure as secretary of war for Washington's administration. Only a few months after starting his role in Washington's administration, Knox returned to his plan to reorganize the militia that he had first proposed almost four years earlier. Knox and Washington reviewed the proposal and made a few revisions. In January 1790, Washington submitted the plan to Congress. On May 8, 1792, Congress finally passed a bill creating a uniform militia system. Under the Confederation system, Knox had also observed Congress's inability to respond to a domestic crisis, and he brought this experience to the cabinet. Although the new federal Congress finally adopted Knox's militia plan, it took the legislature more than two years to pass the bill. Given this glacial pace, he had little faith that Congress could muster decisive military action in the face of a crisis.

Knox's entire career, from brigadier general of the artillery to secretary of war under President Washington, convinced him that the nation required a strong president. During the Revolutionary War, Knox significantly outranked Hamilton. He created the artillery corps in the Continental Army, developed the first school for artillery, and oversaw the expansion of the first military school at West Point. He then served as the secretary of war for several years under Congress's supervision before the Department of War was placed under executive control in 1789, and Knox continued in the office in the new federal government. While these experiences taught Knox lessons similar to the ones Hamilton learned during the war, his experiences were entirely his own. It is no surprise that he feared the anarchy of the French Revolution—a mob response was antithetical to the values that he and his beloved Society of the Cincinnati espoused. He also advocated for a decisive presidential response to other important events in the 1790s, such as the Neutrality Crisis in 1793 and the Whiskey Rebellion in 1794, based on these past experiences.[28]

On the evening of August 8, 1794, Knox departed Philadelphia to investigate the state of his farm, then on the brink of bankruptcy in Maine. Washington undoubtedly resented Knox's absence over the next two months, and their relationship cooled upon Knox's return to Philadelphia on October 6. Unfortunately, Washington's frustrations have colored history's assessment of Knox's contributions to the cabinet.[29] Washington himself wrote to Knox that "it would have given me pleasure to have had you with me & advantages might have resulted from it on my present tour [to Western Pennsylvania]."[30] Washington may have been angry with his secretary of war, but he valued Knox's abilities, input, and experience. Knox had been at Washington's side for every major battle of the Revolutionary War and had been a trusted confidant during the Confederation period. Once in office, he helped smooth the transition between the old and new governments by serving as secretary of war under both constitutions. During the first few years of the presidency, Knox and Washington worked closely to navigate tensions between the United States and many Native American nations.[31] Although Knox did not march out with Washington and troops to meet the rebels in western Pennsylvania during the Whiskey Rebellion, he was actively involved in the cabinet until his departure on August 8, and he helped define the administration's strategy. Based on his own experiences, Knox supported a strong executive led by a powerful president and supported by the cabinet.

Although largely forgotten by the history books, Edmund Randolph served as Washington's personal lawyer and one of his trusted advisors for over twenty years. As the first attorney general and second secretary of state, he was a central member of the first cabinet. His storied career led to an ignominious end, however: in 1795, Randolph resigned in disgrace after the other members of the cabinet accused him of selling state secrets to the French. His resignation has overshadowed his very real contributions during his lengthy tenure in Washington's cabinet, both in the minds of his contemporaries and in the eyes of history. In Washington's administration, Randolph served as a valued advisor and confidant while Washington established countless legal precedents in his early years in office. After Jefferson's retirement, Randolph took over the Department of State and played a significant role in the administration's response to the Whiskey Rebellion and the Jay Treaty negotiations, two pivotal moments during Washington's second term. Based on his previous governing experience, he championed federal power over the states and ensured that the cabinet supported a strong, active president.

Randolph's tenure as governor of Virginia from 1786 to 1788 was plagued by violence between Native Americans and settlers on the western border and by the fiscal aftermath of the Revolutionary War. These experiences led Randolph to see significant flaws in the 1776 Virginia Constitution. That constitution obligated the governor to consult with the eight-man Council of State before making numerous decisions, including calling out the militia, making appointments to office, or granting pardons. Under this constitutional arrangement, the Virginia governor essentially shared military authority with the council. Even worse, the governor did not control who would serve as his "advisors"; the House of Delegates in the Virginia Assembly, the legislative branch, determined the reelection, salary, and appointment of Council of State members.[32] Randolph objected to the control that the Virginia Assembly wielded over the executive through the council. He also believed the Virginia governor should initiate policy and

FIGURE 2.2 Edmund Randolph, Constantino Brumidi, 1904. Library of Congress

enforce legislation. Randolph recognized the importance of both executive independence from the legislative branch and the executive's ability to drive a policy agenda. He advocated for their adoption in the first federal administration.

Two military issues plagued Virginia during Randolph's tenure as governor: improving the condition of Virginia's forts and providing adequate militia defense for the western counties. A few months after taking office, he investigated the western posts on the Virginia-Kentucky border.[33] In particular, Randolph devoted considerable attention to the Point of Fork fort, located at the intersection of the Rivanna and upper James Rivers. Because of the fort's central location and access to waterways for transportation, it stored most of the state's military supplies. After traveling fifty miles west from Richmond, Randolph arrived at the fort. He was aghast at its condition: "In every instance disorder prevails. . . . Some of the salted beef so offensive that the men complained, and it was thrown away . . . The match is in the same room with the powder. Iron ball in there also. Not a lock upon any door fit for use."[34] These were unacceptable conditions for the most important fort in the state, especially if western communities faced imminent threats of Native American attacks. Randolph issued orders to improve the conditions at the fort and planned a follow-up visit one year later.

Upon Randolph's second visit to the fort, the troops had made significant progress on a new arsenal and powder magazine. Randolph noted that the houses still needed paint and the troops lacked new flints, and he advised that a second arsenal building should be constructed. Randolph's report ended on a somber note:

> A military establishment never existed with so feeble a power
> of defence. It is exposed to destruction, not only from the

successful attack of a few determined and well-prepared men, but even from the negligence or corruption of a single Centinel. I verily believe that without better defence the military stores will fall a sacrifice to some daring attempt or other.

When he returned to Richmond in June 1788, Randolph submitted a plan for new fortifications to the Virginia Assembly, but the assembly took no action on the report.[35] Randolph discovered that the Virginia executive's inability to create and implement new policies significantly limited his ability to improve border security.

As governor, Randolph was technically the commander in chief of the state, but the Virginia Constitution drastically curtailed the power of the governor over the state militia. He could issue proclamations and executive orders, and he could call up the militia in an emergency. In March 1787, Randolph issued his first proclamation, exhorting all militia officers to "punctually and faithfully discharge their respective duties," and threatened prosecution for those who failed to heed their responsibilities. Yet the law gave Randolph no authority to enforce the terms of his proclamation—they were empty words.[36] Less than a decade later, Randolph encouraged Washington to issue proclamations, because he knew the president had the authority to back up his words with action.

In response to the Indian raids out west, Randolph also called up the militia to defend settler communities. Under the 1785 militia law, however, the counties retained control over most aspects of the militia, leaving Randolph powerless to reform it into an effective fighting force. The law required the governor to fill officer vacancies based on recommendations of the county courts or with the advice of the Council of State. Each local commander trained and directed his own troops with little oversight. In return, the law required each county to submit annual militia returns and financial accounts to the governor for executive review, but the counties rarely complied with this regulation within the appointed time.[37] In theory, the militia law gave local communities the authority to select their own leaders under the assumption that they would know the best military and leadership talent. In practice, communities often selected popular individuals with little regard for their military expertise, as long as they made few demands of local male citizens. The law provided no recourse for Randolph to enforce county compliance, remove incompetent officers, or enforce military policy.

Meanwhile, reports of ongoing hostilities arrived daily. Many citizens, including militia officers, begged Randolph to send help. Lieutenant Colonel John Evans urgently requested "a return of the officers and militia," as the local communities were in a "defenceless situation . . . lying exposed to the ravages of cruel and savage enemy. Expecting an Indian war the ensuing season, prays for assistance, as they have neither arms nor ammunition for defence."[38] Lieutenant Colonel Alexander Barnett pleaded for Randolph's help as well. Barnett said he needed scouts, but the militia law did not provide for them and no other legislation gave Randolph the authority to hire them. Randolph's hands were tied unless he took extraconstitutional action and risked censure from the legislature.

Randolph also understood that no additional assistance would be forthcoming from Congress in New York City. He had witnessed his predecessor struggle with the same problems. On May 16, 1786, Governor Patrick Henry had written to John Hancock, the president of the Confederation Congress, "anxious . . . for the peace & safety of the people" of Virginia in light of recent intelligence that settlers had been "attacked by the Indians on the Eastern, Southern & Western Borders of the District." Furthermore, Henry shared his concerns that the Department of Indian Affairs had neglected or mismanaged treaties with Native Americans just outside of Virginia's borders. Eager to provide "against future Evils of a similar nature," Henry urged Hancock to send an agent to negotiate with the Wabash Indians.[39] Nothing came of Henry's pleas. As the attorney general of Virginia during Henry's tenure, Randolph was aware that previous attempts to secure congressional help had failed, so he knew better than to expect a resolution spearheaded by congressional agents. Limited by the state constitution and Congress's unwillingness or inability to assist, the best Randolph could do was offer condolences.[40]

Randolph also learned the importance of an active executive as he worked to settle Virginia's Revolutionary War accounts with the Confederation Congress. The Articles of Confederation required each state to submit a complete report of expenses incurred during the war. Congress would then determine the proper share for each state and issue a credit or debit based on how much the state had already paid. Virginia suffered greater wartime expenses and losses than most of the twelve other states. Yet despite the damage, Virginia was able to use its considerable resources to pay off most of its wartime debts by 1787. The Virginia Assembly confidently believed it would receive a large credit from the Confederation Congress in return. In January 1787, the assembly directed Randolph to appoint an agent to organize, categorize, and compile the state's expenses into a report. With the advice of the executive council, he appointed Andrew Dunscomb to complete the job.[41]

The task quickly became much more daunting than the Virginia Assembly, the council, or Dunscomb expected. Most state papers—including all the vouchers for payments made by Virginia to the Confederation—had been destroyed during the British invasion in 1781.

Dunscomb deposited the remaining papers into large bags and labeled them "not arranged."[42] Dunscomb sought to recreate proof of these payments through other sources, such as paperwork documenting bounties, payments to soldiers, advances of supplies, and advances to the militia. Eight clerks toiled away under Dunscomb's supervision, while he peppered Randolph with letters requesting advice, pleading for assistance, and detailing the difficulties of the project.[43] Randolph sympathized with Dunscomb's plight, but the assembly had not granted him power to assist Dunscomb or oversee the project.

In 1788, the assembly finally authorized the governor and council to intervene. Randolph went to work, simultaneously overseeing Dunscomb's work and lobbying the Continental Congress for an extension to fully provide the necessary proof. He instituted a complex system for categorizing the documents and expenses. He created four categories of accounts: money, specifics, miscellanies, and the executive departments (hospital, marine, and clothing). Next, Randolph outlined seven different types of acceptable proof if the original documents were unavailable. He also listed ten subcategories under the "money" account and eleven subcategories under the "specifics" account. Finally, to guide Dunscomb and his aides, Randolph provided test cases and advised how they should be handled.[44]

Randolph also secured legal counsel to represent the state's claims. On September 27, 1788, after months of correspondence, Colonel William Davies agreed to oversee the project. As a former commissioner of Virginia's Board of War, Davies understood army accounts. He knew where to look for proof of payment, having been privy to the initial transactions. In May 1791, Davies submitted Virginia's final expense report to Congress. Although the Federal Board reduced Davies's claims, it granted Virginia a credit for $19,085,981—the largest of any state.[45] With his brilliant legal mind, Randolph provided the necessary analytical and organizational skills to oversee the project and used his increased authority to hire talented subordinates. But the Virginia Assembly came frighteningly close to failing to grant Randolph enough power to manage the state's claims.

As secretary of state, Randolph brought these past experiences and frustrations with him to the cabinet. He encouraged Washington to exert the full power of the presidency over both domestic and diplomatic issues. Randolph insisted on the president's right to assert executive privilege, defended executive authority over foreign policy, and encouraged Washington to lead a federal response to the Whiskey Rebellion. He did not trust the states, especially those with weak governors, to exercise control over their militias, and he knew how slowly Congress could move on military issues. Randolph's experience with Virginia's war debts also taught him the value of a powerful president who could assert control over the administration's agenda. But his cabinet experience was also unique. He didn't always agree with Hamilton, Knox, and Jefferson, and he was not afraid to say so. He was also the first cabinet member to hold two different positions, first as attorney general and then secretary of state, and served as Washington's trusted advisor for twenty years.[46]

Thomas Jefferson served as governor of Virginia from 1779 to 1781, which were some of the darkest days of the Revolutionary War. The British invaded Virginia during Jefferson's tenure, and he struggled in vain to piece together a military response. During moments of military emergency, Jefferson chafed against the constitutional limitations of his office and pursued more extreme measures to execute the war effort in Virginia. In February 1779, Lieutenant Colonel George Rogers Clark of Virginia had captured several high-ranking British officials.

Typically, captured officers were kept under parole, meaning they were expected to stay in town, but they were treated like gentlemen and given access to most luxuries until they could be swapped in prisoner-of-war exchanges. In this case, Jefferson and the Council of State believed exaggerated accounts that Lieutenant Governor Henry Hamilton, the British commander of Fort Detroit and one of the captured British officials, had incited local Indians to attack Americans, offered bounties for the scalps of white settlers, and mistreated American prisoners of war.[47]

Jefferson had previously taken pains to offer kind and generous treatment to British officers captured in Virginia, so he bristled at these reports. On June 16, 1779, Jefferson learned of Hamilton's capture and ordered, in agreement with his Council of State, that the prisoners be "put into irons, confined in the dungeon of the publick jail, debarred the use of pen, ink, and paper, and excluded all converse except with their keeper."[48] He welcomed the opportunity to inflict vengeance, even if his orders violated established prisoner-of-war protocol.[49]

British officers protested the new conditions and threatened to discontinue further prisoner-of-war exchanges until Hamilton's conditions improved. Major General William Phillips, a British officer who had grown close to Jefferson during his own parole, appealed to Jefferson's "lively sentiments and those liberal principles." Phillips insisted that the terms of Hamilton's surrender amounted to a sacred contract that Jefferson must observe. Under this contract, Jefferson should treat Hamilton as a typical prisoner of war and allow him a parole.[50] Jefferson responded that Hamilton's surrender failed to include any stipulations about his treatment as a prisoner of war. Jefferson admitted, however, that he had "the highest idea of the sacredness of those Contracts which take place between Nation and Nation at war, and would be among the last on earth who should do any thing in violation of them."[51]

FIGURE 2.3 Thomas Jefferson, Charles Willson Peale, 1791. Courtesy of Independence National Historical Park

In July 1779, he requested Commander in Chief George Washington's advice on the matter. Washington replied that he "had no doubt of the propriety of the treatment decreed against Mr. Hamilton, as being founded in principles of a just retaliation."[52] A few months later, Washington appeared to change his mind after reading a letter from Joshua Loring, the British commissary of prisoners. In the letter, Loring announced his intention to retaliate for Hamilton's poor treatment by refusing to release any Virginia soldiers. Washington passed the letter along to Jefferson. Out of respect for Jefferson's authority as governor, Washington refrained from demanding that Jefferson release Hamilton, but added that the Virginia officers held by the British requested Jefferson's leniency.[53] Based on Washington's advice, Jefferson and the Council amended their orders and allowed Hamilton to be released on parole in September.[54] Jefferson's temporary enforcement of harsher penalties—throwing a prisoner into a dungeon in shackles, without access to pen or paper—without a court-martial demonstrated his willingness to stretch the powers of the Virginia executive branch.

Sometimes Jefferson also acted without the approval of his council or the legislature, even though his actions were strictly prohibited by the Virginia Constitution. In May 1779, British forces under the command of Sir George Collier burned Norfolk, the city of Portsmouth, and the shipyard of Gosport, and destroyed a valuable supply depot at Kemp's Landing. At the Gosport shipyard alone, the British destroyed 137 vessels and "five thousand loads of fine seasoned oak-knees for shipbuilding, and infinite quantity of masts, cordage, and numbers of beautiful ships of war on the stocks."[55] In June 1779, news slowly trickled into Williamsburg, the capital at the time, describing the extent of the damage done by the recent British invasion. Jefferson didn't wait for input from the legislature before taking action—he immediately moved to acquire accurate intelligence about the destruction. A few days later, the Virginia Assembly passed a resolution instructing him to do what he had already begun: investigate the situation and report back to Congress.[56]

In early January 1781, as a British force commanded by Benedict Arnold approached the capital in Richmond, the council members and delegates fled to avoid capture. The council lacked a quorum to meet again until January 19. In the meantime, Jefferson continued to govern, exercising powers beyond those outlined in the Virginia constitution.[57] He oversaw the relocation of state papers, issued orders, and raised troops in response to Arnold's invasion.[58] On January 16 and January 18, he wrote to Colonel George Weedon and Lieutenant Richard Claiborne, authorizing the temporary seizure of all boats on the James and Chickahominy Rivers to transport horses and troops.[59]

Other times, Jefferson defied council orders directly. On February 16, 1781, the council met to discuss the state's need for additional naval armaments to shore up the meager defenses. He proposed authorizing temporary impressment measures. The council disagreed and only authorized Jefferson and the officers in Virginia to "engage the willing."[60] Over the next few weeks, it became clear that few owners had volunteered their boats. On March 4, he overrode the council's decision and authorized Captain William Lewis to "impress all the armed vessels of private property which can be had immediately, together with their crews, arms, etc., and the crews of other vessels as far as necessary to man these."[61]

Despite his expansion of executive power in Virginia, Jefferson received widespread criticism for not doing enough to protect the state of Virginia from British forces.[62] Edmund Pendleton, the former president of Virginia's Committee of Safety, wrote a letter to Washington slamming Jefferson as "incredulous and not sufficiently attentive." Pendleton reported that state troops felt "disgrace in having Our

Metropolis, at 100 miles distance from the Sea Coast, Surprized and taken without resistance by a handful of Banditti."[63] Jefferson also received criticism for his flight from Charlottesville in June 1781 in the face of the approaching British troops. When Jefferson's term ended a few weeks after his retreat, most assemblymen were still scattered about the state and could not assemble to elect his replacement. Rather than staying in office until the House selected the next governor, he returned to his home at Monticello, relieved to have completed his term. Many of his critics, including his most vocal opponent—Patrick Henry—believed that Jefferson abandoned Virginia in its hour of need. Henry convinced the House of Delegates to introduce a resolution requiring that "an inquiry be made into the conduct of the Executive of this State for the last twelve months."[64]

When the assembly gathered to consider the charges six months later, the threat of invasion had passed and the members viewed Jefferson's actions in a more reasoned mood. The assembly acquitted Jefferson of all wrongdoing, dismissed the charges as overly partisan, and unanimously passed a declaration declaring "the high opinion which they entertain of Mr. Jefferson's Ability, Rectitude, and Integrity as [Chief] Magistrate of this Commonwealth."[65] Although he was cleared, the charge of cowardice lingered and forced Jefferson to address the charges in the 1796, 1800, and 1804 elections.

Jefferson later defended his deployment of executive power in his *Notes on the State of Virginia*. He analyzed the Virginia constitution and contended that the executive and judiciary branches were subordinate and dependent on the legislature, even though they shouldn't be. He suggested that this imbalance stymied government efficiency, and he proposed a new constitution to remedy the defects of the 1776 government by providing greater separation between the branches of government, as well as more power for the executive.[66] He believed the governor should act independently of the council and the legislature. In the event of another war, Jefferson's constitution would allow the governor to protect the state without requiring a grant of dictatorial powers by the assembly.[67]

Jefferson shared these ideas with both Washington and Randolph. On May 28, 1781, Jefferson had confided to Washington his relief at his imminent retirement from the governorship: "A few days will bring to me that period of relief which the Constitution has prepared for those oppressed with the labours of my office."[68] In February 1783, as Jefferson sailed to Paris to accept a new position as minister to France, he wrote to Randolph and confessed his low opinion of politics in their home state: "I have seen with depression of spirit the very low state to which that body has been reduced. I am satisfied there is in it much good intention, but little knowle[d]ge of the science to which they are called." Jefferson was thrilled that Randolph planned to stand for a seat in the legislature but warned his friend about the burdens of office: "I only fear you will find the unremitting drudgery, to which any one man must be exposed who undertakes to stem the torrent, will be too much for any degree of perseverance."[69]

As a member of Washington's cabinet, Jefferson pursued his goals for an independent, active executive. Although his opinions about executive power differed from Hamilton's and eventually from Washington's, Jefferson initially worked in the cabinet to shape a powerful president based on his own governing experiences. He promoted presidential authority over the diplomatic process, supported executive privilege, and defended Washington's authority against attacks from the French minister. His ideas about executive power continued to influence the administration after he retired as secretary of state. In

1794, Washington purchased a published copy of Jefferson's *Notes on the State of Virginia* for $1.50.[70]

While Alexander Hamilton's importance is sometimes overstated, no chapter on the central figures of Washington's cabinet would be complete without an introduction to Hamilton's wartime experiences. During the Revolutionary War, Hamilton observed Congress's failure to prosecute the war effort and began a long career of advocacy on behalf of a powerful, independent executive. While the army shivered at Valley Forge in the winter of 1777–1778, Hamilton corresponded with George Clinton, the rebel Governor of New York. He did not mince words when he shared his concern that Congress and the state governments would undermine the army's sacrifices: "The weakness of our [legislative] councils will, in all probability, ruin us. Arrangements on which, the existence of the army depends, and almost the possibility of another campaign, are delayed in a most astonishing manner; and I doubt whether they will be adopted at all."[71]

Hamilton's letter to Clinton was just one of many he sent to state and congressional leaders imploring them to reform the government to adequately supply the army. In 1781, Hamilton and Robert Morris, the superintendent of finance, proposed an amendment to the Articles of Confederation giving Congress the power to raise revenue through taxes. In particular, he worried about the back pay due to the officers. Congress had just passed a resolution granting half pay to retired soldiers, yet could not scrounge up the funds to pay the troops. Alas, nothing came of Hamilton's proposed amendment.[72] While the army survived, Hamilton resigned in 1781, disgusted with Congress and its inability to support the troops. He spent the rest of his career promoting

FIGURE 2.4 Alexander Hamilton, John Trumbull, 1792. National Portrait Gallery, Smithsonian Institution

a federal government, and an executive, that avoided the Continental Congress's weaknesses.

After the war, the Nevis-born Hamilton returned to New York, his adopted home state. He practiced law while dabbling in public service, but he quickly became disillusioned with the postwar government. Under the Articles of Confederation, Congress did not levy taxes; it passed requisitions—essentially requests for funds from the states—but had no enforcement mechanism to ensure that the states contributed. Hamilton served as the national government's requisition collector for New York, but he struggled in vain to collect taxes with no power to secure payment. New York treasurer Comfort Sands and the state legislature offered only empty promises that they would raise money in the future. After a short term of service, Hamilton offered his resignation in August 1782.[73] He would later confess to Robert Livingston his fears about the future of the state of New York: "The situation of the state at this time is so critical that it is become a serious object of attention to those who are concerned for the *security of property* or the prosperity of government. . . . The spirit of the present Legislature is truly alarming, and appears evidently directed to the confusion of all property and principle."[74] Hamilton saw flaws in the other states' constitutions as well. In 1787, the Massachusetts legislature repealed tax laws in response to Shays' Rebellion. Somewhat ironically, as he was a former revolutionary himself, Hamilton was disgusted that the government wavered in the face of populist resistance.

These experiences shaped Hamilton's understanding of credit, taxes, and the government's role in monetary policy. He was convinced that if the states retained authority over fiscal policy and taxation, they would devastate the new nation's credit.[75] Less than a decade later, he again witnessed populist resistance during the Whiskey Rebellion. As we will see, Hamilton campaigned vigorously in the cabinet for a strong government-led military response against the rebels.

To rectify the weaknesses of the state and Confederation governments, Hamilton supported early efforts to reform the Articles of Confederation. In September 1786, he arrived in Annapolis, Maryland, with high hopes that the delegates would draft meaningful reform proposals for the Confederation Congress. When only representatives from five states arrived, Hamilton drafted an address to the states from the Annapolis Convention. The address stated that the delegates were "deeply impressed . . . with the magnitude and importance of the object confided to them on this occasion" and wished to make the most of the opportunity. They regretted the absence of delegates from the other eight states, especially since the "defects in the system of the Fœderal Government . . . may be found greater and more numerous, than even these acts imply." The address closed by inviting all thirteen states to send delegates to "Philadelphia on the second Monday in May [1787]" with the goal of considering "the situation of the United States" and "devising such further provisions as shall appear to them necessary to render the constitution of the Fœderal Government adequate to the exigencies of the Union."[76] That gathering would become known as the Constitutional Convention

In 1787, Governor George Clinton appointed Hamilton to serve as a New York delegate to the Constitutional Convention in Philadelphia. On June 18, Hamilton proposed the creation of an executive with magisterial powers that many of his colleagues shunned as suspiciously monarchical. His suggestion was essentially ignored.[77] Once the convention approved the Constitution, Hamilton devoted himself to securing ratification even though he had argued in favor of a much stronger federal government. He famously spearheaded an essay project with James Madison and John Jay to influence undecided delegates in the Virginia and New York State Ratification Conventions. Hamilton himself wrote fifty-one of the eighty-five essays published under the pseudonym "Publius" in defense of the new Constitution, which became known as the *Federalist Papers*.[78]

After his appointment as the first secretary of the treasury, Hamilton finally had the opportunity to help shape a strong executive and powerful federal government. He wasted no time making the most of this moment and crafted an ambitious legislative agenda that transformed the nation's credit from nonexistent to robust, and that required extensive federal powers exercised by an energetic executive branch. First, he drafted a bill authorizing the federal government to assume the states' debts remaining from the Revolutionary War. By assuming the debt, the federal government could ensure that the states' creditors would be repaid and thus would be willing to extend future loans to the new government.[79] Next, Hamilton proposed an excise tax that would provide necessary income for the federal government to discharge its debt.[80] Finally, Hamilton favored the creation of the first national bank to support tax collection and cultivate safe borrowing of money.[81]

After the creation of his financial system, Hamilton continued to promote a strong, independent executive. As we'll discuss in more detail later, in 1793 he asserted the president's right to declare neutrality in the face of foreign war. When Edmond Charles Genêt, the French minister, challenged Washington's authority over foreign policy, Hamilton pushed for Genêt's recall and masterminded a public relations campaign to discredit Genêt. When the Whiskey Rebellion broke out in 1794, he supported federal enforcement of the excise tax he had proposed and convinced Congress to pass. His advocacy for a military suppression of the insurrection was consistent with the goals he pursued during the entirety of his public service career.[82]

Yet while Hamilton reveled in utilizing the power of the federal government, he did not seek to bolster the power of the secretary of the treasury in relation to the president. Based on his military and early governing experience, Hamilton believed that the government needed one strong executive that could actively pursue an agenda. The cabinet needed to encourage and buttress the president, but never undermine or steal his authority, as Hamilton as witnessed in the states.

William Bradford served as the second attorney general of the United States. While he served in the cabinet for only nineteen months before his death on August 23, 1795, he was Washington's trusted advisor and played an important role in the Whiskey Rebellion in 1794. As with the other secretaries, Bradford's background shaped his advice to the president and his cabinet participation. Like Hamilton and Knox, Bradford served in the Continental Army before transitioning to government service. These experiences convinced him of the value of a strong president, which he promoted as attorney general.

In the 1770s, Bradford was an early supporter of the independence movement. After completing his schooling at Princeton, he regularly sent letters to his Princeton classmate James Madison on the proceedings of the Continental Congress in Philadelphia: "I have but little to tell you of the Congress; they keep their proceeding so secret that scarce any thing transpires but what they think proper to publish in the papers. They meet every day & continue long in debate but it is said are very unanimous."[83] While struggling to decide whether to enter the ministry, study law, or become a doctor, Bradford joined the local militia. He boasted to Madison that the Philadelphia militia could soon meet the British army without fear: "We are equally industrious in Philada. and propose having a General review next monday: & I hope

FIGURE 2.5 William Bradford, William E. Winner, 1872.
Department of Justice

in a month or two we shall be able to meet without dread the most disciplined troops."[84] In the fall of 1775, Bradford traveled to Cambridge to witness the siege of Boston.[85]

Bradford's militia term expired one year later, at which point he joined the 11th Pennsylvania Regiment as a company commander. As a part of Washington's Continental Army, Bradford participated in major battles over the next couple of years. In late December 1776, Bradford and the rest of the Pennsylvania 11th were assigned to Thomas Mifflin's brigade. Mifflin's troops succeeded in their own dangerous crossing of the Delaware River on December 28. On the night of January 1, 1778, Mifflin's troops covered the final leg of their journey and met up with Washington's forces as the sun rose on January 2. They arrived in time to participate in the Second Battle of Trenton and helped fight off three British attacks across Assunpink Creek.[86] That night, General Mifflin attended Washington's council of war before leading his troops on a night march to Princeton. Bradford and the other soldiers in the Pennsylvania 11th fought at the Battle of Princeton and forced the surrender of British troops holed up in Nassau Hall.[87] After two night marches and two battles in two days (with no break for sleep), Bradford and the other soldiers collapsed in a tired heap. The experience was one he did not soon forget.

Perhaps more important, Bradford endured the harsh and unforgiving winter at Valley Forge. In the fall of 1777, Congress expressed its wish that the Continental Army establish winter quarters in Pennsylvania to protect the countryside from the British forces cozily quartered in Philadelphia. While Washington worried that supplying his troops would be difficult if they all stayed in once place, he acquiesced to Congress's request and selected Valley Forge as the best defensible location. Washington's fears proved prescient, as the troops struggled to find wood to build shelter and the residents resisted selling food or supplies to the army. Most days, the troops received meager rations of beef, bread, and alcohol. At one point the troops went six days without a ration of beef, their main food staple, and on three separate days received no rations at all.[88] Unwilling to see his troops starve, Washington reluctantly issued orders to confiscate food and clothing from local farms. Sensitive to the importance of public opinion, he ordered that civilians be paid "a reasonable Rate" for the items the army seized.[89]

As a junior officer, Bradford suffered slightly less than the rank-and-file soldiers. Bradford established his headquarters a local home owned by David Havard near Valley Forge. The dwelling was fairly small, and Bradford shared the space with his father, William Bradford Sr., his older brother, Thomas Bradford, and his brother-in-law, Elias Boudinot—all Continental Army soldiers. But it was a solid house and warm in the winter—a large step up from the drafty huts available to average soldiers in Valley Forge.[90]

Although he had a warm place to sleep, Bradford witnessed the pain and hunger of the men under his command. While there are no records showing that Bradford met with congressional representatives who visited camp, reports of Washington's meetings with them certainly circulated among the officer corps.[91] Bradford shared the other officers' frustrations that Congress and locals appeared indifferent at times or moved too slowly to alleviate the suffering of the army. Bradford brought these observations with him to his state and federal governing positions and worked to increase executive authority.

By 1779, two years of fighting had taken its toll on Bradford. He was worn down, suffering from chronic illness, and injured, so he resigned his commission as a lieutenant colonel and returned home to Philadelphia. Over the next few months, Bradford finished his legal studies and joined the bar before the Pennsylvania Supreme Court. The very next year, Pennsylvania named Bradford the state attorney general, a position he held for the next eleven years.

During his tenure as a Pennsylvania state official, Bradford's military experience was never far from his mind. In November 1780, Bradford represented Pennsylvania in the Hartford Convention and served as president of the proceedings. The Hartford Convention was a gathering of representatives from New Hampshire, Massachusetts, Rhode Island, Connecticut, and New York to discuss a more effective way to support the Continental Army and "[draw] forth the necessary Supplies from the States."[92] The Convention passed several resolutions urging the states to call up their militias and immediately comply with the army and congressional requisitions. The resolutions stressed that the failure to supply the materials requested by Congress led "the Army [to] greatly suffer and been frequently brought into a very Critical and dangerous situation."[93] At the conclusion of the Convention, Bradford forwarded the resolutions to the governors of states not present—including Governor Thomas Jefferson of Virginia.

In late 1793, Thomas Jefferson retired as secretary of state and returned to his home at Monticello. Washington selected Attorney General Edmund Randolph to be the next secretary of state. To fill the opening, Washington nominated Bradford as the second attorney general of the United States.[94] Bradford was a solid political choice. In 1791, Governor Thomas Mifflin, Bradford's old military commander, had appointed Bradford to the Pennsylvania Supreme Court. Bradford's tenure on the court, combined with his eleven years as the Pennsylvania attorney general, made him one of the premier legal minds in the country. In addition, no other secretaries in the cabinet represented the middle states of Pennsylvania, Maryland, Delaware, and Rhode Island, so Bradford offered important geographic diversity. Perhaps most important, Washington knew Bradford personally from their time together in the Continental Army and trusted that he would be a firm advocate for a strong executive based on their shared military experience. This trust proved well founded. During his nineteen months in office, Bradford regularly encouraged Washington to assert presidential authority over both domestic and diplomatic issues.

These five men—Hamilton, Knox, Randolph, Jefferson, and Bradford—brought extensive military and leadership experience with them to the president's cabinet. Some of their experiences taught similar lessons. Hamilton, Knox, and Bradford all came away from the Revolutionary

War with a deep distrust of Congress's ability to act decisively; Jefferson and Randolph left the Virginia governorship convinced that executive power must be free from legislative limitations. When they entered Washington's private study to gather as a cabinet, they eagerly participated in a new institution and shared a commitment to expanding presidential authority.

3

Setting the Stage

WHILE WASHINGTON LED the Continental Army and the future secretaries served in the army and state offices, the new nation grappled with what it meant to be independent. On July 2, 1776, the United States declared its separation from Great Britain, but it did not achieve full independence until September 1783, when the Treaty of Paris officially ended the war and Britain recognized the United States as a sovereign nation. Even then, true sovereignty required recognition from other European powers and loyalty from American citizens.[1] In the final years of the war and the first years of nationhood, Americans struggled to define a common culture, identity, and purpose. How would they interact with other nations? How would they comport themselves as citizens? How much power would the state and federal governments have over the American people? Most important, how would their nation differ from the empire they had just left? These questions and Americans' struggle to create a new society reflected their ongoing efforts to grapple with their Anglo-American political heritage. Their beliefs about power, government, and virtue shaped every aspect of the new society and government.

In 1787, the efforts to answer these questions about the future of the nation led to the Federal Constitutional Convention. The convention displayed the Americans' ongoing distrust of the British government, especially the British cabinet, and the delegates' anxieties that their republic would devolve into a similar monarchy. The American preoccupation with the British cabinet influenced the articles of the Constitution that created the executive branch, including the provisions that provided advisors for the president. These fears also played a pivotal role in the state ratification conventions. Delegates at those conventions wanted to provide the president enough support, but they feared the British cabinet even more.

Washington had a front-row seat to this process. He served as a delegate to the Continental Congress before taking up his role as commander in chief of the Continental Army. He observed the new nation's attempts to define a political and social culture separate from its Anglo-American heritage, and he participated in the Constitutional Convention. This experience offered him a unique understanding of the new government and the delegates' efforts to keep their distance from the British monarchy. After the convention, he carefully followed the ratification debates to understand how American citizens received the Constitution and their expectations for the first generation of public officials. For Washington, the outcome of the decades-long struggle to achieve independence and create a new nation had personal ramifications. He did not want his years of sacrifice to go to waste, and he knew he might be called to serve once again.

The 1780s created an atmosphere and social culture that produced the Constitutional Convention, the new federal government, and eventually, the cabinet.

In the 150 years before the American Revolution, the British monarchy underwent significant transformations that altered the colonists' relationship with Britain. The sixteenth-century Tudor monarchs based their authority on divine right—the concept that kings received their authority from God to govern a specific body of people. As a result, their judgment and behavior were unimpeachable. Parliament did, however, offer an occasional check on the monarch's absolute authority through its control of the purse strings. If the king's personal finances could not cover the government's expenses, he would convene a session of Parliament to approve new tax measures. When in session, Parliament could deny his tax requests, but its effect on the king's authority was limited. In the seventeenth century, British kings attempted to continue this model, but profligate spending, religious conflict, and expensive wars drove a wedge between the monarchy and the British people. The monarchy reached a low point in January 1649 when Oliver Cromwell's New Model Army put on trial, convicted, and executed Charles I for treason. After a period of civil war and military rule, Charles II was restored to the monarchy in 1660. In 1685, the English quickly grew dissatisfied again, especially when James II, a Catholic, ascended the throne. James II packed the highest offices with Catholic supporters and threatened to repeal the penal laws, alienating a predominately Protestant populace. When the queen gave birth to a male heir, Catholic rule seemed inevitable for the next generation. Unwilling to accept a Catholic king, Protestant leaders set events in motion when they invited William, Prince of Orange, and his wife, Mary (James II's daughter), to sail from the Netherlands to England and seize the throne. When James II fled rather than face the Dutch forces, supporters of William and Mary named the bloodless coup the Glorious Revolution.[2]

In return for the British throne, William and Mary agreed to a bill of rights that prevented future monarchs from practicing Catholicism, limited the powers of the monarch, and defined Parliament's rights. Most important, the document required regular sessions of Parliament, free elections, and freedom of speech in Parliament. The king could not suspend or create laws or levy taxes without Parliament's consent. Furthermore, the king could not prosecute subjects for petitioning the monarch.[3]

The new power arrangement between Parliament and the king operated under the principle of shared powers. The branches of government did not divide power as the future US government would, but instead shared authority to achieve balance between the executive and legislative power. The monarchy functioned as a head of state but did not hold most of the ruling power. That role fell to Parliament, made up of the House of Commons and the House of Lords. Members of the House of Commons were elected, and members of the House of Lords were appointed by the king or inherited their seats along with land and titles. The House of Lords served as a check on the whims of the populace, while the House of Commons represented the people. When members were elected to the House of Commons, the party with the most members elected ministers to form a governmental body called the Privy Council.

In the mid-1600s, the Privy Council was a small group of ministers from Parliament gathered together to advise the king. As the size of the Privy Council grew over the second half of the seventeenth century, it became too unwieldy to govern, so a small group of ministers from the Privy Council formed a smaller, secret "cabinet council." This subgroup derived its name from its meeting place: the small, private room—or "cabinet"—that belonged to the king. Eventually "council" was dropped and the king's select advisors were known as the cabinet.

The king worked with both houses of Parliament to lead the nation and represent all subjects. Most Britons supported William Blackstone's legal theory that the king could do no wrong. In his *Commentaries,* Blackstone argued that

> the law therefore ascribes to the king . . . large powers and emoluments which form his prerogative and revenue [and] certain attributes of a great and transcendent nature; by which the people are led to consider him in the light of a superior being, and to pay him that awful respect, which may enable him with greater ease to carry on the business of government.[4]

Although Blackstone attributed great power and respect to the king, someone had to be responsible for the government's policies, especially if they were unpopular. So under Blackstone's widely accepted interpretation, the king's ministers took ownership of the government's policies, effectively absolving the king of all responsibility for wrongdoing.[5]

The Glorious Revolution also cemented the role of the cabinet at the center of the British government. After William and Mary came to power, the cabinet ran the government and effectively wielded most of the governing power, so long as it collectively could manage a majority in Parliament.[6] Critics referred to the cabinet derogatorily as a "cabal" or "the conciliabulum." Defined by neither statute nor custom, the cabinet evolved to meet the needs of administration as the kingdom became an empire with transoceanic responsibilities.[7]

The restoration of a Protestant monarchy and the codification of Parliament's rights produced an outpouring of support and celebration for the British monarchy. Officials established annual holidays to celebrate the monarchy and its history, artisans produced an assortment of objects with royal images and symbols, and composers crafted masterpieces to celebrate the new British state. The description of the recent turnover in power as the Glorious Revolution embodied the new cult of monarchy in England, but even more so in the North American colonies.[8] In the 1750s, Washington shared these sentiments: "We have the same Spirit to serve our Gracious King . . . and are as ready, and willing to sacrafice our lives for our Country's good."[9]

These changes produced very real ramifications for North American colonists. In the sixteenth and seventeenth centuries, most of the colonies operated as royal colonies or under the supervision of private companies. As a result, the colonies carefully monitored the fortunes of the monarchy. Colonists resented the Catholic monarchs, who threatened to revoke the governing charters of the colonies, implement a more authoritarian regime, and force religious toleration for Catholics in the colonies in the 1660s. As a predominately Protestant population, the colonists banished religious dissenters, tried to enforce religious homogeneity, and enthusiastically applauded the Glorious Revolution's restoration of a Protestant monarchy.[10]

The British government did not have the funds to oversee a large colonial project, and monarchs were loath to convene a session of Parliament to raise additional revenue. Instead, monarchs in the late seventeenth and early eighteenth centuries focused primarily on stability in Britain and military conflicts in Europe, and largely ignored the colonies. With little attention from the mainland, the colonies flourished under what they called "salutary neglect." They happily governed their domestic affairs through colonial legislatures and enthusiastically participated in the British Empire. They celebrated the Glorious Revolution and eagerly bought into the cult of monarchy that followed. They marched in processions, offered toasts to the monarchy, hosted bonfires with copious alcohol to mark anniversaries and royal birthdays, illuminated their homes, and partook in lengthy feasts—all designed to celebrate the monarchy and their connection to the empire.[11]

In addition to their ideological ties to the monarchy, colonists sought tangible material, economic, legal, and education connections with Britain. As part of the empire, they enjoyed access to silk, porcelain china, and tea from Asia, sold their commodities to the Caribbean and Europe, purchased slaves from British merchants, and bought fine goods produced in Britain. They sought the newest fashions and trends displayed in London to demonstrate their gentility and membership in the empire. Elites sent their children to Britain for the best education and conducted a vibrant correspondence with acquaintances across the globe. In 1774, when the Continental Congress met for the first time, more delegates had visited London than Philadelphia.[12] Colonists considered themselves to be among the best British citizens—they were proud of their heritage and celebrated it.[13]

The Seven Years' War marked the beginning of a new phase in the relationship between the colonies and England. From 1756 to 1763, Britain, its colonies, and its allies fought France, Spain, and their colonies. British won a decisive victory and acquired substantial new territory in the peace settlement. The new lands presented George III and his government with an unprecedented opportunity to reform the empire and assume greater oversight of colonial settlement. For the first time, the cabinet permanently stationed British troops in the colonies to protect their new acquisitions and prevent further conflict with the French and Native Americans. The cabinet also sought a number of reforms to bind the North American colonies more closely to the mother country and make them more productive for the British Empire. The government encouraged the settlement of new colonies in Canada and Florida, attempted to slow the pace of westward expansion, tried to mitigate conflict between white and Native communities by preserving the North American interior for Native peoples, and created new revenue streams to reduce the debt that the government had contracted to prosecute the war.[14]

Eager to reduce domestic taxes to avoid riots in England, the cabinet explored new ways to raise revenue. Starting in 1764, they enacted a series of bills designed to force the colonists to contribute more to the empire's coffers. The Sugar Act in 1764, the Currency Act in 1764, the Stamp Act in 1765, and the Tea Act in 1773 all outraged the colonists.[15] But it was the Coercive Acts, passed in the spring of 1774 in response to the Boston Tea Party, that unified colonial resistance. The Coercive Acts closed the port of Boston, restricted Massachusetts's rights under its governing charter, allowed royal officials and soldiers to face trial in Britain instead of in the colonies, and permitted British military commanders to house troops in private homes.[16] Many colonists felt that the Coercive Acts punished all Massachusetts residents for the actions of a few, and their ire fell on the ministers in the British cabinet. American newspaper writers asserted that the cabinet had created the punitive policies: "The late violent measures, and some others equally vindictive, which are now carrying on, were all concerted in a cabinet-council."[17] Another writer declared that in the "Cabinet . . . the voice of the people is only heard with contempt."[18]

Many newspapers printed cartoons illustrating the colonists' outrage. One example, "Mirror of Truth," depicts angels holding up a mirror to the British ministers, forcing them to confess their many sins as demons drag them down into hell: "Your whole proceedings were contrary to Equity & Justice," "Their duplicity as Ministers is beyond parallel," and "Your crimes stink stronger than all the Taxes in England."[19]

FIGURE 3.1 "The Political Mirror," 1782. Courtesy of the Society of the Cincinnati

The colonies felt betrayed by their British brethren. During the war, they had contributed funds, food, uniforms, supplies, and troops to fight the French and their allies. They had served as partners and fought with distinction. They did not ask for a permanent army to protect their interests. In fact, they believed their militia had proven more than capable of defending their homes and families. Furthermore, they argued that they had already contributed to the war effort and should not be taxed further under the Stamp, Sugar, and Currency Acts.[20]

When Parliament passed these broadly despised bills, colonists initially blamed the cabinet instead of the king. The evolution of the Privy Council and the smaller cabinet had taken place behind closed doors, but most Britons and colonists understood that power dynamics were changing from the larger Privy Council to a few select advisors. They knew that a cabinet existed, and the term "cabinet" pervaded the political lexicon, but many colonists distrusted an institution that they couldn't see or scrutinize. They could not tell who wielded power, who made crucial decisions, and whom they should hold responsible for policies they opposed.[21]

American colonists also noted several constitutional objections to the cabinet's oversight of the colonies through parliamentary legislation. Colonists loudly proclaimed "no taxation without representation," but the reality was a bit more complicated. In response to the first few bills, many colonists accepted Parliament's right to pass legislation that governed the entire empire, at least in principle. They were not trying to implement widespread government reform. They took no issue with legislation such as the Navigation Acts, which restricted how the colonies could buy, sell, and transport goods, because those acts monitored interactions between the colonies and Britain. However, unlike the Navigation Acts, which affected the entire empire, many of the recent tax bills only targeted the North American colonies. Because they had no voice in Parliament, colonists challenged this legislation and insisted their own colonial legislatures were the more appropriate body to pass domestic fiscal legislation. Just a few years later, they took their argument one step further and insisted that their legislatures and Parliament were equals in a loose confederation under the king's supervision.[22]

As the tensions between the colonies and Britain grew, many colonists sought assistance from the king. They believed that he supported their cause and would force his cabinet to rescind the offending legislation. When the king took no action, the colonists blamed the British cabinet for blocking their reconciliation with him. An unnamed gen-

tleman in London reported to the *Virginia Gazette* that the king had welcomed a petition for peace from the Continental Congress, but that
the ministers in the cabinet "are determined to persevere in the great
system of American taxation."[23] In early 1775, Lieutenant John Barker,
a British officer, made a similar observation while he served with his
regiment in Boston. Barker noted in his diary that the Americans demonstrated their displeasure by raising their flag as the "King's Troops"
and referring to the British soldiers as "the Parliaments."[24]

Later that year, the Continental Congress also pointed fingers at the
British cabinet for instigating conflict. In July 1775, the Continental Congress worked to establish friendly diplomatic relations with Native
American nations allied with Great Britain. In an address to the Haude-
nosaunee, also known as the Six Nations Iroquois confederation of
Iroquoian-speaking peoples in Northern New York, Congress expressed
its desire that it could preserve peace between Americans and the Native confederation. Congress also squarely placed blame for the tensions on the king's cabinet: "The king's ministers grew jealous of
us . . . they sent armies to rob & kill us."[25] Washington shared similar
thoughts with a friend, writing, "You must, undoubtedly, have received
an Account of the engagement in the Massachusetts Bay between the
Ministerial Troops (for we do not, nor cannot yet prevail upon our-
selves to call them the King's Troops) and the Provincials."[26]

Americans' anger toward the king's cabinet was shaped by their understanding of the British government and the powers of each branch.
While Americans expected that Parliament and the king's cabinet
would create and implement policy, the king was supposed to act as
the father and protector of all British citizens, including the colonists.
Americans argued that the king had abandoned his constitutional responsibility to restrain the cabinet when it advocated policies that
would threaten the liberties of British citizens. On July 8, 1775, the

Continental Congress sent a second petition to King George III, the "Olive Branch Petition," outlining their understanding of the relationship between the king and his subjects. They wrote, "We therefore beseech your Majesty, that your royal authority and influence may be graciously interposed to procure us relief from our afflicting fears and jealousies . . . and to settle peace through every part of your dominions."[27] The petition pleaded with the king to intervene in the conflict between the colonies and Parliament, believing it was his duty to protect citizens on both sides of the Atlantic Ocean. The Americans were not asking the king to assume unconstitutional powers or return to the absolute monarchy of the Stuart kings. Instead, they urged the king to revive his constitutional right to use the "royal negative," essentially a veto, against legislation that unfairly targeted certain citizens.[28]

Not many delegates to the Continental Congress expected the Olive Branch Petition to change the king's mind, but his response still struck most Americans as especially harsh. The king refused to receive the colonists' petition while sitting on the throne, which would have legitimated American grievances. Instead, on October 27, 1775, the king recited to Parliament the Proclamation for Suppressing Rebellion and Sedition, which declared the colonies to be in a state of "open and avowed rebellion" and urged British officials to "to use their utmost endeavours to withstand and suppress such rebellion."[29] When the king made it clear that he sided with his ministers, Americans turned their rage against the monarch as well.[30] John Adams was one of the first Americans to recognize that the king was no friend to the colonists' pleas, writing: "The Sum total of all Intelligence from England is that the first Man is 'unalterable determined, Let the Event and Consequences be what they will to compel the Colonies to absolute Obedience.' Poor, deluded Man!"[31] By mid-1776, Washington referred to George III as "Our Enemy the King of Great Britain."[32] Mr. Page, a preacher who remained loyal to the king during the Revolution, remarked on the spread of similar sentiment across the colonies, expressing that he was "grieved to hear the King so much vilified & abused in New Engld & America."[33]

Washington carefully tracked Americans' shifting sentiment toward the king. As commander in chief of the Continental Army, Washington interacted with Americans from all thirteen colonies. He received reports from state committees of safety (which governed the states when their legislatures were not in session), welcomed visitors to his army headquarters, and heard the concerns of citizens near the army's camp sites.[34] For example, on October 26, 1775, Washington hosted several luminaries at headquarters, including Benjamin Franklin; Samuel Cooper, a famed Congregational minister; Judith Cooper, his wife; James Bowdoin, president of the Massachusetts Provincial Congress; John Winthrop, a Harvard professor; and Hannah Winthrop, his wife.[35] But Washington did not just interact with elites. In March 1776, enslaved poet Phillis Wheatley accepted Washington's invitation to visit him at his Cambridge headquarters.[36] Through these communications, Washington engaged Americans of every walk of life and learned their fears, hopes, and motivations—including their suspicions of the British government.

The Confederation period, from 1778 to 1789, was a turbulent, anxiety-ridden decade for the new American nation. The country grappled with the physical and psychological damage left in the wake of the Revolutionary War. Congress struggled to govern and address the conflicting needs of the thirteen states. The nation also had to define its purpose, goals, and culture on the international stage. Americans undertook a complete social regeneration. It was no longer sufficient to say they were "not British"; they needed to determine what it meant to be "American." Many leading Americans recognized that they were experiencing a pivotal moment for the nation and its culture. Washington, before submitting his resignation as commander in chief to Congress, wrote to the states encouraging them to come together as one nation: "This is the time of their political probation: this is the moment when the eyes of the whole World are turned upon them—This is the moment to establish or ruin their National Character for ever."[37]

In the 1780s, American culture prioritized republican virtue, which they defined as a dedication to public service, especially through self-sacrifice. A republican gentleman took care to improve his manners and education, but avoided appearing haughty. He dressed meticulously, but not lavishly. He commanded respect through his actions, not merely because of his fortune. In that atmosphere, a politician's reputation served as his political and social currency and determined his election to government, alliances with other politicians, and promotion to higher office.[38] Republican virtue inherently defined itself in opposition to the aristocracy and monarchy ingrained in the British government. The future of the Republic depended on maintaining a virtuous citizenry, specifically contrasted with the corruption Americans perceived in the British cabinet. It wasn't enough for Americans to be virtuous; they needed to be more virtuous than the British.

The Confederation years were marked by intense anxiety that the United States would fail to meet this lofty goal. Perhaps government officials would pursue their own agendas and the new nation would splinter into rival factions. The economic situation certainly inspired little hope. The value of currencies issued by the states and Congress plummeted, and debts owed to both domestic and international creditors spiraled. The economy shrunk as American merchants found themselves shut out of ports previously available to them as citizens of the British Empire. Most European nations still operated under the protectionism of mercantilist legislation, which shut out foreign supplies and merchants in favor of those within their empires. Prior to the Revolution, southerners had sold most of their cotton to British factories; New Englanders had depended on the British to buy American lumber and ships for their navy, and fish caught by New England fishermen to feed enslaved workers in British Caribbean colonies; and the Middle Atlantic had sold most of its excess grain and liquor to British merchants. As an independent nation, the United States had to pay steep tariffs to access British markets—if the British navy permitted American ships to enter the port at all.[39]

Congress could do nothing to solve these economic issues. The Articles of Confederation gave Congress little power to raise revenue. The Articles envisioned a system in which Congress passed requisitions, essentially requests for money, and then each state decided for itself the best way to raise the desired funds. In reality, when Congress issued a requisition, the states debated whether to raise any money at all, instead of how best to meet the demand. Often the states simply ignored Congress's requests. Without funds, Congress was helpless to pay its employees, pay its debts, or defend against military threats. In 1786, Congress's impotence was on full display. Shays' Rebellion forcibly closed courts to prevent the collection of unfair and burdensome taxes. When the states failed to raise funds to pay a federal militia force, Congress could only watch helplessly as Massachusetts merchants, elites, and government officials raised funds and hired a private army.[40]

Regional and sectional divisions compounded economic tensions. Some states threatened to break off from the Union to form regional blocs based on shared economic and cultural values. For example, states in western regions prioritized access to the Mississippi River and the port of New Orleans, as well as defense from Native American attacks.

States in the Northeast blamed white settlers for instigating conflict with Native American nations and resented military expenditures accrued in defending aggressive settlement. They preferred trade agreements that would provide access to Atlantic fisheries and Caribbean ports, which meant nothing to western and southern states. Rather than contribute funds and resources to Congress to pursue national goals, states hoarded money and supplies for their own aims.[41]

Many elite Americans, well versed in the details of ancient governments, knew history was stacked against them. In December 1787, John Adams noted that a few republics had emerged in fifteenth-century Italy, but had all failed: "They were all alike ill-constituted: all alike miserable: and all ended in similar disgrace and despotism."[42] No other republic, especially one as geographically large and dispersed as the United States, had survived. Elite Americans, like Washington, Jefferson, Hamilton, and other officials in the first government, had even more to lose if the Republic failed. They were men of property and wealth. If the Republic crumbled and anarchy reigned, their estates, business, law practices, and trade networks would have suffered irreparable harm.[43]

The Articles of Confederation did not empower the Confederation Congress to solve these problems. Under the Articles, Congress could pass reforms only with unanimous approval by the thirteen states, which was nearly impossible to obtain. These circumstances combined to convince many American leaders that something needed to be done quickly to preserve the fledgling nation.

The first effort to secure reform fizzled before it even started. In September 1786, twelve delegates from five states, New Jersey, New York, Pennsylvania, Delaware, and Virginia, met in Annapolis, Maryland. They waited in vain for more delegates to arrive before concluding that another convention would be necessary. The delegates also quickly realized the trade issues between the states could not be solved without addressing the other economic and governing challenges facing the new nation. Hoping to build some momentum for reform, Alexander Hamilton and James Madison drafted a recommendation to convene another gathering in Philadelphia the following May.[44] All twelve delegates unanimously approved the recommendation and submitted it to the Confederation Congress and the states. Congress sanctioned the recommendation and officially invited each state to appoint delegates to attend a convention the next summer. This gathering became the Federal Constitutional Convention.[45]

On December 4, 1786, the Virginia legislature passed a bill appointing delegates to the convention: George Washington, Edmund Randolph, James Madison, George Wythe, John Blair, and George Mason. It was a distinguished group, full of noted jurists, former governors, experienced legislators, and the one and only commander in chief of the Continental Army. In cahoots with Madison, Randolph included Washington's name on the list without consulting him. Perhaps Madison and Randolph knew that Washington would be reluctant to participate: after eight years of military service, he was enjoying his retirement.

When Randolph announced the nomination, Washington turned him down. Washington had publicly returned his military commission and worried Americans might look unfavorably upon his return to service. Furthermore, he had rejected an invitation to attend a meeting of the Society of Cincinnati in Philadelphia the next summer. Attending the convention after declining the society's company would surely offend his fellow officers.[46] Lastly, Washington feared that the convention would fail. He was reluctant to risk his reputation and political clout on an endeavor that might not work. If the convention did not succeed, Washington and the other Federalists—those who supported a stronger federal government—knew it would be nearly impossible to organize another one. He confided to David Humphreys, his former aide and confidant, that "if this second attempt to convene the States . . . should also prove abortive it may be considered as an unequivocal proof that the States are not likely to agree in any general measure which is to pervade the Union, & consequently, that there is an end put to Fœderal Government."[47] He wanted to make sure that he preserved his political capital for the moment when the nation most needed it.[48]

Randolph, Madison, Knox, and Washington's other correspondents understood his dilemma. But they also understood that the convention would not succeed without him. Randolph elected not to tell the legislature that Washington had refused his nomination and did not appoint anyone to replace him. Randolph knew that Washington's name would lend credibility to the convention and force other states to take the venture seriously. Over the next few months, Randolph and Madison continued to send Washington letters imploring him to attend. Finally, in late April, he begrudgingly agreed to join them.[49] He left Mount Vernon on May 8 and arrived in Philadelphia a few days later.

For the next few weeks, Washington, Madison, and the other members of the Virginia delegation anxiously awaited the arrival of the other states' representatives and hoped all states would attend. They used this time to strategize, build coalitions, and craft proposals for the eventual start of the convention. On May 25, they breathed a sigh of relief when the New Jersey delegation arrived, and the convention reached a quorum.[50] In July, the New Hampshire delegation arrived in Philadelphia, providing almost complete attendance.[51]

On May 25, fifty-five delegates to the Federal Constitutional Convention gathered in the assembly room on the first floor of Independence Hall. As they settled into their seats, they all acknowledged that the British government constantly factored into their deliberations. The

British monarchy and their experience with it colored every proposal, comment, and discussion over the next several months. Many Americans fixated on certain features in the British system as problematic and likely to foster corruption. They objected to the king's lack of responsibility over government policy. They balked at the ministers' dual roles in Parliament and in the king's council, which allowed the ministers to control the king and removed his power to check legislation.[52] Finally, they criticized the commingling of powers between branches under the shared powers system because there was little oversight of, or transparency about, the decision-making process.

These concerns revealed a much larger question about the nature of executive power in a republic. How could the delegates create a single executive with enough power and influence to govern the nation without risking monarchy? How could they maintain their republican virtue and protect individual and states' rights without risking anarchy or the overwhelming malaise of the Confederation? No nation in history had solved this conundrum without eventually succumbing to anarchy or authoritarianism.

The delegates created a presidency with many key provisions designed to address their concerns about the British monarchy. First, they inserted a rule in the Constitution to prevent a power-sharing system in the United States. Article I contains a clause that prevents a member of Congress from holding another position in the federal government, making it much more difficult for an influential congressman or a small group of powerful officials to exercise significant power in the executive branch.[53] The rule protects Congress as well—it forbids the department secretaries from holding another position in the executive or legislative branch.

Next, the delegates decided that the executive branch should be run by one person, rather than a committee. The delegates believed that having one individual in charge of the entire branch would force the president to take ownership of the entire operation. The delegates also included regular elections to hold the president accountable and so that voters could replace him relatively easily.[54] Elections ensured that the president would serve the people, but also implied that fault could be found with the executive. Britons could not vote the king out of office for bad policies, but Americans could replace the president if they disapproved of his actions in office. The delegates crafted the presidency to maximize responsibility and transparency in government. They created an executive that rejected the concept that the king could not be held liable for the actions of his government.[55]

As with all aspects of the presidency, the British cabinet played an important symbolic role in this discussion. The delegates acknowledged that they thought of the British example often during their deliberations, frequently citing the British cabinet as a model to avoid. James Wilson of Pennsylvania insisted that a council often "serves to cover, [rather] than prevent malpractices."[56] Benjamin Franklin similarly suggested that "the many bad Governors appointed in Great Britain for the Colonies" that had frustrated the colonies before the Revolutionary War had been appointed by a corrupt cabinet.[57] Colonel George Mason, an early and ardent support of the Revolution, voiced concerns that the delegates were too preoccupied with the British government: "We all feel too strongly the remains of antient prejudices, and view things too much through a British Medium."[58]

The delegates understood that the president would need assistance governing the nation, but they feared an organized, established council. Over the course of the debates, they considered three types of executive councils to provide advice and support for the president, and they ultimately rejected all three. The first option, a council of revision, would help the president review legislation and check the power of

Congress. The Virginia Plan, written by James Madison and presented by Edmund Randolph on May 29, 1787, included a "council of revision" consisting of members of the executive and judicial branches. The president and the justices of the Supreme Court would sit together to examine and enforce legislation.

On the same day, Charles Cotesworth Pinckney proposed a second type of executive council. Pinckney's plan authorized the president to create his own advisory council with the heads of the future departments.[59] This council avoided the blurring of separation of powers between the branches that occurred in the proposed council of revision. Pinckney's council would provide advice, so the president would not be left without advisors. The president would not be bound to follow their recommendations, however, so the council would not limit executive power.

For the next two months, the delegates debated potential provisions for the executive, judicial, and legislative branches using the Virginia Plan as their guide. After two months of discussion with relatively little progress, the delegates appointed a Committee of Detail to pull together a comprehensive draft constitution based on the few proposals that they had agreed to adopt. From July 26 to August 6, the Committee of Detail met and rejected both the council of revision from the Virginia Plan and the advisory council proposed by Pinckney. The committee members—which included Edmund Randolph—instead favored a strong, independent executive unencumbered by a council.[60]

The six members unequivocally rejected the notion of a council by omitting it from the draft constitution. It's impossible to know exactly why the committee chose to reject the council of revision and Pinckney's proposal, since none of the committee's meeting notes survived, if any were taken. Their decision was most likely driven by fear that a council would limit the power of the president. The committee members were also influenced by the governments of several states, including the Council of State that had stymied Randolph during his tenure as governor. The Pennsylvania, North Carolina, and Maryland state constitutions all included similar councils. While on the Committee of Detail, Randolph helped reject a federal council of revision.

On August 6, the Committee of Detail reported to the entire convention, and the delegates debated each provision of the draft constitution. After viewing the draft, Pinckney introduced another proposal to insert an advisory council consisting of the president, the chief justice of the Supreme Court, the heads of the executive departments, and the president's secretary. Pinckney knew that the Committee of Detail had rejected his earlier council proposal because they believed it would weaken the president, just as the British cabinet allegedly had corrupted the king. Yet Pinckney was not to be deterred and believed the issue deserved further consideration. To address their concerns about limitations on executive power, Pinckney reminded the other delegates that under his proposal, the president could request advice at his leisure and was not required to follow the council's recommendations.

On August 31, the convention created the aptly named Committee of Postponed Matters, also known as the Committee of Eleven, to address the remaining issues. This committee included representatives from each state present at the convention except New York: Nicholas Gilman from New Hampshire, Rufus King from Massachusetts, Roger Sherman from Connecticut, David Brearly from New Jersey, Gouverneur Morris from Pennsylvania, John Dickinson from Delaware, Daniel Carroll from Maryland, James Madison from Virginia, Hugh Williamson from North Carolina, Pierce Butler from South Carolina, and Abraham Baldwin from Georgia. One of the issues on the agenda of the Committee of Postponed Matters was Pinckney's proposed council to advise the president. This committee reconsidered Pinckney's council and again rejected it. While no notes survive from the committee's deliberations, when the committee presented its recommendations to the full convention on September 3, its report included no mention of a council.[61]

On September 7, George Mason introduced a third and final option for an executive council. He asserted that an executive without a council challenged historical precedents for good government: "In rejecting a Council to the President [the delegates] were about to try an experiment on which the most despotic Governments had never ventured." He offered an amendment that would create an executive council of six members chosen by the Senate: two from the eastern states, two from the middle states, and two from the southern states. This council would provide advice for the president and assist in appointing federal officials. Opposing Mason's proposal, Gouverneur Morris argued that such a council would provide cover for a weak president or would obscure responsibility for controversial decisions. Morris didn't have to work hard to remind his fellow delegates of their recent Revolutionary War experience: they had all read Blackstone and witnessed what they viewed as British ministers corrupting King George III. A council seemed like a recipe for ministerial corruption. After considering the arguments, the delegates rejected Mason's proposal by a vote of eight states against three.[62] After rejecting all three proposed councils, the delegates considered no further proposals for an advisory council. The decision was made: the Constitution would neither include nor authorize such an executive body.

Instead of the councils proposed by Madison, Pinckney, and Mason, the delegates inserted two options in the final version of the Constitution that would enable the president to obtain advice. First, Article II, Section 2 grants the president the right to "require the

Opinion, in writing, of the principal Officer in each of the executive Departments, upon any Subject relating to the Duties of their respective Offices."[63] This clause was drafted carefully to limit the power of the president's advisors and the manner in which he interacted with them. In February 1788, James Iredell, a respected jurist from North Carolina and one of the original Supreme Court justices, published several influential pamphlets in the *Norfolk and Portsmouth Journal* analyzing the Constitution. He emphasized the importance of the word "written" in Article II, Section 2. By only permitting the president to request written advice, Iredell argued that the delegates intentionally rejected a cabinet: "The president is not to be assisted by a Council, summoned to a jovial dinner perhaps, and giving their opinions according to the nod of the President—but the opinion is to be given with the utmost solemnity, *in writing*."[64] According to Iredell, the delegates attempted to prevent the department secretaries from forming a cabal around the executive. In addition, by limiting advice to written opinions, the delegates tried to ensure that communications between the president and his advisors would be transparent. A written paper trail created hard physical evidence of each secretary's advice and who advocated which position.

Written opinions also placed physical distance between the president and the secretaries and emphasized that the president was responsible for making all decisions. Written opinions submitted to the president inherently conveyed subordination and highlighted the president's final say on all issues. Article II, Section 2 further required the secretaries to limit their advice to issues pertaining to their departments. The delegates hoped to prevent secretaries from shaping policy outside their areas of expertise.

The delegates also offered a second option for the president to seek additional support on foreign affairs. As Article II, Section 2 provided:

He shall have Power, by and with the Advice and Consent of the Senate, to make Treaties, provided two thirds of the Senators present concur; and he shall nominate, and by and with the Advice and Consent of the Senate, shall appoint Ambassadors, other public Ministers and Consuls, Judges of the supreme Court, and all other Officers of the United States.[65]

Twenty-first-century audiences interpret this clause as a grant of power to the Senate to confirm presidential appointments and ratify treaties. The clause certainly did assign those duties to the Senate, but it had a secondary meaning as well. The delegates meant for the president to request the Senate's advice on treaties and other matters of foreign affairs. They expected the Senate to serve as a council on foreign affairs.[66]

When Washington departed Philadelphia in September 1787, he left knowing that the delegates had considered and affirmatively rejected a cabinet. As president of the Constitutional Convention, Washington attended every session. During the debates, he either sat on a raised dais at the front of the room or with the Virginia delegation. He heard Gouverneur Morris argue that a cabinet would obscure responsibility in the executive branch, he saw the delegates vote against Pinckney's proposed council, and he saw them reject the council of revision in the Virginia Plan. He also reviewed the drafts produced by the Committee of Detail and the Committee of Postponed Matters, and he heard them explain why they rejected an executive council. Washington knew that the delegates rejected an executive council in favor of written advice and the Senate.

Washington also maintained close working relationships with many of the most influential members of the Convention. After the end of the workday, he attended the theater, ate meals and drank tea with his friends, visited former army officers, and listened to music with elite families in Philadelphia. The other delegates joined Washington at these events. During the first week of June, he dined "with a large company" at the homes of George Clymer, Benjamin Franklin, and Robert Morris—all Pennsylvania representatives to the convention. The next week he "Dined with a Club of Convention Members" at the Indian Queen, a lodging house for many of the convention delegates.[67] These social gatherings provided an opportunity for the delegates to discuss their positions on articles of the Constitution, negotiate compromises, and curry favor for proposals in a more private, informal setting. Washington used these events to gauge the expectations of his fellow delegates. If the states ratified the Constitution, Washington knew he would be elected the first president. He needed to know what would be expected of him.

On September 17, 1787, the delegates submitted the proposed constitution to the Confederation Congress for review. On September 28, the Confederation Congress delivered the document to the states and instructed the state legislatures to convene their own ratification conventions. By endorsing a new constitution and submitting it to the states, Congress approved the plan to dismantle the existing government and build a new one. Essentially, it admitted its inability to reform itself or govern the nation. Over the next few years, each state convened a ratification convention to debate the proposed constitution. On June 21, 1788, the new United States federal government officially existed after New Hampshire became the ninth state to ratify the Constitution.[68]

The debates in the state ratification conventions reveal how Americans received the Constitution, their expectations for the new government, and how the delegates anticipated the Constitution would address citizens' concerns. Many delegates in the state debates noted the Constitution's silence on an executive council. A small minority of state delegates argued in favor of including an advisory council specifically outlined in the Constitution. Back in Virginia, Mason resumed his efforts to include an executive council in the Virginia ratification convention. Before the start of the convention, Mason wrote and published his "Objections to This Constitution of Government." Mason protested the lack of an executive council and cited the precedent of councils in all "safe" governments. Although Mason published his "Objections" to sway votes in the Virginia convention, both Federalists (supporters of the Constitution) and Anti-Federalists (opponents of the Constitution) hoped to influence the outcomes in other states. Anti-Federalists in other states republished Mason's pamphlet broadly.

Many of the Anti-Federalists worried about what would happen without an established executive council. In the Pennsylvania ratification convention, Anti-Federalists objected to the Senate's role as a council on foreign affairs. They worried the Senate would usurp executive powers or would be forced to remain in town even when Congress was not in session, to provide advice to the president. Year-round service would be onerous for senators, and citizens would be forced to bear the tax burden of supporting government officials for the entire year. After the majority of Pennsylvania delegates voted in favor of ratification, those opposed to it drafted a document titled "Dissent of the Minority." The official dissent included a proposal to create "a constitutional council . . . to advise and assist the president, who shall be responsible for the advice they give, hereby the senators would be relieved from almost constant attendance; and also, that the judges be made completely independent."[69]

On the other side of the debate, many delegates feared a council and rejoiced in the fact that the Constitution did not authorize one. They believed a council would corrupt the executive or become a den of cronies and favorites—just as they believed the British cabinet had corrupted the king. In a series of published letters, a writer using the pseudonym "Federal Farmer" emphasized the potential for corruption in an executive council. The author of the "Federal Farmer" letters remains a secret, but the most likely candidate is Richard Henry Lee from Virginia.[70]

Opponents of a council, including the "Federal Farmer," viewed the Senate as a more effective and less risky source of advice for the president. The Senate would be a safer advisory body because of its constitutional limitations. First, the Constitution ensures government transparency by permitting the Senate to advise and consent only on matters of foreign affairs. Second, the Senate would be accountable to the people through regular elections. Unlike an appointed council, senators could be removed from office if they served as inept or pernicious advisors. On December 19, "Americanus," whose identity remains unknown, published a letter in the *Virginia Independent Chronicle* defending the constitutional role of the Senate because of the accountability of senators to the state legislatures: "There are thirteen collateral checks, whose united powers, like an overbearing torrent, could not be resisted—I mean the legislatures of the thirteen states. For, as the senate is elected by the legislature of each state, it must be confessed, that each member is responsible to that body, which respectively elect him."[71]

The state debates over a council continued to reflect a widespread preoccupation with the British cabinet. In his "Objections to This Constitution of Government," Mason had referenced the presence of executive councils in other "safe governments," particularly Britain. Iredell published "Marcus II" to refute Mason's claims. Iredell rejected Mason's claim that the British government was safe because it had a council. Iredell described the British council system and demonstrated why each of the various councils and cabinets had no place in the new US government. He argued that the Privy Council best resembled the sort of constitutional council favored by Mason, but it would not limit executive power as Mason hoped: "It is a mere creature of the crown, dependent on its will both for number and duration," and nothing would exist to prevent the president from being "governed by 'minions and favorites.'"[72] In *Federalist 70*, Alexander Hamilton played on Americans' long-standing suspicion of corrupt councils. He argued that a strong council would result in a plural executive, which "tends to conceal faults and destroy responsibility."[73]

The debates in the state ratification conventions demonstrated that many delegates still worried that the Constitution did not provide enough advisors for the president. Despite these concerns, all of the states ratified the Constitution without proposing an amendment to establish an advisory council. The dissenting minority in Pennsylvania was the only one that requested a provision to create a new council. Although the delegates worried about providing appropriate advisors for the president, the fear of the British cabinet proved to be a stronger motivator when crafting the executive branch.

From his perch atop Mount Vernon, Washington anxiously followed the reports leaking out of the state ratification debates. He requested reports from his closest correspondents all over the country, including Benjamin Lincoln, a former Continental Army officer, in Massachusetts: "I feel myself much obliged by your promise to inform me of whatever transpires in your Convention worthy of attention, and assure you that it will be gratefully received."[74] He believed the future of the new nation depended on the proposed federal government, and for him, waiting for news was excruciating. Plus, his personal fortunes were deeply entwined with those of the new government. He had staked his unblemished personal reputation on the success of the Constitutional Convention, and he feared that he would suffer great embarrassment if the state ratification conventions rejected the proposed government. And, as has been previously noted, Washington knew he would be called upon to serve as the nation's first president should the states accept the Constitution. For Washington, there was much riding on the reports that arrived over the next ten months.[75]

Washington went to great lengths to stay abreast of public opinion, the developments in the state conventions, and the likelihood of ratification. He subscribed to at least seven newspapers: *Wyntrop's Journal,* the *Philadelphia Gazette,* the *Pennsylvania Packet,* the *Gazette of the United States, Dunlap & Claypoole, Oswald's Bill,* and the *Virginia Journal.* He also collected volumes of eleven magazines from across the country that included publications of the debates in the state ratification conventions of Massachusetts, Pennsylvania, and Virginia.[76] Washington relied on word-of-mouth news as well. When guests arrived at Mount Vernon, he quizzed them on the progress of ratification in their home states.[77] Lastly, he carried on an extensive correspondence with friends and colleagues across the country and repeatedly requested updates on the status of the Constitution in their private letters. Washington's contacts frequently forwarded him articles of interest or copied key passages into their correspondence.[78] When their letters did not arrive promptly, Washington sent his enslaved manservant William Lee down to Alexandria to fetch the mail.[79]

Washington preferred not to publicly defend the Constitution himself. He swore not to comment on the Constitution in public, but he made no such promises about pulling strings behind the scenes. Shortly after the conclusion of the Constitutional Convention, Washington sent a copy of the Constitution to three former governors of Virginia.

Acknowledging that the document contained some flaws, Washington nonetheless expressed his belief that the new government was better than nothing: "It is the best that could be obtained at this time. . . . If nothing had been agreed to by [the convention] anarchy would soon have ensued."[80] He also passed along speeches and articles to newspaper editors and requested their publication. For example, on October 6, 1787, James Wilson delivered a speech in favor of the Constitution at a public meeting in Philadelphia. Washington read the speech when it was published in the *General Advertiser* and approved of Wilson's interpretation. On October 17, 1787, he sent the speech to David Stuart, a friend and newspaper editor, and asked him to republish it so that it would reach a broader audience: "As the enclosed Advertiser contains a speech of Mr Wilson's (as able, candid, & honest a member as any in Convention) which will place the most of Colo. Mason's objections in their true point of light . . . [t]he republication (if you can get it done) will be of service at this juncture."[81] Over the next several months, Washington sent Stuart additional materials for republication, including "An American Citizen," a broadside written by Tench Coxe and originally published in Philadelphia.[82] While he made no public statement about the Constitution, Washington hoped that these articles would turn the tide in favor of ratification.

Washington also distributed copies of the *Federalist* essays that he received from James Madison, Alexander Hamilton, and John Jay. They all trumpeted the need for "a Government to perpetuate, protect and dignify" the union of the states. Washington thanked the authors for their efforts on behalf of their Constitution: "I am indebted to you . . . for the Pamphlet you were so obliging as to send me. The good sense, forceable observations, temper and moderation with which it is written cannot fail . . . of making a serious impression even upon the antifœderal mind."[83] Washington gave out so many copies of the *Federalist* essays that on May 15, 1788, he had to ask John Jay to send him additional copies: "Could you, conveniently, furnish me with another of these pamphlets I would thank you, having sent the last to a friend of mine."[84]

Washington went to such great lengths to acquire and disseminate news in part because he cared deeply about the outcome of the ratification conventions. But he also needed to know what the American people were saying about the government and the presidency. He needed to know what they expected of him as he prepared to enter office.

On Saturday, June 28, Washington received news that the Constitution had been officially ratified, and he attended a dinner in Alexandria to celebrate. He shared his fellow citizens' "exhilaration," "zest," and conviction that "Providence seems still disposed to favour the members of [the new nation]."[85]

After the states ratified the Constitution, the lame-duck Confederation Congress passed a law requiring each state to choose its electors by January 1789. The law also stipulated that the electors would vote in February and the new government would convene in March. On April 6, 1789, Congress held a joint session and counted the votes for president and vice president.[86] On April 14, Washington received the official communication that he had been elected the first president of the United States.[87] The results were not a surprise—he had been preparing for months.[88]

On April 16, 1789, George Washington left Mount Vernon to begin his trek to New York City, the seat of the new federal government. Along the way, citizens fêted and celebrated Washington and his service to the nation. Towns along the route hosted balls, drank countless toasts, and decorated bridges to welcome the new president. On the morning of April 23, Washington arrived at Elizabeth Town Point, New Jersey, where he boarded an elaborately decorated barge to carry him across New York Harbor. Thirteen "Masters of Vessels," outfitted in white uniforms and black caps, manned the oars. Six other barges loaded with congressmen and dignitaries accompanied him. Once they reached the harbor, private vessels flooded the harbor to greet Washington. Crowds filled the banks of the river and cheered at the firing of a thirteen-gun salute. After Washington reached the shore, a military escort led him to a public levee. Fireworks and cannons capped off the night's festivities.[89]

Washington brought to the presidency a unique perspective of the challenges of the previous decade, the nascent American political culture, and the public's expectations of the new federal government. The combination of Washington's war service, his extensive travels across several states during the war, his interactions with thousands of colonists, and the symbolic leadership he provided to the American cause gave Washington a deep sense of nationalism and American's shared commitment to republican virtue. As part of this American identity, Washington understood and embraced a distrust for all things British, especially the cabinet. As president of the Constitutional Convention, he had gained an invaluable understanding of the intended workings of the federal government. He had listened to delegates share their concerns about the British cabinet and had witnessed the delegates reject proposals for advisory councils. Washington also noted that the delegates intended for the Senate to serve as a council on foreign affairs and that the department secretaries would provide written opinions on matters in their departments. He entered the presidency intending to utilize these two options, and no others.

4

The Early Years

WHEN GEORGE WASHINGTON took the oath of office on April 30, 1789, he was tasked with establishing the functions of the executive branch. The Constitution provided scant information to guide the president as he interacted with the public at events and holidays, welcomed private citizens in his home, and worked with the other branches of government. During the first two years of his administration, Washington designed a social schedule, established relations with the legislature and judiciary, and explored options for obtaining advice. Washington visited the Senate, experimented with a prime-minister-type relationship based on the British model, and sought advice from the Supreme Court before rejecting these options as viable advisory bodies. As Washington established these executive practices—both public and private—he relied on his leadership experience as commander in chief of the Continental Army.

In the months leading up to Washington's inauguration, he expressed misgivings about the decisions and burdens that accompanied his new position. He understood that his every action would set precedents for his successors and invite controversy and judgment from his fellow Americans. As a result, both Washington and other public officials operated under constant, pervasive anxiety about whether they were making the correct choice at any given moment. As Washington confessed to Henry Knox shortly before taking office, "My movements to the chair of Government will be accompanied with feelings not unlike those of a culprit who is going to the place of his execution."[1] One year into his administration, Washington acknowledged to his friend Catharine Macaulay Graham that he felt every decision carried enormous weight. "I walk on untrodden ground," he wrote. "There is scarcely any action, whose motives may not be subject to a double interpretation. There is scarcely any part of my conduct which may not hereafter be drawn into precedent."[2] Given these high stakes, Washington established each precedent with precision. He understood that the nation's future depended on his forging a safe path—an almost impossible task.

In the Early Republic, a man's reputation determined every social, political, and economic opportunity and interaction. It opened doors for trade partnerships, decided who could obtain credit, and served as political currency. Reputations were so important that men engaged in a highly regulated system of written warfare, which sometimes culminated in duels to defend slights to their honor.[3] In order to carve out a successful career in public service, gentlemen had to establish a reputation as virtuous republicans. They were supposed to be talented and exceptional, "live modestly, dress practically, and behave forthrightly in a spirit of accommodation."[4] They were expected to carry these principles into their federal positions—to bring honor and prestige to the office, but not aristocracy. Yet the meaning of these generalities differed from one person to another. What appeared republican to a New Yorker might seem downright aristocratic to a North Carolinian.

Furthermore, no existing governing customs or legal precedents existed to guide Washington and the first generation of officeholders. The lack of guidelines filled each new scenario with additional pressure, but also left officials without a rubric to assess their actions. With no other benchmark, officials turned to public opinion to measure their successes and failures—a highly contested process. Some public figures, such as Hamilton, argued that the opinions of public creditors—elite men of substance—should be considered first. He wanted to use their opinions to support his fiscal legislation. Madison, who opposed Hamilton's agenda, countered that the opinions of average farmers and laborers were more important. He planned to use their opinions to provide transparency and check the corruption and encroachment of government power that he saw in Hamilton's legislation.[5] Thus, depending on the perspective, public opinion could have indicated an official's likelihood of reelection, but also carried enormous implications for that person's reputation and life after political office.

All Early Republic officials shared a constant dread that their fellow citizens might condemn their actions. Washington in particular wanted feedback "not so much of what may be thought the commendable parts, if any, of my conduct, as of those wch are conceived to be blemishes."[6] Finding that careful balance between strength and virtue proved challenging. David Stuart, who had married Washington's stepdaughter-in-law in 1783, regularly funneled reports to Washington from Virginia. A few months after Washington's inauguration, Stuart shared criticism that he had heard in Virginia about Vice President John Adams appearing too monarchical. Washington offered a half-hearted defense of Adams. He replied that although Adams sometimes adopted a high tone, he only used a carriage with two horses. Washington expected Stuart to understand that Adams's use of a relatively modest form of transportation conveyed his republican character.[7] While this distinction might seem silly in the twenty-first century, it demonstrates how Washington, Adams, and others in the Early Republic carefully crafted and dissected each action for hidden republican and aristocratic meaning.

Before the advent of sophisticated polling measures and widespread suffrage, public opinion was hard to gauge. Politicians relied on a few methods to deduce the thoughts of their fellow citizens. First, a network of private correspondents passed along the opinions of their friends, family, colleagues, and acquaintances. These networks expanded far beyond their local communities and allowed politicians to keep tabs on developments across the United States and around the world.[8] Politicians also collected pamphlets, which articulated specific arguments. They were usually signed by the author, which conveyed a great deal of seriousness because the author was willing to stake his name and reputation on the argument contained in the pamphlet. Because they were expensive to produce, pamphlets afforded the wealthy and connected a venue to share their ideas. Pamphlets were printed in relatively small numbers for a limited audience with very specific circulation. Broadsides, large printed sheets similar to posters, and newspaper editorials offered a more informal approach. They were cheaper to create, often anonymous, and recirculated through numerous newspapers. As a result, they were generally considered "beneath the notice of elite politicians."[9] That is not to say elite politicians did not notice them, but they considered the medium too undignified to merit a response.

The combination of letters, pamphlets, broadsides, and newspapers offered politicians a fairly thorough report on the opinions of white, literate males. Although politicians often exchanged letters with female family members or friends, these types of published and private communications rarely conveyed the emotions of working-class women, illiterate men, Native Americans, or freed or enslaved African Americans. These were not the constituencies politicians worked to represent.

Not all of this correspondence was petty gossiping. In the absence of precedent, government officials relied on cultural and social traditions to help determine how the new government should work. Given these enormously high stakes, elites meticulously cultivated professional and personal networks both to provide and to disseminate information. These networks offered critical opportunities to develop trade partners, extend credit, open social circles, and promote political aspirations—indeed, they made or destroyed careers. Politicians at every level managed their own information pipelines through families, friends, and colleagues. They expected these contacts to provide crucial intelligence, but also to pass along select data to their own communities, effectively pursuing their own governing agendas through shadow networks.[10] Through these connections, politicians could reach wide audiences to promote or defend their political positions. For example, Senator William Maclay from Pennsylvania exchanged letters with other elite Pennsylvanians, wrote newspaper essays for his constituents, and obsessed over the Senate record. He fussed over the terse entries, ensuring that any mention of his name accurately reflected his position. He fumed when the Senate closed its debates to the public and worried that voters would not learn of his efforts to represent their interests in a virtuous republican manner. To overcome the lack of official information, Maclay meticulously recorded Senate interactions in his diary. He narrated the debates, offered his interpretations, and speculated about his opponents' motives. Maclay did not transcribe his thoughts for his own benefit—he intended this diary for a higher purpose. Every time he traveled home from New

York City, he brought his diary in his saddlebag, ready to share it with friends, colleagues, and state legislators in Pennsylvania.[11]

Long before Washington gathered the department secretaries in the first cabinet meeting, each one of them had created his own network to support his agenda, supply information, and disseminate reports. Secretary of Treasury Alexander Hamilton depended on his own circle of contacts based largely in New York and Philadelphia. Unsurprisingly, Hamilton's contacts concentrated in elite commercial communities cultivated during his time as a lawyer and politician in New York. As secretary of the treasury, he often consulted these contacts to test how merchant and commercial elites would receive proposed navigation laws and treaties. Reaching out to experts made good business sense, but it also indicates that Hamilton shared the widespread and pervasive anxiety about the future of the nation. His proposed financial system—which depended on the approval of merchant and commercial leaders—would completely transform the nation's economy. If Hamilton failed, he believed, the Republic would fail along with him, and his personal reputation would be in tatters; this was a fear shared by many of the first officeholders.

Immediately after taking office, Hamilton began building the infrastructure required to implement and enforce his financial system. Hamilton, with Washington's approval, needed to fill hundreds of positions in ports and customs collections offices across the nation. While the other departments remained quite small, the Treasury Department's responsibilities and employees stretched across the thirteen states.

As he created this web of employees and new policies to guide their actions, Hamilton reached out to several close associates, including William Bingham and John Fitzgerald. Hamilton and Bingham probably met during the Revolutionary War, when Bingham led the Second Troop of Philadelphia Light Horse dragoons. Bingham came from an elite Pennsylvania family and had enhanced his fortune during the war with several merchant and mercantile businesses. After the war, he enjoyed a prominent position in the financial and political community in Philadelphia. Bingham also played a central role in forming the first Bank of North America—a project near and dear to Hamilton's heart. In 1787, they likely spent time together discussing new financial institutions for the nation when Hamilton visited Philadelphia for the Constitutional Convention. At the time, Bingham represented Pennsylvania in the Confederation Congress and owned one of the finest homes in Philadelphia. Over the course of the summer, Bingham hosted visiting delegates, including George Washington, for afternoon tea and dinner parties "in great Splender."[12]

Hamilton and Fitzgerald developed a close bond while serving together as aides-de-camp for Washington during the war. Both of them fought in the Battles of Brandywine, Germantown, and Monmouth before Fitzgerald retired from the army. In the fall of 1777, they had schemed to defend Washington's reputation and defeat a cabal in Congress that plotted to replace Washington with General Horatio Gates. In the 1780s, Fitzgerald served as the mayor of Alexandria, one of the largest ports in Virginia. He also ran a profitable mercantile business and worked as a collector of customs under Washington's administration.[13] He was the exact type of person Hamilton relied on for news and advice.

When Hamilton reached out to Bingham and Fitzgerald in the fall of 1789, he asked them to supply information about the Philadelphia and Alexandria ports respectively: "It is my earnest wish to obtain all the lights I can on these Subjects in order that I may be the better able to discharge the trust reposed in me."[14] To accurately craft navigation laws and negotiate trade treaties, he wanted to compile a complete picture of the shipbuilding industry, the number of voyages each vessel sailed between various American and international ports, the number of sailors employed by each vessel, and the wages and other privileges afforded to sailors.[15] Hamilton sent these questions to the collectors of customs employed by the Treasury Department, as well as his close friends.[16] Since he valued their opinions, he also requested that Bingham and Fitzgerald send periodic updates on their home states and suggestions to facilitate the growth of trade. Finally, Hamilton encouraged them to offer "any thoughts that may occur to you concerning the Finances and Debts of the United States."[17] If anything was going wrong in his new system, he desperately wanted to know about it.

As secretary of the treasury, Hamilton also took advantage of the built-in network at his fingertips in the Treasury Department to collect and distribute information. He utilized the customs collectors stationed at every American port as invaluable assets. In addition to their regular paperwork, Hamilton requested reports whenever "breaches of the Revenue Laws [took] place."[18] He also expected them to provide updates after the administration implemented a new policy.[19] On August 10, 1790, Congress passed a new law levying additional duties on goods, including spirits and liquors imported from outside the United States. On December 18, Hamilton sent out instructions to his collectors on how they should assess these new taxes. He concluded his letter by encouraging them to "communicate to me, from time to time, such observations concerning the matter as shall be suggested by the course of practice."[20]

Hamilton understood that the financial system required finesse and flexibility. He could not expect Congress to pass legislation, his employees to enforce it, merchants and ship captains to pay their taxes, and the government to obtain revenue without some tension. After all, the rebellious colonies had ostensibly declared independence over unfair taxes. Hamilton relied on his network to let him know when merchants complained of heavy tax burdens, and he counted on them to use judgment and discretion when enforcing taxes on imports— even if that meant turning a blind eye every now and again.[21] The network provided crucial feedback about how his policies were received by his key constituents: the merchants, bankers, and elites. His Treasury Department network continued to supply him with updates after his retirement from the administration in 1795. Oliver Wolcott Jr., Hamilton's protégé, assumed control of the Treasury Department and funneled information to his former boss—often sharing updates with Hamilton before he sent them to President Washington.

In both his private and official correspondence, Hamilton acknowledged the importance of public opinion. He recognized that the American public had a long history of opposing new taxation measures and might resist additional duties under the new administration. Hamilton thought that unimpeachable conduct by the customs collectors might help the public accept new taxes, and he urged his customs collectors to collect payment on imports with "the *most exact punctuality.*" He admitted that state laws often permitted procrastination of duties. Going forward, however, Hamilton considered "*strict observance . . . essential . . .* as well as necessary to the Public."[22]

While Hamilton built a network using Treasury Department employees to further his financial agenda, Secretary of State Thomas Jefferson cultivated his own support network, especially in his home state of Virginia. Jefferson's closest friend, James Madison, served as the cornerstone of this network. Their five-decade-long partnership began during the Revolutionary War, when Madison supplied Jefferson with war updates from Philadelphia and the other seats of government. At every step of the way, until Jefferson's death in 1826, they shared intelligence about the state of the Union and their efforts to preserve it in the face of perceived threats, both foreign and domestic. In 1780, Madison alluded to the private nature of their correspondence. He asked Jefferson to confirm the receipt of his recent letters: "I have written several private letters to you since my arrival here, which as they contained matters that I should be sorry should fall into other hands, I could wish to know had been received."[23] The secret nature of their correspondence was crucial, especially when they broke written or unwritten rules by sending each other intelligence while serving in Congress or the cabinet. Washington expected cabinet deliberations to remain private. Jefferson understood Washington's expectations but elected to share critical information with his closest confidants anyway.[24]

Jefferson primarily relied on Madison to supply information about political developments and conversations out of his reach. While Jefferson served as the American minister to France, Madison sent updates on the Virginia legislature and the Constitutional Convention. On March 19, 1787, Madison anxiously awaited the start of the convention and shared his concerns with Jefferson: "The difficulties which present themselves are on one side almost sufficient to dismay the most sanguine, whilst on the other side the most timid are compelled to encounter them by the mortal diseases of the existing constitution."[25] Once Jefferson joined Washington's administration, he often found himself stuck in New York City and then Philadelphia with a full plate of State Department responsibilities. Madison took advantage of congressional recesses to travel home, visit with neighbors and his own informants, and send reports on public morale back to Jefferson.

During these trips, Madison mined a blend of his personal and professional connections for useful information, and created a hierarchy of communications with Jefferson at the top, then Madison, then local contacts. Madison's local connections supplied information to him, and he in turn supplied reports to Jefferson. If it served his purposes,

Jefferson then passed material on to Washington. When Congress was in session, Madison leaked to Jefferson key details about private conversations not found in the official record of congressional debates. He began this practice when Jefferson traveled back to the United States from France. For example, in February 1790, Madison ensured that Jefferson understood the political scene in New York City before arriving to take office as secretary of state. On February 14, he wrote, "The Report of Mr. Hamilton has been, of late, the principal subject of debate." Madison's letter referred to Hamilton's proposal for the national government to pay off bonds issued during the Revolutionary War. Madison shared that the House had voted unanimously to fund the foreign debt but fractured over the domestic debt. At issue was whether the federal government would pay off the initial bondholders, such as soldiers and farmers, or pay off the speculators who then held most of the bonds. Madison favored a split payment plan that would minimally reward speculators while also repaying the original, virtuous bond owners. He confessed to Jefferson, "The equity of this proposition is not contested. Its impracticability will be urged as an insuperable objection."[26] After Jefferson's retirement from the State Department, Madison continued to serve in the House of Representatives and regularly relayed information from Philadelphia back to Jefferson in Virginia.

James Monroe also provided important information from Virginia and abroad about how the world perceived the administration, Hamilton, and Jefferson. From 1790 to 1794, Monroe served as a senator from Virginia. During congressional recesses, Monroe traveled back to Virginia to tend to his law practice. Unlike Madison, who spent most of his time in Albemarle and Orange Counties in the central region of Virginia, Monroe frequently sent Jefferson dispatches from Fredericksburg, Williamsburg, and Richmond.[27] For example, on October 16, 1792, Monroe reported important personal news, including the death of Colonel George Mason, as well as political developments, such as Richard Henry Lee's retirement from the Virginia governor's office. Monroe also passed along significant political gossip: "Dr. Lee, Harvie, and F. Corbin were mentioned to me by the last post as the only competitors [to replace Henry]. I think it probably some other person may be brought forward, but this is conjecture only."[28] After his appointment as the Minister to France, Monroe proved even more useful to Jefferson. Monroe sent a steady supply of updates on the French Revolution and the war in Europe, filled with colorful assessments inspired by their shared Francophilia. In his first letter after arriving in Paris, Monroe reported: "It happened that I took my station a few days after Robertspierre had left his in the Convention, by means of the guillitin, so that every thing was in commotion, as was natural upon such an event; but it was the agitation of universal joy occasioned by a deliverance from a terrible oppression."[29]

Washington also maintained an extensive information network independent from his subordinates in the executive branch. He received updates from correspondents on his pet projects, including the Potowmack Company, his extensive land holdings out west, and the development of the District of Columbia as the nation's capital city. For example, on September 2, 1789, George Gilpin sent Washington a full account of his recent adventures up the Potomac River. Gilpin and Washington probably met before the start of the Revolutionary War. Gilpin had established himself as a successful wheat merchant in Alexandria, where Washington frequently sold his harvests. In May 1780, Washington rented a steady mare from Gilpin to calm one of his flightier horses.[30] After the war, they developed a closer relationship over their shared passion for the Potowmack Company.[31] Washington believed that the new nation needed to develop economic bonds between the western and eastern regions to foster nationalism. A canal system transporting goods from western farms to eastern markets and ports would facilitate these tenuous bonds. The Virginia legislature created the Potowmack Company to "[open] and [extend] the navigation of Potowmack river." In May 1785, the company met for the first time, electing Washington as the first president and Gilpin as one of the directors.[32] When Gilpin wrote to Washington in September 1789, he had completed his voyage up the Potomac River and shared detailed notes of the distances, waterfalls, rapids, and water depths.[33]

Washington also frequently requested that his trusted advisors pass along reports on public opinion. David Stuart, James Madison, and Chief Justice John Jay were all trusted correspondents in the early years of Washington's administration.[34] Washington also welcomed advice from other friends and government officials. When Edmund Pendleton, president of the Virginia Supreme Court of Appeals, shared his unsolicited opinion on the recent treasury legislation that created the national bank, Washington assured him, "With the most scrupulous truth I can assure you, that your free & unreserved opinion upon any public measure of importance will always be acceptable to me, whether it respects men, or measures—and on no man do I wish it to be expressed more fully than on myself."[35]

Washington's extensive newspaper and magazine subscriptions demonstrate his significant financial and emotional investment in staying informed of developments and public opinion in communities across the United States.[36] He cared deeply about what American citizens thought of the administration and him personally, and he knew that his success, and the nation's future, depended on their support.

Washington experienced a more complicated relationship with public opinion than many other public officials. As president, he felt that his position prevented him from responding to attacks or taking active steps to shape his image. In presidential decisions both big and small, Washington acknowledged the importance of republican virtue and widespread anti-British sentiment. In 1783, officers of the Continental Army formed the Society of the Cincinnati with Washington's blessing and encouragement. Washington believed that the members established the organization to erect a "memorial of their common services, sufferings, and friendships" and were driven "by motivates of sensibility, charity, and patriotism."[37] Yet public outcry forced Washington to distance himself from the society, at least officially. Much to his surprise, the public objected to the organization, especially the hereditary membership, which reminded many of British aristocracy. Critics labeled the organization a subversion of "the principles of republican government" and accused Washington of "wanting in patriotism for not discouraging an establishment calculated to create distinctions in society."[38] In response to these critiques, he encouraged the organization to amend its membership policies. While Washington continued to host many members of the society in his home and visit them in their cities—all appropriate private social interactions—he avoided an official presence in the society.[39] For example, he declined to attend the society's first annual meeting, scheduled to take place in Philadelphia in the summer of 1787.[40] Washington's sensitivity to criticism and his eagerness to avoid it demonstrate how he incorporated public opinion into his decision-making process.

Washington learned a valuable lesson from the backlash over the Society of the Cincinnati and subsequently worked to avoid similar accusations of aristocracy.[41] On August 28, 1788, William Barton, a specialist on the art of heraldry, wrote to Washington offering to create a special seal for the executive branch that would be "consonant to the purest spirit of Republicanism." Washington replied that he believed heraldry could be of great use to the new nation, but that "the minds of a certain portion of the community . . . believ[e] that the proposed general government is pregnant with the seeds of discrimination, oligarchy, and despotism." He assured Barton that while he supported the proposal, he must decline the offer out of "some respect [for] prevalent opinions," and that in this instance, "some sacrifices might innocently be made to well-meant prejudices, in a popular government."[42] While Washington may have agreed with Barton about the utility of heraldry, he refused to attach his name to the project out of fear that it would appear unrepublican.

Washington's efforts to sidestep criticism often worked. On April 23, 1789, Senator Richard Henry Lee brought forth the issue of how Congress should address the president. Although the constitution labels the office "President," it does not specify how the individual should be addressed. On one side, Vice President John Adams and the majority of the Senate advocated for a more extravagant title that would bestow prestige and respect on the new executive branch. Adams endorsed "His Highness the President of the United States of America, and Protector of their Liberties." The House of Representatives, and most American citizens, preferred something simpler, such as "President."[43] Washington studiously avoided giving any indication of his preference. On May 14, 1789, Senator Maclay confessed in his diary that he had no clue how Washington felt about the dispute that became known as the Title Controversy. Maclay served as one of the most vocal opponents of the more regal titles proposed in the Senate and noted his contempt for Vice President Adams for advocating "titles & honors."[44] He asserted that Washington had not expressed opposition to titles or else he "would have heard of it." Edmund Randolph shared with James Madison a popular report circulating in Virginia, holding that Washington had written to John Adams threatening to resign if Congress approved an ostentatious title for the president. Many newspaper editorials assured American citizens that Washington bore no blame for the proposed titles. The *New York Daily Advertiser* claimed, "Our amiable and truly excellent President, we are credibly informed, wishes no badge, which the constitution has not expressly allowed, to distinguish him from his fellow citizens in general."[45]

Although Washington did not reveal his position while the Title Controversy raged in Congress, he later expressed relief at the outcome. On July 26, 1789, Washington wrote to David Stuart that the question of titles "was moved before I arrived, without my privity or knowledge—and urged after I was apprised of it, contrary to my opinion; for I (foresaw and predicted the reception it has) met with . . . Happily, the matter is now done with, I hope never to be revived."[46] Perhaps Washington felt relief at avoiding the awkward title recommended by John Adams, or perhaps he was just glad to have escaped the criticism levied against his vice president.

While Washington and the secretaries' efforts to gather news may seem excessive to us, this information and these relationships served an important purpose. Reports on public opinion helped the first officeholders evaluate their own behavior and that of their colleagues. Furthermore, maintaining these pipelines of information was a critical part of public service. These relationships ensured that the officeholders would continue to receive updates on how the public viewed their actions and whether their careers would be judged successes or failures.

Armed with the public's opinion, Washington set out to create a working and social environment that befitted a republic. As president, he implemented a similar decision-making process to the one he had established during the Revolutionary War. First, he sought out several advisors to solicit their advice before establishing any social or government policy. Second, he considered their advice in private. Third and finally, he made a decision, which he then implemented with alacrity and firmness. In 1789, he was especially focused on how the president should interact with the public. Washington submitted several questions to Acting Secretary of State John Jay, Vice President John Adams, future secretary of the treasury Hamilton, and Acting Secretary of War Knox. Washington inquired if it would be improper for him to make informal visits to his private acquaintances, whether he should he make a tour of the states in the Union during the congressional recess, and whether he should host four great parties per year to commemorate important occasions. Perhaps more important, Washington wanted to know how and when to engage with audiences. At the bottom of the page, underneath the questions, Washington explained: "The President in all Matters of business or Etiquette can have no Object but to demean himself in his publick Character in such a manner as to maintain the dignity of Office without subjecting himself to the imputation of superciliousness or unnecessary reserve."[47]

After receiving responses from his advisors, Washington's first order of business was to create a social calendar that was sufficiently warm and open, while also establishing respect for the new executive. Twice a year, on February 22 and July 4, Washington opened his home to the public to celebrate his birthday and the birth of the nation. On those days, cannons placed at the end of Market Street boomed to announce the start of the festivities. Units of Society of Cincinnati veterans marched in full regalia to the President's House, where they mingled with upstanding citizens. Hundreds if not thousands of visitors filled the drawing rooms, dining rooms, hallways, and landings. They drank punch, offered cheers to Washington's future health, and enjoyed music played by bands in the street.[48]

Although Washington opened his doors on special occasions, he could not welcome random visitors to the house or else a daily continuous stream of guests and office-seekers would have made his work impossible. Instead, Washington hosted weekly levees: any man dressed in respectable attire could enter the president's home every Tuesday afternoon. Washington balanced the open-door policy with strict protocol. He dressed in a velvet suit, wore a ceremonial sword, and greeted each guest with a formal bow. The attendees were then shown to their place in a large circle. Washington slowly walked around the room and exchanged a few words with each guest. After he concluded his circle, the levee ended.

One step below the formal levees, Martha hosted her weekly drawing room gatherings on Friday evenings, which George attended as a guest. These soirees included both men and women and required an invitation.[49] Martha's drawing rooms provided an opportunity for George to receive diplomats, congressmen, government officials, and prominent families.[50] In the Early Republic, women could not participate in politics or government. Therefore, when women were present, events were considered private and the conversations were outside the realm of masculine politics. Of course the reality was much more political than anyone acknowledged, and women read, discussed, and wrote about these issues.[51] Because Martha hosted the drawing rooms, George was free to mingle with the guests and engage in conversations about theater, literature, and, of course, politics. Washington used the social nature of these events to his advantage—he dropped hints about his preferences on legislation under consideration by Congress without appearing to interfere with the legislature.

Finally, the Washingtons hosted private dinners once a week. They invited politicians, government officials, and their friends. The department secretaries and their families frequently attended these dinners.[52] As Washington planned his dinners over the course of a congressional session, he carefully selected guests from each branch of government and from all states. He made sure to include all members of the federal government, avoid charges of favoritism, and refrain from giving offense to any one delegation. A dinner invitation to the President's House helped foster emotional ties between the guests and Washington—and, by extension, with the new federal government. Furthermore, by inviting officials from differing states, he could subtly build coalitions and support for his policies.

Although Washington was the official host of these dinners, he invited the department secretaries as members of his official family to help him facilitate these events just as he had relied on his aides-de-camp to serve guests and foster lively conversation at headquarters. For example, on January 28, 1790, the Washingtons hosted a dinner with representatives from the executive branch and both houses of Congress. From the executive branch, Washington invited Adams and Hamilton. He also included Senators Philip Schuyler (New York), Tristam Dalton (Massachusetts), Robert Morris (Pennsylvania), and Pierce Butler (South Carolina). From the House of Representatives, Washington invited Michael Stone (Maryland), William Smith (South Carolina), James Schureman (New Jersey), Thomas Fitzsimons (Pennsylvania), Theodore Sedgwick (Massachusetts), Daniel Huger (South Carolina), and James Madison (Virginia). Washington continued these dinners through the end of his presidency, noting in his diary that he hosted the entire diplomatic corps at his home on January 12, 1797.[53]

In June 1792, Edward Thornton, a British citizen, attended one of these dinners. Thornton served as the secretary to George Hammond, the British minister to the United States. While in the United States, Thornton frequently wrote to his mentor and financial backer, James Bland Burges, an undersecretary for the British Foreign Department.

In one of his missives to Burges, Thornton described Washington's efforts to straddle the line between republican virtue and respect for the office of the president. Washington clearly harbored a "certain dislike of monarchy," Thornton reported, noting that this dislike seemed a bit hypocritical given that Washington "love[d] to be treated with great respect" and traveled "in a very *kingly* style."[54]

Thornton also highlighted how Washington carefully orchestrated his every public action and appearance. For most travel, Washington rode in an ornate cream-colored coach pulled by six matching horses and attended by liveried coachmen. The coach was one of the fanciest in the United States and recognizable to all who saw it.[55] Washington knew that his fancy coach might remind some citizens of the trappings of monarchy, however, so he balanced it by taking a daily walk on the streets of New York City and then Philadelphia. Walking must have provided little pleasure to Washington. He much preferred to ride a horse for exercise rather than stain his boots with the muck and waste that flowed onto the city streets. But Washington was a conniving politician who carefully crafted his image. He took his walks to convey that he was no better than the average citizen who trudged through the city streets. Washington's contemporaries understood these walks as a political statement and applauded his assertion of republican virtue.[56] Washington hoped that observers would come to the same conclusion regarding the combination of these three types of social gatherings—that they struck an appropriate balance between "too much state and too great familiarity."[57]

Washington referred to the secretaries as his family and regularly included them in social gatherings, events, and meals. He was a great fan of the theater, and he "[could not] deny himself the gratification of requesting the company" of his friends and colleagues.[58] When the federal government resided in New York City, Washington maintained a box at the John Street Theatre. He frequently sent tickets to the secretaries and their wives, as well as other friends and former military officers. On November 24, Washington attended a performance of "The Toy; or a Trip to Hampton Court," performed by the Old American Company. He sent invitations to Abigail Adams, wife of John Adams; Philip Schuyler, senator from New York, and his wife, Catherine; Rufus King, senator from New York, and his wife, Mary; Alexander Hamilton; and Kitty Greene, the widow of General Nathanael Greene. Less than a week later, on November 30, Washington enjoyed the Old American Company's performance of *Cymon and Sylvia*. He again invited a number of his friends and government officials: Dr. William Samuel Johnson, senator from Connecticut, and his wife, Anne Johnson; Ruth and Tristam Dalton, senator from Massachusetts; Sarah and John Jay, chief justice of the Supreme Court; Lucy and Henry Knox; Baron von Steuben, one of Washington's favorite generals during the war; and Kitty Greene.[59] Washington had learned from his experience as commander-in-chief that these social events fostered an esprit de corps among his subordinates that helped carry the officers through the dark days of the war. He was eager to encourage similar bonds and loyalty with the secretaries.

In addition to his regular social events, Washington also embarked on two major tours of the nation during his first term as president. He aimed to bring the federal government to communities that rarely interacted with the new administration outside of their use of the postal service. Washington was the most notable symbol of the new nation, and he hoped his presence would foster emotional connections to the union and build support for the administration's policies. Finally, he wished to explore regions and communities previously unknown to him and learn about their cultures, economies, and ways of life.[60]

Washington conscientiously planned both tours to showcase his devotion to republican virtue. For example, prior to his arrival in Boston on October 24, 1789, Washington informed John Hancock, governor of Massachusetts, that he wished "to visit your Metropolis without any parade, or extraordinary ceremony."[61] He also had these sentiments published in a local newspaper. Despite his protestations, crowds thronged to view the Revolutionary War hero and first president. Washington greeted the people with signs of respect. He bowed to the crowds and removed his hat to honor the ladies observing from the windows. Through these subtle acknowledgments of the average citizen, he appeared less formal.[62]

Washington also took care to emphasize his civilian, not military, status. This position was consistent with his insistence as commander in chief that the military remain subordinate to civilian authority, but he also may have been wary of reigniting the controversy over the Society of the Cincinnati. On the morning of October 23, he stopped in Worcester for breakfast on his way to Boston. While dining, an aide to Major General John Brooks walked in and delivered a message that the Middlesex militia awaited his arrival to parade and conduct a military review. Frustrated that his efforts to prevent fanfare had failed, Washington confessed in his diary that he "[found] this ceremony was not to be avoided though I had made every effort to do [so]."[63] He sent a message back to General Brooks that "there was an impropriety in my *reviewing* the Militia, or seeing them perform Manoeuvres otherwise[. That] as a private Man I could do no more than pass along the line." Washington understood that reviewing the troops and their maneuvers was something a military commander would do to judge battle readiness. Because the United States was not at war, Washington viewed himself a civilian leader and considered a full military review inappropriate. He recognized the symbolic imagery of a conquering military commander and took pains in Boston to emphasize his status as a civilian leader, lest the American public view him as too militaristic.[64]

Washington also avoided imposing on, or favoring, private citizens. By traveling with very few attendees, he conscientiously distinguished himself from British monarchs, who infamously traveled with enormous royal retinues and lodged the entire caravan at private homes at the expense of the owner. Royal visits could convey favor but also could be used as punishment or as a reminder of royal dominance because of the awesome expense of feeding, housing, and stabling the royal entourage. Queen Elizabeth would frequently force her hosts to feed more than a hundred guests for weeks at a time. These visits served as a costly reminder to the nobility that the monarch ruled the nation.[65] Washington, in contrast, recognized that his presence would place a financial burden on his hosts and sought to bear those expenses himself.

On his own tours of the nation, Washington declared that he would only seek lodging at public accommodations where he could pay for his room and board, even when that meant suffering through uncomfortable conditions. Many public houses only offered small, dirty accommodations with little privacy. They were frequently infested with lice and bedbugs, and rarely provided the high-quality food Washington usually consumed on a daily basis. By paying for his room and board, as well as for those of his slaves and servants, he sought to avoid comparisons to British royal tours. Only rarely were Washington's intentions thwarted. On April 27, 1791, he accepted lodging at Jeremiah Vareen's home believing it to be an inn. When he discovered it was a private home, he offered to pay for food and lodging, but Vareen refused. In his diary, Washington wrote—almost in self-defense—that he had been misled: "To this house we were directed as a

Tavern, but the proprietor of it either did not keep one, or would not acknowledge it."[66]

Washington also received so many offers to lodge with friends, former officers, and government officials that he could not select one offer without risking insult. If he stayed with government officials, he might insult former military officers and the Society of the Cincinnati, or vice versa. Similarly, if he stayed with friends in North Carolina, but in boarding houses in South Carolina, he might give offense to one state or the other. Public accommodations allowed him to visit friends and colleagues while maintaining cordial relations with everyone.[67]

Other than April 27, 1791, Washington lodged at a public house almost every other night of his tours. By resting at public houses, Washington took his meals and interacted with average Americans. He learned about their lives and gathered public opinion. This decision invoked republican simplicity: lodging at public houses conveyed that he did not require special treatment just because he was the president.

Washington also physically endured the hardships of eighteenth-century travel. Especially in the southern states, many of the roads were of poor quality, and Washington complained in his diary of the dust, rain, and rough terrain. On Saturday, April 16, 1791, he hoped to escape a violent storm at a local inn. Upon his arrival, however, he discovered that the inn had "no stables in wch. the horses could be comfortable, & no Rooms or beds which appeared tolerable, & every thing else having a dirty appearance."[68] Unfortunately, these poor conditions were more the norm than the exception. Washington frequently described accommodations as "indifferent" and "tolerable."[69]

Washington's decision to lodge in public accommodations, endure uncomfortable travel, and bear the financial cost of his tours were carefully calculated decisions to highlight his normalcy and position himself in direct contrast to the British monarchy. The American public grasped the symbolism of his actions and applauded his republican virtue. One newspaper in Charleston proclaimed, "The harmony and hilarity which prevailed throughout were strongly demonstrative of the general gratitude and joy; and it must have afforded the highest gratification to every true patriot to have observed the man whom we most venerate—*venerated* by all."[70]

Washington's efforts to create a social calendar that balanced republican virtue and gravitas for the new federal government highlight the sheer number of daily practices of the executive branch that he had to create from scratch. Furthermore, the care and detail that Washington poured into planning his interactions with the public reflect his engagement with the political environment around him. Public officials and elites obsessed over the tiniest details of the new federal government and weighed how certain practices might strengthen or threaten the republic. Washington was no exception.

As president, Washington created a productive governing environment by replicating the intimate working atmosphere that he had established as commander in chief. He selected department secretaries based on many outside factors, including the different regions and interests they represented within the United States and the specific experience they brought to each department. Jefferson and Randolph represented Virginia, Knox came from Massachusetts, and Hamilton made his home in New York. But Washington also selected secretaries with whom he had a personal relationship. For example, Washington could have appointed George Clinton to high office; Clinton had served in the New York militia during the war and had many years of experience in state and national office. But he had opposed the ratification of the Constitution and did not have a close bond with Washington. On the other hand, both Randolph and Hamilton had served as aides-de-camp, and Randolph went on to represent Washington in many private legal matters. Knox was one of Washington's favorite generals and kept Washington apprised of government developments when he served as secretary of war for the Confederation Congress (1785–1789).[71] Jefferson had served with Washington in the Virginia House of Burgesses, and they continued a regular correspondence to manage the war effort in Virginia during Jefferson's tenure as governor (1779–1781).[72] Finally, Washington chose secretaries who could provide knowledge and advice on areas beyond his expertise. Hamilton grasped the complexities of the nation's finances. Jefferson had spent six years abroad as the American minister to France, so he brought firsthand experience with the European courts to the administration. Randolph supplied legal interpretations of administrative policy and helped Washington analyze the federal Constitution and congressional legislation. Finally, Knox had run the War Department for several years, negotiated treaties with Native American nations, and organized national militia efforts.

Washington nurtured his relationships with the department secretaries through social interactions. When healthy, and weather permitting, Washington exercised daily, either on horseback or on foot, and he often incorporated social calls with the department secretaries into his exercise routines. For example, in late October, Washington left New York City to begin his tour of the northern states during the congressional recess. Jay, Knox, and Hamilton joined him on a leisurely ride out of the city before they returned to their work, and Washington headed north.[73]

After selecting his official family and instituting a social calendar, Washington turned to creating the daily practices of the executive branch. Although the president's powers were outlined in the Constitution, it fell to Washington to determine how he was supposed to use them from day to day. Complicating the task, political divisions between the nation's leaders arose just a few months after Congress began its first session. During the 1790s, two political camps emerged: Federalists, who believed that only a stronger federal government could save the United States from anarchy, and Democratic-Republicans, who preferred a decentralized government to protect individual liberties and state sovereignty.[74]

In April 1789, several years before the nation's first political parties formed, the beginnings of the ideological division emerged in the First Federal Congress during the Title Controversy. While the debate was about the president's title in theory, questions about executive and congressional power lingered under the surface. An ostentatious title suggested that the executive would be supreme over the executive, while a modest title protected legislative supremacy. The debate over the president's title demonstrates that both sides believed they were fighting for the future of the republic and that every decision had the potential to secure the nation's survival or precipitate its demise.[75]

Washington's first official visit to the Senate, which we first discussed in the introduction, revived the concerns about the balance of powers between the branches of government that had erupted a few months prior.[76] In 1789, the president and senators understood that the first visit could establish a precedent for their relationship as they jointly conducted foreign affairs in the future. The first issue they confronted involved federal negotiations with the many Native American nations along the United States' extensive western borders.

Most Native American nations had sided with the British during the Revolutionary War, recognizing the threat that American settlers posed to Native land.[77] After the war, the Confederation government had appointed commissioners who dictated coercive treaties with tribes to secure peace, establish borders, compel land cessions, and arrange for the exchange of captives. Those controversial treaties provoked considerable armed resistance, particularly in the federal territory north and west of the Ohio River. In the southeast, relations with the Creeks remained tense, and the Cherokees objected to frequent violations of their treaty by white settlers from North Carolina. Representatives from the national government, the Carolinas, the Creeks, and the Cherokees planned to meet on September 15, 1789, to negotiate a new treaty. Washington sought advice about what instructions to give to the commissioners. Because he considered Indian relations to fall under the heading of foreign affairs, he followed constitutional guidelines and prepared to meet with the Senate.

After meeting with a planning committee and supplying all previous treaties, Washington and Knox arrived at eleven thirty in the morning on Saturday, August 22, 1789. After their introduction, Washington handed Adams his prepared remarks. Noise coming in from the open windows forced Adams to read the remarks twice before opening the floor for the senators to debate Washington's questions. The senators sat in silence.[78] Maclay snarked in his diary that his colleagues were so intimidated by Washington's presence in the Senate chambers that they skulked in embarrassing silence. He suspected that if the Senate failed to provide advice, Washington would not return, and the Senate would lose its constitutional right to advise on foreign affairs. These fears, and the fact that he noted them in his diary, indicate the intensity of every moment of governing in the Early Republic. Maclay worried that one misstep might doom the Republic—a fear shared by many of the first officeholders. Determined to prevent any expansion of presidential authority, Maclay stood up and suggested referring the issue to committee for discussion in detail. Washington lost his temper before agreeing to return a few days later.[79] Although he did return the following Monday, Maclay's concerns proved prescient: Washington never returned to the Senate for advice.[80]

After witnessing the president lose his temper, Maclay was convinced that "the President wishe[d] to tread on the Necks of the Senate."[81] Maclay had served as a vocal Anti-Federalist during the ratification of the Constitution, and he became a Democratic-Republican purist during the Title Controversy. He distrusted executive authority and viewed Washington's actions, both in August 1789 and later, as evidence of a Federalist bid to centralize power. For example, on January 14, 1790, Maclay attended a dinner at the President's House. At the dinner, he interpreted Washington's attention and kindness as an attempt to "soften" his republican ardor.[82] He believed that this behavior was consistent with Washington's efforts to reduce the Senate's power back in August. Maclay wrote in his diary that Washington "wishes Us to see with the Eyes and hear with the ears of his Secretary only, the Secretary to advance the Premisses the President to draw Conclusions, and to bear down our deliberations with his personal Authority & Presence."[83]

For his part, Washington sought a strong presidency and viewed the senators as his advisors. Washington saw no reason for them to refer the issue to committee—they had all the information they needed. He had sent all previous treaties for the senators' review, and Secretary Knox, who had managed earlier treaties with Native Americans, had come along to answer the senators' questions.. Based on this exchange, Washington concluded that the Senate could not provide the prompt advice that he needed to handle pressing diplomatic exchanges.

After rejecting the Senate as a source of advice on matters of foreign affairs, Washington experimented with two other options: a prime minister-style relationship, and he consulted with the Supreme Court. First, a prime minister, like the position in Great Britain, would have been an individual with a position in Congress that would have also served as Washington's spokesperson. Washington could have promoted the development of a position similar to a prime minister in two ways, either by using the vice president as a liaison for the administration or by selecting an influential person in the House—such as James Madison—to promote the president's policy. As the president of the Senate under the federal Constitution, the vice president could also serve as a potential intermediary between the legislative and executive branches. Yet, while Adams and Washington respected each other, they never developed a close or warm relationship. Furthermore, Adams had lost political clout due to his ill-considered leading role in the Title Controversy. Offending republican sensibilities, Adams reaped insulting nicknames, including "the Dangerous Vice" and "His Rotundity." The public outcry embarrassed Washington, who thereafter doubted Adams's political judgment and distanced himself from the vice president. This frostiness made political collaboration unlikely going forward.[84] As a result, when Washington eventually created a cabinet, he never invited Adams to join the deliberations. The relationship between the vice president and the president might have evolved differently if the nation had elected John Jay or another of Washington's confidants as vice president instead of Adams.

A prime minister in the House of Representatives initially seemed a more likely scenario. Washington and Madison had worked closely together during the 1780s. They organized the Mount Vernon Conference, a gathering of delegates from Virginia and Maryland that met at Mount Vernon to discuss economic tensions between the two states and control of the Potomac River. Washington and Madison successfully navigated the group to a compromise that produced the Compact of 1785—an agreement regulating the shared Potomac waterway. Just two years later, Madison helped to convince Washington to attend the Constitutional Convention. They worked together during the convention to draft the Virginia Plan and to drum up support for a strong executive. After Congress sent the constitution to the states for ratification, Madison kept Washington apprised of the Virginia ratification debates in Richmond. Once in office as the first president, Washington consulted with Madison on department appointments and dispatched him to Monticello to persuade Jefferson to accept the post of secretary of state.[85]

After Washington's inauguration, Madison served as his primary advisor. Washington requested Madison's advice as he established executive protocols for private and public social events. He also relied on Madison to guide his interactions with Congress. For example, the day after the inauguration, Congress formed a committee to draft a response to Washington's inaugural address. Congress appointed Madison chairman of this committee, and he was responsible for creating the first draft. A few days later, Washington asked Madison to prepare his own reply to Congress's response. Madison agreed, and thereby composed both sides of the official written conversation between the House of Representatives and the president.[86]

Washington relied on Madison less after the department secretaries commenced their administrative duties in September 1789. Washington and Madison's working relationship began to deteriorate over the summer of 1790 as political differences drove a wedge into their friendship. In the spring of 1790, Madison broke with the administration to oppose Alexander Hamilton's proposal to fully fund wartime bonds and assume the war debts of all thirteen states. Madison thought an enormous national debt would be dangerous, and he favored paying back the bonds to the original holders who had earned them through military service or by lending goods and money to Congress in its time of need. Hamilton favored paying the current holders of the bonds, which meant mostly the speculators and financiers who had bought most of them up at reduced rates during the recession in the 1780s. Hamilton understood the emotional appeal of Madison's position, but he argued that the federal government had to pay its debts at face value or creditors would not trust the government, making them less likely to offer future loans.

Madison and Hamilton's disagreement boiled down to a fundamentally different interpretation of the "necessary and proper" clause of the federal Constitution—the clause that gave Congress power to pass laws to carry out its other responsibilities. Hamilton argued that these powers included debt management and the creation of a national bank to help manage the nation's credit. Madison disagreed.[87] Although he opposed both the bond payment and assumption measures, he worked with Jefferson to broker a compromise in June 1790. Madison agreed to provide the necessary votes to pass Hamilton's bill, and in return, Hamilton swung northern support behind the Residence Act, which would move the federal capital to the banks of the Potomac River in 1800.

Any lingering goodwill from the compromise evaporated in February 1791, when Madison unequivocally split from the administration to oppose Hamilton's new bank bill, "An Act to Incorporate the Subscribers to the Bank of the United States." Madison worried that the national bank would favor northern merchants and speculators at the expense of farmers, particularly those in the South. He also argued that the Constitution did not grant the federal government the power to create a national bank. After much deliberation, Washington sided with Hamilton and signed the bills into law. Notoriously thin-skinned, Washington interpreted Madison's opposition to the administration's policies as a personal attack.

Finally, in October 1791, Madison founded a partisan newspaper called the *National Gazette* and contributed editorials attacking the administration and further alienating the president.[88] Washington did not know with certainty that Madison was behind the creation of the *National Gazette*—at least not in 1791—but after reading the editorials, he may have guessed the author's identity. More important, the bitter political debates in the newspapers deepened the partisan divide, moving Washington and Madison even farther apart.

As their relationship soured, Washington no longer turned to Madison for advice on social etiquette, matters of foreign affairs, or nominees to fill vacancies in the executive branch. Instead, he primarily relied on his department secretaries, Jay, and other Federalist-leaning advisors. While Washington still heard Madison's advice—filtered through Jefferson—he was more inclined to select Federalist nominees, practices, and policies recommended by his Federalist advisors.

The Supreme Court offered another alternative to the president's cabinet. A few delegates to the Constitutional Convention and the state ratification conventions anticipated that the Supreme Court might develop into an alternative advisory body to the president. Samuel Jones and Robert Livingston, both delegates to the New York state convention, had worried that the Supreme Court resembled the Star Chamber in Great Britain. The Star Chamber was made up of common-law judges and the king's Privy Counsellors. The Chamber emerged in the late fifteenth century to hold accountable powerful individuals who frequently escaped punishment in common-law courts. By the seventeenth century, however, the Chamber became known for political oppression and monarchical tyranny. Many delegates at the

Constitutional Convention worried that the Supreme Court justices would become privy councilors to the president and subvert justice rather than remain independent.[89] Robert Whitehill expressed similar fears in the Pennsylvania state ratifying convention. He proposed an additional council to shoulder the burden of advising the president and to ensure that the justices remain independent of the executive branch.[90]

The Supreme Court also fit Washington's requirements for a council. He appointed the first justices, so he selected attorneys who were loyal to the new federal government and who supported a constitutional interpretation consistent with his own opinions. The six-justice Supreme Court also suited Washington's preferences for intimate counsel and had the potential to offer more efficient advice than the twenty-six-man Senate. Additionally, the Constitution appointed the Supreme Court as the arbiter of all laws and treaties, so Washington valued the justices' advice on how to implement the laws. Finally, Jay, one of Washington's trusted advisors, led the Supreme Court. The two men had a long history together, and Jay had unparalleled expertise on foreign affairs and statecraft. Washington and Jay first met during the First Continental Congress in Philadelphia in 1774. They continued their correspondence during Jay's tenure as president of the Continental Congress from 1778 to 1779 and minister to Spain from 1779 to 1782.[91] After the war, Jay served as secretary of foreign affairs under the Articles of Confederation, during which time he and Washington exchanged letters discussing foreign affairs and agreeing on the need for a stronger national government.[92] After the Constitutional Convention in 1787, they shared their hopes of ratification, and Jay forwarded Washington his publications in favor of the new Constitution.[93] In 1789, Jay remained in office as the acting secretary of foreign affairs until Congress established the Department of State in July 1789. Washington trusted Jay's foreign policy and legal expertise, and nominated him to be chief jus-tice of the Supreme Court on September 24, 1789.[94]

Early in his administration, Washington consulted Jay on many pro-cedural questions, legal issues, and diplomatic challenges.[95] He valued Jay's opinions on social etiquette at the start of the administration.[96] He also relied on Jay when faced with constitutional issues, frequently consulting Jay and Randolph on the same questions of law. In June 1790, Washington considered one of the first applications for clemency. He forwarded Jay the application for mercy and requested Jay's legal opinion.[97]

The department secretaries followed Washington's example and sought Jay's legal and diplomatic expertise. In April 1793, Hamilton pro-vided Jay with the latest updates on the diplomatic tensions with France and Great Britain and asked for his advice. A few days later, Jay replied and encouraged the administration to move cautiously: any statement published by the president should avoid mentioning treaties or "neutrality," Jay believed, because it was better "at present that too little shd. be said, than too much."[98] Jay shared Washington and the secretaries' desire for peace and suggested that the administration would have more power to negotiate behind closed doors if the proc-lamation left room for interpretation.[99]

The other justices, however, balked at providing advice for the ex-ecutive. During the summer of 1793, Washington's cabinet secretaries debated how to handle British and French ships and the ships they had captured into American ports. On July 12, the cabinet gathered and re-quested a meeting with the Supreme Court justices to discuss the issue. On July 20, 1793, four of the justices—John Jay, James Wilson, James Iredell, and William Paterson—replied that the question of whether the Supreme Court could provide advice to the president re-quired full participation by all of the justices. They requested additional time to consult their colleagues. On August 8, the justices declined to provide advice. In the letter, they provided their rationale:

> The Lines of Separation drawn by the Constitution between the three Departments of Government—their being in certain Respects checks on each other—and our being Judges of a court in the last Resort—are Considerations which afford strong arguments again the Propriety of our extrajudicially deciding the questions alluded to; especially as the Power given by the Constitution to the President of calling on the heads of Departments for opinions, seems to have been *purposely* as well as expressly limited to *executive* Departments.[100]

The other justices drove the Supreme Court's refusal to provide advice. Jay had favored a more flexible interpretation of the separation of powers among the branches of government and had willingly consulted with Washington and the secretaries in the past. Furthermore, in 1794, he temporarily left his judicial post to accept a diplomatic appointment from Washington to negotiate a new treaty with Great Britain.[101] Clearly Jay was willing to juggle several roles within the federal government without worrying that they would pose a conflict of interest or muddy the separation of powers. Perhaps Jay would have offered Washington guidance if not for the other justices' objections.

Washington's councils of war, and the advice he received from his officers, had been critical to his success during the Revolution, so it is almost surprising that he did not create the cabinet earlier in his presidency. Instead, Washington used every tool available to him under the strict letter of the Constitution before concluding that these options were insufficient. Washington's governing strategies during the years 1789 to 1791—particularly his failed visit to the Senate in August 1789—suggest that a council continued to be on his mind. When Washington did embrace the cabinet as a central part of the executive branch in 1793, he continued to utilize the same strategy. He often brought questions to the cabinet meetings or submitted then in advance to the department secretaries.[102]

In 1789, Washington entered the presidency with little guidance about how to structure his daily activities, manage the executive branch, or interact with his advisors. The Constitution offered scant instructions, and there was no precedent for Washington to follow. In the face of this novel situation, he created a social calendar and work environment modeled after his leadership experience as commander in chief of the Continental Army. When establishing executive precedent, Washington initially tried to follow the constitutionally approved mechanisms for obtaining advice: he visited the Senate for consultation, he engaged the executive departments for written advice, and he experimented with other advisory options, including the Supreme Court and prime minister. All of these options, however, failed to provide Washington with the support he needed to govern effectively. Washington neither planned nor intended to create the cabinet when he first took on the presidency, but he eventually realized that he needed more help than the Constitution could offer.

5

The Cabinet Emerges

By late 1791, George Washington was ready to start creating a new advisory council in the executive branch. In the first years of his presidency, Washington had visited the Senate, contemplated a prime minister relationship with Congress, and consulted with the justices of the Supreme Court. But none of these options was suited to the task— either they proved too inefficient to offer timely advice, as in the case of the Senate, or the personalities in the offices clashed, as in the case of Madison and the Supreme Court. Washington ultimately rejected these alternatives and gradually increased in-person consultations with the department secretaries until he convened his first official cabinet meeting on November 26, 1791. Even after the first meeting, Washington moved slowly. His interactions with the department secretaries occurred organically in response to the real-time challenges that they faced in office. By convening the first cabinet meeting, Washington started the *process* of creating the cabinet; he did not construct an institution that remained unchanged from day one. By the start of 1793, he had held only nine meetings.

As Washington organized his first few cabinet meetings, he experimented with how to bring his council-of-war practices into the executive branch. He relied heavily on his war experience to shape daily executive business, the power hierarchy in the executive branch, and presidential oversight of all major executive issues.[1] He convened councils and the cabinet for similar reasons: to provide advice, to offer political cover for controversial decisions, and to build consensus among subordinates for one of his policies. Washington also used similar strategies to manage the two bodies. He frequently sent questions for his subordinates to consider ahead of time, then used those questions as the agenda for a meeting. If the participants disagreed, he requested written opinions after the meeting. Finally, he hosted social events for his subordinates to help foster amicable relationships. Washington never wavered in his commitment to civilian authority— both as commander in chief and as president—but he approached both positions with a military mindset. By the end of 1792, the cabinet had met nine times and was poised to play a central role in the diplomatic crisis that broke out in April 1793.

Many Americans, however, had not forgotten about their nemesis from the Revolutionary War. Most Americans had blamed the British cabinet for instigating the conflict by crafting oppressive legislation to impose on the colonies. A new advisory body around the president was bound to raise suspicion. Anticipating that their fellow Americans might perceive their meetings as resembling the British cabinet, Washington and the secretaries strove to avoid such comparisons by convincing the American public of their republican virtue.

Article II, Section 2 of the Constitution authorizes the president to request written advice from the department secretaries. Washington initially followed this guideline in his limited interactions with the department secretaries. As soon as he took office, he requested written advice and updates from the acting department secretaries. On May 9, 1789, Washington asked Henry Knox, then acting secretary of war, to compile a summary report on relations with the Cherokee Indians.[2] Washington wrote John Jay, acting secretary for foreign affairs, and requested a "clear account of the Department at the head of which you have been . . . to impress me with a full, precise & distinct *general idea* of the United States, so far as they are comprehended in, or connected with that Department."[3]

In the fall of 1789, the First Federal Congress created the new executive departments and the secretaries assumed office. Thomas Jefferson described the daily flow of business between the executive departments and the president:

> Letters of business came addressed sometimes to the President, but most frequently to the heads of departments. If addressed to himself, he referred them to the proper department to be acted on: if to one of the Secretaries, the letter, if it required no answer, was communicated to the President simply for his information. If an answer was requisite, the Secretary of the department communicated the letter & his proposed answer to the President. Generally they were simply sent back, after perusal, which signified his approbation. Sometimes he returned them with an informal note, suggesting an alteration or a query. If a doubt of any importance arose, he reserved it for conference.[4]

As president, Washington replicated his Revolutionary War management style by employing a similar process for dispatching paperwork and correspondence. Jefferson's depiction of their working relationship closely resembled the picture that James McHenry painted of

Continental Army headquarters in 1779: "The General's usual mode of giving notes to his secretaries or aides for letters of business. Having made out a letter from such notes, it was submitted to the General for his approbation and correction—afterwards copied fair, which it was again copied and signed by him."[5] Jefferson also revealed that Washington insisted "he always [be] in accurate possession of all facts & proceedings in every part of the Union" in order to serve as "a central point for the different branches, preserved an unity of object and action among them." The strict hierarchy that Washington implemented as president replicated the military hierarchy he enforced as commander in chief.[6]

As Washington's comfort with the presidency increased, he experimented with other methods of obtaining advice from his secretaries. In early 1790, he started requesting follow-up meetings with individual secretaries after they had submitted written replies to his questions. For example, at the end of January, Knox drafted plans to rearrange the state militias and sent them to Washington. After exchanging a few letters, Knox arrived at the president's home at nine in the morning on January 21 for a meeting. After discussing and amending the plan, Washington submitted it to Congress.[7]

In late August 1790, Washington inched toward cabinet meetings when he engineered a meeting between the department secretaries. He planned to send an agent to Amsterdam to negotiate additional loans from the Dutch government, but he sought the opinions of his secretaries before he selected a nominee. Rather than requesting individual opinions and waiting for the staggered arrival of four letters, Washington instructed Hamilton to discuss appropriate candidates with Jefferson and report back. The secretaries met, agreed on a candidate, and drafted diplomatic instructions to guide the mission. On

September 3, Hamilton reported the result of the meeting to Washington and attached the draft instructions for Washington's review.[8]

In late March 1791, Washington further expanded the secretaries' responsibilities when he left Philadelphia to complete his tour of the southern states. He recognized that his letters would be unavoidably delayed by the postal service and the poor conditions of the southern roads. To prevent unnecessary interruptions in communication, he provided his travel schedule to the secretaries in advance. He instructed them to send letters to the next stop along the tour so that they would reach him as quickly as possible. Despite his best efforts to ensure efficient communication, Washington knew that they might need more immediate feedback. Before leaving, he authorized the secretaries to meet if an urgent matter arose.[9]

Shortly after Washington's departure, Hamilton received word from William Short, the American minister to France and temporary emissary to the Netherlands. Short wrote that he had negotiated favorable terms on a new loan from the Dutch government, but it had to be approved immediately or the Dutch would rescind the offer.[10] Recognizing how desperately the government needed the new loan to cover its expenses, Hamilton wrote to the other secretaries and Vice President John Adams to request a meeting. On Monday, April 11, the secretaries gathered at Jefferson's house. The secretaries and Adams agreed to approve the new loan of up to 3 million guilders. Hamilton then submitted the group's decision to the president for his review.[11] Almost a month later, Washington finally received Hamilton's report and gave his approval.[12]

Later that year, on November 26, 1791, Washington convened his first cabinet meeting—more than two and a half years into his administration. Commercial relations with Great Britain and France had consumed a great deal of the administration's attention during that time, so Washington gathered the secretaries to discuss how to foster more constructive diplomatic relationships moving forward. He offered two goals for the next year: increase American access to both French and British ports in the West Indies, and take control of the western forts promised by the British to the United States in the 1783 Treaty of Paris. In preparation for the meeting, Washington asked Jefferson to draft a few questions to guide the discussion. Jefferson produced an agenda that directed the secretaries to consider three issues: two potential Franco-American commercial treaties designed to secure more favorable trade terms, strategies for negotiating with British minister George Hammond regarding the western forts, and broader commercial relations between the United States and Great Britain.[13] Over the next several weeks, both Hamilton and Jefferson sent overtures to the British and French ministers. Unfortunately, Britain showed no interest in offering more generous trade terms, which the Washington administration required to open negotiations. Similarly, Jefferson convinced Washington that Short was better positioned to instigate any change in the Franco-American alliance.[14] As a result, nothing came of the treaties proposed during Washington's first cabinet meeting. While the meeting did not produce diplomatic progress, it did preview many of the issues that would challenge the cabinet in years to come.

The second cabinet meeting occurred in December 1791, after news arrived that the American army had suffered an embarrassing defeat to Native Americans in the Battle of the Wabash. In response to this report, Washington instructed Knox to prepare two reports for Congress: one to outline the previous War Department policies that had led to the defeated expedition, and another to suggest a plan to cut military expenditures by seeking a diplomatic resolution to the war. On the morning of December 28, Washington summoned the cabinet to review and amend Knox's reports before submitting them to Congress in early January.[15]

Washington's interactions with his department secretaries over the next year indicate a gradual development toward a permanent presidential cabinet. He gathered the secretaries six times, with meetings evenly dispersed throughout the year. Yet he still had not fully embraced cabinet meetings as his primary method of obtaining advice. He continued to request written advice when the circumstances permitted him extra time to deliberate or he wanted written support for his decision. For example, in April 1792, Washington considered utilizing the presidential veto for the first time. Congress had passed a bill to increase the size of the House of Representatives from 65 to 120 members based on the first census. Washington requested *written* opinions from the department secretaries on the constitutionality of the bill. Hamilton and Knox approved of the bill, while Jefferson and Randolph opposed it. Hamilton and Knox argued that the Constitution did not articulate how Congress should assign representatives for each state, which afforded Congress leeway to decide the matter. They also believed the bill equitably distributed the new representatives. Randolph and Jefferson adopted a stricter interpretation of the Constitution, contending that it *did* specify how Congress should apportion representatives. They said the Constitution required Congress to pick a common number that would divide each *state's* population evenly. The result would be the number of representatives allotted to that state. Instead, the current bill under consideration ignored the states and divided the *nation's* population by 30,000. The result produced fractions in several states' populations and awkwardly doled out extra representatives to cover the largest fractions.[16]

Washington was inclined to side with Jefferson and Randolph, and rule that the bill "was contrary to the common understanding of the Constitution and to what was understood at the time by the makers of it." He still harbored reservations, however. When Congress had voted on the bill, the votes split along geographical lines, with southerners opposing the bill and northerners favoring it. Washington feared accusations of partiality toward the southern states, so he asked Randolph and Jefferson to meet with Madison. If all three men supported the veto, he would agree. But how he should invoke the veto was another question, as no one had ever done so before. Washington asked Randolph, Jefferson, and Madison to draw up an "instrument for him to sign."[17] The three men produced a letter of veto which encouraged the House of Representatives to apportion seats using the mode "prescribed by the Constitution," which Washington delivered to the House on April 5, 1792. After his veto, the House drafted a new apportionment bill adopting Washington's recommendation. On April 14, Congress passed the new bill setting the number of representatives at 105, instead of 120, and Washington immediately signed it into law.[18]

From October to December 1792, Washington convened cabinet meetings more frequently to deal with urgent foreign policy questions, especially if they posed new challenges. One such challenge emerged on October 29, 1792, when Jefferson received a letter from the Spanish diplomats José Ignacio de Viar and José de Jaudenes. The letter tacitly conceded that their government had incited the Creek Indians to oppose American expansion, which Americans viewed as grounds for war.[19] The administration had struggled for three years with conflict between Native Americans and white settlers on the western borders, but this letter was the first time a sovereign European power had admitted to instigating violence. Spanish support of the Creeks presented a direct threat to American sovereignty that could not be ignored.

Washington organized a cabinet meeting to help frame his response to the diplomats. As he had done so many times in councils of war, he presented two questions for his advisors to consider. First, how should they respond to Spain? Second, should Washington include the Spanish diplomats' letter in his upcoming annual address to Congress? Jefferson recommended notifying Congress immediately because the issue pertained to a declaration of war—a power the Constitution reserved for Congress. Hamilton advised against war in general, viewing it as detrimental to the financial well-being and recovery of the nation. He feared that involving Congress would only hasten the start of conflict. Given the differing opinions, Washington decided to consider the issue privately after the cabinet meeting was over. A few days later, he chose to follow Jefferson's recommendations. To deal with Spain, he instructed Jefferson to authorize American agents to lodge complaints with the Spanish government in Louisiana. On November 7, he also submitted a special message to Congress alerting them to the threat— with the Spanish letter attached.[20]

As Washington consulted with the secretaries in person and convened the first few cabinet meetings, similarities increased between his leadership as president and commander in chief. As president, Washington relied on the secretaries to manage their departments and implement his decisions. He also used the secretaries as intermediaries between the president and Congress to procure funding for the administration's policies and to protect presidential power, just as he had used his aides-de-camp during the Revolutionary War.

One striking illustration of this pattern took place in the spring of 1790. In January of that year, the House of Representatives drafted the Foreign Intercourse Bill, which established a fund to provide salaries for American ministers abroad. As the bill worked its way through Congress, Jefferson and Washington developed a strategy to thwart congressional encroachment in diplomacy and set precedent for independent executive control over foreign affairs. This episode also reflected Washington and the secretaries' shared commitment to promoting a powerful and energetic presidency. Perhaps recalling his own frustrating experiences with limited power as governor of Virginia, Jefferson played a significant role in preserving executive authority during this episode.

The Foreign Intercourse Bill proved surprisingly divisive in Congress. If the House of Representatives selected a relatively small fund, the executive could afford to send representatives to only a few nations. The initial amount selected, $30,000, might not have covered ambassadors to Spain, England, France, and the Netherlands—all possible future allies and key power brokers in the Atlantic world.[21] However, many congressmen did not want the president to appoint a large number of ministers. They worried that numerous ministers would require burdensome taxes to support their appointments. Instead, they wanted the government to send temporary emissaries if tensions arose between the United States and a foreign nation. Additionally, a fleet of foreign ministers reminded many Anti-Federalists (and future Republicans) of the aristocratic courts of European monarchies.[22]

The debate over the bill produced two important questions about the extent of executive power. First, did Congress have the right to consult on the location of diplomatic appointments, and therefore the ability to shape the diplomatic corps? If Congress voted to provide limited funds, it would effectively insert itself into foreign policy decisions. The executive would not have sufficient funds to send ministers to all European nations and would be forced to choose between potential European allies. Second, did the Senate have the right to prevent the president from appointing foreigners to consular positions? A consular is also a foreign minister, but Early American presidents usually reserved them for less important countries or sent them to smaller regions outside the capital of a foreign nation. Washington had nominated Thomas Auldjo, Etienne Cathalan, Sieur de La Motte, and John Parish to various vice consul positions. Rather than immediately approving these appointments, the Senate passed a resolution "that it may be expedient to advise and consent to the appointment of Foreigners to the Offices of Consuls or Vice-Consuls for the United States."[23] The Senate did not object to Auldjo, Cathalan, or de La Motte because of their credentials, but rather because of their foreign citizenship.

Washington had selected these men because he believed they were the best candidates for the positions. From Washington's perspective, the Senate could encroach on executive power by blocking the establishment of consular posts for which no acceptable American candidate could be found but which the administration considered essential.[24] The North American colonies had experienced steady immigration up through the Revolution; this trend continued after the end of hostilities. Many immigrants adopted the United States as their home nation and offered firsthand knowledge of foreign nations, even if they had not officially applied for citizenship. Washington cared more about his consuls bringing the appropriate expertise and experience to the position than about their place of birth.

Jefferson and Washington opposed both of Congress's attempts to insert itself into the diplomatic process. The Confederation Congress had spent years battling corruption scandals and inefficient committee systems, which caused endless frustration and suffering for the Continental Army and the states. As a result, Jefferson and Washington had good reason to be wary. Furthermore, in Article II, Section 2, the US Constitution granted the president the right to appoint all "Ambassadors, other public Ministers and Consuls," with the advice and consent of the Senate.[25] Jefferson and Washington interpreted this clause to mean that the Senate could approve or reject Washington's nominees, but that the president had sole discretion to decide how many ambassadors to appoint and where to send them.

On March 23, and again three days later, Washington and Jefferson met privately to discuss diplomatic appointments and to plan a strategy for protecting executive authority over the appointment process. They determined that between $36,000 and $50,000 was necessary to adequately support ministers abroad. They also agreed that Jefferson should use his upcoming visit to the Committee of Congress to demonstrate the need for additional funds.[26] After that visit, Jefferson sent an update to Washington, reaffirming that "the Senate has no right to negative the *grade* [of a foreign mission] . . . the transaction of business with foreign nations is Executive. It belongs to the head of that department."[27]

Jefferson also warned Washington to keep in mind the importance of protecting executive precedent. If Washington agreed to submit to congressional oversight, future presidents—particularly those with a less vaunted reputation—would be bound by the same limitations. A few weeks later, Washington invited James Madison to the President's House for a private consultation. He recorded in his diary that Madison agreed with Jefferson: the Senate had "no Constitutional right to interfere with either, & that it might be impolitic to draw it into a precedent their powers extending no farther than to an approbation or disapprobation of the person nominated by the President all the rest being Executive and vested in the President by the Constitution."[28] Between his written opinions and the advice he provided in meetings, Jefferson encouraged Washington to establish a precedent of independent executive control over diplomacy.

On April 30, 1790, the House resumed discussion on the Foreign Intercourse Bill and approved only $30,000 for the new ministers, $6,000 less than the minimum required by Washington and Jefferson.[29] As the bill progressed to the Senate for its approval, Washington and Jefferson exploited their unique positions to secure additional funds from Congress. On May 7, Martha Washington held her weekly drawing room gathering, which Senators Charles Carroll and Ralph Izard attended. Washington used the unofficial setting to his advantage. If Washington approached the senators on the street or in the halls of Congress, he would have been accused of interfering with legislative affairs. But eighteenth-century social conventions gave Washington a cover to negotiate under the pretense of socializing: in the Early Republic, the presence of women in the state drawing room made the event social, not political, no matter how much politics were discussed.[30] Because Martha was the official host of the event, George could discuss politics with her guests without appearing to be politicking. Fully aware of these expectations, Washington struck up a conversation with Carroll and Izard. He casually mentioned that he planned to send ministers plenipotentiary to England and France, and chargés d'affaires to Spain, Portugal, and Holland, but that the currently allocated sum would make these appointments impossible.[31]

Jefferson reinforced this message a few weeks later when he testified in front of the Senate committee tasked with considering the appropriations bill. Senator Maclay noted in his diary that Jefferson's arguments reminded him of European monarchs: "high Spiced. He has been long enough abroad to catch the tone of European folly."[32] Maclay distrusted foreign courts, foreign ministers, and Jefferson's support of both. Yet, despite Maclay's objections, Washington and Jefferson's combined efforts proved persuasive. When the Senate completed its final reading of the bill, the bill included an amendment for an increase in funds. The amended bill still required approval from the House of Representatives, however. Over the next month, the joint House-Senate Conference Committee jockeyed over the amount of appropriations. On June 23, 1790, the committee settled on a compromise and Maclay grudgingly admitted that the friends of the administration succeeded in increasing the appropriation to $40,000.[33] Washington noted in his diary the administration's victory with the passage of the Foreign Intercourse Act the following week.[34]

Both Jefferson and Washington regarded the bill as an important precedent for the establishment of independent executive control and presidential agency. They had two reasons for this view. First, the president retained the ability to dictate the terms of ambassador appointments, including where they were located, without having to consult with the Senate. The Senate gained no additional powers and could only approve or reject the president's nominee. Second, the Senate removed itself from the debate over foreign-born nominees. The Senate approved Washington's nominees and acknowledged that foreign-born candidates were sometimes the best option.[35] Through their collaboration, Jefferson and Washington ensured that future presidents would enjoy the right to energetically pursue diplomatic relations without obstacles imposed by Congress. Jefferson's role—as an advisor and intermediary between the executive and legislative branches—determined that the emerging cabinet would support a strong presidency.

The cabinet's deliberations at the end of March 1792 also highlight how Washington used his department secretaries as persuasive advocates for his presidency. On November 4, 1791, the Western Confederacy of American Indians, led by the Miamis, Shawnees, and Delawares, had crushed the American army under the command of General Arthur St. Clair. A few months after the defeat, Congress created a committee to investigate the cause of the disastrous defeat. As part of its investigation, the committee requested papers from the Department of War and Department of the Treasury pertaining to the expedition. Because this request represented the first time Congress wished to review executive papers, Washington was quick to include his advisors as he decided whether to comply. Additionally, if he decided to reject the committee's request, he wanted to be sure he had political protection for the decision, just as he had often secured cover from his officers during the Revolutionary War.

On March 31, Washington called a cabinet meeting. In his summons to the secretaries, he acknowledged the weight of the moment, writing that he wished "to consult, merely because it was the first example [of Congress requesting executive papers], & he wished that so far as it shd become a precedent, it should be rightly conducted." The secretaries convened at the President's House, but the high stakes of the situation rendered them speechless—a rare occurrence. They requested more time to consider the issue before offering their opinions. On April 2, the secretaries returned to Washington's study, armed with information and ready to offer their advice. They "were of one mind 1. that the house was an inquest, & therefore might institute enquiries. 2. that they might call for papers generally. 3. that the Executive ought to communicate such papers as the public good would permit, & ought to refuse those the disclosure of which would injure the public."[36] Essentially, the secretaries agreed that the House had the right to form a committee and investigate an issue relating to the executive branch; that the House could request executive papers; and that the president should share the papers with the House unless secrecy was necessary to protect the nation. The secretaries also agreed that no harm would come from sharing the requested papers with Congress. They encouraged Washington to comply—in theory, at least.

There was a problem with the way Congress had phrased its request, however. The House committee had addressed its request for papers to the department secretaries directly, but Washington and the secretaries determined "that neither the Committee nor House had a right to call on the head of a department, who and whose papers were under the Presidt. alone."[37] In other words, the departments belonged to the executive branch and the secretaries were subordinate to the president, so only the president could supply the papers. But Washington did not want to assert executive privilege for the first time over a simple wording issue. Instead, he dispatched the department secretaries to speak privately with the members of the House committee and request a change in phrasing. The committee members agreed to issue a new request that asked Washington "to cause the proper officers to lay before this House such papers of a public nature in the Executive Department, as may be necessary to the investigation of the causes of the failure of the late expedition under Major General St. Clair."[38] While this difference in wording may seem trivial, Washington was determined to protect the president's sovereignty over executive branch operations, and the department secretaries helped ensure that Congress respected his chain of command.

During the first couple of years of his presidency, most of Washington's interactions with the department secretaries still occurred in individual conferences or through letters. But he increasingly found cabinet meetings to be a helpful way to gather advice and promote his agenda, especially when faced with tricky constitutional or diplomatic issues. The cabinet had emerged as a part of the executive branch.

Now that Washington and his secretaries were regularly meeting in person, they feared that the public would draw parallels between their gatherings and the British cabinet, which many had considered the origin of most corruption in the British government. Unfortunately, Washington and the secretaries never wrote down how fears of the British cabinet shaped their own interactions—or if they did, their words have been lost to history. However, the president and secretaries had always taken great care to consider public opinion and adapt their behavior to fit the expectations of the watchful public. Their approach to the nascent cabinet was no different.

The delayed emergence of the cabinet is the strongest evidence showing that Washington sought to avoid comparisons to the British cabinet. He was clearly familiar with the cabinet model given the importance of councils of war to his success during the Revolution. When Washington visited the Senate in 1789, this type of advisory group was likely on his mind; he hoped that the senators would support him in the same way that his officers had during the war. He even prepared for the meeting in the same way—he sent materials ahead of time and brought questions for the senators to discuss. When the Senate failed to meet his expectations, Washington explored other types of advisory relationship before concluding that these options were insufficient. Only then did he turn to creating the cabinet.

When the cabinet emerged in 1792, Americans did not immediately decry the new institution, which is perhaps surprising given their long distrust of the British cabinet. Instead, Americans seemed to understand that Washington needed support and advice during moments of crisis or constitutional uncertainty. As a result, they rarely criticized the cabinet as a group and instead offered objections to how particular individuals operated within the administration.

Hamilton served as a lightning rod for most of the intense critiques of Washington's cabinet. Criticism of Hamilton fixated on two main objections. First, opponents accused him of undermining the separation of powers between the branches of government by med-dling in Congress.[39] On January 14, 1790, Hamilton had delivered the first of two major reports on the development of public credit. The first report called for the federal government to assume responsibility for the states' debts remaining from the Revolutionary War. To pay off the nation's increased debt, he proposed negotiating additional interna-tional loans at more favorable rates and levying taxes on distilled spirits.[40] On December 14, 1790, he submitted his second report to the House of Representatives. This report called for the creation of a national bank to facilitate the collection of taxes, to offer loans, and to regulate currency.[41] Congress eventually passed Hamilton's funding bill on August 4, 1790, and his bank bill on February 25, 1791. But to secure passage of both bills, he had to negotiate, manipulate, cajole, and threaten congressmen to vote for the legislation. This approach rubbed many observers the wrong way. For example, on August 6, 1794, an anonymous pamphlet accused Hamilton of trying to expropriate "the exclusive right of the legislature to originate money bills" for his department and away from the House of Representatives, thereby undermining the constitutional separation of powers. The author believed that Hamilton had "obtained much more influence over the deliberations of both Houses of Congress than either of them over one another."[42]

Senator Maclay's diary reflected similar concerns about Hamilton's growing influence over the legislative branch. In the summer of 1790, as Congress debated treasury legislation, Maclay's journal is littered with complaints about Hamilton's intrigues. He noted: "This Evening Mr. [Robert] Morris & [Thomas] Fitzsimons called on Us. Hamilton has been with them again. [N]ever had a Man a great propensity for bar-gaining than Mr. Morris. Hamilton knows this, and is laboring to make a Tool of him."[43] Not only did Maclay disagree with the financial pro-posals, he also hated Hamilton's methods of securing votes.

The second charge against Hamilton alleged that he created a pro-British faction that controlled the entire executive branch. Hamilton's stance on the French Revolution seemed to confirm his opponents' suspicions. In 1789, many Americans, especially members of the emerging Jeffersonian Republican Party, greeted the start of the French Revolution as the natural evolution of their own successful revolution. However, Hamilton and many other Federalists quickly grew wary of the violence that consumed France and the potential that anarchy would cross the sea and spread in the United States.[44] Hamilton's opposition to the French Revolution caused many to question his commitment to republican ideals.[45]

Republican adversaries also believed that Hamilton conspired to replace their republic with a monarchical aristocracy based on the British model. But they also recognized that Hamilton had spotless Revolutionary War credentials. To undermine his service record, opponents cited his long history as a "champion of monarchy." They alleged that he had advocated for a "monarchical form of government, formed after the British model," in the Constitutional Convention.[46] Writing under the pseudonym "Amicus," Hamilton insisted that these accusations were a "gross misrepresentation." He asserted that he had only supported propositions "conformable to the republican theory" and that other delegates, "pre-eminent for republican character," had supported his proposals in the Convention.[47] The charges stuck, however. In early 1792, Henry Lee articulated similar concerns in a letter to Madison: "Indelibly stained is the wisdom the honor &justice of the govt. by those fashionable treasure s[c]hemes imitative of the base principles & wicked measures adopted thro necessity in corrupt monarchys."[48]

Although still in the administration, Jefferson shared many of the same criticisms of Hamilton in his letters. Writing to Monroe, Jefferson denounced Hamilton and absolved Washington of complicity—a common trope among Republican letters at the time. Jefferson also alleged that Hamilton "brought the P. [President] forward with manifestations that the business of the treasury had got beyond the limits of his comprehension."[49] Many years later, Madison echoed Jefferson's sentiments after Washington delivered his final annual address to Congress, remarking that the speech "shews that he [is] completely in the snares of the British faction."[50]

The accusations hurled at Hamilton directly reflect American anxieties about the British cabinet. Americans did not begrudge Washington for consulting with a cabinet. The public offered no criticism of the institution, and most citizens absolved him of responsibility for any policies they opposed. Instead, Americans criticized the administration the same way they had criticized the British ministry before the Revolutionary War. For example, in the spring of 1772, John Adams jotted down notes on British corruption and historic examples of ministers warped by power:

> In England, the common Rout to Power has been by making clamorous Professions of Patriotism, in early Life, to secure a great Popularity, and to ride upon that Popularity, into the highest Offices of State, and after they have arrived there, they have been generally found, as little zealous to preserve the Constitution, as their Predecessors whom they have hunted down. . . . Sir Robert Walpole. Commited to the Tower the Father of Corruption.[51]

Robert Walpole had served as prime minister from 1721 to 1742. While in office, he had engineered the concentration of executive authority in the king's cabinet under his leadership. Critically, he held this powerful position while still serving in Parliament. In the summer of 1789, as the First Federal Congress debated the creation of the executive departments, they spent ample time considering the position of the secretary of the treasury. While they feared executive meddling in Congress, they ultimately decided to retain a connection with the position because the Treasury Department had too much potential to consolidate power in the executive branch.[52] They passed legislation requiring the secretary to submit reports "respecting all matters referred to him by the Senate or House of Representatives," which gave them limited oversight over the department.[53] This clause offered Hamilton, as secretary of treasury, a unique position: he worked in the executive branch but could suggest policies to Congress without going beyond the limits of his office. However, when Hamilton proposed fiscal legislation, secured its passage, and appeared to concentrate authority in his hands, the American public could not help but see similarities between him and Walpole, as well as between him and the British ministers who had corrupted King George III.

As public awareness of the cabinet increased and criticism of Hamilton and his role in the cabinet accelerated, the president and the secretaries responded. Washington increasingly handled cabinet affairs with discretion and secrecy out of concern for the public's distrust of anything resembling the British cabinet. He expected that cabinet discussions would remain private unless he approved publication of the minutes or debates.

Washington rarely discussed cabinet proceedings with friends, family, or acquaintances. He did not even refer to the gatherings as cabinet meetings, instead saying that he met with the "secretaries" or the "gentlemen of my family." The secretaries, congressmen, and the press all used the label "cabinet" by the end of 1793, so the term existed in the political lexicon. Still, Washington never took the bait—he served another four years as president without using the term "cabinet" even once. After his retirement, he immediately referred to Adams's gatherings with the department secretaries as cabinet meetings—further indicating that he had consciously avoided the term in his presidential letters.[54] Washington's avoidance of the term while in office suggests he was uncomfortable with the connotations of the British cabinet.

As secretary of state, Jefferson coped with public criticism by attempting to differentiate himself from the administration. Initially, Jefferson attempted to sway the executive branch, and Washington in particular, away from Hamilton's financial system. Once he feared that the president was out of his reach, Jefferson waged a campaign to distance himself from any comparisons to the British cabinet. Over the next few years, Jefferson established himself as the silent leader of the opposition movement and encouraged public outrage over Hamilton's legislative agenda. As debates in the cabinet became increasingly intense and hostile, Jefferson reported them to his political allies and enlisted their help to defend his reputation. For example, when the cabinet crafted official letters to send to American ministers abroad, Jefferson sent Madison drafts of the letters before they were finalized. In other words, Jefferson shared privileged cabinet information while the conversations were still ongoing. He also encouraged Madison to show the letters to their mutual allies.[55] Jefferson understood that the pipeline of information between himself and Madison flowed both ways. Madison supplied him with information, and he expected Madison to disseminate select intelligence as well. Jefferson wanted it known among his friends and allies that he disagreed with the administration's policies, and Madison obliged.

Jefferson also fed Madison and others critical information to bolster their fight in Congress against Hamilton's legislation. On December 27, 1792, the House of Representatives had passed a resolution requesting a detailed report on the loans that Hamilton had already negotiated. One week later, Hamilton delivered his report to Congress. Jefferson and other Republicans were unconvinced by Hamilton's explanations and suspected that he had misappropriated foreign funds by lodging them in the new United States bank. Jefferson drew up notes on Hamilton's report, including these suspicions, for Madison's use in Congress.[56] In addition, Jefferson secretly drafted a proposal with six resolutions all sanctioning Hamilton in the House. On February 27, 1793, the House considered a modified version of Jefferson's resolutions.[57] A few days later, the Federalists in the House soundly defeated these resolutions, with none gaining more than fifteen aye votes to thirty-three nay votes.[58] Although Jefferson pulled the strings behind the scenes, Federalists guessed that he was calling the shots and accused him of undermining the very administration he served.[59]

When his efforts in the cabinet failed to discredit Hamilton, Jefferson became convinced that something needed to be done to save the Republic. He devised a plan to create a resistance movement, which became the grassroots beginnings of the Democratic-Republican Party. He started by gathering an informal network of correspondents to pass along information about local opposition to Hamilton's legislation.[60] Next, Jefferson and Madison recruited Philip Freneau to publish a newspaper—the *National Gazette*—to combat the Treasury Department's policies. They desperately wanted a printed voice to counter the *Gazette of the United States,* which operated as Hamilton's unofficial mouthpiece. Jefferson agreed to put Freneau on the State Department payroll to supplement his earnings, and he launched the *National Gazette* in the fall of 1791.[61]

That summer, Jefferson and Madison took their organizing efforts one step further. In May 1791, they departed Philadelphia in a carriage and headed north. First, they met with Aaron Burr and Chancellor

Robert Livingston—two of Hamilton's many enemies in New York. From New York City, they sailed up the Hudson to Albany, where Governor George Clinton, another Hamilton nemesis, greeted them. Next, they spent several weeks traipsing around areas of the countryside where Anti-Federalist sentiment persisted and where the local population would welcome efforts to oppose Hamilton's allegedly monarchical schemes. They dined with officials and greeted citizens in taverns and inns. Technically, they traveled around the state of New York under the guise of inspecting the flora and fauna of a very different climate than their Virginia countryside, but not everyone was fooled by this excuse. Robert Troup, an old friend of Hamilton, reported back to the secretary of the treasury that Jefferson and Madison had traveled north to "engage in a passionate courtship" of Burr, Livingston, and Clinton, hoping that they could "hunt down" Hamilton.[62]

Jefferson did not conduct his resistance movement in front of Washington. He argued against Hamilton's policies in cabinet meetings but never acknowledged his role in organizing the emerging opposition party. In fact, in a private conversation with Washington, he insisted "that I kept myself aloof from all cabal & correspondence on the subject of the government, & saw & spoke with as few as I could."[63] Jefferson did acknowledge that he had "an intimacy" with the new opposition party, but he assured Washington that it only sought to protect congressional authority and was loyal to the federal government: "The Republican party . . . [in] the next Congress would attempt nothing material but to render their own body independant [sic], that that party were firm in their dispositions to support the government."[64]

Washington initially accepted Jefferson's assurances and repeatedly pleaded with him to "coalesce in the measures of the government" with the other secretaries. Hamilton was not so easily convinced of Jefferson's innocence. He complained to friends that "Mr. Madison cooperat[ed] with Mr. Jefferson is at the head of a faction decidedly hostile to me and my administration, and actuated by views in my judgment subversive of the principles of good government and dangerous to the union, peace and happiness of the Country." Hamilton shared these concerns with Washington as well, and accused Jefferson of founding the *National Gazette* to attack the administration.[65]

Washington gave Jefferson and Hamilton wide latitude to complain about each other for several years, but his patience had limits.[66] In August 1793, Jefferson again denounced a monarchical party that criticized the government as "good for nothing . . . a milk and water thing which cannot support itself." Fed up after years of bickering, Washington replied that the accusation was "insanity . . . for the republican spirit of the Union was so manifest and so solid."[67]

By 1793, based on conversations like these, Jefferson reluctantly concluded that Hamilton had duped Washington. Madison confirmed Jefferson's assessment that the administration had taken on a British pallor: "Every Gazette I see . . . exhibits a spirit of criticism on the anglified complexion charged on the Executive politics. I regret extremely the position into which the P. [President] has been thrown. The unpopular cause of Anglomany is openly laying claim to him."[68] Jefferson started to discuss retirement, fearing that his own reputation would be tainted by association and convinced that he could no longer serve in the administration while holding a dramatically different opinion on most major issues. He hoped immediate retirement from the cabinet would affirm his reputation as a virtuous republican and distance him from any claims of British behavior. Washington appealed to Jefferson and convinced him to stay in the administration for a few more months.[69] The demands of the Neutrality Crisis further delayed Jefferson's departure, and he did not retire until the end of the year.

After his return to Monticello, Jefferson continued to build the Democratic-Republican Party in opposition to Hamilton's Federalists for the next two decades. Jefferson's lengthy efforts to sway public opinion against Hamilton and the Washington administration suggests that public animus toward the British cabinet lingered long after one might expect. In 1818, Jefferson read with horror a recent biography of George Washington written by the chief justice of the Supreme Court, John Marshall, in which he wrote: "The party feelings of his biography . . . have called from [his papers,] a composition as different from what Gen. Washington would have offered, as was the candor of the characters."[70] Jefferson considered Marshall's account to be highly biased and partisan, and he was determined to set the record straight on Washington's administration and his role in it. He compiled his personal papers from his time as secretary of state and called it his *Anas*. Although he did not publish his *Anas* while alive, he had hoped the remarks would serve as a rebuttal to Marshall's biography. In this volume, Jefferson detailed his consistent opposition to Hamilton's supposedly monarchical measures in private conversations with Washington and in cabinet debates. He recalled a conversation he had with Washington in October 1792, when he reportedly tried to convince Washington that "there was a squadron devoted to the nod of the Treasury," which had resulted in "the executive swallow[ing] up the legislative branch."[71]

When talking with Washington, Jefferson had assumed the president shared the same fears of the British cabinet and would understand his warnings about Hamilton. He asserted that Hamilton had been "so bewitched and perverted by the British example as to be under thorough conviction that corruption was essential to the government of a nation." Also faulting John Adams, Jefferson insisted that "the glare of royalty and nobility during his mission to England, had made him believe their fascination a necessary ingredient in government."[72] Many years later, he recorded these criticisms for an early nineteenth-century audience that shared his aversion to the British cabinet.

In the *Anas*, Jefferson also defended the Republican Party against Marshall's criticisms that it sought to destroy the new nation. Jefferson insisted that the Republican Party had "endeavor[ed] to keep the government" within the parameters established in the Constitution and to "prevent [the government] being monarchized in practice."[73] In 1818, Jefferson took care to compile these passages and explain his behavior because he worried that Marshall's biography would turn public opinion against him, or perhaps that future readers would judge his behavior harshly. His efforts to discredit Hamilton's legacy and bolster his own—fourteen years after his rival's death—demonstrate the power of public opinion in the Early Republic and his fear of any association with the British cabinet.[74]

On the other side of the public debate, Hamilton conducted his own campaign to distinguish himself from the British ministry. While Hamilton greatly admired the success of the British Empire, he recognized from the very beginning of his tenure as secretary of the treasury that comparisons between the British monarchy and the American executive might be problematic. On August 12, 1791, he met with George Beckwith, an unofficial minister from Britain to the United States.[75] During their conversation, Beckwith asked for information about the new minister plenipotentiary from France, Jean Baptiste Ternant. Hamilton disingenuously reported that he knew very little of Ternant or his mission. Hamilton also insisted that the secretary of state exercised jurisdiction over foreign affairs, and because the federal government had "no Cabinet . . . I am a stranger to any special views, that may be in the contemplation of the French government."[76]

Hamilton's concern about the public's reaction to a cabinet shaped his response to Beckwith. He easily could have conveyed to Beckwith that Jefferson controlled the diplomatic conversations without specifying "we have no Cabinet." Although this conversation was technically private, Hamilton knew that Beckwith sent reports of their interactions to London. Perhaps he assumed the British ministry widely circulated these reports and that the information could leak to the public. Whatever the reason, Hamilton's response implied his belief that the existence of a cabinet would reflect poorly on the administration in 1791.

Hamilton's response was out of character given that he had demonstrated a tendency to interfere with diplomacy behind Jefferson's back.[77] The previous summer, he had confided in Beckwith, "Mr. Jefferson our present Secretary of State is I am persuaded a gentleman of honor . . . but from some opinions which he has given respecting Your government, and possible predilections elsewhere, there may be difficulties which may possibly frustrate the whole." In other words, Jefferson was an ardent Francophile and might frustrate negotiations between Beckwith and the United States. Hamilton suggested that Beckwith inform him if "any such difficulties should occur . . . in order that I may be sure they are clearly understood."[78] Essentially, he encouraged Beckwith to bypass the State Department if conversations with Jefferson did not proceed smoothly. The next August, however, Hamilton downplayed his role in the administration and diplomacy, perhaps because some citizens and their representatives in Congress had started criticizing Hamilton's leadership in the Treasury Department. They already accused him of harboring monarchical ambitions, controlling the legislature, and undermining the separation of powers. While struggling to pass his legislative agenda, Hamilton may have worried that the public would frown upon the cabinet, and his participation in it, as symbolic of the British monarchy.

Although Hamilton took steps to minimize the criticism directed at him, he rejected Jefferson's assessment that his behavior appeared too British. Instead, he worked to build support for his policies and change the minds of American citizens. He embarked on an ambitious publication campaign to defend the presidency, his proposed legislation, and his behavior against charges of monarchism. In August 1792, he published under the pseudonym "An American" to rebut recent attacks on the administration by Freneau in the *National Gazette*. Writing as "An American No. II," Hamilton argued that Jefferson's employment of Freneau set "a pernicious precedent, inconsistent with those pretensions to extraordinary republican purity."[79] He charged that Jefferson employed Freneau as a clerk in the State Department to subsidize the *National Gazette*'s partisan goal of undermining the federal government. Hamilton sought to discredit Freneau and Jefferson as hypocrites.[80] In 1792, writing as "Civis," Hamilton posited that his management of the debt and the Treasury Department made him the "true republican."[81]

This war of words was not just petty infighting between Hamilton, Jefferson, and their supporters. Instead, the flurry of publications demonstrates their shared recognition that public opinion measured their success, protected their reputations, and ensured the survival of the government. One goal of these publications was to distinguish their behavior from their British counterparts. Politicians on both sides dashed off editorials in a desperate attempt to secure the all-important approval of American people and legitimize their actions.

Washington convened his first cabinet meeting two and a half years into his presidency. Over the next fifteen months, he experimented with the best way to use these new meetings. To manage his secretaries, Washington drew on many of the practices that had served him well as commander in chief. He sent questions ahead of time for their consideration, used these questions to guide their meetings, and requested written opinions or additional gatherings if they disagreed.

As they met and formed a new institution, the British cabinet remained the elephant in the room. The American public had not forgotten its animus toward the British ministers and judged the administration by how closely its policies and behavior resembled the British. Eager to avoid these negative associations, Washington and the secretaries crafted their behavior to present themselves as virtuous republicans. When those efforts fell short and criticism emerged anyway, they waged a public relations campaign to win approval for their positions—with mixed results.

Yet Washington's relationship with his advisors would evolve once again. On April 5, 1793, he received news that France had declared war on Great Britain and the Netherlands. Faced with the possibility of international war, Washington embraced frequent cabinet meetings as a central part of executive practice.

6

A Foreign Challenge

On FEBRUARY 1, 1793, France declared war on Great Britain and the Netherlands. The fighting spread to Italy, Germany, and Spain before expanding to the West Indies and engulfing British, French, and Spanish colonial holdings. Two months later, news of the European war reached Washington at his home at Mount Vernon. He immediately sent word to Hamilton and Jefferson that he would end his vacation early and join them shortly in Philadelphia. Washington and his secretaries believed that fighting another war would be nothing short of catastrophic. The Revolutionary War had wreaked havoc on the American economy, which was finally recovering after the economic downturn of the 1780s. Farms had slowly improved their harvests, American credit had gradually been restored, and currency had stabilized. Another conflict would likely paralyze the Atlantic trade so vital to the vulnerable new nation and threaten its fragile economic recovery. American farmers, sailors, and merchants would also be caught in the crossfire as they tried to transport and sell American goods in foreign ports and preserve the small economic advances of the past few years. Those were just the potential economic repercussions, let alone the death and physical destruction of war. Worst-case scenario, if the United

States fought another war with Britain and lost so soon after gaining independence, there was a real possibility that the nation would be forced back into colonial status. While Washington wrapped up his visit and made his way back to Philadelphia with these potential consequences in mind, he instructed Hamilton and Jefferson to prepare strategies to maintain neutrality in the European war.

Once Washington returned to Philadelphia, he entered a new phase in his relationship with the cabinet. In late 1791 and 1792, he utilized the practices he had perfected in councils of war as commander in chief. He occasionally convened cabinet meetings, three times in 1791 and six times in 1792. He almost always submitted questions for consideration ahead of time, asked for written opinions in the event of disagreement, and then decided on a course of action after the meeting. But most of the interactions still took place in writing or in individual consultations. In 1793, Washington continued these practices, but he also began calling regular cabinet meetings to debate ongoing diplomatic and domestic issues. Given the intensity of the situation, he preferred to discuss issues multiple times before making decisions, rather than just relying on written opinions. The year 1793 served as the high-water mark for cabinet meetings. Fifty-one gatherings took place in 1793—over half of all the meetings that Washington organized as president. Rather than meeting once every couple of months, in 1793, the cabinet usually met once or twice each week at the President's House. In times of extreme stress, they gathered up to five times per week. Washington had convened a handful of cabinet meetings before April 1793, but never with the frequency required to resolve the issues surrounding the Neutrality Crisis. Given the potential consequences of each decision, he called these meetings to request advice and support as he carefully established diplomatic precedent for the new nation.

In addition to creating new internal practices, Washington and the cabinet established critical executive precedents. They crafted the first major foreign policy and forged rules of neutrality that regulated periods of peace over the next five decades. They also asserted American independence on an international stage, demonstrating that the administration would not be pushed around by European powers.

By establishing these precedents, the cabinet worked to reinforce the president's authority over diplomatic affairs. As Washington and the secretaries implemented neutrality, they actively sidelined Congress and state authorities in favor of executive-led enforcement of foreign policy. The secretaries' defense of presidential power and rejection of congressional participation reflected their shared experience with the inefficiencies of the state legislatures and the Confederation Congress.

At several points during the Neutrality Crisis, Washington adopted a strong position that could have provoked public reaction. As he navigated these difficult choices, he followed the model he had established with his officers in councils of war before retreats or controversial decisions. Washington convened the cabinet before each major decision, ensuring he had the secretaries' approval before announcing his policy and crafting executive precedent. He often requested written opinions after cabinet meetings to be sure he had evidence of their support. While he never published cabinet deliberations or the secretaries' written opinions regarding the Neutrality Crisis, he had evidence of their support if he needed it and he could have made their correspondence public.

By the end of 1793, Congress and the American public had accepted how the administration handled the Neutrality Crisis, effectively ceding all authority over diplomacy to the executive branch. Additionally, the frequent cabinet meetings exacerbated the Hamilton-Jefferson feud and accelerated the rise of the first two-party system. Finally, the cabinet became a visible institution within the executive branch, and Washington experienced pointed criticism for his relationship with the cabinet for the first time.

Eight days after receiving news of the European war, Washington left Mount Vernon to return to Philadelphia. Anxious to return as quickly as possible, he collected reports on the road conditions to determine the best route. After leaving home, Washington rode down to Alexandria before crossing the Potomac River and landing in Georgetown. Although Washington left no records of this trip or his thoughts along the way, his route can be pieced together based on similar journeys he completed in May 1787, April 1789, November 1790, and July 1795. Washington completed each journey in five days and structured the trip around stops in Alexandria, Georgetown, Baltimore, Havre de Grace, Wilmington, and Chester.[1] Given the urgency of Washington's return to Philadelphia, he preferred to dine and sleep at familiar accommodations. He could not risk poor provisions, faulty care for his horses, or delays caused by unfamiliar innkeepers making a scene when meeting him. Perhaps he enjoyed breakfast at Vanhorn's Tavern in Prince George County before spending the night at Spurrier's Tavern. In the past, Washington had complained of the service at Spurrier's but he continued to stop at the hostelry because there was "no other" along the route.[2] The next day, Washington likely arrived in Baltimore. He may have asked for any news of the foreign conflict, since he could not receive mail while on the road. As he had done on previous visits, Washington may have dined with Dr. James McHenry, his former aide-de-camp and future secretary of war. On April 15, he might have dined at Skerrett's Tavern (also called Cheyns's or Webster's) before he crossed the Susquehanna River on the public ferry at Havre de Grace. The next day, Washington made his way to Wilmington. To complete his journey, Washington probably enjoyed breakfast in Chester before arriving in Philadelphia on the evening of April 17, anxious to receive updates on the state of the war.

When Washington woke in Philadelphia, he drafted a letter to the department secretaries summoning them to a meeting at nine o'clock the next morning. He also sent them thirteen questions about the European conflict to consider in advance of their meeting.[3] On April 19, the cabinet gathered at the President's House, meeting in Washington's private study on the second floor.[4] Washington's study was fifteen by twenty-one feet—not a particularly large room for five large adult men. The space was further restricted by Washington's ornate desk (which measured more than five feet long), his dressing table, a wood-burning stove, a large globe, bookshelves along the walls, and the temporary table and chairs brought in for the meeting. When Washington and the four secretaries gathered in the room, it would have been rather cozy at best, claustrophobic at worst.

Washington's pre-circulated questions and the April 19 cabinet meeting set the agenda for the rest of the year. The European war posed four main issues that dominated the cabinet's attention: Should the administration issue a neutrality proclamation, and if so, with what wording? Should the administration receive a minister from France, and if so, under what terms? How would the crisis affect treaty relations with France and Great Britain? What role would Congress play in resolving the crisis?

From the moment Washington sent his questions, political tensions rippled under the surface. Jefferson and Hamilton had spent the previous year and a half battling over financial legislation and jockeying for influence in the executive branch. By 1793, they hated each other and were predisposed to assume the worst. Although Washington penned the letter with the thirteen questions to the department secretaries, Jefferson was convinced Hamilton had drafted the questions: "Though those sent me were in [the president's] own hand writing, yet it was palpable from the style . . . that they were not the President's . . . in short that the language was Hamilton's, and the doubts his alone." After receiving the letter, Jefferson conferred with Randolph, who shared the same suspicions. A few days earlier, Randolph and Hamilton had discussed similar questions. When Randolph received Washington's letter, he immediately recognized the same questions Hamilton had raised.[5]

Although Washington adopted the questions proposed by Hamilton, Jefferson was wrong to assume that the president had passed along the questions without editing them. These issues had been on Washington's mind for weeks. On April 12, before departing for Philadelphia, he wrote to Jefferson and Hamilton that the administration needed "to use every means in its power to prevent [American] citizens from embroiling us with either [France and Great Britain], by endeavouring to maintain a strict neutrality."[6] He considered neutrality essential long before Hamilton shared his thoughts. Furthermore, Washington had added several significant questions to Hamilton's draft. Hamilton's original list no longer exists, but we can likely tell what he shared with Washington based on a similar letter he sent to John Jay the week before. In Washington's April 18 letter to the secretaries, he voiced concerns about a neutrality proclamation, transmitting information to Congress, and how to interpret the French-American treaty—all of which are absent in Hamilton's letter to Jay.[7]

Despite apparent tension between Hamilton and Jefferson, the cabinet initially made progress in addressing Washington's questions when they gathered on April 19. Washington understood that the administration needed to formally declare its position in the war so that other European nations knew whether to treat the United States as an ally or an enemy, but he wasn't sure how that would affect American citizens. The first question asked if the administration should take steps to keep Americans out of the European conflict: "Shall a proclamation issue for the purpose of preventing interferences of the Citizens of the United States in the War between France & Great Britain &ca? Shall it contain a declaration of Neutrality or not? What shall it contain?" The cabinet agreed that the administration would issue a proclamation forbidding American citizens from "all acts and proceedings" that would give the appearance of assisting any of the belligerent powers, including fighting or carrying contraband or items related to war such as weapons and ammunition.[8]

Washington and the secretaries agreed to leave the word "neutrality" out of the proclamation. Under international law, that term would require strict enforcement and might interfere with other American treaties. Jay had similarly advised Hamilton that "it [is] better at present that too little shd. be said, than too much."[9] The Neutrality Crisis presented an entirely new set of circumstances for the members of the administration. The cabinet had no experience trying to keep citizens *out* of an international conflict—during the Revolutionary War, the Continental Congress and the Continental Army had barely scraped together enough men, financial support, and war matériel to keep the war effort afloat. Overexuberance was unfamiliar. Given these uncertainties, Washington and the secretaries agreed that avoiding the word "neutrality" left the administration with room to enforce the proclamation flexibly. They recognized that they were setting important precedent—the Neutrality Crisis was the first time the nation was forced to choose sides between European belligerents—and Washington preferred to move slowly when establishing decisions that would mold the executive branch for his successors.

Jefferson encouraged the vague language in the proclamation as the best course of action for the administration, but he also harbored ulterior motives. A strict American neutrality would have favored Britain. Jefferson knew that France needed supplies for its war against Britain and the Netherlands. Furthermore, Jefferson suspected that France desperately depended on American funds, repaid from Revolutionary War debts, to purchase those supplies. He hoped that he could negotiate a neutrality that would subtly favor the French.[10] He planned to try to secure faster repayment of American debts to France, to allow French ships to purchase supplies, and to permit France to sell captured British goods in US ports. To achieve these goals, Jefferson needed the proclamation to avoid the word "neutral."

At the April 19 cabinet meeting, Washington instructed Randolph to draft the proclamation. The cabinet had agreed to issue a proclamation forbidding American citizens from engaging with hostile powers. Much to Jefferson's chagrin, Randolph managed to slip "impartial" into the statement at the last minute without Jefferson noticing. The key clause now read that the United States would "adopt and pursue a conduct friendly and impartial toward the belligerent powers." Although "impartial" did not make as bold a statement, the message was clear, and the announcement became known as the Neutrality Proclamation.[11]

After resolving the first question, the cabinet turned to the imminent arrival of the new French minister. Citizen Edmond Charles Genêt was on a ship headed toward Philadelphia to replace his predecessor, Jean Baptiste Ternant. All the secretaries concluded that the government should receive a minister from France, but they disagreed over how friendly that reception should be. Eighteenth-century diplomatic customs dictated how countries would treat emissaries from other nations. If two nations signed an alliance, then their ministers would be welcomed "absolutely," and the ministers would enjoy more privileges and access to the home government. On the other hand, if two nations did not have a treaty that defined their relationship, ministers might be received "with qualifications," and they would operate under limited diplomatic privileges until the two nations established a more formal diplomatic relationship.[12]

While France and the United States had signed treaties of alliance during the Revolutionary War, the political situation in France had changed significantly since 1783.[13] The French Revolution had begun on May 5, 1789, when King Louis XVI convened the Estates-General for the first time since 1614. Most Americans had initially applauded the constitutional reforms of the French Revolution, which promised to bring more rights to the French people. However, by late 1792, the revolution had taken a radical turn. On January 17, 1793, the National Convention convicted King Louis XVI of high treason. While the king had driven the nation into enormous debt, his true crime was ruling a society that had lost patience with the monarchy. On the morning of January 21, the king was led from the Temple prison to the Place de la Revolution (now the Place de la Concorde), where he was executed by guillotine. At 10:22 A.M., the king's head fell into a basket while the crowds roared "Vive la Nation! Vive la République!"[14]

Despite the conditions on the ground in France, Jefferson argued that the Franco-American diplomatic relationship remained the same, while Hamilton insisted that France's unstable political climate posed a danger to the United States. He suggested that the French Revolution could produce military despotism, so the treaties should be "suspended till their government shall be settled in the form it is ultimately to take."[15] Hamilton advised Washington to limit his interactions with the new French minister until that time. Recognizing that Hamilton and Jefferson were unlikely to agree, Washington called a time-out to allow cooler heads to prevail.

A few days later, the cabinet returned to Washington's house.[16] When the secretaries reassembled, Hamilton and Jefferson remained deadlocked over the French minister and whether the Neutrality Proclamation affected the United States' diplomatic relationships with France and Britain.

The Federalists, represented in the cabinet by Hamilton and Knox, abhorred the violence and the anarchy of the French Revolution. While Hamilton and Knox appreciated French support during the Revolutionary War, the French Revolution had devolved into senseless violence. The Committee of Safety, led by the radical Jacobins, ordered the execution of 17,000 people and the arrest of 300,000. There was also a real fear that the violence that had consumed the French Revolution would make its way across the Atlantic. Abigail Adams wrote to her husband, John, the Vice President, that she hoped Republicans would "not follow the French example & Lop of[f] Heads, even of departments."[17] After their experience with Shays' Rebellion during the Confederation, Hamilton and Knox were unwilling to risk further uprisings. They argued that the administration had a responsibility to secure the nation's safety.

The tumultuous political scene in Paris caused Federalists to question France's value as an ally. They argued that the French leadership could shift at any moment, making an alliance uneasy at best. Lastly, Hamilton and Knox claimed that the execution of King Louis XVI abrogated the Franco-American Treaty. Because the diplomatic relationship had been severed, the administration should accept the minister with qualifications until the administration established a new diplomatic relationship with France.[18] The administration could not afford to favor France, risk alienating the country's largest trading partner, Britain, and derail the economic system Hamilton had recently engineered.

Republicans, represented in the cabinet by Jefferson and Randolph, held deep emotional attachments to France. At the very least, they insisted that Americans owed France for its support during the Revolutionary War on principle. Republicans also pointed to the two Franco-American treaties signed in February 1778. The treaties had outlined France's military, economic, and diplomatic commitment to the United States during the Revolutionary War. In the Treaty of Amity and Commerce, France had effectively recognized American independence and the two countries had established a mutually beneficial trade relationship. In the Treaty of Alliance, both countries pledged to come to each other's defense if Britain attacked them or interfered with their trade. Most Republicans argued that these treaties obligated the United States to assist France in its current war against Britain. They asserted that "the *real* alliance is affixed to the *body* of the [French] *state*," not the monarch. Finally, many Americans believed they should support the French Revolution as the republican ideological successor to the American Revolution. They also nursed a lasting distrust of the British and feared that an Anglo-American alliance would foster the growth of a monarchy within the United States. Based on all these factors, Jefferson and Randolph argued that the Franco-American relationship remained intact and that a French minister ought to be received without qualification.[19]

The personal spat between Hamilton and Jefferson belied a much larger conflict over the future of the United States. Hamilton and the Federalists envisioned a nation that prioritized manufacturing, trade, financial institutions, and industrialization. The growing American population would naturally flock to urban centers to pursue employment and education. A close relationship with Britain facilitated these goals. On the other side, Jefferson and the Republicans promoted a future of yeoman farmers, each with a farm and livelihood enough to feed a family. Supported by their own labor (and that of their slaves), farmers remained independent from the influence of employers or landlords, and thus could serve as virtuous republican citizens. Additionally, family farms kept citizens out of cities, which many Republicans viewed as dens of sin and corruption. They did not shun trade—farmers needed to sell their products, after all—but they believed the government should not prioritize merchant interests. Hamilton and Jefferson's cabinet debates took on additional seriousness in the context of this fight for the future character of their new nation.[20]

Washington recognized that no amount of cabinet debate would resolve these issues, so he requested written opinions from the department secretaries, just as he had often done when his officers reached an impasse in councils of war. All the secretaries submitted their opinions by May 6. After receiving the written opinions, Washington decided to accept Genêt and confessed to Jefferson that "he had never had a doubt about the validity of the treaty: but since a question had been suggested he thought it ought to be considered."[21] His decision amounted to a wait-and-see approach. He would accept the French minister and he would not suspend the Treaty of Alliance for fear that a strong position might provoke war with France. Yet, he also took the secretaries' advice to exploit the wiggle room inherent in the treaties. Article XI of the Treaty of Alliance required both countries to protect each other's possessions if *attacked* by Great Britain. Jefferson suggested that because France had declared war on Britain, the conflict was *offensive,* not *defensive,* and therefore did not require the United States to provide aid—a convenient interpretation given that the United States did not have a navy and could offer little support anyway.

Washington also accepted Jefferson's interpretation of Article XXIV of the Treaty of Amity and Commerce. This article stipulated that enemies of France could not "fit their Ships" or "sell what they have taken" in American ports. Put another way, because France was at war with Britain, the United States must prohibit Britain from arming its warships or selling war booty in American ports. But the treaty did not require the administration to grant these privileges to France either. Technically, a neutral policy did not invalidate the treaties. According to Jefferson's interpretation, Washington could abide by the Franco-American treaties in good faith *and* enforce neutrality.[22]

Unbeknownst to Washington and the secretaries, Genêt had arrived in Charleston, South Carolina, on April 8, 1793. After spending two months tossed about at sea during a particularly stormy spring, the *Embuscade* finally spotted land and limped into Charleston harbor. Although Philadelphia was his intended destination, a large storm had driven Genêt's ship off course and he landed 680 miles to the south. Battered by the Atlantic crossing, the *Embuscade* nevertheless offered an enthusiastic salutation. Genêt had designed the ship to speak to Americans' revolutionary spirit. The figurehead was a liberty cap, the foremast had been carved into a liberty pole, and the sails had large messages printed in English. The rear sail (mizzen-top) declared: "FREEMEN, WE ARE YOUR BROTHERS AND FRIENDS." The front sail (foretop) warned: "Enemies of Equality, relinquish your principles or tremble!"[23] Charleston warmly received Genêt's unsubtle message and offered an equally effusive welcome. The new French minister was treated to fêtes, dinners, balls, and receptions. French merchants residing in Charleston outfitted their private vessels to fight the British navy and offered them to Genêt free of charge.[24]

Genêt's mission was to secure three key concessions from the American government. First, Genêt assumed that French ships—both warships and privateers—would be granted access to American ports for repairs and provisioning. He also expected French privateers would be permitted to sell their captured British goods in American ports. Privateers were ships outfitted and operated by private citizens during wartime under licenses from a national government, authorizing them to attack and plunder enemy ships on the high seas. Privateers towed their captured prizes back into port to sell off the goods and supplies, often making a fortune. During wartime, each nation relied on its own band of privateers to wreak havoc on enemy nations and their trade. Second, Genêt intended to oversee the landing of French troops in American ports, purchase supplies, and then launch attacks on British and Spanish territories from US territory. Genêt planned to coordinate with the French fleet to attack British fisheries in Canadian waters and burn Halifax to the ground. The fleet would then sail to New Orleans to rendezvous with his new army (filled with American citizens) to liberate all of Louisiana.[25] Finally, Genêt demanded immediate and full payment of Revolutionary War debts to fund the new French war. He insisted immediate payment would benefit the American economy because France was generously prepared to purchase all its war supplies from American farmers and merchants. Unsurprisingly, Genêt's agenda received a mixed reception from Washington's administration.[26]

Overcome by the joyous welcome he received in Charleston, Genêt abandoned all diplomatic protocol. He should have quickly made his way to Philadelphia to present his credentials to the administration. Instead, he commissioned four private vessels and hired American soldiers to man the ships. He also instructed the local French consul to adjudicate any prizes (foreign ships captured by French vessels) that privateers brought into Charleston. Essentially, Genêt established French law in an American port.[27] He then made his way to Philadelphia, not quickly by sea but slowly over land. Over the course of the twenty-eight-day journey, he relished the affection shown to him by the American people. Upon arriving in Philadelphia, Genêt was greeted by a committee and a throng of ebullient citizens. The crowd marched to the French minister's house and delivered an address from local citizens' organizations, which were followed by cheers and applause.[28] Later that evening, he sent a missive back to the French government in Paris gleefully reporting on his first few weeks in the United States: "My journey [between Charleston and Philadelphia] has been a succession of uninterrupted civic festivals and my entering Philadelphia has been a triumph for liberty. Real Americans have reached the climax of happiness."[29] This reception blinded Genêt to the complicated diplomatic realities facing Washington and the new nation.

While Genêt was indulging in festivals and balls, Washington and the secretaries learned of his actions in Charleston. On May 2, 1793, Washington and the secretaries received a report from George Hammond, the British minister to the United States. Hammond revealed that Genêt's ship, the *Embuscade,* had been lurking within US sovereign waters in the Bay of Delaware. On April 25, the *Embuscade* had captured a British ship, the *Grange,* and imprisoned its crew. Hammond asserted that the capture violated American neutrality and expressed his certainty that the United States would "adopt such measures . . . [to] procure the immediate restoration . . . of the British Ship Grange and the liberation of her crew."[30]

The British complaints and Genêt's reckless behavior forced the cabinet to establish a privateer policy. Washington's Neutrality Proclamation prohibited foreign ship captains from anchoring in American ports to acquire supplies and weapons or to recruit crew members. Yet the proclamation contained many legal gaps. The proclamation did not outline which branch of the federal or state governments would enforce the administration's neutrality policy. Neither Congress nor any state government had passed laws regarding the proclamation, so if American citizens violated the terms, it was not clear which court should hear the case, under which statute they would be prosecuted, what would happen to the ships in the interim, or who would enforce the judgment.[31] Put another way, it was not clear what specific crime they had committed or how they should be punished. These were just a few of the questions raised by the Neutrality Proclamation.

Over the course of the summer, Washington and the secretaries formulated foreign policy through a process of trial and error. On May 16, Genêt finally arrived to present his credentials to the administration. When he reached Philadelphia, Jefferson immediately warned him to cease licensing American vessels as French privateers. Perhaps blinded by his sympathy for the French cause, Jefferson believed that Genêt took the warning to heart and would henceforth comply with the administration's neutrality policy.

After Genêt's arrival, Washington gathered the cabinet to discuss a new privateer case. On May 3, the *Citoyen Genêt* had captured the British ship *William,* and a few days later, it had captured the *Active.* The *Citoyen Genêt* was one of the privateers Genêt had outfitted while he was in Charleston, and in a fantastic display of ego, he had named the ship after himself. On May 14, the *Citoyen Genêt* had arrived in Philadelphia with its two prizes in tow, meaning that Genêt defied the administration's neutral policy right under Washington's nose. Despite his behavior, Jefferson encouraged the rest of the cabinet to view Genêt's conduct in Charleston as a "slight offense." Jefferson argued that Washington had not yet issued the Neutrality Proclamation when Genêt first landed. Jefferson argued that the administration had little power over the legality of the privateers and their prizes. The president could not force restitution of prizes—that power belonged to Congress.

On the other side, Hamilton and Knox feared that overlooking Genêt's conduct and ignoring French seizures of British ships would provoke reprisals from Britain. Furthermore, they viewed the power dynamic between the president and Congress very differently. Based on their own experiences with Congress, they did not trust the legislature to act forcefully. They argued that the administration must compel France to give up the prize ship and free the captured crew, or the French vessels should be sent away immediately.

Randolph suggested a more moderate approach. He agreed with Jefferson's view that Washington could not force the restitution of the prizes, but he argued that the president should banish French privateers from American ports.[32] At this point, Washington had yet to fully articulate the president's power to enforce diplomatic policy, so he adopted a restrained approach. He followed Randolph's advice and Jefferson conveyed the administration's decision to Genêt a few days later. Washington also instructed Jefferson to apologize to Britain for not restoring their ships. Washington hoped the apology would suffice to ward off any future conflict.[33] At this early stage in the Neutrality Crisis, his decision reflected his cautious approach to establishing precedent and the cabinet's uncertainty about the executive's powers to enforce diplomatic policy.

Genêt was not content to keep his prizes and continued to push his luck. Over the next several weeks, he peppered Jefferson with numerous letters protesting American neutrality and asserting French rights. He also offered several foreign policy suggestions—each more outlandish than the last. On May 22, Genêt suggested the administration reorganize its debt payment plan so that it could immediately pay off the French loans remaining from the Revolutionary War. On

May 27, Genêt sent two letters. First, he demanded the release of Gideon Henfield. Henfield was an American captain born in Massachusetts whom Genêt had hired to sail the *Citoyen Genêt*. Pennsylvania authorities had arrested Henfield for violating American neutrality when the *Citoyen Genêt* arrived in Philadelphia. In his letter to Jefferson, Genêt insisted that Henfield should be released because he was under the protection of the French government as a captain of a privateer. Essentially, he denied that the US government had any right to control its own citizens. Genêt then sent his second letter, this time proclaiming the French consul's right to adjudicate cases of French prizes brought into American ports.[34]

Jefferson carefully crafted replies to Genêt's letters to explain the administration's position and defend the powers of the executive branch. In response to the May 22 letter, Jefferson informed Genêt that full payment of French debt was impossible. Repaying such a large sum in one payment would cripple the American economy.[35] No matter how much the administration might wish to aid France (or not), that solution was not possible.

Jefferson next turned to Genêt's May 27 letters. Jefferson denied Henfield's release. He explained that each government had power over its citizens. By "granting military commissions within the United States," Genêt had "infringe[d] on [American] Sovereignty" and led American citizens "to commit acts contrary to the duties they owe their own country."[36] Jefferson also denied Genêt's claim that the French consul had jurisdiction over French prize cases. He asserted "the *right* of every nation to prohibit acts of sovereignty from being exercised by any other within its limits." In other words, French consuls in American ports could not rule on the status of French privateers and their prizes. Jefferson defended "the *duty* of a neutral nation to prohibit such as would injure one of the warring powers." Lastly, Jefferson tried to show Genêt that American neutrality did not intend to be cruel. The proclamation permitted privateers to enter American harbors for defensive repairs but prohibited offensive arming. Genêt did not appreciate the nuance or simply chose to ignore it.

At the end of June, Washington received word that his plantation manager was dying. He left Philadelphia for a quick visit to Mount Vernon, planning to return less than two weeks later. While he was out of town, Thomas Mifflin, the governor of Pennsylvania, received word of Genêt's latest antics. Agents in the Philadelphia port reported that Genêt was arming a new privateer, the *Petite Democrate*. The *Petite Democrate* was a British ship formerly named the *Little Sarah,* which had been captured by the *Embuscade.* Not only was Genêt flagrantly violating the administration's Neutrality Proclamation, but by converting a British ship into a privateer just a few blocks from the President's House, he publicly flaunted his disregard for Washington's orders. Mifflin forwarded the news to Washington, who asked to be kept apprised if Genêt began arming any additional vessels.

Mifflin, a devout Republican and no friend of the president, gladly let the matter drop. Mifflin and Washington had a historically sour relationship dating back to his brief tenure as one of Washington's first aides-de-camp in the Revolutionary War. In August 1775, the position of quartermaster general had become available. Mifflin had requested the promotion, which Washington had granted. By March 1776, however, rumors swirled around Congress accusing Mifflin of mismanagement and corruption in the administration of the quartermaster department. While Mifflin had initially approached his new duties with enthusiasm, by the summer of 1777 he felt overwhelmed by the burdens of the department. On October 8, 1777, Mifflin sent his resignation to Congress, but congressmen pleaded with him to continue in the position until they found a replacement.[37] Although Mifflin agreed to stay on as acting quartermaster general, he ignored his duties for the next several months, leaving the critical department at a standstill. Washington blamed many of the hardships suffered by the army at Valley Forge on Mifflin's misconduct and never forgave his former aide.[38]

Mifflin also harbored ill will toward Washington. In the summer of 1777, as the British army circled Philadelphia, he requested that the Continental Army defend Philadelphia at all costs. Conveniently, Mifflin also lobbied for a line command. He asserted that as a native Pennsylvanian, he deserved a promotion. Washington disagreed and insisted he remain in the quartermaster department. Washington also excluded the quartermaster general from his inner circle of advisors, which further injured Mifflin's pride.

Mifflin sought revenge against Washington for the perceived slights to his honor. After he resigned from the quartermaster department, Congress appointed him to the Board of War. The Board of War oversaw Washington's operations, which Washington and his aides interpreted as a slight against his capabilities as commander in chief. As a member of the board, Mifflin voted to promote General Thomas Conway despite Washington's protests. Mifflin also vocally criticized Washington's command and played a role in the plot to replace Washington with General Horatio Gates during the winter of 1777. But by March 1778, any congressional resistance to Washington's command disintegrated and Washington could not help but gloat: "Genl Mifflin it is commonly supposed, bore the second part in the Cabal; and General Conway, I know, was a very active, and malignant partizan but I have good reasons to believe that their machinations have recoiled most sensibly upon themselves."[39] Given their decades-long dislike of each other, Mifflin was in no rush to help Washington enforce his neutral policy in 1793.

On July 6, the *Petite Democrate* prepared to set sail. Alexander Dallas, the Pennsylvania secretary of state and a Republican himself, hoped that he could convince Genêt to pause his operations. The meeting went badly. Genêt failed to sense that Mifflin and Dallas were allies, and "he flew into a great passion, talked extravagantly & concluded by refusing to order the vessel to stay."[40] He denounced the administration's neutral policy and threatened to take his appeal directly to the American people. While Mifflin hated to assist the administration, he could not aid a foreigner in breaking the law. He called out the militia and sent word to Knox and Jefferson.[41] Dallas also relayed his conversation with Genêt to Jefferson and Knox—including the French minister's threat to take his appeal directly to the people.

Envisioning a bloody battle on the docks of Philadelphia, Jefferson rushed to Genêt and urged caution. According to Jefferson's report compiled later that day, he asked Genêt to "detain" the *Petite Democrate* until they could lay the issue "before the President who would [return] Wednesday." Genêt "went into an immense field of declamation &complaint." He took the opportunity to further challenge the administration and Washington in particular. He insisted, "in a very high tone," that the president had overstepped his authority in denying French privateers access to American ports, and he shared his plans to appeal to Congress. According to Jefferson's account of the meeting, he interrupted Genêt and explained that the Constitution divided the "functions of government among three different authorities" and that all foreign affairs responsibilities "belonged to the executive department." When Genêt insisted that Congress was the sovereign, Jefferson countered that Congress was sovereign "in making laws only," but that the executive was responsible for enforcing them.[42] Although he disagreed with many of Washington's policies by this point, Jefferson still defended the power of the executive and rejected Genêt's attempts to increase congressional oversight.

After some convincing on Jefferson's part, Genêt said "that he could not make any promise [to retain the ship], it would be out of his duty, but that he was very happy in being able to inform [Jefferson] that the vessel was not in readiness." Jefferson again pressed Genêt to promise that the ship would not depart before the president's return. He "gave the same answer that [the *Petite Democrate*] would not be ready for some time, but with the look & gesture which shewed he meant I should understand she would not be gone before that."[43] Still blinded by his fierce Anglophobia, Jefferson interpreted these words as a promise that the ship would not depart until Washington's return. Despite Genêt's evasiveness and threats to appeal to the American people, Jefferson left the meeting believing the French minister would honor his word. He reassured Dallas and Mifflin that the *Petite Democrate* would not leave Philadelphia until Washington got back and that they could safely disband the militia.[44] Eager to avoid conflict, Mifflin followed Jefferson's recommendation and sent the troops home.

Two days later, Hamilton, Knox, and Jefferson gathered to discuss Genêt's latest actions. Hamilton argued that the administration must stop Genêt's departure. He proposed installing cannons on Mud Island, a small island at the mouth of the Philadelphia harbor, and recommended that they issue orders to stop the *Petite Democrate* if she tried to leave American waters. Reluctant to start a violent confrontation and confident that Genêt would act prudently, Jefferson suggested that they await Washington's arrival in Philadelphia before deciding.[45] Unwilling to act without unanimous cabinet support, Hamilton and Knox reluctantly agreed to wait for Washington.

The next day Washington returned to Philadelphia and discovered that Genêt had moved the *Petite Democrate* down the river and out of reach of the proposed cannons on Mud Island. Eager to get to the bottom of the situation, Washington reviewed Jefferson's accounts of his negotiations with Genêt. He also read reports from Dallas, Mifflin, Hamilton, and Knox, which revealed Genêt's threat to go above the president's head and to appeal to the American people for support. Jefferson also had this information and he knew that Genêt's threat challenged the president's authority over diplomacy—yet he had conveniently left this portion of the story out of his dispatch. Irate, Washington wrote to Jefferson. His anger was palpable: "Is the Minister of the French Republic to set the Acts of this Government at defiance—*with impunity?*" Washington then challenged Jefferson to offer a solution: "Circumstances press for decision—and as you have had time to consider them (upon me they have come unexpected) I wish to receive your opinion upon them—even before tomorrow." Jefferson was on the road to his summer home outside of Philadelphia, but Washington did not care. He demanded immediate answers.[46] Flustered, Jefferson wrote back and reiterated that "he [had] received assurance from mister Genet to-day that she will not be gone before the President's decision." Should Washington wish to discuss how to further proceed, Jefferson said it would be his honor to "confer with the President, or any others, whenever [Washington] pleases."[47]

The next morning, Jefferson ominously noted that the secretaries gathered "on summons" from the president. Tired from his rushed journey back from Mount Vernon, annoyed with the above-average summer heat, and faced with an impending showdown with France and Britain, Washington must have been in quite a dark mood. The cabinet meeting notes, or rather the lack of documentation, reflect the somber feeling in the president's private study that morning. In his private notes on cabinet meetings, Jefferson typically described the back and forth between the secretaries and offered his own editorializing on each position. But on the morning of July 12, Jefferson only transcribed the final decisions of the cabinet with brisk, efficient language. The cabinet agreed to order all French ships and prizes to remain in harbor until further notice. Mifflin would be instructed to keep the ships under close surveillance and forcibly stop the ships if necessary. The cabinet also planned to consult the Supreme Court justices for advice on how to proceed.[48]

A few weeks later, Washington gathered Hamilton, Jefferson, and Knox to discuss Genêt's conduct. They agreed to request Genêt's recall from France, but Washington wanted to maintain cordial relations with France. He wished to "express our friendship to [France]" but would make clear that administration "insist[ed] on the recall of Genet."[49] Hamilton also urged Washington to place all Genêt's correspondence before Congress. He perceived that Genêt's outrageous behavior presented a unique opportunity to score political points at the expense of his political rivals who were more closely aligned with France. Jefferson balked at this suggestion. He recognized that Genêt's unpredictable behavior discredited the Republicans who had ardently cheered his arrival. Genêt's letters would only highlight his fundamental misunderstanding of the US Constitution, challenges to the administration, and violations of Washington's neutrality policy. When these indiscretions were made public, Jefferson knew that Genêt's behavior would turn public opinion against France. Genêt's letters would also harm Jefferson's personal reputation as the unofficial leader of the Republican Party, for they revealed Jefferson's efforts to enforce the administration's neutrality policy. Although many Republicans had turned against Genêt, they still wanted to support France in the European war. They would not look favorably on Jefferson's efforts to enforce neutrality.[50]

On August 1, Washington summoned cabinet members to a meeting to get Randolph's opinion. Randolph had left the city briefly, but upon his return to Philadelphia, he quickly approved the cabinet's decision to request Genêt's recall. Washington knew this step was a bold move and might incur the wrath of some radical Republicans. He obtained the unanimous agreement of all his secretaries before taking this momentous step, just in case he needed political cover down the road. This cabinet meeting proved to have lasting influence on the development of the executive branch and American diplomacy. By requesting Genêt's recall, the administration sent the message that it would defend American sovereignty against foreign influence and diplomatic machinations. When the French government granted Washington's request, it tacitly acknowledged the United States' right to dictate rules of neutrality on domestic soil and to demand that foreign nations abide by those rules. Genêt still had some supporters, but the American public largely acquiesced to his removal.[51]

The cabinet may have decided how to resolve their Genêt problem, but events soon made clear that the administration needed to legally define the rules of neutrality. At the end of July, a Pennsylvania jury issued a verdict in *United States v. Henfield,* acquitting Henfield of all privateering charges.[52] The case posed a major problem for the administration. Washington and the cabinet had instructed William Rawle, the United States district attorney in Pennsylvania, to prosecute the case.[53] Edmund Randolph had written the indictment himself and Supreme Court justice James Wilson delivered the grand jury charge, proclaiming, "That a Citizen, who, in our State of Neutrality . . . takes an hostile Part with either of the belligerent Powers, violates . . . his Duty and the laws of his Country."[54] Republican presses gleefully reported the verdict, praising the "independent jury" that had "firmly withstood the violence of an aristocratic torrent, whose sluices were opened upon them."[55] The verdict embarrassed the administration and highlighted the legal vulnerabilities present in the Neutrality Proclamation. Although the proclamation prohibited citizens from engaging in privateering, there was no legal code under which a district attorney could prosecute the case.

To prevent that embarrassment from happening again, Washington instructed the secretaries to meet and craft more formal rules of neutrality. In early August, the secretaries met and drafted eight rules to govern American interactions with foreign nations going forward, which they sent to Washington for his review. After considering the secretaries' draft, Washington convened another meeting a few weeks later and the cabinet finalized the rules of American neutrality.[56]

These rules emphasized that foreign nations must take "efficacious measures to prevent the future fitting out of Privateers in the Ports of The UStates." The administration did not care if France and Britain outfitted privateers, but they could not do so in American ports. The cabinet also took a harsher stance against privateers than it had earlier in the summer. No longer would the administration turn a blind eye to prizes. Now, if France brought captured British ships into American harbors, the president intended to "indemnify the Owners of those prizes" and expected "to be reimbursed by the French Nation."[57] These new rules represented a development in the cabinet's interpretation of the president's power to enforce diplomatic policy. Congress had been out of session since March 4 and could offer no solution to curb privateering while adjourned. Perhaps Congress's inability to take action while out of session reminded the secretaries of their previous frustrating experiences with the state legislatures and the Confederation Congress. By the end of August, they were convinced that the legislature was too inefficient to provide forceful implementation of the administration's policy and they claimed the power for the executive to enforce domestic policy, effectively sidelining Congress from this process. On June 4, 1794, Congress passed legislation confirming Washington's rules of neutrality and affirming the president's new powers.[58]

In 1793, Washington's cabinet established important executive and diplomatic precedents, but that year also witnessed the crystallization of the first two-party political system, helmed by Hamilton on one side and Jefferson on the other. The previous fall, Jefferson had warned Washington this breach was coming. On September 27, 1792, Jefferson had left his home in Charlottesville, Virginia, to return to his office in Philadelphia. Along the way, Jefferson made a minor detour from his route to visit Mount Vernon. Washington and Jefferson enjoyed breakfast together before turning to politics. During their conversation, Washington confessed his disappointment at "the difference which he found to subsist between the Sec. of the Treasury and [Jefferson]." He acknowledged the disagreement in their political positions, but "he had never suspected it had gone so far in producing a personal difference."[59] Washington's efforts to serve as a mediator over the next several months failed, and by 1793, Hamilton and Jefferson loathed each other. The increasing animosity between the two festered during periods of crisis. Washington's small private study exacerbated the existing tensions between Hamilton and Jefferson by confining them together in a small space. Furthermore, the summer that year was so hot and muggy that a severe yellow fever epidemic broke out in October. Washington's second-story study would have been stifling in the Philadelphia heat, even on the coolest of summer days. Almost twenty years later, Jefferson described his interactions with Hamilton as "daily pitted in the cabinet like two cocks."[60] His word choice conveyed a violent, bloody spectacle and reveals a great deal about the nature of cabinet debates.

Jefferson and the Republicans believed that Hamilton and the Federalists sought to turn the government into a monarchy modeled after Britain. While Jefferson did not think the president agreed with this plan, he thought Washington oblivious to Hamilton's machinations. On the other side, the Federalists were convinced Jefferson and the Republicans were blinded by their rabid love of all things French to the dangers of anarchy and the violence of the French Revolution.

Washington did his best to manage the conflict. He hosted the secretaries at regular family dinners, invited them to the theater, and included them at other social events. He hoped that social interactions would foster an esprit de corps and diminish political divisions, just as social occasions had cultivated bonds among his officers during the war. Washington invited the secretaries to dine with him after many cabinet meetings to smooth hurt feelings that developed during the debates. For example, on July 31, 1793, he welcomed the secretaries to one such dinner. The day before, he had written to Jefferson: "As the consideration of this business may require some time, I should be glad if you & the other Gentlemen would take a family dinner with me at 4 'Oclock. No other company is, or will be envited."[61]

Similarly, on November 18, 1793, Washington hoped that a family dinner would encourage the cabinet to reach a consensus. Earlier that month, the cabinet had met four times in five days, on each occasion gathering for several hours in Washington's office. On November 18, the cabinet members paused their deliberations halfway through the meeting to sit for dinner. During this gathering, Jefferson and Hamilton clashed over whether the administration should banish Genêt from American soil. Although the cabinet had agreed to request Genêt's recall in late July, the administration had yet to receive a reply from

France because of the slow transportation time across the Atlantic Ocean. While the administration waited for France to respond, Genêt proceeded with his outlandish plans to launch invasions into British and Spanish territories from the United States. Washington had tired of Genêt's continuously offensive conduct and wanted to act. Hamilton argued in favor of Genêt's immediate banishment. He suggested that the dignity of the nation was at stake and "that our conduct now would tempt or deter other foreign ministers from treating us in the same manner." Jefferson protested that expelling the French minister would provoke war: "The measure [would be] so harsh a one that no precedent is produced where it has not been followed by war." Counseling patience, Jefferson urged Washington to wait for an official reply from the French government.[62] After the meal ended and the debates resumed, Jefferson and Hamilton still did not agree. Washington "lamented there was not an unanimity among [them], that as it was [they] had left him exactly where [they] found him." At the bottom of his meeting minutes Jefferson noted ominously, "And so it ended."[63]

Washington also employed flattery to keep Jefferson in the administration. Appealing to Jefferson's sense of duty to encourage good behavior, he emphasized the importance of hearing both sides of each debate in cabinet meetings. During their breakfast in September 1792, Jefferson had first mentioned his wish to retire. Washington tried to convince him of his value, and of the value of the Republican perspective, in the cabinet. He assured Jefferson that his opinions were important and that having both perspectives in the cabinet kept the administration on a moderate course: "[Washington] thought it important to preserve the check of my opinions in the administration in order to keep things in their proper channel and prevent them from going too far."[64] The president implored him to stay and confessed "that he could not see where he should find another character to fill [the] office."

He had benefited from hearing multiple opinions in his councils of war and sought to maintain a similar situation in the cabinet.

Whenever possible, Washington also tried to balance his decisions between the two sides. If he could not force these powerful secretaries to get along, he could at least make them feel important. In a private conversation with Jefferson prior to the outbreak of the Neutrality Crisis, Washington evidently said, "There was no nation on whom we could rely at all times but France, and that if we did not prepare in time some support in the event of rupture with Spain & England we might be charged with a criminal negligence." In his notes on the meeting, Jefferson confessed, "I was much pleased with the tone of these observations. it was the very doctrine which had been my polar star."[65]

While Washington's opinions on France shifted during the course of 1793, he continued his efforts to make Jefferson feel valued. In late November 1793, Washington sided very conspicuously with Jefferson during a cabinet meeting. The cabinet had gathered to discuss Washington's upcoming annual address to Congress. Washington often provided Congress with an update on the state of diplomatic relations with foreign nations in his addresses, and 1793 was no different. Over the last year, Jefferson had been in negotiations with George Hammond, the British ambassador, to resolve lingering issues from the end of the Revolutionary War. The British insisted that Americans repay prewar debts and restore loyalist property. Americans promised that they would pay their debts once Britain evacuated western forts and indemnified slave owners for the enslaved people who had escaped with the British army.

A few days before the cabinet meeting, British ambassador George Hammond acknowledged that the British had suspended their negotiations with the Americans until the end of the war with France. Both Jefferson and Washington were outraged at Hammond's letter. Jefferson had been waiting months for a reply from London and had sent several reminders to Hammond inquiring when he might receive an answer. After learning that London had arbitrarily decided to pause negotiations without their input, Washington and Jefferson concluded that Britain did not take the United States seriously. Recognizing an opportunity to score a few political points of his own, Jefferson urged Washington to lay his recent communications with Hammond before Congress.[66] Hamilton, Knox, and Randolph all favored withholding the communications from Congress and preserving secrecy to protect the possibility of future negotiations. Much to Jefferson's surprise, Washington lost his usual composure and vented his frustrations with Britain and Hammond. Jefferson described Washington's decision: "The Presidt. Took up the subject with more vehemence than I have seen him shew, and decided without reserve . . . (wherein H. K. and R. had been against me). This was the first instance I had seen of his deciding on the opinion of one against that of three others, which proved his own to have been very strong."[67] While it is likely that Washington went against the cabinet majority because he simply lost his temper, it is also possible that he expressed his opinion in such strong terms to assure Jefferson he still had an important role in the cabinet.

Washington may have also used cabinet meetings for a political purpose as the partisan tensions between Hamilton and Jefferson intensified and his other efforts to mediate failed. Although the extent of Jefferson's connections with the nascent Republican Party remained obscure in 1793, Hamilton did his very best to paint Jefferson in the worst possible light when he wrote to Washington,

> I have long seen a formed party in the Legislature, under his auspices, bent upon my subversion. I cannot doubt, from the evidence I possess, that the National Gazette was instituted

by him for political purposes and that one leading object of
it has been to render me and all the measures connect with
my department as odious as possible.[68]

Hamilton knew these charges would bother Washington, who considered attacks on the Department of the Treasury's policies to be attacks on his administration. In 1793, the *National Gazette* expanded its
criticism and hounded Washington with stories that extolled Genêt's
virtues and denounced the administration for its neutrality policy.
The evidence against Jefferson was convincing. He had hired Philip
Freneau, the publisher of the *National Gazette,* as a translator in the
Department of State. However, the only other language Freneau spoke
was French. As the longtime minister to France and an avowed
Francophile, Jefferson needed little assistance with that particular
language.

Washington raised the issue with Jefferson and said that while "he
despised all their attacks on him personally," he was more upset that
the paper criticized every "act of the government." Washington may
have complained about Freneau's attacks and made it clear that he
saw Freneau's hiring as a partisan act, but he never accused Jefferson
outright. Jefferson interpreted this conversation as a suggestion that
he should fire Freneau from the State Department, which he refused
to do.[69]

Washington did not force Jefferson to fire Freneau, but he ensured
that Jefferson took part in administrative decisions. As commander in
chief, he had learned the value of covering his bases, and he applied
those lessons to the cabinet. If Jefferson was present at cabinet meetings, he could not later claim ignorance or protest that he had been
excluded from the decision-making process. Furthermore, Jefferson
would look rather foolish if he tried to distance himself from the ad-

ministration's position while still serving as secretary of state. Jefferson discovered this conundrum when he tried to defend his role in the Neutrality Crisis to fellow Republicans, who accused the administration of adopting pro-British policies. When Madison and other Republicans criticized the Neutrality Proclamation, Jefferson quickly distanced himself from the document, making sure that his allies knew he had not written the statement: "I dare say you will have judged from the pusillanimity of the proclamation, from whose pen it came."[70] As early as May 1793, Jefferson acknowledged that this tactic had limited success, and he lamented his situation: "A proclamation is to be issued, and another instance of my being forced to appear to approve what I have condemned uniformly from its first conception."[71]

The year 1793 also proved to be a major turning point for the cabinet's visibility as an executive institution. For the first time, the press and the public used the word "cabinet" to describe Washington's meetings with his department secretaries. On June 13, Madison wrote to Jefferson criticizing the Neutrality Proclamation. Madison argued that the proclamation usurped Congress's power. According to Madison, the Constitution granted Congress the power to declare war, and therefore only Congress could declare peace. He asked Jefferson, "Did no such view of the subject present itself in the discussions of the Cabinet?"[72] Significantly, the secretaries also described their interactions as cabinet meetings, suggesting that they recognized that their actions created a new institution. In 1793, Jefferson and Hamilton described their gatherings as "cabinet meetings" and their decisions as "cabinet opinions" in their private notes.[73]

Increased public awareness of the cabinet's existence raised new objections to the administration. Members of the federal government had received ample criticism before 1793. In 1789, the public denounced Adams for his role in the Title Controversy, and Hamilton dealt with his fair share of critiques for his financial legislation in 1791 and 1792. But 1793 marked the first time the public targeted Washington and the presidency. One anonymous letter to the president, printed in the *National Gazette,* lamented the government's "shamefully pusillanimous" conduct toward Britain. The author warned Washington to "shut his ears against the whispers of servile adulation, and to listen to solemn admonitions of patriotic truth." If the president did not follow this advice, "the people . . . [would take] the law into their own hands . . . and wipe off the disgrace of the nation."[74] Madison and other Republicans shared similar sentiments behind closed doors.[75] Jefferson exonerated Washington from willfully complying with Hamilton's monarchical plans by suggesting that he had simply become senile: "His memory was already sensibly impaired by age, the firm tone of mind for which he had been remarkable was beginning to relax, its energy was abated; a listlessness of labor, a desire for tranquility had crept on him, and a willingness to let others act and even think for him."[76]

While Washington felt he could not respond publicly to these attacks, he used the cabinet as a hierarchy of communication and channeled responses through his secretaries and other supporters. He never personally authored replies to newspaper attacks, but he supported efforts by Hamilton and others to defend the administration.[77] He encouraged his subordinates to publish replies to the attacks, he responded to private letters, and he worked to prevent further critiques of the administration. On June 29, 1793, Hamilton published an article under the name "Pacificus" to defend the Neutrality Proclamation. He asserted the president's power in diplomatic matters: "The President is the constitutional Executor of the laws. Our Treaties and the laws of Nations form a part of the law of the land." Hamilton argued that as part of

Washington's constitutional duties, "it was necessary for the President to judge for himself whether there was any thing in our treaties incompatible with an adherence to neutrality." Washington had determined that neutrality was compatible with the Franco-American treaties. Accordingly, it was the president's duty, he argued, to enforce laws and treaties domestically: "As Executor of the laws, to proclaim the neutrality of the Nation, to exhort all persons to observe it, and to warn them of the penalties which would attend its non-observance."[78] While no evidence exists that Washington approved the editorial before publication, Jefferson confided to Madison that the author behind the "Pacificus" letter was "universally known."[79] Given that Hamilton and Washington saw each other almost every day, they likely spoke about Hamilton's writing plans.

Other leading Federalists joined in the fray. Chief Justice John Jay and Senator Rufus King worked to turn public opinion against Genêt and the French cause. During one of the cabinet meetings in July, Hamilton had learned of Genêt's threat to appeal to the American people. He quickly wrote a series of anonymous articles attacking Genêt under the collective title "No Jacobin."[80] The very first line of the series stated: "It is publicly rumoured in this City that the Minister of the French Republic *has threatened to appeal from The President of The United States to the People.*"[81] Early the next month, Jay concluded the Supreme Court's regular session in Philadelphia and left to return to New York. Before departing Philadelphia, Jay likely consulted with Hamilton and learned of Genêt's threats. They were close friends and frequently discussed legal matters and diplomacy. On August 13, Hamilton also passed along this damaging information to King, another Federalist ally. The very next day, Jay and King published Genêt's remarks in a New York newspaper, which was then reprinted widely.[82] Unlike most editorials at the time, they published this article under their own names, lending credence to the report. Their article confirming Genêt's threats was the first publication backed by two well-respected public officials, rather than cloaked in anonymity.

Early Republic political culture included unwritten rules for published materials. There were four categories of documents: newspaper editorials, broadsides, pamphlets, and letters. Newspaper editorials were usually anonymous, intended for a lower-class audience, and carried less weight. Broadsides were short, hastily written, anonymous documents. They were cheap to print, intended to incite emotions in the crowd, and were tacked to a pole, tree, or side of a building. Pamphlets were usually published by wealthier men or those with connections to printers. They were intended for the "first and second" classes, articulated detailed arguments, and the author usually signed his name. Private letters, often intended to be shared among select circles, were the most powerful weapon because the audience assumed the author spoke freely.[83] Readers understood that not all documents were the same—an anonymous newspaper editorial was much less credible and serious than a private letter. When Jay and King published a letter in the newspaper with their names attached, readers grasped the severity of the allegations.

Washington probably approved Jay's and King's article. They were two high-ranking Federalists and federal officials with extensive diplomatic experience and many overlapping ties to the president and the cabinet—they understood the political and diplomatic ramifications of their publication. They likely would not have issued such a public statement without Washington's tacit blessing. Furthermore, Jay "seldom visited [Philadelphia] without a long conference with the President."[84] After conversing with Hamilton, Jay may have visited Washington to get his blessing to publish the article.

The Federalists' collective efforts paid off. Genêt's insolence toward the president outraged the American public. In the late eighteenth century, the American flag had not yet taken on its symbolic importance. Instead, as the most famous American, Washington embodied the nation.[85] An attack on Washington by a foreigner inspired many Americans to rally behind the president and defend neutrality, even if they did not necessarily support the policy itself. Neutrality, and the president's authority over diplomacy, became a matter of national pride.

By the end of 1793, Genêt's behavior and the ongoing violence of the French Revolution vindicated the administration's strict adherence to neutrality. That December, Washington delivered his annual address to Congress in which he included a separate message notifying Congress that he had requested Genêt's recall as French minister and expected France's reply imminently: "From a sense of their friendship towards us, from a conviction that they would not suffer us to remain long exposed to the action of a person who has so little respected our mutual dispositions." Along with his announcement, Washington submitted Genêt's correspondence with Jefferson: "The papers now communicated will more particularly apprize you of these transactions."[86] Genêt's letters convinced many of the most ardent Francophiles that Washington was justified in requesting the removal of the French minister.

In February 1794, Genêt's replacement, Jean Antoine Fauchet, arrived from France. Fauchet brought a warrant for Genêt's arrest and a warning that if he continued his rabble-rousing, his family in France would be held hostage.[87] Aware that banishing Genêt to France would result in his near-certain execution, Washington agreed to allow the disgraced French minister to remain in the United States. King, one of the former French minister's harshest critics, encouraged Washington to grant Genêt asylum. He suggested that because Genêt no longer posed a threat to the nation, he should be treated with compassion and perhaps pity.[88] Washington was not a forgiving man, but he sensed the public's lingering affection for France and the harsh criticism that would await him if he permitted Genêt's execution.

Although the public approved the administration's neutrality policy by the end of the year, the uproar had caused significant damage. Washington was deeply hurt by the criticism of his leadership and sometimes vented his frustration to the cabinet. For example, in August, as the cabinet discussed Genêt's behavior, Washington shared his fears that Genêt would incite violence by encouraging public resistance to the administration. Perhaps goading him a bit, Knox brought up a recent political cartoon that depicted the president's execution by guillotine in the National Gazette. Jefferson noted that Washington lost his temper and railed against the criticism. He vented "on the personal abuse which had been bestowed on him." What he said next revealed the origins of his hurt feelings: Washington "defied any man on earth to produce one single act of his since he had been in the government which was not done on the purest motives."

Washington was notoriously thin-skinned and resented the increase in public criticism. He had accepted the presidency out of a sense of duty, rather than an inherent interest in wielding power. He would have much rather spent his final years at Mount Vernon, and the presidency made him cranky.[89] Keenly aware of what he was sacrificing, Washington felt entitled to a certain amount of gratitude from the public and lost his temper when Freneau, the editor of the National Gazette, did not show the appropriate appreciation. Washington had initially subscribed to the National Gazette but canceled his subscription once the newspaper increased its criticism of the administration. To irritate the president, Freneau continued to send three copies of the daily newspaper to the President's House on Market Street. Washington was unaccustomed to outright impertinence, and it galled him: "The *rascal Freneau* sent [me] three of his papers every day, as if he thought [I] would become the distributor of his papers, [I] could see in this nothing but an impudent design to insult [me]."[90]

Perhaps the shift in public opinion offended Washington the most. When Washington had first taken office, the public had greeted him with overwhelming adoration.[91] Although a small minority criticized his levees and expensive coach and horses, most citizens approved of Washington's early decisions as president. Opposition grew in response to Hamilton's financial measures and the administration's decision to declare neutrality in 1793, which many Republicans viewed as a betrayal of their French allies.[92] In Washington's second term, the rise of partisan strife and a Republican press provided numerous public outlets for this increasingly ferocious criticism. When Bache first published the *General Advertiser and Aurora* in October 1790, Washington was an early subscriber. He loved newspapers and eagerly perused their pages for news and reports on the state of the nation. However, by 1793, Bache had assumed Freneau's mantle. The *Aurora* emerged as the leading Republican newspaper and dominated the anti-Washington press. In 1792, Washington canceled his subscription. Not to be deterred, or perhaps to get under the president's skin, Bache followed Freneau's example and continued to deliver several copies of his newspaper six days a week to the front door of the President's House on the corner of Sixth and Market Streets.[93] Washington could not escape the critiques, despite his best efforts.

Washington believed that as president, he had to hold himself to a higher standard of propriety and discretion. He could not write editorials or share public letters, but he did selectively respond to private letters of criticism. On September 11, 1793, Washington replied to a private letter sent by Edmund Pendleton. Pendleton had shared his concerns about Hamilton and Treasury Department policies. Washington replied with typical non-committal politeness: "With respect to the fiscal conduct of the S—t—y of the Tr—s—y I will say nothing; because an enquiry . . . will be instituted next Session of Congress into some of the Alligations against him. . . . A fair opportunity will then be given to the impartial world to form a just estimate of his Acts, and probably of his motives."[94] He made exceptions to his tight-lipped policy when he received letters from old acquaintances, if they were respectable men of substance and wisdom.

Washington also used his annual addresses to Congress to respond to his critics and to promote the administration's agenda. In his October 1791 address, he could barely contain his glee over the success of the new United States Bank: "The rapid subscriptions to the Bank of the United States . . . is among the striking and pleasing evidences which present themselves, not only of confidence in the government, but of resource in the community."[95] In his address on November 6, 1792, he defended the new fiscal system and its taxes. He stated that the revenue was in a "prosperous state," but lamented the "impediments, which in some places continue to embarrass the collection of duties on spirits distilled within the United States." Washington threatened the offenders with prosecution, for "nothing within constitutional and legal limits . . . shall be wanting to assert and maintain the just authority of the laws."[96]

In 1793, Washington delivered several dispatches to Congress in addition to his annual address. He included all the administration's correspondence with Genêt. He also provided a brief explanation of their tumultuous relationship. He expected this information to counter Republican criticism of the administration for declaring neutrality and refusing aid to France in its war against Britain:

It is with extreme concern I have to inform you that the proceedings of the person [France has] unfortunately appointed
their Minister Plenipy here, have breathed nothing of the
friendly spirit of the Nation which sent him. Their tendency
on the contrary has been to involve us in war abroad, & dis-
cord & anarchy at home. So far as his Acts, or those of his
agents, have threatned our immediate commitment in the
war, or flagrant insult to the authority of the laws, their effect has been counteracted by the ordinary cognisance of the
laws, and by an exertion of the powers confided to me.[97]

Congress largely met his expectations. They approved his decision to
request the recall of Genêt and supported his efforts to establish American neutrality.

Washington's pride was not the only casualty of the Neutrality Crisis.
On December 31, 1793, Jefferson retired as secretary of state. He could
stomach the conflict with Hamilton no longer; furthermore, he increasingly felt himself at odds with the administration's position and
wanted to be freed from his responsibilities as secretary of state, which
required him to defend (at least publicly) and execute the president's
policies. Jefferson's retirement marked the first major departure from
Washington's administration, and firmly drew the lines between the
two nascent political parties and their international loyalties. It also
began an exodus of cabinet retirements over the next year.

After Jefferson's retirement, Washington adopted a new policy for
his cabinet appointments in light of rising political conflict. Starting in
1794, Washington required demonstrated loyalty to the administration
as a precondition for nomination to his cabinet. In October 1795, he

discussed possible candidates for open positions with Hamilton and approved of those individuals who had "been a steady friend to the general government since it has been in operation."[98] He refused to have his cabinet torn apart again by political divisions during his final years in office.

As we have seen, the cabinet supervised several key developments during the Neutrality Crisis that solidified executive power and confirmed the president's prerogative over foreign affairs. Washington's Neutrality Proclamation claimed for the president the authority to shape domestic policy relating to treaties. The rules of neutrality crafted by the cabinet affirmed the president's right to enforce administrative policy. Washington's call for Genêt's removal demonstrated the president's power to request a recall and the government's right to have its policies respected by foreign nations. When Congress and the public supported the Washington administration's handling of the Neutrality Crisis, Congress ceded these powers to Washington and the president. Furthermore, when France recalled Genêt, it tacitly accepted the United States' authority to establish its own foreign policy as an independent nation. Washington relied on the cabinet when determining every one of these administrative decisions and policies, and the secretaries willingly participated in this process. The resolution of the Neutrality Crisis was a product of the cabinet's participation—the secretaries brought their previous frustrations with the Confederation Congress, weak governors, and state legislatures to the cabinet. They worked to sideline Congress and promoted the president's power over the diplomatic process.

The unique composition of the cabinet, with both French and British interests represented by the Republicans and the Federalists, respectively, produced a neutrality that preserved trade relationships with Britain and avoided an outright break with France. The absence of

Hamilton or Jefferson from the cabinet likely would have produced a significantly different outcome. Jefferson may have disagreed with Washington's decisions, but he routinely defended Washington and the presidency against Genêt's attacks. The secretaries' participation ensured that the cabinet, as an institution, facilitated and supported a strong presidency in diplomatic affairs. After Jefferson's departure, the administration faced another significant challenge to its authority. This time, the threat came not from a mighty European power across the Atlantic but from a band of rebels in western Pennsylvania.

7

A Domestic Threat

On July 15, 1794, a group of about thirty militiamen surrounded Bower Hill, the home of General John Neville. Bower Hill, the largest and most ornate mansion in western Pennsylvania, sat atop a hill overlooking the Pittsburgh region. Neville served as the federal tax inspector for western Pennsylvania and was charged with inspecting local whiskey stills and collecting an excise tax. When he refused to surrender to the militia on July 15, the rebels returned the next day with more than 500 additional reinforcements, forcing Neville to flee to a local ravine, while a small handful of US Army soldiers tried to defend the home. In the fighting, Major James McFarlane, a Revolutionary War veteran and leader of the rebel force, was killed. Outraged, the rebels burned Bower Hill to the ground.

While the Washington administration had faced resistance to its tax measures before and had grappled with diplomatic challenges the previous year during the Neutrality Crisis, this rebellion posed the first major domestic threat to the presidency, the Constitution, and the rule of law. The rebellion was a moment of reckoning that raised significant questions for the new government. Did the Constitution grant the federal government power to levy an excise tax? If so, could the federal government enforce the law, or would the states lead the enforcement effort? If the federal government took responsibility, would the president craft a federal response or would Congress? Finally, how would the public respond to these enforcement measures?

If the government failed to repress the rebellion, the consequences would have been unthinkable. The federal government would have set a precedent that citizens could evade taxes, while forfeiting its ability to raise money and its credibility on the foreign stage. The location of the insurrection further compounded the pressure of the situation. Western Pennsylvania offered a direct connection to the Great Lakes and Canada. Since the Revolutionary War had ended in 1783, the United States and Britain had squabbled over borders and the possession of western forts. Washington and the secretaries suspected that Britain or other European empires might exploit any sign of weakness and encourage western communities to break off from the United States and join a foreign empire. The cabinet concluded that the survival of the federal government, the future of its fiscal system, and the nation's capacity to internationally project its military strength depended on the administration's ability to collect taxes and enforce compliance with federal laws.[1]

Over the next several months, Washington and the secretaries crafted a response to the insurrection that defended federal power to levy taxes, asserted the president's right to establish domestic policy, sidelined Congress, and forced the state governments to comply with the president's orders—much as they had done during the Neutrality Crisis, but this time the cabinet focused on asserting executive authority over domestic issues. When creating policy, they drew on their previous governing and leadership experiences. Washington followed his council-of-war practices by convening cabinet meetings to build consensus among his advisors and requesting written opinions to provide political cover before making a controversial decision. In cabinet deliberations, the secretaries drew on their own frustrating experiences with the Confederation Congress and state governments. They encouraged Washington to oversee a federal response to the rebellion, rather than relying on Congress or state authorities. When the secretaries advocated decisive action, their advice encouraged Washington's predilection to adopt forceful measures.

Public opinion also played a crucial role in shaping cabinet deliberations in 1794. At each stage of the decision-making process, Washington and the secretaries considered popular responses to their actions. Rather than immediately resorting to force, they elected to send a peace delegation to negotiate with the rebels. In late August, reports trickled back to Philadelphia that the peace commission would fail. Despite their dwindling hopes, Washington and the secretaries waited to call up the militia until they received official notice that the rebels had rejected peace. They adopted this cautious approach to shore up public support for the administration's eventual military action. On September 9, 1794, Washington finally issued orders for the Virginia, Maryland, New Jersey, and Pennsylvania militias to meet in Carlisle, Pennsylvania.[2] Yet Washington did not leave Philadelphia until September 30. He lingered for three weeks to make sure public opinion supported this step. Once the prominent Republican newspapers endorsed the administration's policy, Washington confidently rode out to meet the militia in Carlisle.[3]

In January 1791, Congress had passed an excise tax on domestic liquors to help pay off the national debt. An excise tax made good political sense. The government desperately needed funds to pay its debts and to pay for government services, including employee salaries and basic defense measures. An excise tax would not offend foreign trade part-ners because it did not apply to exports or imports. It avoided the poten-tial backlash sparked by direct taxes, which applied to all citizens in the nation. Direct taxes also weighed more heavily on the poor because they were applied based on the number of individuals per household, rather than scaled based on income. Additionally, direct taxes required government officials to go door-to-door collecting taxes from families. The administration also favored excise taxes to avoid the pitfalls of land taxes, which infuriated the landowning elite, and property taxes, which outraged the slave-owning elite who would have paid taxes based on the number of enslaved persons they owned. The administration depended on the support of these interest groups and so it avoided taxation mea-sures that would alienate these constituencies. Finally, the excise tax would be paid by whiskey distillers. Distillers would pass the costs on to consumers, but the consumers would not interact directly with tax officials, which would preserve the popularity of the administration.[4]

Almost immediately, however, the tax faced backlash and exacer-bated existing regional tensions. Farmers in western regions of Virginia, Kentucky, North Carolina, and Pennsylvania cultivated fertile lands and produced sizable harvests to sell on the market. But wheat and corn are heavy and were expensive to transport on wagons over long dis-tances to distant port cities. Furthermore, roads in North Carolina and Kentucky were nearly impassable several months of the year. Nor was river transport an option, as Spain barred Americans from accessing the Mississippi River and the port of New Orleans. Whiskey was the one commodity that brought farmers enough profit to cover the exor-bitant shipping costs. Furthermore, cash-poor farmers often distilled whiskey from their leftover corn to use as a trading commodity in lieu of currency. These farmers protested the excise tax as unfairly burden-some on the poor communities in western counties of the states.

In North Carolina, farmers evaded and violently resisted the tax. In June 1792, Daniel Huger, a Federalist from South Carolina, reported to Hamilton that many North Carolinian farmers found ingenious methods to avoid the tax. They shipped their whiskey to Virginia, where they sold their spirits for lower prices, thus undercutting Virginian competitors and avoiding the excise tax. Distillers also threatened violence to avoid taxation. When Joseph McDowell Jr. tried to inspect a still in North Carolina's Fifth District, he discovered how creative distillers could be with their threats. Inspired by the materials at hand, the owner of one distillery threatened to grind off McDowell's nose on the mill's grindstone. In August 1792, McDowell reported this treatment to Hamilton and Washington.[5]

The administration found even less success enforcing the excise tax in Kentucky. Kentuckians resented the federal government for failing to force Spain to grant access to the Mississippi River. They also felt abandoned by the federal government when the administration did not provide a more robust defense against Native American attacks on their farms. As a result, Kentuckians were not especially eager to support an administration that appeared to have ignored their interests. When the tax went into effect on July 1, 1791, Kentucky simply disregarded it.[6] Kentucky chief revenue officer Colonel Thomas Marshall could not find candidates willing to serve as tax collectors, even with the promise of extra financial incentives. Distillers in compliance with the tax refused to report their neighbors who rejected the excise, even for financial rewards. Most distillers would not even fill out the paperwork necessary for collectors to inspect stills.

The state legal system also refused to cooperate. Kentucky grand juries refused to charge individuals with crimes, and the first federal attorney declined to bring a single case before the courts. When the federal attorney retired, Washington offered the position to several prominent lawyers, but all turned him down. Desperate to bring the state into compliance, Hamilton offered to forgive the first year of taxes if Kentucky's distillers promised to pay after 1793. The distillers ignored this offer. By 1795, Hamilton offered three years of tax forgiveness. They also ignored this offer.[7]

For the time being, the administration was willing to overlook Kentucky's insubordination. The secretaries feared that too harsh a response would push western communities into the arms of the Spanish, British, or French. Kentucky did not become a state until June 1792, and even then, the state's bonds to the new nation were tenuous. In May 1794, hundreds of people gathered in Lexington, Kentucky, to pass a series of resolutions condemning the government for abandoning them to Indian attacks and forsaking their economic needs by not prioritizing Americans' access to the Mississippi River. Attorney General William Bradford encouraged Washington to ignore the resistance efforts in Kentucky for the moment. He suggested that the administration give them "no formal notice . . . at present, unless for the purpose of directing a prosecution. They are clearly libellous in some parts of them, tending to excite sedition & disaffection to the Government; and therefore are indictable. But, generally speaking, publications of this nature are best counteracted by silence and contempt."[8]

In August 1792, discontent in Pennsylvania also bubbled to the surface. Local leaders passed resolutions that called for "legal action to obstruct the operation of the Law," as well as the formation of committees of correspondence and intimidation of collectors and any distillers who were in compliance with the law.[9] Although Hamilton immediately advocated a military response, Washington and Randolph recognized that military suppression would be wildly unpopular at that moment. Instead, the administration offered leniency. At Washington's request, Hamilton drafted a proclamation, but Randolph edited out some of the most inflammatory language. Randolph insisted that Hamilton remove the phrase "criminality" and any reference to the military. He recognized that "the charge to the military would inflame the Country."[10] The final proclamation denounced the protests and urged citizens to abide by the law, but it did not threaten military action.

In July 1794, the rebellion accelerated when the armed rebels attacked Neville's home.[11] Washington's hands may have been tied with North Carolina and Kentucky—North Carolina was far from the seat of government, and Kentucky appeared to be on the brink of secession, so one wrong move might send it into the arms of the Spanish or British—but western Pennsylvania was a different story. The protests were at the administration's back door, and Washington was disinclined to extend mercy more than once.

In late July, Washington learned of the rebels' attack on Bower Hill. He called an emergency cabinet meeting to discuss the crisis.[12] Each secretary brought with him years of experience with state governments; this familiarity colored their advice to Washington and their participation in the cabinet over the following two months. The crisis forced Washington to decide if his administration would spearhead a military response, allow Congress to take the lead, or leave containment to Pennsylvania.

On July 25, 1794, the secretaries piled into Washington's study and gathered around the small table set up for the meeting. The cabinet expressed a unanimous "indignation . . . at the outrages committed" by the rebels.[13] Hamilton and Knox advocated immediate military action against the rebels in western Pennsylvania. Some contemporaries, including Jefferson, and many historians have accused Knox of blindly following Hamilton's lead. Yet his prior experience in the Revolutionary

War and during the Confederation period instilled in him a firm commitment to a powerful, active executive—independent of Hamilton's agenda. Knox distrusted Congress as well as the states' ability to pull together a coordinated approach to the insurrection. He believed the president was the natural person to craft and enforce a federal response to the rebellion.

As the new secretary of state, Randolph brought with him the same analytical, methodical approach that he had utilized as governor of Virginia. He appreciated that the time for leniency had passed, but he was mindful of clashing opinions on the tax and sympathy for the farmers.[14] He suggested that Washington negotiate with the alleged rebels before turning to a military response. The new attorney general, William Bradford, also counseled Washington to engage the rebels in negotiations—but only as political cover while the president readied troops for action.[15] The cabinet also agreed that the president should not request congressional approval to direct the federal army under the command of General Anthony Wayne to crush the rebellion. A multi-state militia force would be much more palatable to the American public, which already nursed a distrust of a standing army. The army was busy in the Ohio Territory, anyway; it was marching west to the Ohio River Valley, and later that summer it would win a decisive victory against a confederation of the Shawnee, Miami, and Delaware Indians at the Battle of Fallen Timbers.[16]

The secretaries also dismissed congressional action. After receiving the news of the continuing violence in western Pennsylvania, Washington and the cabinet could have waited for Congress to reassemble in the fall. But the stakes of the rebellion were too high, and they could not risk the possibility that the rebellion would escalate. They all remembered how Shays' Rebellion had spread across western Massachusetts in 1786, shut down the court system, and prevented tax collection while Congress struggled to raise money and troops. Alternatively, Washington could have cited the pressing circumstances and convened an emergency session of Congress. Because of the secretaries' previous experiences with Congress, these options were never seriously considered. The tax had never enjoyed bipartisan support, and the secretaries knew that the Republicans in Congress would stall a military response. Instead, the secretaries made the unanimous decision to seek authorization for the president to call up the militia. It was an extraordinary moment—almost right away the secretaries elected to immediately sideline Congress in the nation's first major domestic crisis.

The cabinet agreed that the president should spearhead the federal response to the rebellion, but Washington needed legal authority to call up state troops. On May 2, 1792, Congress had passed a new law that provided for "calling forth the Militia to execute the laws of the Union, suppress insurrections and repel invasions." The law recognized that a foreign country might invade the nation, or a domestic rebellion might crop up during congressional recess. In the case of a domestic crisis, the president could present the facts to an associate justice of the Supreme Court or a district judge. If the justice or judge approved military action, the president could then call forth the militia in the necessary states.[17]

The secretaries mapped out their strategy during the July 25 cabinet meeting. Eager to secure approval and move forward with military preparations, Washington and the cabinet took no chances. They decided to share their materials with Supreme Court Justice James Wilson. Wilson was a safe choice. He was a longtime Federalist, a Washington supporter, and an advocate of executive authority.[18] The secretaries also advised Bradford on how to make his approach to Wilson. Bradford should avoid revealing the president's wish "that the certificate should be granted." If events forced Washington to order military action, the cabinet wanted undisputed legal authorization.[19] There could be no hint that he had coerced or influenced Wilson's decision. After the cabinet meeting ended, Randolph gathered the appropriate materials and Bradford submitted them to Justice Wilson.

The following week, Washington convened a cabinet meeting, which several Pennsylvania officials joined, including Governor Thomas Mifflin, Secretary of the Commonwealth Alexander James Dallas, Chief Justice Thomas McKean, and Attorney General Jared Ingersoll.[20] According to Hamilton's records of the meeting, Washington opened by declaring that

> the circumstances which accompanied it were such as to strike at the root of all law & order; That he was clearly of opinion that the most spirited & firm measures were necessary to rescue the State as well as the General Government from the impending danger; for if such proceedings were tolerated there was an end to our Constitutions & laws.

Washington explained that he hoped a peaceful outcome would be possible. If not, the administration would move forward with a military response. Anticipating that he would soon receive the necessary approval from Justice Wilson to convene and deploy federal forces, Washington asked Governor Mifflin to call out the Pennsylvania militia.

The Pennsylvania officers in attendance were shocked. They completely disagreed with Washington's assertion of federal control. From their perspective, the insurrection was a Pennsylvania problem. The rebels were Pennsylvanians, the victims were Pennsylvanians, and the alleged crimes had taken place in Pennsylvania. Any federal government action would be massive overreach. They insisted the state judiciary alone could punish the rioters.[21]

The Whiskey Rebellion raised several questions about whether the rebels committed crimes under state or federal jurisdiction, and thus whether the state or federal government should drive the response. The rebels' defiance of the excise law was a federal crime. The rebels' attack on the Bower Hill home of General Neville appeared to be the only state crime. Governor Mifflin suggested that while federal enforcement had failed, the state had not explored its enforcement options. Mifflin argued that "the employment of a military force, at this period, would be as bad as anything that the Rioters had done—equally unconstitutional and illegal." Others warned that the use of force might provoke further resistance.[22] The Pennsylvania delegation urged Washington to allow the state judiciary time to prosecute the insurgents.

Mifflin's suggestion that they ignore the rioters' federal crimes appalled Washington and his secretaries. Outraged, Hamilton suggested that perhaps Pennsylvania officials didn't want to enforce the laws because they supported the rebels. Additionally, he argued that if the use of federal force would increase local resistance, then state justice had already failed in the western counties and federal forces needed to take over.[23]

After the meeting, Washington asked each cabinet member—Randolph, Hamilton, Knox, and Bradford—to draft a written opinion recommending a course of action. While he genuinely desired their opinions, he also followed his previous military experience and ensured that he had written proof for the secretaries' agreement on controversial action. Washington never published their correspondence, but he had it if he needed it. In their written opinions, the secretaries unanimously rejected the argument that Pennsylvania could quell the insurrection and instead advocated a federal response. The secretaries, however, split over how to shape the administration's strategy and submitted opinions consistent with the positions they had articulated during the July 25 cabinet meeting. Hamilton and Knox again advocated immediate military action. Randolph recognized that military action might be necessary but preferred to pursue diplomacy first. Bradford again recommended that Washington send a peace commission for political cover even as he prepared a military strategy. Washington selected this last approach—it appealed to his desire to demonstrate strength while also cultivating public opinion in his favor.[24]

On August 4, 1794, Justice Wilson granted Washington the necessary authority to call out the militia and initiate a three-phase plan.[25] First, on August 7, 1794, the administration issued a proclamation denouncing the rebellion, outlining the legal violations, instructing the rebels to disperse, and warning that military action would follow if peaceful negotiation failed.[26] Hamilton and Knox drafted the proclamation and Randolph and Washington approved the text. This proclamation, unlike the 1792 version, pulled no punches, accusing "persons in the said western parts of Pennsylvania" of "perpetrat[ing] acts which . . . amount to treason." The proclamation directed all insurgents to "disperse and retire peaceably to their respective abodes." Should the resistance continue, Washington announced his intention to call up the militia to protect "the very existence of Government and the fundamental principles of social order."[27]

The strong language reflected the ongoing resistance to the excise tax, but also the cabinet's prior experience with rebellions. Knox never forgot the chaos of Shays' Rebellion in Massachusetts, nor did he overlook Congress's inability to organize the militia or raise money to curb the insurrection. Furthermore, Knox had his own personal history with Mifflin, including the contentious debates between the cabinet and Mifflin over Genêt and the Neutrality Crisis. Hamilton shared Knox's enthusiasm. He had urged military action in 1792 and was convinced that if a proclamation had failed to stymie resistance to the excise tax two years earlier, it would fail again. The cabinet was determined to respond more forcefully this time.

As the second step, Washington sent commissioners to negotiate a peaceful settlement to the conflict. Washington carefully selected all three commissioners: Bradford, the attorney general; Pennsylvania Supreme Court Judge Jasper Yeates; and Senator James Ross. All three were native Pennsylvanians, government officials, and loyal Federalists.[28] Ross also resided in one of the most rebellious counties, but as one of Washington's closest friends, he could be trusted to enforce the federal government's power. Randolph drafted instructions and sent them to the peace commissioners with Washington's approval. The instructions urged the commissioners to stress how painful it would be for the president to use military force against American citizens and his "earnest wish" for "peace and tranquility" to prevail. The commissioners were to state explicitly that only Congress could repeal the excise legislation, and so the Pennsylvanians needed to address their concerns to their elected officials. They should also share that the president was prepared to "grant an amnesty and perpetual oblivion for every thing which has past" if the insurgents agreed to certain unequivocal conditions: the insurgents must not obstruct the enforcement of the laws and distilleries must pay the duties moving forward.[29]

As the final step, Washington would summon the militia. On August 7, he announced his *intention* to call up the militia, to gauge the reaction and to prepare the public for future military engagement. Critically, Washington did not actually summon troops in early August. Instead, he allowed the public several weeks to get comfortable with the idea and slowly built support for military action *only* if negotiations failed. In the meantime, Washington planned to secretly gather the militia in Pennsylvania and nearby states if the commissioners failed to reach an agreement with the rebels. If necessary, the militia would march west.[30]

The next night, Knox left Philadelphia to sort out the finances for his farm in Maine. His estate was on the brink of bankruptcy and he could put off his visit no longer. He wrote to Washington pleading for a temporary release of duties. He could barely contain his anxiety and fear for his family's future: "Accustomed to consider even your desires, much less your orders, as paramount to every other consideration, I shall certainly defer my journey, or even renounce it altogether, if your view of the subject should render my continuance here of public importance although permanent pecuniary ruin or something very like it attends either one or the other."[31] Significantly, Knox was willing to risk his reputation, his fortune, and his family to stay by the president's side. Washington hated to see his secretary of war leave in the middle of the crisis and generally disapproved of "the absence of the Officers of the government . . . Under these circumstances." He reluctantly approved Knox's departure, however, while encouraging "a safe & speedy return."[32] Knox traveled first to Boston and then to Maine to visit his new home in Thomaston. He dispatched with his estate business in a few weeks, but then inexplicably lingered, enjoying the site of his future estate rather than returning to Philadelphia.[33]

In Knox's absence, Hamilton gleefully took over the administration of the Department of War. Because he had been pushing for military action for years to protect and expand his fiscal system, he eagerly oversaw the organization of the state militias and the supplies needed to support the troops. Hamilton's role in the administration's response in the fall of 1794 and his subsequent command of the state militias have caused history to remember his role in the Whiskey Rebellion as larger than it was in reality. He certainly served as an essential figure, but

Knox's role cannot be discredited. Knox participated in the formation of the administration's strategy and encouraged Washington to lead a federal response to the rebellion. Of all the secretaries, Knox had the most experience with Congress and the challenges of organizing state militias. The president trusted his advice. Furthermore, prior to his departure, Knox issued the initial orders to militias in New Jersey, Pennsylvania, Maryland, Virginia, and New York to prepare them for future advances.[34] He was not just Hamilton's lackey, and Washington sorely missed his presence after August 8.

Knox's absence was especially notable as the cabinet grappled with the state militias. The cooperation of the states' governors would be needed to call up the militia in each state. After the August 2 meeting, it appeared that cooperation would not be widely forthcoming. After their meeting, Governor Mifflin sent his own written opinion to Washington. He argued that the Pennsylvania judiciary should have the opportunity to prove whether it could adequately handle the insurrection. Washington assigned Randolph—with Hamilton's assistance—to correspond with Mifflin. In his capacity as acting secretary of war, Hamilton drew up the first draft of the administration's response each time Mifflin objected to federal policy. At Washington's instruction, however, Randolph reviewed these letters and sent the responses under his name and from the office of the secretary of state. Prior to this moment, Washington never assigned one secretary to deal with the states' governors. Instead, he usually directed a secretary to correspond with the governors when the issue fell under his department's jurisdiction.[35] Hamilton certainly could have sent the responses in his capacity as acting secretary of war, or Bradford could have replied to the numerous legal questions in Mifflin's letter.

Washington intentionally arranged for Hamilton and Randolph to work together on this task. He understood Hamilton's personality and his tendency to antagonize opponents. By filtering Hamilton through Randolph, he created an important institutional check. He would use Randolph's moderation to limit Hamilton's aggressive nature. Washington also had political motivates for ordering Randolph to send the letters. Recognizing the political tensions in the August 2 meeting, he selected Randolph as the most palatable option: Mifflin ardently supported Jefferson and the emerging Republican Party, and Randolph remained the most Republican-leaning of Washington's department secretaries. Additionally, Randolph favored pursuing peaceful options before involving troops. The administration's response to Mifflin would appear more conciliatory if it came from him.[36] Finally, although Randolph personally disagreed with a military response in the beginning, Washington trusted his legal expertise to defend the administration's position.

As we have seen, Mifflin and Washington had long detested each other. Their animosity dated back to the Revolutionary War, when Mifflin criticized Washington's command and tried to have him replaced with General Horatio Gates. Mifflin and Washington had clashed over enforcement of the administration's neutrality policy in the summer of 1793. Mifflin and Washington had also battled over state and federal power just a few months before the outbreak of the Whiskey Rebellion. In April 1793, the Pennsylvania legislature empowered Mifflin to survey the Presque Isle area, near Erie, Pennsylvania, and lay out a town for settlement. Mifflin's first attempt to send surveyors failed due to threats of Native American violence. On March 1, 1794, Mifflin issued orders to raise a militia company to accompany surveyors to the Presque Isle region. Further reports of Native American unrest reached Knox as the militia prepared to march west. Given the threat of hostilities, Knox advised Mifflin to postpone the venture. At the end of May, Mifflin wrote to Washington declaring his intentions to proceed with the survey. Washington, in no uncertain terms, instructed him to "suspend for the present the establishment at Presque-isle."[37] As he had done so many times during the Revolutionary War, Washington obtained the unanimous support of his cabinet before taking the bold step of asserting his federal authority over state officials.[38] Mifflin reluctantly agreed to postpone the mission. But by mid-June, he felt he had waited long enough, and he impatiently wrote to Washington about the delay. When Washington against instructed him to postpone the surveys, Mifflin denounced Washington's actions as unconstitutional:

> Can the requisition or advice of the Executive Authority of the United States justify the Act which suspends the operation of a positive law of Pennsylvania? The Constitutional supremacy of the Laws of the Union will not be disputed: but may it not be Asked, what law of the Union . . . furnish[es] an Executive Magistrate with an authority to Substitute his opinions for Legislative institutions.[39]

Finally, on July 21, after several heated letters had been exchanged, Washington assured Mifflin that he had never intended to infringe on the governor's constitutional duties. He also acknowledged that he would accept full responsibility for the consequences of the delay in the surveying mission.[40]

Given their complicated history, Washington perceived Governor Mifflin's behavior in August 1794 as a further challenge to the president's authority. After the outbreak of the insurrection in western Pennsylvania, Washington and the secretaries believed Mifflin sought to thwart Randolph's efforts to coordinate the federal response to reserve power for the states; perhaps he even harbored secret sympathies for the rebels.[41] Unstintingly loyal to Washington, Knox had resented

Mifflin's criticism of his commander in chief during the war. As secretary of war, he had overseen the correspondence between Washington and Mifflin over the Presque Isle squabble. He doubted Mifflin would willingly fulfill his national obligations and call up the state militia to crush the rebellion.[42] The cabinet's response to Mifflin reflected its determination to carve out space for the president to determine domestic policy, free from limitations placed by state governors. The cabinet ensured that the state governments would answer to the federal government—led by the president.

In his August 5 written opinion, Mifflin reiterated that Washington had not provided the Pennsylvania judicial system the time and opportunity to bring the rebels to justice. He argued that "the Military power of the Government ought not be employed until its Judiciary authority, after a fair experiment, has proved incompetent to enforce obedience.[43] Washington and the secretaries were incredulous; resistance had erupted two years earlier, and since then Pennsylvania officials had made little effort to enforce the law. Hamilton drafted a reply to Mifflin's letter and forwarded it to Randolph for review. Randolph made a few small adjustments and sent the letter to Mifflin. The Hamilton-Randolph letter trumpeted the administration's goal to assert the power of the federal government and an independent executive. They acknowledged that Mifflin's suggestion to rely on state enforcement would be a good one—"if there were no Fœderal Government, Fœderal laws, Fœderal Judiciary, or Fœderal Officers." Furthermore, the administration might be willing to trust Mifflin to enforce the laws if they, "by a series of violent, as well as of artful expedients, had not been frustrated in their execution for more than three years."[44]

When editing and approving Hamilton's drafts, Randolph probably recalled his frustrated attempts as Virginia governor to control the militia. As governor of Virginia from 1787 to 1788, Randolph had been able to do little other than urge county militia officers to act when Indian attacks threatened the safety of the western counties. In 1794, the Constitution granted the president the authority to call up, deploy, and lead the militia, and Randolph encouraged and helped Washington to utilize this power. Additionally, the inability or unwillingness of Pennsylvania officials to subdue the insurrection echoed the incompetency of Virginia county officials during the 1780s. Randolph spoke from personal experience when he asserted that the excise laws could not be effectively enforced in the western Pennsylvanian counties without federal assistance.[45]

Although Mifflin grudgingly agreed to follow Washington's command and prepare the Pennsylvania militia, he wrote additional letters challenging the administration. One week later, he assured Washington that he would comply with the administration's orders and tried to assure the president of his personal fidelity. He argued, however, that the law required him to pursue a judicial resolution to the rebellion before turning to the militia. Additionally, he insinuated that Washington entered their August 2 conference determined to use force against the insurgents.[46]

Meanwhile, the cabinet received an update on the state of the rebellion. On August 15, Hamilton forwarded Washington a letter from Hugh H. Brackenridge, a prominent figure in western Pennsylvania politics. Brackenridge warned that the insurgents were gaining strength and would march on Philadelphia to demand a repeal of the whiskey excise laws.[47] Bradford also sent Washington a letter a few days later. While Bradford supplied Randolph with official reports in his capacity as commissioner, he also gave his private opinion that "the people cannot be induced by conciliatory offers to relinquish their opposition to the excise laws." Based on conversations and rumors, Bradford had come to this conclusion before his official meeting with the rebel leaders. He shared this opinion to encourage Washington to move forward with "those preparatory measures which are not inconsistent with the mission." He also reminded Washington of the value of time: "The more artful men among the insurgents will endeavor to gain time to prepare themselves—& the moderate party will join them in hopes of putting off the evil day."[48] Washington understood Bradford's message—the administration should not delay military preparations and risk the rebels gaining strength.

On August 24, Washington met with Hamilton and Randolph as the commissioners, led by Bradford, demanded unconditional surrender from the rebels. Fearing the peace commissioners would have little success, Washington, Hamilton, and Randolph readied the militia in nearby states, but they conducted these preparations under the strictest secrecy. They determined that to maintain full public support, the administration could deploy the militia only *after* the peace commission had failed.[49] They did not expect news of the commissioners' meeting with the rebels to reach Philadelphia until September. The next day, Hamilton wrote two letters to Virginia governor Henry Lee. The first letter issued the president's official instructions to gather the militia. The second letter contained private instructions to summon the militia after September 1: "Your orders for assembling the Militia cannot well issue before the first of September. For particular reasons, it is wished they may be dated on that day."[50]

By August 22, 1794, it had become clear that the peace negotiations had failed and that Washington would send out the militia. That day Mifflin sent a letter taking issue with a particular phrase in Washington's August 7 proclamation against the insurrection. Washington had asserted that local officers of Pennsylvania failed to enforce the laws of the Union and that the officers expressed friendly sentiments toward the rebels.[51] Mifflin replied that he hoped to "manifest in every way a zealous co-operation in the views of the General Government." To comply with Washington's requests, he needed to see "the evidence, on which the above charge is founded," so that he "may take the proper steps to vindicate the honor of the State Government, and to remove the delinquent officers." The request was heavily laden with sarcasm. At the end of the letter Mifflin challenged Washington and his administration to support these charges: "In its present form, however, the charge is so indiscriminate, that those Citizens who may be involved in its obloquy do not enjoy a fair opportunity for defence, nor does the Government possess the means to discover the proper objects for its indignation and censure."[52]

Washington asked Hamilton to prepare a report of the alleged violations. In his capacity as secretary of the treasury, Hamilton had long seethed over the western counties' resistance to the whiskey excise tax and kept extensive records of potential crimes. He drew up an eight-page letter, naming thirty-three officials and military leaders who unequivocally "opposed" and "discounted" the whiskey excise laws or sympathized with the rebels. He also offered a detailed report of their alleged crimes and the evidence offered against them.[53] Washington then forwarded the report to Randolph. Although Randolph usually edited Hamilton's drafts, in this instance he forwarded Hamilton's report directly to Mifflin without making any alterations. Randolph had abandoned hope that a peaceful solution would end the rebellion, and he expressed his full support for a federal military response. More important, he fought back against Mifflin's attacks on presidential power, regardless of his own opinions on the administration's policy.

In the meantime, the cabinet worked to ensure that public opinion backed military action. Although Hamilton authored most of the materials, Washington approved the publications as part of a broader strategy to build public consensus.[54] On August 21, Hamilton submitted a detailed report of the rebels' actions in *Dunlap and Claypoole's American Daily Advertiser.*[55] Shortly thereafter, Hamilton published a series of letters under the name "Tully." The series of essays warned readers to ignore the emotional pleas employed by the rebels in western Pennsylvania: "Shun the artful snare which may be laid to entangle your feelings and your judgment." Hamilton positioned the crisis as one between a duly elected government and insurgents committed to turning the populace against the people's representatives. The second essay outlined how the excise bill had been passed and emphasized the constitutional process followed by all branches of government. The third essay worked to undermine support for the rebels by emphasizing "a sacred respect for the constitutional law is the vital principle, the sustaining energy of a free government." Without respect for the Constitution and "authority of the laws," society would devolve from freedom to slavery. Hamilton concluded by sharing his confidence that the public "will not fail to do what your rights, your best interests, your character as a people, your security as members of society conspire to demand of you."[56]

These propaganda efforts had the intended effect. On September 10, the Philadelphia militia turned out in full force. The next day, the *General Adviser,* the Republican-backed newspaper in Philadelphia, lauded the federal government's military response to the crisis.[57] Later that month, Randolph wrote to the peace commissioners and thanked them for trying to secure a peaceful resolution. He passed along the cabinet's belief that their efforts helped secure a positive public response to military action:

> Altho' the insurrection was not absolutely extinguished, [the president] is persuaded, that everything which could have

been done under the existing circumstances has been accomplished by your labours. Indeed he ascribes to your conduct the prospect of finding but a feeble opposition. . . . [Y]ou have . . . amply prepared the public mind for the support of any measures, which may be necessary.[58]

The public response also helped bring Mifflin in line with the administration's position. In early September, the administration had received the peace commissioners' reports from their negotiations with the rebels. The report confirmed the cabinet's suspicions that diplomacy would fail. The leaders of the rebellion had voted 34 to 23 in favor of accepting the government's terms for peace, but Bradford, Yeates, and Ross knew that enforcing the law in western Pennsylvania would be impossible if twenty-three leaders failed to cooperate.[59] Washington and the cabinet came to the same conclusion and passed on the news to Mifflin. After the militia enthusiastically responded to the call for service and the Republican press sided with the administration, Mifflin followed the tide of public opinion. He could not risk charges of disloyalty while the rest of his party supported the president. On September 12, 1794, he wrote again and assured Washington that he would comply with the president's orders with "the utmost dispatch and alacrity."[60]

As Randolph grappled with these interpersonal and constitutional complications, he consistently asserted the power of the presidency. When replying to Mifflin's letters from August 5, August 12, and August 22, Randolph adopted most of Hamilton's drafts. Each letter dismantled or refuted Mifflin's claims, including his proposal that the administration leave enforcement to the judiciary. All three letters also asserted the power and independence of the president. Randolph responded that if Washington adopted the plan Mifflin recommended, it would require a complete "abdication of the undoubted rights and authorities of the United States and of his Duty," and would force the president to "postpone the measures for which the laws of the United States provide."[61] Essentially, Randolph asserted that the Constitution required the president to lead a firm federal response to the rebellion.

These letters reveal an important dynamic within the cabinet, especially after Jefferson's retirement at the end of 1793. When he was in the cabinet, Jefferson thought little of Randolph's contributions. He frequently lamented to his close confidants that the cabinet often split 2½ votes to 1½ because of Randolph's indecisiveness.[62] In fact, Jefferson complained to Madison that Randolph was "the most indecisive one I ever had to do business with."[63] Jefferson's frustrations grew out of his expectations that he would always have Randolph's support for his positions. When Randolph articulated a middle ground between the two sides, Jefferson attributed the disagreement to splitting hairs, but he begrudgingly admitted that Washington frequently adopted Randolph's middle-ground policies.[64] Despite Jefferson's venting, Randolph was the most accomplished legal mind in the cabinet, and Washington and the other secretaries depended on his expertise. Hamilton, himself a lawyer, frequently requested Randolph's legal assessment before advocating new policies.[65] Hamilton was unquestionably the loudest, most forceful personality in cabinet meetings, but as the new secretary of state, Randolph frequently challenged Hamilton's interpretations. Randolph's review of Hamilton's letters meant far more than a simple rubber stamp of approval.

On September 9, Washington ordered all militia units to meet in Carlisle, Pennsylvania.[66] Then he waited a few weeks longer to ensure that public opinion would back the administration's military response.[67] He had also secured unanimous cabinet support for military action. The Constitution did not require him to secure the approval of the secretary of state in order to undertake this military expedition against the rebels. But Washington wanted Randolph's endorsement anyway. He recognized that crushing a domestic insurrection established a significant executive precedent, and he worked within the cabinet to build consensus before taking this important step, just as he had often built consensus within his councils of war during the Revolution.

By the end of September, Knox had been absent two weeks longer than he had originally promised, and Washington had received no communication from him in months. He was worried and annoyed. He had hoped that Knox would return in time to lead the militia west against the rebels. He sent Knox a letter expressing his displeasure and concern: "Under the circumstances which exist to exceed your proposed time of absence so long, is to be regretted—but hearing nothing from you for a considerable time has given alarm, lest some untoward accident may have been the cause of it."[68] Washington also shared that he was departing for western Pennsylvania and regretted that his trusted secretary of war was not at his side. Traveling back from Maine at the same moment and delayed by weather, Knox did not receive the letter. He would arrive in Philadelphia on October 6, only to discover the president had already left. By the time Washington returned to Philadelphia, their relationship had cooled significantly. Washington believed the good of the nation should always trump individual needs, and he resented Knox's absence during a moment of crisis. Although he was grateful for Knox's many years of service, he never fully forgave the misstep.[69]

At the end of September, Washington finally left Philadelphia to meet the Pennsylvania, Virginia, Maryland, and New Jersey militias at the predetermined rendezvous point.[70] Over the next five days, he rode west with Hamilton and his private secretary, Bartholomew Dandridge Jr. During their travels, the small group met up with infantry detachments in Reading, a New Jersey regiment in Harrisburg, and Mifflin and Richard Howell, governor of New Jersey, two miles short of Carlisle. A detachment of Philadelphia troops greeted Washington just after he crossed the Susquehanna River and escorted him to Carlisle for the final leg of his journey.[71]

At 12:00 P.M. on October 4, a hush fell over the camp as the president's imminent arrival was announced. Upon entering camp, Washington carefully surveyed the parade of troops, cavalry, and artillery.[72] On October 9, 1794, the army began its march west through the Cumberland Valley and over the Allegheny Mountains, while Washington headed back to Philadelphia.[73] By the time the troops reached Pittsburgh, the rebel leaders had fled, and the insurrection crumbled in the face of the federal forces. Troops led by Hamilton and General Henry Lee rounded up any rebels they could find. In the end, only twelve cases went to trial and only two were convicted; most cases were dismissed due to lack of evidence.[74] But the arrests were not intended to imprison hundreds of rebels; rather, the point was to drive home the message that the federal government had the authority to tax its people and enforce the collection of the tax.[75]

As with so many other aspects of his presidency—his journeys to visit the states, his transportation, his social engagements—Washington carefully managed the details of public opinion and his reputation. He was perfectly happy for Hamilton to conduct widespread arrests while he traveled back to Philadelphia with his reputation unsullied.[76]

The military response ended the rebellion and asserted federal authority, but it also served as a visible embodiment of Hamilton's new financial system. In order to pay the militiamen's salaries and buy food, clothing, and matériel, the administration requested a large loan of up to $1 million from the new Bank of the United States.[77] Commanders of each state militia then received blank drafts to withdraw up to $15,000 to pay for provisions, including the daily whiskey rations for each soldier.[78] Ironically, the army's incursion into western Pennsylvania infused much-needed specie into the region. The army purchased clothing, food, supplies, and whiskey for its troops and their horses.[79] Many local farmers used this specie to purchase land or pay off their tax debts.

Most Americans approved of Washington's handling of the Whiskey Rebellion, and historians have largely shared the public's assessment.[80] In mid-October, Bradford sent a letter to Washington as he traveled to New Jersey. He had talked with local gentlemen and was pleased to share that "attachment to the general government" had increased "in every part of the state in a wonderful degree." Furthermore, Bradford's acquaintances had expressed "great indignation against the insurgents." They had heard rumors that the militia would not march to confront the rebels and had expressed their fears that "the wound should not be thoroughly probed."[81] Washington did not write a reply to this letter, but he must have been gratified to hear that so many Americans approved of his actions.

Not everyone applauded the administration's response. Farmers out west did not change their mind about the tax and continued to request tax relief.[82] When Washington insisted on regional atonement, many westerners felt betrayed. William Findley, one of Hamilton's political rivals from western Pennsylvania, resented the concept of regional atonement instead of individual atonement, but he blamed Hamilton, not the president.[83] Other Republican leaders, including Jefferson and Madison, criticized the administration behind closed doors for launching "an armament against people at their ploughs."[84] They grew more vocal in their opposition after Washington delivered his annual speech to Congress in November. In his speech, Washington accused

Democratic-Republican societies of fomenting the rebellion. Jefferson was outraged. He could not believe Washington had "permitted himself to be the organ of such an attack on the freedom of discussion, the freedom of writing, printing & publishing." He blamed Hamilton and "the faction of Monocrats" for brainwashing the president.[85] Once again, Washington had escaped most of the blame.

In 1794, the Washington administration adopted a strong federal reaction to the Whiskey Rebellion. While Washington favored sending a powerful message to the insurrection, he preferred to act with the agreement of his cabinet, based on his previous council-of-war interactions. He relied on his cabinet secretaries to provide advice and shape administration policy. He also convened cabinet meetings to build consensus and provide political cover for his controversial and precedent-setting decisions. The cabinet worked to sideline Congress and to bring the state governments under federal oversight during this process. The secretaries all brought previous governing experience to the cabinet, and this expertise colored their response to the rebellion. As a result, Washington and the cabinet worked toward a shared goal—they asserted the president's authority over domestic issues at the expense of congressional and state power. Through their participation in cabinet deliberations, Hamilton, Knox, and Randolph helped ensure that the cabinet supported and promoted presidential leadership. The Whiskey Rebellion served as the culmination of the cabinet's prior experiences and the fulfillment of their goals for the presidency. But after suppressing the Whiskey Rebellion, the cabinet again underwent a huge change and faced yet another new challenge.

8

A Cabinet in Crisis

THE WASHINGTON ADMINISTRATION and the cabinet experienced a significant turning point in 1795. John Jay, chief justice of the Supreme Court and envoy extraordinary to Great Britain, signed the Treaty of Amity, Commerce, and Navigation, which became known as the Jay Treaty. The Jay Treaty finally produced a détente in Anglo-American tensions after many years of effort and offered hope that the United States could avoid war with Great Britain. But it also produced a violent domestic response. Criticism of Washington and the Federalists reached new heights. Amid the public uproar, the cabinet faced unfamiliar challenges. A rash of retirements produced a different cast of characters, and in the summer of 1795, the cabinet experienced an unprecedented crisis. The new secretary of war, Timothy Pickering, and secretary of the treasury, Oliver Wolcott Jr., accused Edmund Randolph of treason. Randolph's subsequent resignation left Washington without his closest advisor, and the president increasingly distanced himself from the cabinet. The cabinet's behavior during Washington's final years in office shows the more intimate side of state-building. The personal relationships between Washington and the secretaries shaped the evolution of the cabinet as a new institution and its influence on the executive branch, domestic politics, and diplomacy.

The final years of Washington's administration also produced many important precedents for the executive branch and the cabinet. First, the ratification and eventual public acceptance of the Jay Treaty emphasized the president's authority over foreign affairs. Second, Washington asserted executive privilege for the first time—further sidelining Congress in the diplomatic process. Third, he again tinkered with cabinet practices in his final years in office. Although he convened a handful of cabinet meetings in the final years of his presidency, he primarily relied on individual conferences, written advice, and support from trusted advisors outside of the administration. Washington's evolving relationship with the secretaries reinforced the personal nature of the cabinet as an advisory body. The president summoned a cabinet meeting when the deliberations would be beneficial, but he was under no legal obligation to meet with his cabinet. He remained acutely aware of the precedents he established until the end of his administration, and he reinforced that the cabinet served at the president's pleasure.

On November 6, 1793, the British Privy Council issued a secret order instructing British naval commanders to capture all ships heading toward or leaving French colonial ports. The king's councilors crafted this order as part of their war strategy against France. The French merchant marine was occupied fighting an international war and French merchants eagerly employed neutral American ships to transport their goods back to France. Unsurprisingly, the British sought to thwart this practice and seize French goods for themselves. The order was issued in secret so that Thomas Pinckney, the American minister, could not give advance warning to the Washington administration or American captains. As a result, the British navy captured 250 American vessels and their crews. Most were condemned as war prizes and their cargoes seized—all without indemnifying American merchants and investors.[1] In March 1794, news of the secret order and subsequent seizure of ships reached the United States. Americans were aghast. Reports that the British had treated American captains and crews badly after their capture further compounded the initial outrage.[2]

In late March, Washington received news of fresh disturbances out west between Native Americans and settlers. Guy Carleton, Lord Dorchester, the governor of the province of Quebec, had gathered representatives from the Seven Villages Nations. He hosted the delegates at the Château Saint-Louis, a large castle on the cliffs overlooking the St. Lawrence River. At the council, Dorchester declared that recent American settlement in western territories was illegal under the Treaty of Paris.[3] Dorchester argued that the widespread American breach of the treaty terms effectively nullified any peace agreement. In fact, he argued, that American actions amounted to "an infringement on the King's rights." He finished his address by stating that Americans needed to abandon their "improvements and houses on our side" and return to the United States or the villages would be destroyed.[4] The Washington administration and the American public read these reports as British war-mongering and feared an uptick of Native violence toward settlers in western territories.[5]

With all signs pointing toward a war with Britain, Washington received reports that the Privy Council had passed new, milder orders to mitigate the effects of the November 1793 decision. Washington chose to interpret this order as a sign that Britain would be receptive to a diplomatic solution. Before the sun rose on the morning of April 15, Washington sent Chief Justice John Jay a message inviting him to breakfast at the President's House. While the two men were enjoying the meal, Washington asked Jay if he would be willing to travel to London to negotiate a new treaty with Britain.[6] While no record of the meeting exists, Jay evidently expressed his willingness to serve. The next day, Washington wrote to the Senate and emphasized the importance of pursuing all peaceful solutions before turning to war: "Peace ought to be pursued with unremitted zeal, before the last resource, which has so often been the scourge of Nations, and cannot fail to check the advanced prosperity of the United States, is contemplated." With these aims in mind, Washington nominated Jay to serve as envoy extraordinary to Britain.[7]

On Sunday, June 15, Jay landed in London with a few goals.[8] First, find a satisfactory solution to the recent British seizures of American ships and goods. Second, resolve outstanding issues from the Treaty of Paris, including American debts owed to British creditors and western forts occupied by British soldiers. Third, come to terms for the Anglo-American commercial relationship. Americans desired a "free ships, free goods" international community. This principle argued that neutral ships should be able to carry goods free from attack by belligerent nations, regardless of which nation owned the contested goods. Under this policy, American ships should be able to transport French or British goods and travel unmolested by the other nation. Yet Jay's instructions were fluid, and Washington and Randolph did not outline strict terms. They recognized that events and developments outpaced their ability to communicate and instructed Jay to consider "the ideas, herein expressed, as amounting to recommendations only, which in your discretion you may modify, as seems most beneficial to the United

States." This general grant of negotiating power had two firm exceptions: "the Government of the United States will not derogate from our treaties and engagements with France" and the government would not sign a treaty of commerce abrogating the preexisting American treaty with France.[9]

Jay conducted diplomacy with Britain pragmatically. He understood that he approached the bargaining table from a position of weakness. Americans insisted that British soldiers vacate western forts and cease inciting Native Americans to make war against them. American merchants also wanted more liberal trade policies that would allow them to sell their goods in most ports, but they had little leverage to force these changes. While Britain did not want the United States to enter the war on France's side, British ministers understood that Americans placed an even higher premium on neutrality. British colonies relied on Americans imports, especially foodstuffs to feed colonists and slaves, but they had other available sources. Conversely, Americans desperately depended on British trade to fuel their economy. If Britain wielded the most powerful navy in the world, retained a military presence in Canada, and cultivated diplomatic ties with Native Americans, British ministers could dictate where they would compromise and where they would stand firm.

With a clear grasp of these realities, Jay arrived in London and worked to establish cordial relations with the British ministers. A few weeks after his arrival, Jay related his social calls to Hamilton: "Shortly after my arrival I dined with Lord Grenville; the cabinet Ministers were present, but not a Single Foreigner. On Monday next I am to dine with the Lord Chancellor, & on next Friday with [Prime Minister William] Pitt." In the same letter, he described his guiding principles for his negotiations: "I will do every thing that Prudence and Integrity may dictate and permit. I will endeavor to accommodate rather than dispute—and if this plan shd. fail, decent and firm Representations must conclude the Business of my mission."[10] Above all, Jay wished to avoid further aggravating relations between the United States and Britain. He understood that making unrealistic demands in negotiations and employing theatrical threats could push the British ministers to call off negotiations—making war more likely, not less.[11]

Jay's approach endeared him to Lord William Grenville, the secretary of state for foreign affairs. Grenville and Jay both valued integrity above all other qualities. Early on, Jay and Grenville agreed to keep their negotiations secret. They also excluded all other personnel from their conversations. Colonel John Trumbull, Jay's private secretary, described his exclusion from the meetings and the complete secrecy surrounding the negotiations: "Sir James Bland Burgess and myself, had a real holiday for a month."[12] As a result, very little written documentation of their negotiations exists.

At the end of September, after initial conversations and social interactions, Jay submitted a draft treaty to Lord Grenville. This draft included provisions that would prevent both sides from employing Native Americans in a war with each other, provided for free trade on neutral ships, and exempted raw materials and important foodstuffs from contraband rules during war. Except for more permissive rules on transportation of foodstuffs, Jay secured almost none of these provisions in the final treaty. He likely never expected to—Britain would never agree to "free ships, free goods." Instead, Jay started from a position that gave him room to negotiate and compromise. On September 13, 1794, Jay revealed his strategy in a private letter to Washington:

My Letter to Mr Randolph which accompanies this, contains very full and accurate Information respecting our negociations here. You will perceive that many points are *under*

Consideration, and that alterations will probably yet take place in several articles. altho it is uncertain, yet it is not altogether improbable that Lord Grenville and myself may agree on Terms which in my opinion should not be rejected.[13]

On November 19, 1794, John Jay signed and sent the new Anglo-American treaty to Washington.[14] Jay wrote to Randolph that the treaty was the best outcome possible given the circumstances: "My opinion of the treaty is apparent from my having signed it. I have no reason to believe or conjecture that one more favorable to us is attainable."[15] His assessment was probably correct. He secured for the Americans three important concessions: a slightly more liberal trade policy that granted American ships limited access to the British West Indies; the creation of a commission to award restitution for American ships captured by the British; and British evacuation of western forts. In return, British ministers gained three important concessions: a commission to adjudicate outstanding pre-Revolutionary debts to British merchants; a twelve-year grace period before American ports could raise duties on British goods; and the creation of a loophole in the trade agreement that allowed the British navy to purchase provisions seized as contraband (rather than returning the provisions, as the Americans desired). Because the British had instigated tensions by seizing American ships, the British viewed their limited concessions as a victory.

Many Americans felt the final treaty betrayed their interests. Madison shared with Jefferson that "in Portsmouth, Boston and Philada. *unanimous* Remonstrances have also issued from Town Meetings and been sent by express to the P." to declare their opposition to the treaty.[16] Jefferson declared that "no man in the US. has had the effrontery to affirm that it was not a very bad one except [Alexander Hamilton] under

the signature of Camillus."[17] Opponents of the treaty wanted more access to British markets and resented the imbalanced nature of the
commercial agreement. Although the treaty prevented Americans
from raising duties on British goods for twelve years, Britain was free
to increase taxes on American goods immediately.[18] Additionally, the
agreement permitted British traders to cross the Canadian border and
sell goods in American territory, but prohibited American merchants
from trading in Canadian territory. Finally, southerners howled that
the treaty addressed American prewar debts to British creditors but provided no settlement for runaway slaves who escaped on British ships.[19]
Given the widespread American objections to the treaty, ratification
seemed uncertain.

As Jay finalized his negotiations, the cabinet underwent major personnel changes. On December 31, 1794, Knox retired; Hamilton followed one month later. Randolph's role changed: he took over the prestigious and powerful Department of State. As the sole remaining
secretary from Washington's original cabinet, Randolph became the
senior statesmen among the secretaries and enjoyed a privileged relationship with the president. Randolph was privy to private conversations and confidential information that Washington kept from the
other secretaries. Washington appointed Timothy Pickering as the new
secretary of war and Oliver Wolcott Jr. as the new secretary of the treasury. Both men had previous federal government experience, and
Washington knew them personally. Pickering had served as an Indian
agent for the government and as postmaster general. Wolcott was
Hamilton's second-in-command as the comptroller of the Treasury Department. But there was no doubt that the new appointees did not
match up to their predecessors. After his retirement, Washington

acknowledged that the replacements had failed to meet his expectations. After Randolph's resignation in August 1795, Pickering took over the Department of State. Pickering was fine as a secretary of war, though he did not have the same close relationship with the president that Knox had enjoyed. But as secretary of state, he was a disappointment. Washington had approached at least six other candidates, leaving the important office vacant from August to December, before finally settling for Pickering.[20] Washington selected James McHenry for secretary of war after a long and frustrating search. On August 9, 1798, Washington wrote to Hamilton and confessed his disappointment in his final secretary of war: "Your opinion respecting the unfitness of a certain Gentleman for the Office he holds, accords with mine, and it is to be regretted, *sorely,* at this time, that these opinions are so well founded. I early discovered, after he entered upon the Duties of his Office, that his talents were unequal to great exertions, or deep resources."[21]

Washington handled the changing personnel by convening fewer cabinet meetings. He continued to use the cabinet as a tool to process difficult decisions, but the secretaries no longer gathered to decide collectively on every single diplomatic detail, as they had done in 1793. Washington never wrote down why he convened so few cabinet meetings during his final years in office. It is possible Washington turned away from the cabinet because he was tired of governing or did not feel that he needed the cabinet to make decisions. Perhaps Washington and the secretaries felt increasingly confident in their ability to execute policy and cabinet deliberations weren't necessary.

However, Washington's withholding of critical information suggests an ulterior motive for his distance from the cabinet. His interactions with his department secretaries during the debates over the Jay Treaty revealed his distrust of most of the cabinet in 1795 and 1796. In late 1794,

FIGURE 8.1 Timothy Pickering. Department of State

Oliver Wolcott.

FIGURE 8.2 Engraved Portrait of Secretary of the Treasury Oliver Wolcott Jr.
Bureau of Engraving and Printing

FIGURE 8.3 James McHenry, Charles Balthazar Julien Fevret de Saint-Mémin, Baltimore, 1803. Library of Congress

rumors began to circulate that Jay had signed a treaty with Great Britain, but official papers moved much slower. On March 7, 1795, Washington finally received the long-awaited package from Jay. He immediately shared the contents of the treaty with Randolph. Congress had adjourned just a few days prior, so Washington and Randolph elected to call a special session of the Senate. They sent out messages summoning the senators to Philadelphia by June 8, 1795.[22] Until the senators could vote on the treaty, Washington resolved to keep the contents of the treaty under wraps.

Amazingly, Washington and Randolph kept the terms of the treaty secret for more than three months. In London, Jay also worked hard to keep the treaty contents private. He refused to send the complete treaty to James Monroe, the American minister to France. Instead, Jay sent his secretary, John Trumbull, to Paris and gave Trumbull instructions to share with Monroe the "nature of the treaty *orally and in confidence.*"[23] On March 11, Madison wrote to Monroe and conveyed the widespread curiosity surrounding the treaty: "What its contents are, the Executive alone as yet know the most impenetrable secresy being observed. You will easily guess the curiosity and disappointment of the public."[24] In April, Randolph wrote to John Adams and noted recent articles about the treaty in Benjamin Franklin Bache's paper, the *Aurora*. Randolph assured Adams that these articles were scandalous lies because "not one word of which [the treaty], I believe, is known thro' a regular channel to any person here, but the President and myself."[25] Many months later, Madison confirmed that the secrecy surrounding the treaty had included the other department secretaries: "I understand that it [the treaty] was even witheld from the Secretaries at war & the Treasury that is Pickering & Wolcott."[26]

During Hamilton's tenure, Washington rarely kept confidential information from his secretary of the treasury. From 1792 to 1794, Wash-

ington regularly included all four secretaries in his deliberations on issues both foreign and domestic. His intentional exclusion of Pickering,
Wolcott, and Bradford (his dying attorney general) spoke volumes
about their personal relationship and his lack of trust in the newer cabinet members. Washington never wrote down why he distrusted
Pickering and Wolcott—or at least why he trusted them so much less
than his previous secretaries. Perhaps their personalities clashed, he
feared their abilities were not up to the challenges of their offices, or
he suspected they were driven by partisan motives. Whatever the
reason, he kept the treaty secret and his secretaries at arm's length.

The secretaries grasped the shift in presidential power. All the participants understood that the president's private study was where Washington made significant decisions. The secretaries continued to administer their own departments with oversight from the president, but
they were only involved in the decision-making process when he welcomed their participation. As a result, access to Washington and the
cabinet equaled the ability to influence major policy and constitutional
decisions.

On June 8, the Senate gathered as planned and Washington delivered the treaty for review. Federalists immediately pushed through a
motion to veil the proceedings with the strictest secrecy.[27] After a few
days of deliberations, Republicans proposed rescinding the veil of secrecy over Senate deliberations. They believed that if the public learned
of the treaty's contents, public outrage would prevent its ratification.
The Senate rejected their proposal 20 to 9. During the debates over the
next week, Republicans made clear they despised every concession
granted to Britain. While Federalists accepted many of the treaty terms,
they were also troubled by Article XII. Although that article permitted
smaller American ships to trade in the British West Indies, it prohibited Americans from selling their goods; they could only purchase

British goods to sell in the United States. Federalists recognized that this provision would further cripple the shipping industry in New England (their largest base of support), while Republicans hated that their constituents in the South could not sell their crops. On June 17, the Senate approved the treaty, with one important qualification—Article XII had to change.[28]

Sensing an impending loss, Republicans worked to divide southern Federalists from their northern colleagues by introducing a new measure regarding enslaved people who had escaped with British aid during the Revolutionary War. Articles VI and VII of the treaty addressed the debts owed by both parties from the last two decades of conflict. Article VI established a commission to review complaints from prewar British creditors whose loans had never been repaid. Article VII created a similar commission to hear complaints from American merchants and citizens whose ships and goods had been seized by the British navy since February 1793.[29] Republicans sought to insert a new clause that read "And also for obtaining adequate compensation for the negroes, or other property of the American inhabitants, tarried off from the United States, in violation of the definitive Treaty of Peace and Friendship, between his said Majesty and the United States."[30] This clause threatened to rekindle a decades-old debate on the role of slavery in the Revolutionary War and sink the tentative peace between Britain and the United States. In late June, Federalists narrowly defeated this proposal 15 to 12. The Senate voted again on the treaty with the same result—Federalists had received the exact two-thirds majority necessary for ratification, 20 votes to 9.[31]

Before adjourning, the senators passed one final motion. As part of the deliberations, each senator had received one copy of the treaty. On Friday, June 26, the Senate voted to rescind the injunction of secrecy surrounding the treaty but instructed its members not to publicize or share their individual copy of the treaty.[32]

Three days later, Washington woke up to the news that the secrecy surrounding the treaty had imploded. After the Senate approved the treaty, many leading Federalists had urged Washington to share the treaty. Rufus King, a senator from New York, and Hamilton had written to Washington and Randolph to urge publication. They argued that secrecy was turning public opinion against the treaty and the administration. Their arguments convinced Washington and Randolph, who spent a few days selecting their preferred venue for distribution. Randolph selected the *Philadelphia Gazette,* edited by Andrew Brown. The *Philadelphia Gazette* had been the first newspaper to report the debates in Congress and had frequently published pieces friendly to the federal government and the Constitution. Randolph submitted a notice that the treaty would be published on Wednesday, July 1, 1795.[33]

Stevens T. Mason, a senator from Virginia, beat Washington and the Federalists to the punch. After the Senate approved the treaty, Mason snuck his copy of the treaty to Benjamin Franklin Bache. As the editor of the *Aurora,* the leading Republican newspaper, Bache was a longtime Washington opponent and had vociferously opposed the secrecy surrounding the treaty debates. On June 29, Bache published an abstract of the treaty. Two days later, on July 1, he followed with the entire treaty—the exact day Washington had planned to release the treaty in the *Philadelphia Gazette.* The *Aurora* articles reflected poorly on Washington and the administration. The Republicans appeared to be the party of government transparency, while the Federalists and the administration sought to keep the public in the dark.[34]

The fate of the treaty now depended on Washington. He shared the Senate's concerns that Article XII would limit American merchants' ability to sell their goods in the Caribbean and had spent the last several months deliberating whether he would sign the treaty. Washington had also finally shared the contents of the treaty with the other department secretaries after the Senate's ratification. At the end of June, Randolph had suggested Washington solicit their opinions and provided several questions for him to send to the other secretaries.[35] Following Randolph's advice, Washington dispatched a letter with the same questions to Pickering, Wolcott, and Bradford, requesting their written opinion. In particular, Washington requested advice about a conditional ratification. Because the Senate had suspended the twelfth article of the treaty, Washington contemplated conditionally ratifying the treaty and sending an emissary to Britain to renegotiate that article. He questioned whether a renegotiation of Article XII would negate the Senate's ratification.[36] He asked his secretaries to advise whether he would need to resubmit a revised treaty for a new ratification, or if the Senate's original approval satisfied their constitutional duties.[37] Given the contentious public debates surrounding the treaty, he worried the Senate would no longer vote to ratify the treaty. Above all, Washington did not want to go through the trouble of renegotiating Article XII and resubmit the treaty for approval if the Senate was going to reject the treaty under pressure from public opinion.

Over the next week, the secretaries sent their opinions to Washington. They all agreed that Washington did not need to resubmit the treaty with a renegotiated Article XII.[38] According to Randolph, the Senate "intended their resolution of the 24th of June 1795 to be a final act; and that they do not expect the proposed article to be submitted to them before the treaty operates."[39] Despite Randolph's Republican leanings and Pickering, Wolcott, and Bradford's staunch Federalism, all of the secretaries offered advice that favored the president's authority in diplomacy and minimized the Senate's role.

As Washington received the secretaries' opinions, he also received troubling news that threatened the future of the treaty. In early June, American newspapers printed reports that the Privy Council had passed a new order-in-council again authorizing the seizure of American ships.[40] Because Jay had already left London, however, the administration did not receive additional information until Randolph spoke with Hammond in early July. Hammond explained that in early April, Lord Grenville had received two critical pieces of news that prompted new British action. First, the French army was desperately in need of provisions and was using neutral nations' flags to cover their supplies in order to get the shipments safely back to France.[41] Second, the United States had just completed the last payment on its debt to France and Hammond had witnessed enormous French purchases of provisions since the payment.[42] Upon receiving this new intelligence, the Privy Council issued the new order, which instructed British captains to seize neutral vessels heading for French ports that might be secretly carrying French provisions.

On July 12, Randolph drew up a plan for dealing with the new order and the ratification of the treaty. He proposed that he meet with Hammond and convey Washington's desire to sign the treaty, with one major reservation. Randolph would tell Hammond that Washington could not sign the treaty while the new order was in effect: "We are informed by the public gazettes, and by letters, tolerably authentic that vessels, even American vessels, laden with provisions for France may be captured and dealt with, as carrying a kind of qualified contraband. . . . [T]he President cannot persuade himself, that he ought to ratify, during the existence of that order." Randolph and Washington both knew that Hammond planned to return home to London at the end of the summer and hoped to bring the ratified treaty with him, so they schemed to use his travel plans to their advantage. Randolph proposed that they write an official dispatch stating Washington's intention to ratify as soon as the April 25 order authorizing the seizure of American ships was rescinded. Hammond could deliver this memorial to King George III and the treaty could be ratified as soon as the Privy Council canceled the order.[43]

The next morning, Randolph visited Washington in his private study, and the president approved this plan. Randolph rushed back to the Department of State offices and shared the approved message with Hammond. Hammond asked if "the President was irrevocably determined not to ratify; if the provision-order was not removed?" Randolph had not expected this question. Unable to answer, Randolph scurried back to the President's House. Washington angrily replied that he would never sign the treaty with the hated order in place. He instructed Randolph to draft the memorial they had previously discussed, the form of ratification, and instructions for the American agent in London. The next morning, Randolph again met with Hammond, this time in the public drawing room at the President's House. He relayed Washington's inflexibility regarding the April 25 order and assured Hammond that he would have the promised memorial before he sailed for London. Confident that Randolph would keep him apprised of communications with Britain, Washington left Philadelphia for his scheduled end-of-summer visit to Mount Vernon without having settling on a final decision on the treaty.[44]

Washington's interactions with his secretaries before he left Philadelphia reveal the interpersonal relationships within the cabinet. His practice in 1795 diverged from the precedent he had established earlier in his administration. In June 1795, Washington and the secretaries were all in Philadelphia. He could have summoned a cabinet meeting to debate conditional ratification, but instead he requested written opinions. If he wanted written opinions to protect him from later criticism, he could have called a cabinet meeting and then requested each secretary send him their opinion in writing—a practice he had employed when discussing the Neutrality Crisis in April 1793, in February 1794 when he convened a cabinet meeting to discuss sharing diplomatic dispatches with Congress, and in August 1794 when the cabinet debated the Whiskey Rebellion.[45] In the summer of 1795, however, he met individually with Randolph and consulted the other secretaries only through writing.

Washington also continued to rely on his other trusted advisors outside the administration. He exchanged numerous letters with Hamilton throughout the Jay Treaty process. Perhaps unbeknownst to Washington, Hamilton had read the contents of the treaty in early June. Senator Rufus King had secretly shared his copy with Hamilton in order to solicit his advice.[46] In early July, Washington opened their correspondence by expressing his "desire is to learn from dispassionate men, who have knowledge of the subject, and abilities to judge of it, the genuine opinion they entertain of *each* article of the instrument; and the *result* of it in the aggregate." Washington assured his former treasury secretary that he had no desire to interfere with Hamilton's business, and if he had no time or inclination to offer advice, Washington would understand. Yet if Hamilton had a few moments, Washington would welcome his general thoughts on the treaty, as well as his opinion on whether the "treaty should again go to the Senate" if King George III "consent[ed] to the suspension of the 12th. article" or whether "the President [is] authorized by the Resolution of that body to ratify it" without the Senate's approval.[47] Washington was not content to hear just his secretaries' opinions on these issues; he wanted Hamilton's input as well.

On July 13, Washington thanked Hamilton for his advice. Hamilton's letters from July 9 and 11 no longer exist, but he evidently neglected to address Washington's questions about Article XII's limitations on American merchants, for Washington again raised the issue: "I asked, or intended to ask in my letter of the 3d. whether you conceived (admitting the suspension of the 12th. Article should be agreed to by the B. Government) there would be a necessity for the treaty going before the Senate again for their advice & consent?" He acknowledged that this issue particularly weighed on him because of the partisan factions in the Senate. His fears were well founded. Around the same time, Senator Henry Tazewell of Virginia wrote to Monroe that he "believe[d] the Condition suspends the whole Treaty, and the manner in which the condition may be fulfilled will require it again to pass before the Senate. If so—I believe the Treaty will never be sanctified."[48]

The next day, Washington received another letter from Hamilton, this time answering his question on Article XII. Hamilton believed that Washington would need to resubmit the treaty with a renegotiated article. This position surprised Washington—perhaps because Hamilton had always served as the most outspoken proponent of unrestricted executive power. On July 14, Washington shared his shock: "The opinion which you have given as to its being necessary to submit the *new* article to the Senate, being in direct opposition to that of the Secretaries and the Attorney general, has occasioned some embarrassment with me."[49] The differing opinions of Hamilton and the department secretaries bothered him so much that he asked Hamilton to communicate further with Randolph:

> I wish you to write to him your ideas, if upon mature reflection you shall think differently from the gentlemen around me; or you find the sense of the Senate to be different from

what I have been led to expect. I have told Mr Randolph that
your sentiments do not agree with those which I received
from the Officers of government; and have desired him to
revise them. I have also told him, that I have requested the
favor of you to write to him on this subject.[50]

Unfortunately, because Hamilton's letters from early July did not survive, and neither did his letter to Randolph, it is unclear why he disagreed with the other secretaries. Whatever the reason, Washington's
request again departed from his previous practice. Washington had
never overruled or sought outside interference when the cabinet decided on an issue unanimously. Washington trusted Hamilton completely and gave his opinions significantly more weight than those of
most members of his cabinet.

Washington and Hamilton continued to correspond about the public's response to the Jay Treaty over the next several months. At the end
of July, Washington complained about the public protests against the
Jay Treaty: "[The treaty] has received the most tortured interpretation,
& that the writings agt. it (which are very industriously circulated) are
pregnant of the most abominable mis-representations."[51] His letter also
demonstrates his stubbornness and resistance to influence from public
pressure. Washington believed that it was his responsibility, and his
alone, to make the final determination on the treaty. When he requested the opinions of men he respected, he was eager to hear their
thoughts, but he had little time for everyone else: "It is, more than ever,
an incumbent duty on me, to do what propriety, and the true interest
of this country shall appear to require at my hands on so important a
subject, under such delicate circumstances."[52]

At the end of the summer, Washington again wrote to Hamilton.
This time the president requested Hamilton's advice on his upcoming

annual address to Congress. He hinted at recent unpleasantness in the cabinet and revealed his loneliness in the cabinet without Hamilton.

> Altho' you are not in the Administration—a thing I sincerely regret—I must, nevertheless, (knowing how intimately acquainted you are with all the concerns of this country) request the favor of you to note down such occurrences as, in your opinion are proper subjects for communication to Congress at their next Session; and particularly as to the manner in which this treaty should be brought forward to that body.[53]

Other private citizens rushed to share their opinions with the president as well. After the *Aurora* published the treaty, Washington had been bombarded by private letters, anonymous editorials, and addresses from civilian organizations. One irked Washington more than most. On July 13, 1795, a group of Boston citizens, self-styled the Boston Selectmen, wrote to Washington with their opinion that the treaty, "if ratified, will be highly injurious to the commercial Interest of the United States, derogatory to their National honor, and Independence, and may be dangerous to the Peace and happiness of their Citizens." They then listed nineteen reasons Washington should reject the treaty. These opinions he likely received with equanimity, but the letter's conclusion rubbed him the wrong way:

> We earnestly hope, and confidently rely, that his prudence, fortitude, and wisdom, which have more than once been eminently instrumental, in the Salvation of his Country, will be equally conspicuous on the present occasion, and that the reasons we have assigned, will have their influence to induce

him to withold his signature from the ratification of this alarming Instrument.[54]

This final passage insulted his honor and sense of duty—the citizens had suggested that Washington would be acting without wisdom and prudence if he ratified the treaty. Furthermore, he considered the letter writers highly presumptuous to assume they could or should influence his final decision.

On July 28, 1795, Washington replied to the Boston citizens in a letter that was published in the *Independent Chronicle and the Universal Advertiser* in Boston. He rarely replied to letters from citizens, unless they were friends and colleagues. However, the Boston Selectmen had published their letter in local newspapers, and Washington felt obliged to reply. The final response barely concealed his displeasure and made very clear who was responsible for the final decision: "I have weighed with attention every argument which has at any time been brought into view. But the Constitution is the guide which I never can abandon. It has assigned to the President the power of making treaties, with the advice and consent of the Senate." He closed his public letter by gently reminding the Boston Selectmen of his previous accomplishments: "While I feel the most lively gratitude for the many instances of approbation from my country; I can no otherwise deserve it than by obeying the dictates of my conscience."[55]

In August 1795, during Washington's deliberations on the Jay Treaty, the cabinet was rocked by scandal. On July 28, 1795, British minister George Hammond had delivered to Wolcott letters that he had intercepted that mentioned Secretary of State Randolph.[56] The letters were a series of dispatches Jean Antoine Fauchet, the French minister, had written to his government and sent back to France aboard the *Jean Bart*. An English ship captured the *Jean Bart* and handed the letters over to the British government. After reviewing the documents, the British Foreign Office sent Hammond the originals, who promptly turned them over to Wolcott.[57]

The early dispatches depicted Randolph as an ally, friendly to the French cause. On June 4, 1794, Fauchet wrote Dispatch #3, describing the Republican victories in the 1793 and 1794 sessions of Congress and mentioning a meeting with the secretary of state. At this meeting, Randolph supposedly confessed to Fauchet that divisions in the nation, and in the administration, were growing.[58] In Dispatch #6, written on September 7, 1794, Fauchet detailed the events surrounding the Whiskey Rebellion. According to Fauchet, Randolph allegedly visited him and suggested that for a few thousand dollars, the French could decide whether the United States remained at peace or erupted into civil war.[59] Fauchet didn't provide a complete explanation, but he probably assumed that Randolph meant that France could influence events on the western border of Pennsylvania by investing in the rebel cause. Fauchet interpreted this confession as Randolph's opposition to Washington's stance on the rebellion.[60]

Cabinet deliberations at the same time challenged Fauchet's account. On August 2, 1794, Washington and his secretaries had met with Pennsylvania state officials to plan a response to the insurrection in western Pennsylvania.[61] On August 5, the same day Randolph supposedly met with Fauchet, he sent Washington his opinion: Randolph preferred to seek a diplomatic solution to the rebellion before turning to military force, but he supported military suppression should diplomacy fail. Randolph's behavior in late August and early September further discredits Fauchet's account. During the Whiskey Rebellion, Randolph worked to support the administration's military approach once Washington adopted this policy. He battled with Governor Thomas Mifflin, a fellow Republican, to ensure that Pennsylvania complied with Washington's orders and did not obstruct the federal response to the rebellion.

On October 31, 1794, Fauchet wrote Dispatch #10 and revealed an enormous shift in his opinion of Randolph and the US government. Events in France shed light on this sudden about-face. The power structure had recently shifted, and national troops had executed Robespierre, Fauchet's mentor. In Dispatch #10, the French minister revealed the failures and flaws of the Washington administration (as he saw them) to demonstrate why he had found so little success persuading the government to adopt pro-French policies. He hoped to endear himself to a new group of factional leaders back home. Fauchet had also personally cooled toward Randolph. He recognized that Randolph had oversold the pro-French sentiment in the United States and within the president's heart. Furthermore, Randolph had suggested to Fauchet that he should adopt more cordial manners toward the president, or his tenure as French minister might meet the same end as that of Edmond Charles Genêt, Fauchet's unfortunate predecessor. Fauchet's portrayal of Randolph hardly reads like a description of a disloyal traitor.

From Randolph's perspective, he had done nothing but serve Washington faithfully. In 1794, Randolph had followed Washington's instructions—he fostered a friendly relationship with Fauchet and worked to allay French suspicions of Jay's mission to negotiate with Britain. Of course he would describe the president as pro-French and blame any pro-British policies on other department secretaries. That's how diplomats and politicians operated.[62]

Hammond, an astute diplomat and skilled politician, had sized up the partisan divide in the president's cabinet. He immediately grasped that the dispatches presented an opportunity to reduce Randolph's influence in the administration as the sole remaining Republican in the cabinet. After Hamilton's retirement, Wolcott had inherited Hamilton's special relationship with Hammond. Hammond knew Pickering and Wolcott, both arch-Federalists, were much friendlier to the British cause. Eager to exploit divisions in the cabinet, he handed over the letters to Wolcott at the end of July 1795.[63]

How the events surrounding these letters unfolded over the next few weeks is difficult to piece together, as many of the crucial exchanges took place in person. Randolph later recounted his experience, but Pickering, Wolcott, and Washington wrote little about their thought processes or motivations.

In later July, Washington remained at Mount Vernon enjoying his annual end-of-summer vacation. He planned to return to Philadelphia in early September unless circumstances demanded his presence earlier. Randolph toiled away in Philadelphia, sending Washington regular updates on the public displays against the Jay Treaty.[64] Upon translating the Fauchet dispatches with their questionable French, Wolcott and Pickering immediately concluded that Randolph had offered to undermine the administration in return for bribes. They consulted with Bradford and devised a plan. On July 31, they visited Randolph and convinced him to request Washington's return to Philadelphia. However, they remained silent on the Fauchet letters and insisted that matters surrounding the treaty required the president's presence. Although Randolph had previously thought Washington could finish his vacation in peace, he acquiesced and wrote the president. Unbeknownst to him, Pickering also wrote Washington and alluded to another secret reason for the hasty return:

> On the subject of the treaty I confess I feel extreme solicitude; and for a *special reason* which can be communicated to

you only in person. I entreat therefore that you will return with all convenient speed to the seat of Government. In the mean time, for the reason above referred to, I pray you to decide on no important political measure, in whatever form it may be presented to you.[65]

Pickering, Wolcott, and Bradford were elite, powerful, well-educated men, deeply concerned with moral philosophy and ideology. But they were also human, and driven by petty rivalries and power struggles within the executive branch. Pickering and Wolcott were both High Federalists, intensely loyal to Hamilton, and motivated by extreme partisanship. As a result, they were eager to eliminate Randolph's Republican-leaning ideas from the cabinet. They viewed his potential positions as dangerous to the administration. Many Federalists believed that French radicals had encouraged the creation of Democratic-Republican societies. Washington and the other secretaries blamed these societies for the growth of partisan tensions and unrest, including the Whiskey Rebellion. Washington had expressed these fears to one of his former aides-de-camp, Burgess Ball, writing that "the Insurrection in the Western counties of this State [Pennsylvania] is a striking evidence" of "the Incendiaries of public peace . . . and may be considered as the first *ripe fruit* of the Democratic Societies."[66] By 1795, many elite French refugees had settled in Philadelphia—too close to the seat of government for many Federalists. Evidence of Randolph's friendliness with the French community fit nicely into Pickering and Wolcott's preconceived notions about the French radical threat.

Randolph's personal history exacerbated fears that his integrity might be compromised. Although he came from an elite Virginia family and owned a large plantation with many enslaved workers, he was chronically in debt. His family depended on the earnings from his law practice to keep them solvent, but his tenure as governor of Virginia and his wife's many illnesses frequently interrupted his meager income.[67] His poor financial situation was perhaps the worst-kept secret in Philadelphia. In August 1793, Jefferson had confided in Washington that Randolph had unpaid bills, which had "injured him with the merchants and shop-keepers." Jefferson suggested that these debts "had affected his character of independence; that these embarrassments were serious, and not likely to cease soon." Jefferson worried that Randolph's debts made him susceptible to bribery, and he offered this information to Washington as a reason Randolph should not be trusted as the next secretary of state.[68] If Jefferson, a fellow Republican, had these concerns, Pickering and Wolcott almost certainly doubted Randolph's integrity.

On a personal level, Pickering and Wolcott resented Randolph's role in the administration and his close relationship with Washington. They must have been embarrassed in June when they realized they had been excluded from secret conversations about the Jay Treaty. At the end of July, Wolcott wrote to Hamilton with an update on the deliberations over the Jay Treaty. This letter reveals that he had shared the Fauchet letters and his suspicions of Randolph with Hamilton prior to showing them to the president. He also wrote, "We have been constantly amused by R—who has said that the President was determined to ratify—the precise state of the business has never been communicated till within a few days—the affairs of his Dept. are solely conducted by himself."[69] Wolcott revealed his desire for a greater role in the conversations on the Jay Treaty and resented Randolph's influence over foreign affairs. Perhaps with Randolph expelled from the administration, Wolcott and Pickering could take on a larger role in the cabinet and further their Federalist ambitions.

On August 11, Washington arrived in Philadelphia. Pickering rushed over to the President's House that evening and delivered the Fauchet letters. The next morning, Washington cloistered himself in his private study and reviewed the documents with great care. He did not speak French and had very limited reading comprehension. As a result, he depended on the translations Pickering offered. He jotted down several questions and notes about how he should approach the situation. He shared these questions with Pickering and Wolcott so that they would all be on the same page before meeting with Randolph.[70]

Washington left no written record of that evening, so it is impossible to know what he was thinking as he pored over the documents accusing Randolph of treason. His leadership and personnel management during this period might seem callous, especially toward Randolph, his longtime friend. Washington and Randolph had been friends and colleagues for twenty years. They first met when Randolph accepted a position as Washington's aide-de-camp in the Continental Army. After Randolph returned to Virginia and pursued a legal career, he served as Washington's private attorney. By August 1795, he had served faithfully in the administration for six years.

In the summer of 1795, after news of the Jay Treaty leaked, Washington suffered constant attacks in the newspapers. He hated the criticism of his presidency and his character. Washington also deeply resented his critics for not appreciating his service and his many decades of sacrifice as a public official.[71] The departure of Washington's trusted advisors and longtime friends, including Jefferson, Hamilton, and Knox, compounded the public criticism. Previously, Washington had offered secretaries the opportunity to explain their behavior in writing or in private consultations. In 1792, when Hamilton and Jefferson's feud escalated and they lobbed allegations at each other, Washington patiently listened to their complaints and attempted to smooth their ruffled feathers. Washington brushed aside Jefferson's concerns that Hamilton was fomenting a movement to produce a monarchy in the

United States: "That as to the idea of transforming this government into a monarchy, he did not believe there were ten men in the United States whose opinions were worth attention, who entertained such a thought."[72] He also assured Jefferson that his participation in the cabinet was valuable and presented a critical balance to Hamilton's opinions. Despite his best efforts, most of his trusted advisors had left the administration. After receiving Pickering's report, Washington acted as though yet another trusted advisor had betrayed or abandoned him, and he was not in a forgiving mood.[73]

On the other hand, Washington may have been motivated to preserve the administration's reputation at all costs. In January 1790, he had written, "There is scarcely any part of my conduct wch may not hereafter be drawn into precedent."[74] Although he had served six years in office by this point, he still felt the burden of precedent. He could have given Randolph the benefit of the doubt or consulted with his longtime friend privately. Instead, Washington acted to ensure that he remained above reproach. The administration had established a precarious foundation for the new nation, and he did not know how the accusations would implicate him or the presidency. The United States had never experienced a treason scandal, and Washington was not sure the nation would survive. Many years later, Wolcott wrote to John Marshall and described Washington's deliberations leading up to the confrontation. According to his recollections, Washington requested that Wolcott and Pickering be present when he confronted Randolph. He felt they all deserved answers, and if Randolph was to continue in the administration, Pickering and Wolcott needed to be able to trust him as a colleague.[75] More important, they would be witnesses to Washington's interactions with Randolph, and they could testify that the president never placed his personal relationship with Randolph above the safety of the nation.

A few days later, Washington signed the Jay Treaty without renegotiating more favorable trade terms for American merchants in the
Caribbean (Article XII) or waiting for the Privy Cabinet to rescind the
April 25 order that mandated the seizure of American ships. Washington instructed Randolph to deliver the ratification documents to
Hammond before he returned to Britain the next day. Randolph was
surprised by this turn of events—Washington had previously insisted
he would never ratify the treaty while the April 25 order was in effect.[76]
Furthermore, every written communication Randolph had exchanged
with the president while he was at Mount Vernon suggested that Washington had not changed his mind. Washington offered Randolph no
explanation for his change of heart.[77]

At 9:00 A.M. on August 19, Randolph arrived at the President's House
for his usual meeting. The president's steward asked Randolph to return at 10:30 A.M. because Washington was "expecting some other gentlemen." Randolph returned as requested and entered the private
study, where he found that Pickering and Wolcott had been meeting
with Washington for some time. Washington greeted Randolph
brusquely before presenting the Fauchet letters. He then offered Pickering and Wolcott the opportunity to question Randolph. After Randolph provided a brief response, Washington instructed him to wait
across the hall in the drawing room while they discussed the situation.
After forty-five painful minutes, Washington called him back into
his study. Unwilling to leave his fate in the hands of Pickering and
Wolcott, Randolph asked for the opportunity to put his response in
writing. Picking up a quill, Randolph painstakingly scratched out a
few lines in response to the accusations leveled against him. He
handed over the piece of paper with its ink still wet, declared that he
"would not continue in the office one second after such treatment,"
and abruptly resigned.[78]

Randolph's response to the accusations of treason makes more sense in the context of 1790s honor culture. In the Early Republic, honor culture dictated that each gentleman's reputation was his political currency. Like most gentlemen, Randolph fiercely protected his reputation. He took pride in his years of service in the administration and the many more decades of friendship he enjoyed with Washington. In many ways, Randolph had devoted his career to serving Washington one way or another. On August 19, when he returned at 10:30 in the morning, he was surprised to find Pickering and Wolcott meeting with Washington without him. Upon learning the subject of their meeting, Randolph was insulted that this meeting had taken place behind his back, before he had the opportunity to explain himself. He could not believe his longtime friend would not speak with him privately. Washington's offer to the other secretaries to question Randolph added to the outrage—he outranked Pickering and Wolcott and had served a much lengthier tenure in the administration. Although Pickering declined to interrogate Randolph, and Wolcott only asked one question, Randolph indicated "it was a style of proceeding, to which I would not have submitted, had it been pursued."[79]

After suffering through this embarrassing experience, Washington then forced Randolph to wait across the hall for forty-five agonizing minutes. Randolph must have paced back and forth across the room while frantically replaying the previous months in his head. It dawned on him that these accusations might explain why Washington had changed his mind and ratified the Jay Treaty without qualifications a few days earlier. The longer Washington kept him waiting, the more betrayed he felt. When Washington finally called him back into the study, Randolph allowed his wounded honor to color his judgment. Sensing he had lost Washington's trust, he acted rashly and resigned immediately. Had Randolph asked for the opportunity to clear himself before resigning, he might have remained in office. At the very least, his reputation would have remained intact.

After leaving the President's House, Randolph went straight to the Department of State offices and ordered his office to be locked and his papers preserved. Later that day, Randolph wrote to Washington requesting access to the Fauchet letters so that he could prepare a vindication of his tenure as secretary of state. Washington granted his request and a few days later provided copies of the requested materials. Washington also promised to keep the scandal quiet until Randolph had completed his report.[80]

That same day, newspapers in Philadelphia began reporting that Randolph had resigned from his office but offered no rationale for the decision. Although no official explanation was forthcoming, the Early Republic rumor mill likely offered ample material for discussion. Political gossip was everywhere. William Seton, a prominent New York merchant, gathered enough material to offer Alexander Hamilton "the whisper of the day."[81] Over the next few weeks, Randolph tracked down copies of his correspondence with Fauchet and transcribed his documents. Each document, often several pages long, had to be copied by hand. When the process took longer than he expected, Randolph started leaking information to the papers. On September 19, the *Philadelphia Gazette* published the first of several letters exchanged between Randolph and Washington.[82]

A few days later, Randolph wrote to update Washington and to request additional materials. He asked when the president had learned of Fauchet's letters and asked for access to any other relevant papers. Washington replied that he had received Fauchet's letters upon his return to Philadelphia on August 11. Washington closed the letter by assuring Randolph, "No man would rejoice more than I should, to find that the suspicions which have resulted from the intercepted letter, were unequivocally, and honorably removed."[83]

Once he accepted Randolph's resignation, Washington probably felt a little sheepish and sad at the loss of his most trusted confidant in the cabinet. He did not form close friendships easily, and to lose one of the few people he let into his inner circle must have been devastating. His letter to Randolph hinted that he regretted the way their last meeting had gone and that he hoped Randolph would return or at least that their relationship could be repaired.

Just a few weeks later, however, the tenor of their correspondence shifted dramatically. On October 8, Randolph wrote to Washington complaining that Pickering had denied him access to certain papers and impeded his investigation. Unbeknownst to Randolph, however, his letter was lost in the mail and never delivered to the president. When Washington did not write back immediately, Randolph sent it to the papers for publication. Washington replied to Randolph and acknowledged that he had read the correspondence printed in the papers. He assured Randolph that he had issued orders to Pickering to provide complete access to the department papers and correspondence. Washington also made several of his own requests in his final letter to his former secretary of state. Since Randolph seemed determined to continue to publish their letters and government papers, Washington asked that the publications include the letter he was currently writing. He wanted the public to know that he had no wish to hamper Randolph's investigation. But he could not resist revealing how he felt about Randolph airing the administration's dirty laundry in the press:

> That public will judge, when it comes to see your vindication, how far, and how proper it has been for you, to publish

private & confidential communications—which, oftentimes have been written in a hurry, and sometimes without even copies being taken. And it will, I hope, appreciate my motives, even if it should condemn my prudence, in allowing you the unlimited license herein contained.

Finally, Washington made clear that he did not wish to hear from his former secretary of state again: "As you are no longer an Officer of the government, and propose to submit your vindication to the Public, it is not my desire, nor is it my intention to receive it otherwise than through the medium of the Press."[84] Had Randolph kept his investigation private and sent his vindication directly to Washington, the outcome might have been very different. But once Randolph exposed the inner workings of the administration and the cabinet, the relationship was irreparably damaged. Even more harmful, Randolph gave into his bitterness and publicly criticized Washington and the Federalists of sabotaging his reputation and his role in the administration as a voice of moderation. From that point onward, Washington cut all ties with Randolph. He excused private critiques, but rarely did he forgive public criticism from a formerly close confidant.

In December 1795, Randolph published his findings in a pamphlet titled *Vindication of Edmund Randolph*.[85] Upon reading the pamphlet, Jefferson remarked, "His narrative is so straight and plain, that even those who did not know him will acquit him of the charge of bribery: those who know him had done it from the first."[86] On the other hand, Abigail Adams read the report with nothing but scorn for Randolph and admiration for Washington: "The President whom Mr Randolph treats so very unhandsomely appears with more dignity for the tenderness he shews a Man Who can never be considerd in any other Light than the Fool of Party, the weak unstable Politician, assumeing

to himself an influence over the mind of a Man infinately his Super-
iour."[87] The public tended to agree with Adams. Rather than reading
the vindication as an impartial review of facts, they saw Randolph as a
failed politician, bitter over his reduced role in the administration and
lashing out at Washington in revenge.[88]

The entire episode had enormous implications for the cabinet as
well. Randolph had been the sole remaining secretary from the beginning of Washington's administration. He was also Washington's closest
advisor after Hamilton's retirement. Washington found it incredibly
difficult to secure an appropriate replacement for secretary of state and
reluctantly settled on Timothy Pickering after many months of
searching. But he clearly missed Randolph's presence, and that of his
other original secretaries, even if he never admitted it. In the final year
and a half of his presidency, Washington convened only eight cabinet
meetings—a tiny number compared to the fifty-one meetings he arranged at the peak of cabinet activity in 1793.

Given the devastating repercussions of Randolph's resignations,
why did this episode develop in this way? Washington and the secretaries operated under unique personal motivations and emotions that
drove their actions, creating a perfect storm of anxieties and tensions.
Randolph's behavior in the late summer and fall of 1795 reveals an increasingly hysterical, outraged man fighting to salvage his crumbling
reputation. He depended on the meager salary from his position as secretary of state and worried that the accusations threatened his ability
to secure another position. His actions became increasingly frantic
and irrational as he grasped for resolution to a problem largely of his
own creation.

Randolph's decision to publish his correspondence with Washington
in mid-September is a bit more puzzling. Two reasons explain Randolph's behavior. First, the letter Randolph wrote after his resignation

reflects his panic and desperation. As gossip began to swirl about his resignation, the pressure to provide an explanation undermined Randolph's judgment and his personal knowledge of Washington. When it took longer than he expected to compile his vindication, he felt compelled to offer an answer to quiet the rumor mill and resorted to publishing private letters.

Second, as Randolph sifted through the letters and the evidence, he began to suspect that the president had known about the Fauchet letters for more than a week before finally confronting him on August 19. He concluded that Washington had acted normally during that time to deceive him, which Washington confirmed after Randolph asked. Reading this reply, Randolph determined that Washington had sided with Pickering and Wolcott and laid a partisan trap to ensnare him. Although Randolph still loved and admired the president, his pain and anger caused him to lash out at Washington to inflict a small measure of vengeance. In late October, Washington and Randolph exchanged their final communications with each other and never spoke again.[89]

Although Washington had lost his secretary of state, matters in the executive department still required his immediate attention. On August 14, Washington resolved the lingering Jay Treaty issues by signing the treaty. Washington never explained why he suddenly changed his mind and decided to ratify the treaty before more favorable trade terms could be negotiated with Britain. Writing about the Jay Treaty many years later, both Wolcott and Pickering believed that Randolph's suspected secret relationship with France had pushed Washington to sign the treaty.[90] Hamilton's evolving views may have also nudged Washington toward ratification: by early August, Hamilton appeared to be leaning in the direction of ratification.[91] Additionally, Washington resented attempts by Republicans and the public to sway his opinion. Their efforts may have had the opposite of their intended effect—the outreach may have driven Washington to support ratification. Lastly, upon returning to Philadelphia and learning that Hammond had set a departure date for his trip home to London, Washington may have seized the opportunity to finally free himself of the treaty debate by sending the ratification documents with Hammond. Whatever reason motivated Washington's change of heart, these personal relationships had large implications for both foreign and domestic policy.

Despite Washington's hopes that the Jay Treaty was behind him, Republicans had other ideas. After he signed the treaty on August 14, Britain countersigned the document in October. On February 29, 1796, Washington officially proclaimed the treaty and shared a copy with Congress on March 1, 1796.[92] Until he proclaimed the treaty at the end of February, however, the public continued to debate provisions in the document—and, perhaps more important, what provisions had been omitted. As the self-proclaimed party of the people, Republicans galvanized popular protests against the treaty. They organized marches, demonstrations, and meetings to discuss the treaty and convey their disapproval. Republicans also distributed petitions, sent letters to representatives in Congress, and published editorials denouncing the treaty.[93] Federalists vocally disdained public protests against government policy as dangerous. They argued that citizens elected representatives to use their best judgment on complicated issues, rather than blindly following instructions from their constituents. Although Federalists considered themselves to be elite leaders who guided the rabble, they also participated in democratic organizing to build support for the treaty. They circulated petitions, organized demonstrations of their own, and published countless editorials.[94]

In March, the months-long debate reached a breaking point. On March 2, 1796, Congressman Edward Livingston from New York submitted a resolution: "The President of the United States be requested to lay before this House a copy of the instructions to the Minister of the United States, who negotiated the Treaty with the King of Great Britain, communicated by his Message of the first of March, together with the correspondence and other documents relative to the said Treaty."[95]

Over the next several weeks, the House debated Livingston's proposal. While most Federalists outright objected to the proposal, many Republicans, including James Madison, also expressed concern. On March 6, Madison wrote to Jefferson that the proposal "is so questionable that he [Livingston] will probably let it sleep or withdraw it."[96] Madison evidently shared his displeasure with Livingston as well. Livingston refused to withdraw his motion, but he amended his original proposal the next day on the suggestion of a "gentlemen for whose opinion he had a high respect." He requested the addition of the phrase "excepting such of said papers as any existing negotiation may render improper to be disclosed." The House of Representatives adopted the resolution, with Livingston's addition, 62 to 37, and appointed Congressmen Livingston and Albert Gallatin to present the resolution to the president.[97]

Washington received word of Livingston's motion on March 2, the same day it was made, and contemplated what action he would take if the House passed the resolution. The next morning, he asked Wolcott to meet with Hamilton and gather information about the 1792 cabinet meeting when they had first considered asserting executive privilege.[98] In March 1792, the House of Representatives had requested War and Treasury Department papers pertaining to Arthur St. Clair's disastrous expedition against Native Americans in the Ohio Territory. Ultimately,

Washington had complied with the House's request and shared the relevant papers. Either Washington did not remember clearly the cabinet discussions from April 1792 or he wanted Hamilton's opinion on why this House request might differ from the 1792 request. Hamilton sent Washington a brief note arguing that he should resist a broad incursion by the House into executive rights (and presidential papers).[99] Washington thanked him for the letter and indicated that he was leaning toward complying with the House's request. But just a few days later, Washington had changed his mind.

After receiving the House's request from Livingston and Gallatin, Washington wrote to his secretaries with three questions. First, did the House have a constitutional right to request the president's papers? Second, did they think he should relinquish the desired papers? Third, what was the best method to comply with or refuse the House's request? Washington requested written opinions and summoned the secretaries to a cabinet meeting the next day at 10:00 A.M.[100] In this instance, he resorted to his earlier cabinet practices. He called a cabinet meeting because he contemplated setting precedent by asserting executive privilege for the first time. He wanted the secretaries to share their positions and debate with each other if necessary, but he also needed to make the decision at his own pace. He requested written opinions so that he could have all the facts laid out on his desk as he contemplated his next step. Written opinions would provide political cover if Washington selected a politically unpopular option.

When they gathered in Washington's private study, Pickering, Wolcott, and McHenry all strenuously argued that Washington should reject the House's request.[101] The new attorney general, Charles Lee, offered a slightly different take. He argued that the House of Representatives did not have "a right by the constitution to demand and obtain the papers" pertaining to the Jay Treaty. However, Lee sug-

FIGURE 8.4 Charles Lee, Cephas Giovanni Thompson. Department of Justice

gested that "it [would] be expedient under the circumstances of this particular case to comply with the request" as long as the papers "contain nothing" that would be inappropriate to "[disclose] to the public."[102]

At some point after the cabinet meeting, Washington decided to assert executive privilege for the first time. He asked Pickering to draft a reply to the House's request and then had Lee review and amend the document.[103] On March 30, Washington sent his reply to the House. He assured Congress that he was always inclined to share information with it and to "harmonize with the other branches" of government. He suggested, however, that diplomatic negotiations require additional secrecy to maintain relationships and future negotiations. While he wanted to comply with the request, "to admit . . . a right in the House of Representatives, to demand, and to have, as a matter of course, all the papers respecting a negociation with a foreign power, would be, to establish a dangerous precedent."

Washington also seized the opportunity to remind the House of its constitutional responsibilities—and limitations. He recalled his time in the 1787 Constitutional Convention in Philadelphia and the determination of the delegates to vest "the power of making treaties . . . exclusively . . . in the President, by and with the advice and consent of the Senate." He reminded the congressmen that the House had acquiesced to the president and Senate's primacy in foreign affairs up to this point. Challenging anyone to disagree with his recollection, Washington encouraged the House to revisit the journals of the Constitutional Convention, which he kept safe in the Department of State offices. Having fully explained his understanding of the constitutional powers of each branch, he concluded: "It is perfectly clear to my understanding, that the assent of the House of Representatives is not n[e]cessary to the validity of a treaty."[104]

If Washington struggled with any lingering doubts, Hamilton's next letter likely ended any remaining questions. Hamilton had prepared a draft of a response for him to send to the House, which Washington received on March 30. Because of its tardy arrival, Washington used Pickering's draft instead. But he assured Hamilton that his draft was incredibly helpful. He only submitted Pickering's draft once he confirmed that both drafts articulated the same argument.[105]

Over the next month, the House debated the president's response and appropriations for the treaty. Both Federalists and Republicans kept up their war for public opinion by writing petitions and publishing editorials. Under constant bombardment from Federalist petitions and the weight of Washington's reputation, Republicans in the House saw their majority against the treaty gradually slipping away. On May 2, the House finally passed a bill allocating the necessary resources to enforce the Jay Treaty, 51 to 48. Two days later, the Senate passed the bill and it became law on May 6, 1796.[106]

Washington's assertion of executive privilege established a critical precedent for his successors. Presidents have exercised their right to keep certain communications private to protect ongoing missions, relationships, or negotiations. The cabinet played a central role in this formative moment for presidential power. The cabinet secretaries defended the president's right to conduct diplomacy in private, not because they sought to increase their own power or the profile of their departments but bolster the president's position vis-à-vis the House when conducting foreign affairs. Without the secretaries' encouragement, Washington might have decided to comply with the House's request.

From 1795 to 1797, Washington entered his final phase with the cabinet. He convened few cabinet meetings, preferring written advice from the secretaries and individual meetings with his favored advisors. Washington and the cabinet also established important precedents for diplomacy and presidential power. The secretaries supported the first use of executive privilege to protect executive authority over foreign affairs and sideline the House of Representatives.

The final years of Washington's administration also established important precedents for the cabinet as an institution. By distancing himself from the cabinet, Washington asserted his right to consult with the advisors of his choice. He also ensured that the cabinet developed very little institutional power. The secretaries had a great deal of autonomy over their own branches, but they had no power in the president's decision-making process unless Washington invited them to participate. As a result, the cabinet remained a personal advisory body that served at the pleasure of the president. When he wanted to consult with advisors outside of the government, he was free to do so. Washington's successors would soon discover that this precedent was more challenging to manage than they expected.

Epilogue

Wᴴᴱɴ ɢᴇᴏʀɢᴇ ᴡᴀsʜɪɴɢᴛᴏɴ accepted the presidency, the Constitution articulated few details of the daily functions of the executive branch. When he retired in 1797, he had created precedent for how the president would interact with Congress, the Supreme Court, the public, and the department secretaries. The cabinet, however, remains one of Washington's most influential creations. He crafted the cabinet to serve as a private advisory body at the president's pleasure, which had several important ramifications for his successors. Rather than following a written guide or legislative direction, each president would decide how his or her cabinet operated. The flexibility of the institution offered an excellent opportunity for strong leaders but could serve as a liability for weaker presidents. If a president managed the cabinet with diplomacy or exerted firm management, the secretaries served as indispensable aides and powerful spokesmen for the administration. If a president lacked authority within his cabinet or failed to control the agenda, the cabinet undermined the administration. Lastly, the public accepted the cabinet because Washington, the father of the country, had created it. Although the scope of the cabinet has changed, the character of the institution remains the same. Each president determines his own relationship with his advisors free from public or congressional oversight.

John Adams's and Thomas Jefferson's cabinets demonstrate the consequences of Washington's cabinet precedent. Both Adams and Jefferson willingly adopted Washington's cabinet structure. No constitutional clause or congressional legislation obligated them to consult with a cabinet, but neither Adams nor Jefferson ever experimented with an alternative method for obtaining advice. They also retained several of Washington's key practices: submitting questions prior to group meetings, requesting written opinions after a cabinet gathering, including cabinet members in the creation of the president's annual address to Congress, and fostering an official family environment. Their cabinet experiences demonstrated the potential strength and volatility of the new institution. Adams struggled with hostile secretaries who followed Hamilton's marching orders, undermined his agenda, and challenged his bid for reelection. In his final year in office, Adams finally asserted presidential control over the executive branch and affirmed the cabinet's subservience to the president. Jefferson created an effective cabinet formula that co-opted the strengths of Washington's and Adams's administrations while avoiding their partisan divisions. Adams's and Jefferson's relationships with their department secretaries reflected the private, idiosyncratic nature of the cabinet—just the type of institution Washington intended.

In the summer of 1796, Washington decided to retire to private life at Mount Vernon. Washington had originally wanted to leave the presidency after his first term in 1792, but Madison, Jefferson, Knox, and Hamilton prevailed upon him to stay in office for one more term. However, 1796 was a different story. He was finished with public service and no amount of persuasion could convince him otherwise. He was tired of the constant criticism in the press, tired of the public events in Philadelphia, and tired of the responsibility. No matter how earnestly Hamilton, Pickering, Wolcott, and McHenry begged him to remain in office, Washington would not budge. On September 19, 1796, he published a Farewell Address in Philadelphia's *American Daily Advertiser*. Other newspapers quickly reprinted the address, and it spread throughout the states. Washington selected publication in a newspaper so that he could speak directly to the American people, rather than through Congress or some other official channel. The final message combined a draft from 1792 that Madison had written when Washington first threatened to retire and a draft that Hamilton wrote in September 1796. The message encouraged the American people to put aside their partisan and sectional differences and focus on the emotional, economic, and national ties holding them together. The message also encouraged future leaders to avoid alliances with foreign nations that would drag the United States into international conflicts. Finally, Washington assured the American people that he had served the nation to the best of his abilities and humbly requested they assess his shortcomings with indulgence.[1]

Washington's immediate successor faced an impossible task. No other statesman could match his reputation, and every candidate would inevitably fall short in comparison. The issue of the cabinet was practically absent from the 1796 and 1800 presidential elections. Washington's precedent was so powerful that no one seriously considered abandoning the cabinet as an integral part of the executive branch. No popular protests, petitions, or legislative proposals emerged to replace the cabinet with an alternative advisory body. Neither Adams nor Jefferson ever mentioned abandoning the cabinet when they assumed office, though in a private letter to Dr. James Currie, Benjamin Rush speculated that Adams would "govern without a Council, for he possesses great knowledge, and the most vigorous internal resources of mind."[2] Contrary to Rush's expectations, however, Adams retained the secretaries from Washington's administration.

In Washington's administration, the secretaries had played a central role in crafting the president's message. For his inaugural address and his first annual address to Congress, Washington requested James Madison's input. Congress did not create the executive departments until September 1789, and Thomas Jefferson finally took office as secretary of state in January 1790. Once the secretaries were up and running, he requested that they submit items to be included in the address. After he compiled the first draft, Washington shared certain sections of the draft with the cabinet and requested feedback. He then incorporated much of this feedback into the final message.

Adams continued Washington's precedent by including the secretaries in drafting the annual addresses to Congress. He developed a formula that he utilized for all four of his addresses. First, while still at home in Quincy, Massachusetts, for his summer vacations, he sent letters to his cabinet soliciting papers on topics he should mention in his address. Next, he requested the secretaries prepare drafts of the speech. Finally, he compiled the suggestions and produced a final product. Adams's addresses always included contributions from each secretary but packaged in his own words. For example, in 1799, Wolcott and Pickering submitted drafts that included vitriolic language against France. Rewriting the draft, Adams kept the substance of their suggestions but adopted a much more conciliatory tone.[3] In 1800, the new secretary of state, John Marshall, created the first draft of the annual address. Adams adopted much of Marshall's prose but added important provisions offered by Attorney General Charles Lee and Treasury Secretary Oliver Wolcott Jr. on topics including judiciary reform, disbanding the Provisional Army, and improving the manufacture of arms.[4]

Jefferson also used his annual addresses to Congress as an opportunity to stress the importance of cabinet teamwork. Unlike Washington and Adams, who asked for drafts from their secretaries and then compiled their speeches privately, Jefferson typically wrote an outline or first draft himself, circulated it to his secretaries, and then called a cabinet meeting to discuss any final revisions. Gallatin and Madison crafted entire sections on fiscal and foreign policy to fit into the final version, but the lower-ranking cabinet members also put their stamp on the final product. With all of his secretaries, Jefferson accepted some of their ideas and rejected others. For example, in November 1801, Jefferson sent a draft of the address to the department secretaries. Secretary of the Navy Robert Smith replied to Jefferson's draft with six full pages of suggestions, including specific recommendations on proposed immigration legislation. He counseled Jefferson to avoid making a specific recommendation about the length of a residency requirement for new citizens. According to Smith, so much division existed within the Republican ranks that no matter what position Jefferson adopted, he would offend a section of the party. He preferred to encourage Congress to draft the legislation and take responsibility for the decision. Jefferson followed this advice, and the final version of the address recommended a revision of the naturalization laws but did not suggest any particulars.[5]

Adams also relied on official family dinners, another of Washington's practices, to foster amicable relationships with the department secretaries and to make them feel included in the process of governing. In November 1798, he reported to his wife, Abigail, "We had the Ministry & General Officers to dine on Monday and all agreeable."[6]

Jefferson, too, approved of the practice of dining with his cabinet secretaries as an official family. As a widower whose two daughters were often home in Virginia, Jefferson used official family dinners to help fill the void in the White House. In June 1803 when Albert Gallatin first arrived in the District of Columbia, Jefferson invited him to dinner at the White House: "Th: Jefferson asks the favor of mr & mrs Gallatin to dine with him today; and requests that while they are arranging matters at their new quarters they will dine with him every day. It may give them more time for other arrangements, and will be conferring a real favor on Th:J."[7] These dinners served a dual purpose: they provided much-needed social interaction for Jefferson, and they solidified the relationships between the secretaries and the president. Intimate social gatherings helped foster a sense of esprit de corps within his cabinet, which prevented divisions between the secretaries and encouraged the secretaries to feel invested in the success of the administration.

Both Adams and Jefferson also retained Washington's structure of cabinet deliberations. They frequently submitted a topic of conversation, or questions for consideration, and then called an in-person meeting, but they always reserved the final decision for themselves. For example, in early 1797, Adams learned that France rejected Charles Cotesworth Pinckney as a special envoy. Rumors also abounded that the French ministry had forced Pinckney to leave the country or suffer imprisonment. Adams sent a list of fourteen questions to his cabinet asking them to consider whether the administration should send another mission to France. If so, Adams asked, under what conditions and terms should negotiations take place?[8] On March 19, Adams put to paper several of his own observations in preparation for the cabinet meeting.[9] At the meeting the next day, he used his initial list of questions to guide the conversation. Afterward, he drafted additional questions based on the discussion and requested written opinions from the secretaries.[10] In late April, McHenry and Wolcott wrote back in response.[11] On May 1, Pickering sent his own written replies.[12]

Jefferson employed the same method of convening and managing cabinet meetings. For example, on December 31, 1802, Jefferson sent a letter to his secretaries requesting a consultation the next day at eleven in the morning. He indicated that he wished to discuss "the subject of N. Orleans & the Floridas."[13] After deliberating with his secretaries, on January 11, Jefferson nominated James Monroe as minister extraordinary to France. Monroe's mission was to partner with Robert Livingston, the current minister to France, to purchase New Orleans and secure permanent American access to the Mississippi River.[14]

Finally, Adams and Jefferson followed Washington's model of nominating secretaries who offered diverse geographic, economic, and social representation in the cabinet. Washington had selected two secretaries from Virginia, one from Maine, and one from New York, each of whom offered differing diplomatic, economic, legal, and military experience. Finally, Washington's secretaries shared ideological affinities with different interest groups. Hamilton cozied up to the merchant and banking elite, Knox remained involved in the military community, and Jefferson represented the slave-owning southern elite. Washington tried to retain balance when nominating replacements for open positions. Timothy Pickering was from Massachusetts, James McHenry was from Maryland, Oliver Wolcott, Jr. was from Connecticut, William Bradford was from Pennsylvania, and Charles Lee was from Virginia. While they were all Federalists, they still brought differing backgrounds and experiences to the cabinet.

Adams inherited this balance when he retained Washington's secretaries for his cabinet. After removing McHenry and Pickering in 1800, he sought to retain an equilibrium among regional and factional interests. John Marshall of Virginia became the next secretary of state, and Samuel Dexter of Massachusetts filled the role of secretary of war.

While Jefferson dismissed Adams's secretaries and nominated his own Republican candidates, he followed the model of representing different parts of the nation. He first selected James Madison as secretary of state. Madison served as Jefferson's closest confidant for most of his adult life, and they frequently enjoyed extended stays at each other's homes—which was relatively easy, as Madison owned a large plantation not far from Jefferson's home at Monticello. Next, Jefferson chose Albert Gallatin as his secretary of the treasury. An immigrant from Switzerland, Gallatin had made his home in western Pennsylvania. He was known for his more radical positions, sympathy for the rebels during the Whiskey Rebellion, and affiliation with western territories. Both Madison and Gallatin had led partisan attacks on the previous Federalist administrations and possessed unassailable Republican credentials. Federalists disliked Gallatin so much that Jefferson delayed his nomination as secretary of the treasury until Congress adjourned, out of fear that the Federalist senators would wreak havoc on the confirmation process.[15]

For the lesser departments, Jefferson selected Henry Dearborn, a Revolutionary War veteran from New Hampshire, as his secretary of war. Jefferson tapped Levi Lincoln of Massachusetts as his attorney general. Prior to Jefferson's administration, Lincoln worked as an attorney, served in both houses of the Massachusetts legislature, and even defended his home state as a member of the Minute Men. For his secretary of the navy, Jefferson approached Samuel Smith of Maryland. When Smith repeatedly turned down the offer, Jefferson settled for Samuel's brother, Robert, to maintain ties to the powerful mid-Atlantic family. An ardent Anglophile, Robert provided important ideological diversity to Jefferson's cabinet. Jefferson followed Washington's example by selecting political leaders who represented various economic, regional, religious, and political interests. These appointments strengthened Jefferson's position as the head of the Republican Party and shored up support among different regions of the country.[16]

For the next 207 years, presidents adhered to this precedent. Until the election of Donald Trump in 2016, presidents have followed Washington, Adams, and Jefferson's example of representing the nation through their cabinet secretaries. Abraham Lincoln famously stitched together a coalition of different factions of the nation by selecting secretaries from Missouri, Ohio, Pennsylvania, New England, and New York. Over the course of two centuries, presidents have also expanded their ideas about who should be represented in the cabinet. Barack Obama kept registered Republicans from the Bush administration in his cabinet, and also appointed female, African American, Asian American, and Latinx secretaries. On the other hand, Trump has nominated few women or people of color to secretary positions, instead relegating them to lower-level posts, and has tapped former businessmen and friends who all appear to support his views. He also selected nominees, such as Stephen Bannon and Jeff Sessions, who risked alienating racial, religious, and ethnic communities. Perhaps as a result, Trump's cabinet has seen frequent, protracted vacancies and the highest rate of turnover in US history.

For all of their similarities, Adams's and Jefferson's cabinet experiences also demonstrated the flexibility, potential, and peril of the cabinet legacy that Washington left behind. Adams struggled with the legacy that each president would determine his own relationship with his secretaries. This flexible arrangement worked when the president supervised the secretaries in a diplomatic manner or when his reputation and stature ensured complete loyalty. When the president could not match Washington's management skills or did not command the respect of his secretaries, the system failed. Adams discovered the hard way how difficult it was to recreate Washington's leadership.

Eager to provide continuity between the first two administrations, Adams elected to retain Washington's department secretaries. He knew that the department secretaries enjoyed close relationships with former treasury secretary Alexander Hamilton, but he initially believed that the secretaries would be loyal to the office of the president. He even defended their actions in the 1796 election, assuring his friend Elbridge Gerry: "I believe there were no very dishonest Intrigues in this Business. The Zeal of some was not very ardent for me but I believe none opposed me."[17] This trust proved misguided. A few months later, he wrote to his wife, Abigail: "From the Situation, where I now am, I see a Scene of Ambition, beyond all my former suspicions or Imaginations.—An Emulation which will turn our Government topsy turvy. Jealousies & Rivelries have been my Theme and Checks and Ballances as their Antidotes."[18] Wolcott, Pickering, and McHenry turned out to be staunch Hamilton allies and actively colluded to undermine Adams's foreign policy, weaken his administration, and prevent his reelection. They also conspired to thwart Adams's attempts to pursue peace with France, encouraged his absences so they could plot undisturbed, and leaked private government documents to Hamilton for publication.[19]

In the summer of 1798, the cabinet challenged Adams's right as president to seek peace and prepare for war simultaneously—a situation Washington never experienced. Adams's first peace commission, led by John Marshall, Charles Cotesworth Pinckney, and Elbridge Gerry, had brought the United States and France to the brink of war. Charles Maurice de Talleyrand, the French foreign minister, had demanded bribes and embarrassing concessions from the commissioners before summarily throwing them out of the country. Outraged, Federalists in Congress passed legislation authorizing the expansion of the army, navy, and local defenses.

In August 1799, Talleyrand sent assurances to Adams through diplomatic back channels that a new delegation would be received by the French Directory. Without consulting his cabinet or leaders in Congress, Adams nominated William Vans Murray as a new envoy extraordinary. Under significant pressure from members of his own party, Adams agreed to also send Oliver Ellsworth and William Richardson Davie—two staunch Federalists—to join Murray in Paris. As the commissioners moved forward with preparations for their mission, Adams vacationed in Quincy. Taking full advantage of the president's absence, Pickering and the other Hamiltonian Federalists worked to prevent the commissioners' departure. Such blatant disloyalty never occurred in Washington's administration. Jefferson may have naively trusted French minister Edmond Charles Genêt during the Neutrality Crisis in 1793, but he never intentionally undermined the president's final decision. Adams's inability to control his secretaries demonstrated the potential downside of a flexible cabinet.[20]

When Pickering, Wolcott, and McHenry failed to change Adams's mind about sending the commissioners, they called in reinforcements. Sometime between October 19 and 21, 1799, Hamilton arrived in Trenton and called on the president. Hamilton's presumption that he could lecture on Adams on foreign policy enraged the president. Not only had Hamilton treated Washington with the utmost respect, but a private citizen would never have stormed into Washington's study and challenged his authority. The cabinet divisions had taken their toll on Adams's administration and his stature as president.[21]

Despite Hamilton's best efforts, Adams's diplomatic efforts produced the Treaty of Mortefontaine in 1800, which addressed many of the lingering issues from the Jay Treaty and preserved peace between the United States and France. News of the treaty returned too late to influence the election, however. Convinced that they could not control Adams, many of the leading Federalists threw their support to Charles Cotesworth Pinckney, a reliable Federalist from South Carolina. Jefferson and Aaron Burr tied for first place in the electoral college, with Adams coming in a distant third. After thirty-six rounds of balloting, the House of Representatives selected Jefferson as the third president of the United States.[22]

Jefferson had observed Pickering, Wolcott, and McHenry conspire with Hamilton to undermine Adams's peace mission and sabotage his reelection chances. Once in office, Jefferson intended to keep a close eye on his secretaries. Based on his observations of the two previous administrations, Jefferson also pursued two additional goals: avoid confrontation with his cabinet in order to preserve a harmonious, effective working environment, and preserve and strengthen presidential authority by limiting cabinet meetings and controlling the flow of information so that the cabinet secretaries could not pursue their own agendas.

Jefferson relied on a few strategies to achieve these goals. He drew on his years of diplomatic experience to manage his relationships with the secretaries. Averse to conflict, Jefferson promoted comity between the secretaries. In 1810, he wrote to his friend Dr. Walter Jones and reminisced about his success in maintaining cordial relationships between his cabinet members: "The harmony was so cordial among us all, that we never failed, by a contribution of mutual views, of the subject, to form and opinion acceptable to the whole."[23] He had observed how cabinet divisions and disloyalty disrupted both Washington's second term and Adams's administration, and he worked tirelessly to prevent any erosion of authority in the executive branch. In the absence of written rules to guide cabinet interactions, he knew how much personal relationships mattered.

Jefferson carefully organized cabinet meetings to ensure that he retained control over the administration's policies and interactions. He meticulously managed the structure of cabinet discussions to create an inclusive cabinet environment. Rather than bringing up a general topic of discussion, he posed a series of questions in the meeting designed to find common ground among his department secretaries. Whereas Washington preferred to hear the secretaries' conflicting opinions and then make a decision, Jefferson hated confrontation and feared its effect on cabinet interactions. Washington's precedent and the lack of written guidelines afforded Jefferson the flexibility to create cabinet practices that suited his preferences and skills.[24]

By restricting interactions between secretaries, Jefferson ensured that he alone possessed all the facts and strengthened his position as the center of executive government. He turned toward group gatherings only when an unexpected situation required detailed advice. The unpredictable nature of cabinet meetings emphasized the role of the cabinet as an advisory body and an instrument of the president's leadership to be used at his discretion. Jefferson's cabinet noticed his efforts to underscore the president's authority. In a letter to his brother-in-law, Secretary of State Robert Smith complained of Jefferson's complete control: "Nay I . . . did not dare to bring forward the measure until I had first obtained his approbation. Never was there a time when executive influence so completely governed the nation."[25]

Finally, Jefferson fostered loyalty among his cabinet members by convincing each secretary that he valued his contributions. He never forgot how powerless he had felt to influence Washington's decisions in 1793, and he worked to ensure that his secretaries were heard. These efforts worked. Caesar A. Rodney, Jefferson's second attorney general, believed that the president desired and respected his opinion, even though he was the lowest-ranking cabinet member. In July 1807, Rodney wrote to his brother that he needed to delay his trip to Richmond because "the President could not spare me from head-quarters."[26]

Adams's and Jefferson's administrations demonstrate the legacy Washington left behind: that every president would have to create his or her own strategies to manage the cabinet. Regardless of how loyal secretaries have been to presidents, they are still a team of rivals who fight over resources, time, attention, and career advancement. Successful administrations require presidents to deftly handle the egos and ambitions of their secretaries, while not sacrificing their agendas to their subordinates' demands. It can be a nearly impossible task.

Washington shaped the cabinet to serve his needs as president and left a legacy in which the president would select his own advisors and determine how they would interact. There were no rules or written guidelines for future presidents to follow. Each president crafted his own relationships with his secretaries—for better or for worse. Whether the cabinet would support the president's agenda and provide meaningful advice, or undermine policy and create divisions within the executive branch, depended entirely on the president's ability to manage his secretaries through a combination of leadership skills and diplomacy. Adams and Jefferson followed Washington's lead with mixed results. Although the cabinet has grown and evolved in step with the expansion of the executive branch and the federal government over the last two centuries, Washington's legacy remains.

In the twenty-first century, the American public well understands the potential influence of the advisors whom the president chooses for the cabinet. Advisors are considered such an important part of the presidency that presidential candidates are expected to name their foreign policy advisors during their campaigns. This expectation uniquely illustrates the power of Washington's cabinet legacy. The delegates to the Constitutional Convention determined—and stated forcefully in the Constitution—that the Senate should serve as a council on foreign affairs. Nonetheless, each president has disregarded these expectations and instead chosen his own advisors. As long as Washington's precedent endures, each president will start his or her term by appointing fifteen department secretaries with whom he or she can work closely, or largely ignore. Other individuals may play advisory roles as well. For example, unlike many of his predecessors, Obama enjoyed a close relationship with his vice president, Joe Biden. Trump has largely eschewed traditional advisor relationships, instead relying on his daughter and son-in-law, Ivanka and Jared Kushner, and on television personalities to guide his agenda. These are just two examples of how each president determines how, when, and where he or she will consult advisors or follow their advice. These interactions are hidden from Congress's prying eyes and the public's examination. This dynamic has become an accepted part of American political tradition largely because the cabinet was George Washington's creation.

Citation and Abbreviation Guide

The Adams Papers, Adams Family Correspondence, ed. Lyman H. Butterfield et al. Cambridge, MA: Harvard University Press, 1963–.

The Adams Papers, Diary and Autobiography of John Adams, ed. L.H. Butterfield et al. Cambridge, MA: Harvard University Press, 1962.

The Adams Papers, Papers of John Adams, ed. Robert J. Taylor et al. Cambridge, MA: Harvard University Press, 1977–.

DHFFC: Documentary History of the First Federal Congress, ed. Linda Grant De Pauw et al. Baltimore: Johns Hopkins University Press, 1972–2012, 20 vols.

DHRC: Documentary History of the Ratification of the Constitution, ed. Merrill Jensen et al. Madison: Wisconsin Historical Society Press, 1976–.

Diaries: The Papers of George Washington, Diaries, ed. Donald Jackson et al. Charlottesville: University of Virginia Press, 1976–1979.

Journals of the Continental Congress, 1774–1789, ed. Worthington C. Ford et al. Washington, DC: Library of Congress, 1904–1937.

Letters to Delegates of Congress, 1774–1789, ed. Paul H. Smith et al. Washington, DC: Library of Congress, 1976–2000, 25 vols.

PAH: The Papers of Alexander Hamilton, ed. Harold C. Syrett. New York: Columbia University Press, 1961–1987.

PGW: The Papers of George Washington, Colonial Series, ed. W. W. Abbot et al. Charlottesville: University of Virginia Press, 1987–.

PGW: The Papers of George Washington, Confederation Series, ed. W. W. Abbot et al. Charlottesville: University of Virginia Press, 1987–.

PGW: The Papers of George Washington, Presidential Series, ed. W. W. Abbot et al. Charlottesville: University of Virginia Press, 1987–.

PGW: The Papers of George Washington, Retirement Series, ed. W. W. Abbot et al. Charlottesville: University of Virginia Press, 1987–.

PGW: The Papers of George Washington, Revolutionary War Series, ed. W. W. Abbot et al. Charlottesville: University of Virginia Press, 1987–.

PJM: The Papers of James Madison, Congressional Series, ed. William T. Hutchinson et al. Chicago: University of Chicago Press, 1962–1977, vols. 1–10.

PJM: The Papers of James Madison, Congressional Series, ed. William T. Hutchinson et al. Charlottesville: University of Virginia Press, 1962–1977, vols. 11–17.

PTJ: The Papers of Thomas Jefferson, ed. Julian P. Boyd et al. Princeton, NJ: Princeton University Press, 1950–.

PTJ: The Papers of Thomas Jefferson, Retirement Series, ed. J. Jefferson Looney et al. Princeton, NJ: Princeton University Press, 2004–.

Notes

Introduction

1. For a few examples, see George Washington to John Adams, May 10, 1789, *PGW*, 2:245–250; George Washington to Catharine Sawbridge Macaulay Graham, January 9, 1790, *PGW*, 4:551–554; "Memoranda of Consultations with the President (11 March–9 April 1792)," *PTJ*, 23:258–265, March 31 entry.

2. Richard M. Ketchum, *Saratoga: Turning Point of America's Revolutionary War* (New York: Henry Holt and Company, 1997), 265.

3. *DHFFC*, 2:5–6.

4. George Washington to United States Senate, August 21, 1789, *PGW*, Presidential Series, 3:515; Charlene Bangs Bickford, "'Public Attention Is Very Much Fixed on the Proceedings of the New Congress': The First Federal Congress Organizes Itself," in *Inventing Congress: Origins and Establishment of the First Federal Congress,* ed. Kenneth R. Bowling and Donald R. Kennon (Athens: Ohio University Press, 1999), 153–154.

5. William Maclay, *The Diary of William Maclay,* ed. Kenneth R. Bowling and Helen E. Veit (Baltimore: Johns Hopkins University Press, 1988), 128.

6. *DHFFC*, 2:31–35; George Washington to the United States Senate, August 22, 1789, *PGW*, 3:521–527.

7. Maclay, *The Diary of William Maclay*, 128.

8. Fergus M. Bordewich, *The First Congress: How James Madison, George Washington, and a Group of Extraordinary Men Invented the Government* (New York: Simon & Schuster, 2016), 133–135.

9. Legally, the attorney general was an inferior position, as Congress did not create a Justice Department until 1870. In Washington's administration, the attorney general acted as legal counsel for the administration. Washington, however, did not treat Edmund Randolph, his first attorney general and longtime friend, any differently than the other secretaries. For the sake of brevity and in the spirit of equality demonstrated in Washington's cabinet meetings, I will refer to the three department secretaries and the attorney general as "the department secretaries" moving forward.

10. For a few examples, see Kathleen Bartoloni-Tuazon, *For Fear of an Elective King: George Washington and the Presidential Title Controversy of 1789* (Ithaca, NY: Cornell University Press, 2014); John Ferling, *Jefferson and Hamilton: The Rivalry That Forged a Nation* (New York: Bloomsbury Press, 2013).

11. Henry Barrett Learned, *The President's Cabinet: Studies in the Origin, Formation and Structure of an American Institution* (New Haven, CT: Yale University Press, 1912); Carol Berkin, *A Sovereign People: The Crises of the 1790s and the Birth of American Nationalism* (New York: Basic Books, 2017); William Hogeland, *The Whiskey Rebellion: George Washington, Alexander Hamilton, and the Frontier Rebels Who Challenged America's Newfound Sovereignty* (New York: Simon & Schuster, 2010); Todd Estes, *The Jay Treaty Debate, Public Opinion, and the Evolution of American Political Culture* (Amherst: University of Massachusetts Press, 2008).

12. Joanne Freeman, *Affairs of Honor: National Politics in the New Republic* (New Haven, CT: Yale University Press, 2001); James Sterling Young, *The Washington Community, 1800–1828* (New York: Columbia University Press, 1966), 141–150; Bartoloni-Tuazon, *For Fear of an Elective King*.

13. Catherine Allgor, *Parlor Politics: In Which the Ladies of Washington Help Build a City and Government* (Charlottesville: University Press of Virginia, 2000); David S. Shields and Fredrika J. Teute, "The Republican Court and the Historiography of a Women's Domain in the Public Sphere"; "The Court of Abigail Adams"; "Jefferson in Washington: Domesticating Manners in the Republican Court," *Journal of the Early Republic* 35 (Summer 2015): 169–183, 228–235, 238–259. For an example of work that builds off Shields and Teute, see Amy Hudson Henderson, "Material Matters: Reading the Chairs of the Republican Court," *Journal of the Early Republic* 35 (Summer 2015): 287–294.

14. Gautham Rao, *National Duties: Custom Houses and the Making of the American State* (Chicago: University of Chicago Press, 2016); Max Edling, *Hercules in the Cradle: War, Money, and the American State, 1783–1867* (Chicago: University of Chicago Press, 2014). See also the articles on the state by Ariel Ron, Gautham Rao, Hannah Farber, Ryan Quintana, Rachel St. John, Stephen Skowronek, and Richard R. John in *Journal of the Early Republic* 38, no. 1 (Spring 2018): 61–118.

15. On the "executive turn," see, for example, Saladin M. Ambar, *How Governors Built the Modern Presidency* (Philadelphia: University of Pennsylvania Press, 2012); Ari Hoogenboom, *Rutherford B. Hayes: Warrior and President* (Lawrence: University of Kansas Press, 1995); Arthur M. Schlesinger Jr., *The Imperial Presidency* (New York: Houghton Mifflin, 1973); Woodrow Wilson, *Constitutional Government in the United States* (New York: Columbia University Press, 1908). For studies that situate the modern presidency within other parts of the state, see Richard Bensel,

Yankee Leviathan: The Origins of Central State Authority in America, 1859–1977 (Cambridge, UK: Cambridge University Press, 1990); Stephen Skowronek, *Building a New American State: The Expansion of National Administrative Capacities, 1877–1920* (Cambridge, UK: Cambridge University Press, 1982); Daniel P. Carpenter, "The Multiple and Material Legacies of Stephen Skowronek," *Social Science History* 27, no. 3 (2003): 465–474; William J. Novak, "The Myth of the Weak American State," *American Historical Review* 113, no. 3 (2008): 752–772.

1 · Forged in War

1. "Journey to the French Commandant: Narrative," *Diaries*, 1:130–161.

2. "Expedition to the Ohio: Narrative," *The Diaries of George Washington*, 1:174–210.

3. "Early Military Career," George Washington: A National Treasure, Smithsonian Institution, https://www.georgewashington.si.edu/life/chrono_military.html, accessed July 4, 2019.

4. "May 1775," *Diaries*, 3:325–332.

5. John Adams to Abigail Adams, May 29, 1775, *The Adams Papers*, Adams Family Correspondence, 1:207–208.

6. "Commission from the Continental Congress, 19 June 1775," *PGW*, Revolutionary War Series, 1:6–8.

7. David Hackett Fischer, *Washington's Crossing* (Oxford: Oxford University Press, 2006), 310–319; Edward G. Lengel, *General George Washington: A Military Life* (New York: Random House, 2005), 118–123.

8. "Instructions from the Continental Congress, 22 June 1775," *PGW*, Revolutionary War Series, 1:21–23.

9. "Instructions from the Continental Congress, 22 June 1775," *PGW*, Revolutionary War Series, 1:21–23.

10. Don Higginbotham, *The War of American Independence* (New York: Macmillan Press, 1971), 211; Lengel, *General George Washington,* 164–167.

11. John Adams to Abigail Adams, April 6, 1777, *The Adams Papers,* Adams Family Correspondence, 2:199–201.

12. "Council of War, 8 October 1775," *PGW*, Revolutionary War Series, 2:123–128.

13. Lengel, *General George Washington,* 110.

14. "Council of War, 18 October 1775," *PGW*, Revolutionary War Series, 2:183–184.

15. "Council of War, 2 November 1775," *PGW*, Revolutionary War Series, 2:279–284.

16. "Instructions to Colonel Henry Knox, 16 November 1775"; Colonel Henry Knox to George Washington, December 17, 1775; Colonel Henry Knox to George Washington, January 5, 1776, *PGW*, Revolutionary War Series, 2:384–385, 563–565; 3:29–30; Thomas Fleming, *The Strategy of Victory: How General George Washington Won the American Revolution* (New York: Da Capo Press, 2017), 19.

17. Council of War, February 16, 1776, *PGW*, Revolutionary War Series, 3:320–324; Dave Richard Palmer, *The Way of the Fox* (Westport, CT: Greenwood Press, 1975), 108; Robert Middlekauff, *Washington's Revolution: The Making of America's First Leader* (New York: Alfred A. Knopf, 2015), 108–111; Higginbotham, *The War of American Independence,* 98–106; Stephen Brumwell, *George Washington: Gentleman Warrior* (New York: Quercus, 2012), 218–225.

18. General Howe to the Earl of Dartmouth, November 26, 1775, *Documents in the American Revolution,* ed. K. G. Davies (Dublin: Irish University Press, 1972–1981), 11:193, cited in John Ferling, *The Ascent of George Washington: The Hidden Political Genius of an American Icon* (New York: Bloomsbury Press, 2009), 100–101.

19. George Washington to John Hancock, March 19, 1776, *PGW*, Revolutionary War Series, 3:489–491.

20. John Hancock to George Washington, May 16, 1776, *PGW*, Revolutionary War Series, 4:312–313; Fleming, *The Strategy of Victory*, 25–39. Chapter 7 of Brumwell, *George Washington: Gentleman Warrior* offers a thorough overview of the New York campaign.

21. George Washington to John Hancock, May 20, 1776, *PGW*, Revolutionary War Series, 4:346.

22. Higginbotham, *The War of American Independence*, 156–159; Brumwell, *George Washington: Gentleman Warrior*, chapter 7.

23. Lengel, *General George Washington*, 146–148.

24. "Council of War, 29 August 1776," *PGW*, Revolutionary War Series, 6:153–155.

25. George Washington to John Hancock, August 31, 1776, *PGW*, Revolutionary War Series, 6:177–179.

26. Lengel, *General George Washington*, 148; Arthur Lefkowitz, *George Washington's Indispensable Men* (New York: Stackpole Books, 2003), 67.

27. George Washington to John Hancock, September 16, 1776, *PGW*, Revolutionary War Series, 6:313–317.

28. George Washington to John Hancock, September 18, 1776, *PGW*, Revolutionary War Series, 6:331–337.

29. "Council of War, 16 October 1776," *PGW*, Revolutionary War Series, 6:576–577; "Council Chamber, Washington's Headquarters, Morris-Jumel Mansion," Detroit Publishing Co. [1905–1915], Library of Congress Prints and Photographs Division, LC-D4-40386.

30. Fischer, *Washington's Crossing*, 89–114.

31. Joseph Reed to Charles Lee in Lefkowitz, November 21, 1776, *George Washington's Indispensable Men*, 86.

32. "Council of War, 12 September 1776," *PGW*, Revolutionary War Series, 6:288–289.

33. Andrew Jackson O'Shaughnessy, *The Men Who Lost America: British Leadership, the American Revolution, and the Fate of the Empire* (New Haven, CT: Yale University Press, 2013), 251–252.

34. John Ferling, *Almost a Miracle: The American Victory in the War of Independence* (Oxford: Oxford University Press, 2007), 175–186; Higginbotham, *The War of American Independence*, 166–170.

35. "Bright-Douglass House, Mahlon Stacy Park, Trenton, Mercer County, NJ," Library of Congress Prints and Photographs Division, HABS, NJ, 11-TRET, 8- (sheet 3 of 5); Dorothy Troth Muir, *General Washington's Headquarters, 1775–1783* (Troy, AL: Troy State University Press, 1977).

36. Fischer, *Washington's Crossing*, 313–315.

37. General James Wilkinson, *Memoirs of My Own Times* (Philadelphia: Abraham Small, 1816), 1:139–140; Henry Knox to Mrs. Knox, January 7, 1777, in William S. Stryker, *The Battles of Trenton and Princeton* (Boston, 1898), 449; Fischer, *Washington's Crossing*, 313–315.

38. George Washington to John Hancock, January 5, 1777, *PGW*, Revolutionary War Series, 7:519–530.

39. Fischer, *Washington's Crossing*, 315–323; George Washington to John Hancock, January 5, 1777, *PGW*, Revolutionary War Series, 7:519–530; Lengel, *General George Washington*, 203–206.

40. Fischer, *Washington's Crossing*, 324–340; George Washington to John Hancock, January 5, 1777, *PGW*, Revolutionary War Series, 7:519–530.

41. Fischer, *Washington's Crossing*, 310–312.

42. Fischer, *Washington's Crossing*, 310–317.

43. George Washington to Robert Dinwiddie, April 25, 1754, *PGW*, Colonial Series, 1:87–91 n. 2 "Washington and the French & Indian War," *Digital Encyclopedia of George Washington*, https://www.mountvernon.org /george-washington/french-indian-war/washington-and-the-french -indian-war.

44. "Memorandum, 30 May–11 June 1755," *PGW*, Colonial Series, 1:293–298.

45. George Washington to John Augustine Washington, June 28–July 2, 1755, *PGW*, Colonial Series, 1:319–328.

46. "Council of War, 12 July 1776," *PGW*, Revolutionary War Series, 5:280.

47. George Washington to John Hancock, July 30, 1776, *PGW*, Revolutionary War Series, 5:517–520.

48. Major General Nathanael Greene to George Washington, November 24, 1777, *PGW*, Revolutionary War Series, 12:376–379.

49. "Council of War, 29 October 1777"; Brigadier General John Cadwalader's Plan for Attacking Philadelphia, November 24, 1777; Circular to the General Officers of the Continental Army, December 3, 1777, *PGW*, Revolutionary War Series, 12:46–49, 371–373, 506.

50. Circular to the General Officers of the Continental Army, December 3, 1777, *PGW*, Revolutionary War Series, 12:506; Brumwell, *George Washington: Gentleman Warrior*, 318–321.

51. Major General Nathanael Greene to George Washington, November 24, 1777, *PGW*, Revolutionary War Series, 12:376–379.

52. George Washington to Lieutenant Colonel Robert Hanson Harrison, January 9, 1777, *PGW*, Revolutionary War Series, 8:25–26; Lefkowitz, *George Washington's Indispensable Men*, 6–9; Fischer, *Washington's Crossing*, 17–19.

53. *PGW*, Revolutionary War Series, 1:xvii.

54. Bernard C. Steiner, *The Life and Correspondence of James McHenry, Secretary of War under Washington and Adams* (Cleveland: Burrows Brothers Company, 1907), 27n.

55. *Memoir of Lieutenant Colonel Tench Tilghman*, ed. S. A. Harrison (Albany, NY: J. Munsell, 1876), 135.

56. Mark Edward Lender and Garry Wheeler Stone, *Fatal Sunday: George Washington, the Monmouth Campaign, and the Politics of Battle* (Norman: University of Oklahoma Press, 2016), 237; Fleming, *The Strategy of Victory*, 87.

57. Lender and Stone, *Fatal Sunday*, 285.

58. Lender and Stone, *Fatal Sunday*, 290–293.

59. Gerald Edward Kahler, "Gentleman of the Family: General George Washington's Aides-de-Camp and Military Secretaries," MA thesis, University of Richmond, 1997, 86.

60. Robert Hanson Harrison to President of Congress, August 27, 1776, *PGW*, Revolutionary War Series, 6:140–144; Lefkowitz, *George Washington's Indispensable Men*, 67; Ferling, *The Ascent of George Washington*, 160–163.

61. Executive Committee to George Washington, February 26, 1777, *Letters of Delegates to Congress*, 6:373–374n.

62. "Farm Structure," George Washington's Mount Vernon, Digital Encyclopedia, http://www.mountvernon.org/digital-encyclopedia/article /farm-structure, accessed December 19, 2017.

63. Brumwell, *George Washington: Gentleman Warrior*, 217, 270.

64. Lund Washington to George Washington, November 5, 1775, *PGW*, Revolutionary War Series, 2:304–308.

65. George Washington to Lund Washington, August 26, 1776, *PGW*, Revolutionary War Series, 6:135–137.

66. "Agreement with William Pearce, 23 September 1793," *PGW*, Presidential Series, 14:120–123.

67. George Washington to Robert Orme, March 15, 1755, *PGW*, Colonial Series, 1:242–245.

68. Brumwell, *George Washington: Gentleman Warrior*, 67–70; Ferling, *The Ascent of George Washington*, 27–30.

69. Steiner, *The Life and Correspondence of James McHenry*, 24.

70. Martha Washington to Mercy Otis Warren, March 7, 1778, quoted in Louise V. North, Janet M. Wedge, and Landa M. Freeman, *In the Words of Women: The Revolutionary War and the Birth of the Nation, 1765–1799* (Lanham, MD: Lexington Books, 2011), 122; Ferling, *The Ascent of George Washington*, 226.

71. Marquis de Chastellux, *Travels in North America in the Years 1780, 1781 and 1782*, ed. Howard C. Rice Jr. (Chapel Hill: University of North Carolina Press, 1963), 2:513.

72. "June 15, 1778," *New-York Journal*, quoted in North, Wedge, and Freeman, *In the Words of Women*, 121; Lefkowitz, *George Washington's Indispensable Men*, 198, 309; Middlekauff, *Washington's Revolution*, 178, 218.

73. North, Wedge, and Freeman, *In the Words of Women*, 109.

74. Ferling, *The Ascent of George Washington*, 156, 226.

75. John Trumbull, *The Autobiography of John Trumbull*, ed. Theodore Sizer (New Haven, CT: Yale University Press, 1953), 22–23.

76. Chastellux, *Travels in North America*, 1:105–110.

77. George Washington to Lieutenant Colonel Robert Hanson Harrison, January 20, 1777, *PGW*, Revolutionary War Series, 8:116–117; Ferling, *The Ascent of George Washington*, 166–168.

78. "Brigadier General John Cadwalader's Plan for Attacking Philadelphia, 24 November 1777," and Continental Congress Camp Committee to George Washington, December 10, 1777, *PGW*, Revolutionary War Series, 12:371–373, 588–589; Committee at Headquarters to Henry Laurens, December 6, 1777; Elbridge Gerry to John Adams, December 3, 1777; Elbridge Gerry to James Warren, December 12, 1777, *Letters of Members of the Continental Congress*, ed. Paul H. Smith (Washington, DC: Library of Congress, 1982), 8:374, 381, 404.

79. George Washington to Lieutenant Colonel Joseph Reed, December 15, 1775, *PGW*, Revolutionary War Series, 2:551–554; Fleming, *The Strategy of Victory*, 17–19.

80. Ferling, *The Ascent of George Washington*, 100.

81. Abigail Adams to John Adams, July 16, 1775, *The Adams Papers*, Adams Family Correspondence, 1:245–251.

82. Lefkowitz. *George Washington's Indispensable Men*, 74–75.

83. Lefkowitz, *George Washington's Indispensable Men,* 74–75; David Humphreys to Alexander Scammell, June 28, 1781, Founders Online, National Archives, http://founders.archives.gov/documents/Washington /99-01-02-06209; Ferling, *The Ascent of George Washington,* 156, 226.

84. Chastellux, *Travels in North America,* 1:105–110; Ferling, *The Ascent of George Washington,* 156, 226.

85. Lefkowitz. *George Washington's Indispensable Men,* 74–76.

86. *Journals of the Continental Congress, 1774–1789,* 1:42.

87. Edmund Cody Burnett, *The Continental Congress* (New York: W. W. Norton & Company, 1941), 218–219.

88. Henry Laurens to John Laurens, May 16, 1778, *Letters of Members of the Continental Congress,* 684–685.

89. George Washington to Henry Laurens, December 23, 1777, *PGW,* Revolutionary War Series, 12:683–687; Middlekauff, *Washington's Revolution,* 147–150; Fleming, *The Strategy of Victory,* 77, 116–117; Brumwell, *George Washington: Gentleman Soldier,* 249–252, 324; Lengel, *General George Washington,* 159–160, 175–177, 275–276, 290.

90. George Washington to Henry Laurens, December 23, 1777, *PGW,* Revolutionary War Series, 12:683–687.

91. George Washington to Continental Congress Camp Committee, January 29, 1778, *PGW,* Revolutionary War Series, 13:376–409; Fleming, *The Strategy of Victory,* 77.

92. Nathanael Greene to George Washington, May 23, 1780, Founders Online, National Archives, http://founders.archives.gov/documents/Washington /99010201834; Middlekauff, *Washington's Revolution,* 147–150; Fleming, *The Strategy of Victory,* 77, 116–117; Brumwell, *George Washington: Gentleman Soldier,* 249–252, 324; Lengel, *General George Washington,* 159–160, 175–177, 275–276, 290.

93. May 15, 1780, and August 29, 1780, *Journals of the Continental Congress,* 17:426–429, 790–792.

94. Joseph Jones to James Madison, October 2, 1780, *PJM,* Congressional Series, 2:105–109.

95. Burnett, *The Continental Congress,* 492.

96. December 15, 1780, *Journals of the Continental Congress,* 18:1154–1156; January–February 1781, 19:42–44, 123–124, 180, 203; August–October 1781, 21:851–852, 1030.

97. John Hancock to George Washington, December 22, 1775, and "I. Questions for the Committee, 18 October 1775," *PGW,* Revolutionary War Series, 2:185–190, 589–590; Continental Congress Committee on Fortifying Ports to George Washington, April 17, 1776, and Board of War to George Washington, June 21, 1776, *PGW,* Revolutionary War Series, 4:75–76, 321–322.

98. George Washington to John Sullivan, November 20, 1780, Founders Online, National Archives, Early Access document, http://founders .archives.gov/documents/Washington/99-01-02-04002, accessed August 14, 2017.

99. Middlekauff, *Washington's Revolution,* 147–150; Fleming, *The Strategy of Victory,* 77, 116–117; Brumwell, *George Washington: Gentleman Soldier,* 249–252, 324; Lengel, *General George Washington,* 159–160, 175–177, 275–276, 290.

100. "Diary: November 26, 1781," "Diary: November 30, 1781," *The Papers of Robert Morris, 1781–1784,* ed. E. James Ferguson et al. (Pittsburgh: University of Pittsburgh Press, 1977), 3:253, 303.

101. "Diary: December 3, 1782," *The Papers of Robert Morris, 1781–1784,* 3:317.

102. "Diary: February 18, 25, 1782," *The Papers of Robert Morris,* 4:249, 300.

103. George Washington to Benjamin Lincoln, December 30, 1781, Founders Online, National Archives, Early Access document, http://founders .archives.gov/documents/Washington/99-01-02-07609, accessed August 9, 2017.

104. George Washington to Nathanael Greene, December 15, 1781, Founders Online, National Archives, Early Access document, http://founders.archives.gov/documents/Washington/99-01-02-07535, accessed August 9, 2017.

105. Alexander Hamilton, "Federalist No. 74," *The Federalist Papers*, ed. Clinton Rossiter (New York: New American Library, 1961), 447.

106. James Madison, *Notes of Debates in the Federal Convention of 1787* (New York: W. W. Norton & Company, 1987), 485–488.

107. "20 May 1789," *Gazette of the United States*, in Linda Grant de Pauw, ed., *Documentary History of the First Federal Congress of the United States of America* (Baltimore: Johns Hopkins University Press, 1974), 10:720–721.

108. *Annals of Congress*, 1st Cong., 1st sess., 76.

2 · *The Original Team of Rivals*

1. For just a few examples, see William Hogeland, *Founding Finance: How Debt, Speculation, Foreclosures, Protects, and Crackdowns Made Us a Nation* (Austin: University of Texas Press, 2012); Stephen F. Knott and Tony Williams, *Washington and Hamilton: The Alliance That Forged America* (New York: Sourcebooks, 2015); Kate Elizabeth Brown, *Alexander Hamilton and the Development of American Law* (Lawrence: University Press of Kansas, 2017); John Ferling, *Jefferson and Hamilton: The Rivalry That Forged a Nation* (New York: Bloomsbury Press, 2013).

2. *Journals of the Continental Congress*, 10:144.

3. Brigadier General Henry Knox to George Washington, June 15, 1778, *PGW*, Revolutionary War Series, 15:401–402; E. Wayne Carp, *To Starve the Army at Pleasure: Continental Army Administration and American Political Culture, 1775–1783* (Chapel Hill: University of North Carolina Press, 1984), 33–75.

4. Brigadier General Henry Knox to George Washington, December 30, 1778, *PGW*, Revolutionary War Series, 18:532–533.

5. Harry M. Ward, *The Department of War, 1781–1795* (Pittsburgh: University of Pittsburgh Press, 1962), 5–6.

6. North Callahan, *Henry Knox: General Washington's General* (New York: Rinehart, 1958), 191.

7. Henry Knox to Robert Morris, February 21, 1783, *The Papers of Robert Morris, 1781–1784,* ed. E. James Ferguson et al. (Pittsburgh: University of Pittsburgh Press, 1977), 7:448–449.

8. Tom Cutterham, *Gentlemen Revolutionaries: Power and Justice in the New American Republic* (Princeton, NJ: Princeton University Press, 2017), 22–23.

9. "Rough Draft of Society to Be Formed etc.," April 15, 1783, Knox Papers, Massachusetts Historical Society, Boston.

10. Henry Knox to George Washington, March 24, 1785, *PGW,* Confederation Series, 2:458–460; Ward, *The Department of War,* 49–54.

11. Ward, *The Department of War,* 53–54.

12. Ward, *The Department of War,* 56; George William Van Cleve, *We Have Not a Government: The Articles of Confederation and the Road to the Constitution* (Chicago: University of Chicago Press, 2017), 133–160.

13. "Report of Mr. Philip Liebert," *The St. Clair Papers: The Life and Public Services of Arthur St. Clair,* ed. William Henry Smith (Cincinnati: R. Clark, 1882), 2:17–19; Ward, *The Department of War,* 67.

14. June 19, 1786, Reports of Henry Knox, Papers of Continental Congress, 1774–1789, National Archives, 360.2.4, Vol. 151; Ward, *The Department of War,* 57.

15. *Journals of the Continental Congress,* 31:892–893; Van Cleve, *We Have Not a Government,* 214–242; Robert Middlekauff, *The Glorious Cause: The American Revolution, 1763–1789* (Oxford: Oxford University Press, 1982, 2005), 621.

16. "December Meeting. Indian Necropolis in West Medford: General Arrangement of the Militia: Cotton Mather's 'Magnalia,'" *Proceedings of the Massachusetts Historical Society* 6 (1862–1863): 361–414; Ward, *The War Department, 63.*

17. "Treaty with the Cherokee, 1785," *Indian Affairs: Laws and Treaties,* ed. Charles Joseph Kappler (Washington, DC: Government Printing Office, 1903, 57th Cong., 1st Ser.), 2:9–11.

18. Andrew Pickens to Alexander McGillivray, October 20, 1786, Andrew Pickens Papers, Huntington Library; Edmund Cody Burnett, *The Continental Congress* (New York: W. W. Norton & Company, 1941), 622–629; Van Cleve, *We Have Not a Government,* 48–73.

19. Board of Treasury to Henry Knox, June 14, 1786, Letters of Henry Knox, Papers of Continental Congress, 1774–1789, National Archives, 360.2.4, Vol. 150; Ward, *The Department of War,* 59.

20. Henry Knox to George Washington, October 23, 1786, *PGW,* Confederation Series, 4:299–302.

21. Mark Puls, *Henry Knox: Visionary General of the American Revolution* (New York: Palgrave Macmillan, 2008), 193–196.

22. Puls, *Henry Knox,* 27–28.

23. Joseph Parker Warren, "The Confederation and the Shays Rebellion," *American Historical Review* 11, no. 1 (October 1905): 46–49.

24. *Journals of the Continental Congress,* 31:892–893.

25. Cutterham, *Gentlemen Revolutionaries,* 135–136.

26. Hogeland, *Founding Finance,* 138–139.

27. Cutterham, *Gentlemen Revolutionaries,* 136–139.

28. Henry Knox to George Washington, January 18, 1790, *PGW,* Presidential Series, 5:10–15; George Washington, "December 1789," *Diaries,* 5:503–512.

29. Richard H. Kohn, "The Washington Administration's Decision to Crush the Whiskey Rebellion," *Journal of American History* 59, no. 3 (1972):

567–584; Mary K. Bonsteel Tachau, "The Whiskey Rebellion in Kentucky: A Forgotten Episode of Civil Disobedience," *Journal of the Early Republic* 2, no. 3 (1982): 239–259; Jeffrey J. Crow, "The Whiskey Rebellion in North Carolina," *North Carolina Historical Review* 66, no. 1 (1989): 1–28; Thomas P. Slaughter, *The Whiskey Rebellion: Frontier Epilogue to the American Revolution* (Oxford: Oxford University Press, 1986); William Hogeland, *The Whiskey Rebellion: George Washington, Alexander Hamilton, and the Frontier Rebels Who Challenged America's Newfound Sovereignty* (New York: Scribner, 2006).

30. George Washington to Henry Knox, October 9, 1794, *PGW*, Presidential Series, 17:43.

31. Ward, *The Department of War*, 103–112.

32. Francis D. Cogliano, *Emperor of Liberty: Thomas Jefferson's Foreign Policy* (New Haven, CT: Yale University Press, 2014), 15.

33. Kentucky was a district of Virginia until it gained statehood in 1792.

34. "Inspection of the Post," April 23, 1787, *Calendar of Virginia State Papers and Other Manuscripts*, ed. William P. Palmer (Richmond: R. U. Derr, Superintendent of Public Printing, 1884), 4:272.

35. "Report of the Condition of the Post at the Point of Fork by Edmund Randolph, Esquire," May 5, 1788, *Calendar of Virginia State Papers*, 4:434–435.

36. "A Proclamation," March 24, 1787, *Calendar of Virginia State Papers*, 4:260.

37. William Waller Hening, ed. *Statutes at Large; A Collection of All the Laws of Virginia* (Richmond: George Cochran, Printers, 1823), 12:10–17.

38. John Evans, Co. Lieut., to Gov. Ed. Randolph, January 27, 1787, *Calendar of Virginia State Papers*, 4:232.

39. Patrick Henry to the President of Congress, May 16, 1786, *Patrick Henry: Life, Correspondence and Speeches*, ed. William Wirt Henry (New York: Charles Scribner's Sons, 1891), 3:353–355.

40. Charles Frederic Hobson, "The Early Career of Edmund Randolph, 1753–1789," Ph.D. dissertation, Emory University, 1971, 234; Joseph Martin to

Governor Randolph, February 10, 1787; Arthur Campbell to Governor Edmund Randolph, March 9, 1787; Alexander Barnett, Co. Lieut., to Governor Edmund Randolph, March 26, 1787, *Calendar of Virginia State Papers,* 4:235, 254, 262–263; "5 January 1788," *Journal of the Council of the State of Virginia,* ed. George H. Reese (Richmond: Virginia State Library, 1967), 4:197–199.

41. Hobson, "The Early Career of Edmund Randolph," 236.

42. Andrew Dunscomb to Edmund Randolph, June 22, 1788, *Calendar of Virginia State Papers,* 4:459.

43. Hobson, "The Early Career of Edmund Randolph," 238–240.

44. "September 8, 1788," *Journal of the Council of the State of Virginia,* 4:363–371; Van Cleve, *We Have Not a Government,* 65–73; Burnett, *The Continental Congress,* 618–628.

45. Colonel William Davies to the Governor, May 21, 1791, *Calendar of Virginia State Papers,* 5:156–157; E. James Ferguson, *The Power of the Purse: A History of American Public Finance, 1776–1790* (Chapel Hill: University of North Carolina Press, 1961), 324.

46. Edmund Randolph to George Washington, February 12, 1791, *PGW,* Presidential Series, 7:330–31.

47. Order of Virginia Council Placing Hamilton and Others in Irons, June 16, 1779, *PTJ,* 2:292–295.

48. Order of Virginia Council Placing Hamilton and Others in Irons, June 16, 1779, *PTJ,* 2:292–295.

49. William Phillips to Thomas Jefferson, July 5, 1779, *PTJ,* 3:25–28; Michael Kranish, *Flight from Monticello: Thomas Jefferson at War* (Oxford: Oxford University Press, 2010), 105–110.

50. Enclose: Major General William Phillips to Thomas Jefferson, July 5, 1779, *PGW,* Revolutionary War Series, 21:536–540.

51. Thomas Jefferson to George Washington, July 17, 1779, *PGW,* Revolutionary War Series, 21:534–536.

52. George Washington to Thomas Jefferson, July 10, 1779, *PGW*, Revolutionary War Series, 21:419–421.

53. George Washington to Thomas Jefferson, September 13, 1779, *PTJ*, 3:86–87.

54. Thomas Jefferson to George Washington, July 17, 1779, and October 1, 1779; George Washington to Thomas Jefferson, August 6, 1779; September 13, 1779, *PGW*, Revolutionary War Series, 21:534–536, 22:53–54, 413, 414, 580–581.

55. Ithiel Town, "A Detail of Some Particular Services Performed in America (Journal of Collier and Matthew's Invasion of Virginia)," *Virginia Historical Register and Literary Notebook* 4 (October 1851): 181–195, cited in Kranish, *Flight from Monticello*, 116–117.

56. Thomas Jefferson to William Fleming, June 8, 1779, *PTJ*, 2:288–289.

57. *Journals of the Council of the State of Virginia*, ed. H. R. McIlwaine (Richmond: Virginia State Library, 1932), 2:272–273.

58. Cogliano, *Emperor of Liberty*, 36.

59. Thomas Jefferson to Richard Claiborne, January 18, 1781, *PTJ*, 4:393.

60. Thomas Jefferson to Baron von Steuben, February 16, 1781, *PTJ*, 4:633.

61. Thomas Jefferson to William Lewis, March 4, 1781, *PTJ*, 5:57; Cogliano, *Emperor of Liberty*, 35–37.

62. John Beckley to Thomas Jefferson, enclosing a Resolution of the House of Delegates, June 12, 1781, *PTJ*, 6:88–90.

63. Edmund Pendleton to George Washington, February 16, 1781, Founders Online, National Archives, http://founders.archives.gov/documents /Washington/99-01-02-04880.

64. Henry Young to William Davies, June 9, 1781, *PTJ*, 6:84–86n; Kranish, *Flight from Monticello*, 294–295; Cogliano, *Emperor of Liberty*, 26–28.

65. Cogliano, *Emperor of Liberty*, 29.

66. Thomas Jefferson, Notes on the State of Virginia, 72, Coolidge Collection of Thomas Jefferson Manuscripts, Massachusetts Historical Society, Boston, http://www.masshist.org/thomasjeffersonpapers/notes/nsvviewer.php?page=72.

67. Cogliano, *Emperor of Liberty*, 38–39.

68. Thomas Jefferson to George Washington, May 28, 1781, *PTJ*, 6:32–33.

69. Thomas Jefferson to Edmund Randolph, February 15, 1793, *PTJ*, 6:246–250.

70. LibraryThing, "George Washington," https://www.librarything.com/catalog/GeorgeWashington, accessed January 10, 2018.

71. Alexander Hamilton to George Clinton, March 12, 1778, *PAH*, 1:439–442.

72. Michael Hattem, "Newburgh Conspiracy," *Digital Encyclopedia of George Washington*, https://www.mountvernon.org/library/digitalhistory/digital-encyclopedia/article/newburgh-conspiracy.

73. Rao, *National Duties*, 59.

74. Alexander Hamilton to Robert Livingston, April 25, 1785, *PAH*, 3:608–610.

75. Hogeland, *Founding Finance*, 140.

76. "Annapolis Convention. Address of the Annapolis Convention, [September 14, 1786]," *PAH*, 3:686–690.

77. "Constitutional Convention. Plan of Government, 18 June 1787," *PAH*, 4:207–211. Christopher Collier and James Lincoln Collier, *Decision in Philadelphia: The Constitutional Convention of 1787* (New York: Ballantine Books, 2007), 76–86.

78. "Introductory Note: The Federalist [October 27, 1787–May 28, 1788]," *PAH*, 4:287–301.

79. "First Draft: First Report on the Further Provision Necessary for Establishing Public Credit [December 13, 1790]," *PAH*, 7:210–225; Hogeland, *Founding Finance*, 160–161.

80. Hogeland, *Founding Finance,* 176–182.

81. "Final Version of an Opinion on the Constitutionality of an Act to Establish a Bank [February 23, 1791]," *PAH,* 8:97–134; Hogeland, *Founding Finance,* 183–185; Gordon S. Wood, *Empire of Liberty: A History of the Early Republic, 1789–1815* (Oxford: Oxford University Press, 2009), 91–107.

82. For examples of scholarship that include these arguments, see Stanley Elkins and Eric McKitrick, *The Age of Federalism* (New York: Oxford University Press, 1993); Ferling, *Jefferson and Hamilton;* Leonard D. White, *The Federalists: A Study in Administrative History, 1789–1801* (New York: The Free Press, 1948).

83. William Bradford to James Madison, June 2, 1775, *The Papers of James Madison,* 1:148–151.

84. Ibid.

85. William Bradford to James Madison, June 3, 1776, *The Papers of James Madison,* 1:184. Evidence suggests he may have participated in the siege, but it's inconclusive.

86. David Hackett Fischer, *Washington's Crossing* (Oxford: Oxford University Press, 2006), 293–307.

87. Richard M. Ketchum, *The Winter Soldiers: The Battles for Trenton and Princeton* (New York: Holt, 1999), 361–364.

88. James Kirby Martin and Mark Edward Lender, *"A Respectable Army": The Military Origins of the Republic, 1763–1789,* 3rd ed. (New York: Wiley Blackwell, 2015), 104.

89. George Washington to Richard Peters, December 14, 1777, *PGW,* Revolutionary War Series, 12:607–609.

90. Edward Pinkowski, *Washington's Officers Slept Here: Historic Homes of Valley Forge and Its Neighborhood* (Philadelphia: Sunshine Press, 1953), 126–127.

91. Martin and Lender, *A Respectable Army,* 105.

92. William Bradford to Thomas Jefferson, November 22, 1780, *PTJ*, 4:138–141.

93. William Bradford to Thomas Jefferson, November 22, 1780, *PTJ*, 4:138–141.

94. George Washington to the United States Senate, January 24, 1794, *PGW*, Presidential Series, 15:113.

3 · Setting the Stage

1. David Golove and Daniel Hulsebosch, "A Civilized Nation: The Early American Constitution, The Law of Nations, and the Pursuit of International Recognition," *New York University Law Review* 54, no. 4 (2010): 932–1066; Eliga H. Gould, *Among the Powers of the Earth: The American Revolution and the Making of a New World Order* (Cambridge, MA: Harvard University Press, 2012).

2. Eliga Gould, *The Persistence of Empire: British Political Culture in the Age of the American Revolution* (Chapel Hill: University of North Carolina Press, 2000), 14–30; Brendan McConville, *The King's Three Faces: The Rise and Fall of Royal America, 1688–1776* (Chapel Hill: Omohundro Institute of Early American History and Culture by the University of North Carolina Press, 2006), 22; G. M. Trevelyan, *The English Revolution, 1688–1689* (Oxford: Oxford University Press, 1938), 3–98.

3. Gould, *Persistence of Empire*, 14–30; Trevelyan, *The English Revolution*, 3–98.

4. William Blackstone, *Commentaries on the Laws of England* (Oxford: Clarendon Press, 1765–1770), 1:234.

5. Jeremy Black, *George III: America's Last King* (New Haven, CT: Yale University Press, 2006); Andrew Jackson O'Shaughnessy, "'If Others Will Not Be Active, I Must Drive': George III and the American Revolution," *Early American Studies*, 2, no. 1 (2004): 1–46; Gould, *Persistence of*

Empire, 14–30; McConville, *King's Three Faces,* 17; Eric Nelson, *Royalist Revolution: Monarchy and the American Founding* (Cambridge, MA: Harvard University Press, 2014), 19–20.

6. Edmund Raymond Turner, *The Cabinet Council of England, 1622–1784* (New York: Russell & Russell, 1932), 1:7, 19–21.

7. Edmund Burke, *Thoughts on the Cause of the Present Discontents, 1770,* in Edmund Raymond Turner, *The Cabinet Council of England in the Seventeenth and Eighteenth Centuries* (Baltimore: John Hopkins University Press, 1930), 2:319–320; Saikrishna Bangalore Prakash, *Imperial from the Beginning: The Constitution of the Original Executive* (New Haven, CT: Yale University Press, 205), 39–41.

8. McConville, *King's Three Faces,* 49–50; Steven C. Bullock, *Tea Sets and Tyranny: The Politics of Politeness in Early America* (Philadelphia: University of Pennsylvania Press, 2017), 8–14; Linda Colley, *Britons: Forging the Nation, 1707–1837* (New Haven, CT: Yale University Press, 1992).

9. George Washington to Robert Dinwiddie, June 10, 1754, *PGW,* Colonial Series, 1:129–140.

10. McConville, *King's Three Faces,* 15–36.

11. McConville, *King's Three Faces,* 17, 49–50; Don Higginbotham, "War and State Formation in Revolutionary America," in *Empire and Nation: The American Revolution in the Atlantic World,* ed. Eliga H. Gould and Peter S. Onuf (Baltimore: Johns Hopkins University Press, 2005), 56–57, 61; Gould, *Persistence of Empire,* 14–30; Nick Bunker, *An Empire on Edge: How Britain Came to Fight America* (New York: Alfred A. Knopf, 2014), 13–17; Nelson, *The Royalist Revolution,* 3–22.

12. Sarah Knott, *Sensibility and the American Revolution* (Chapel Hill: University of North Carolina Press, 2009), 106.

13. Knott, *Sensibility and the American Revolution,* 23–24; McConville, *King's Three Faces,* 7–8; T. H. Breen, "'Baubles of Britain': The Amer-

ican and Consumer Revolutions of the Eighteenth Century," *Past and Present* 119, no. 1 (1988): 73–104.

14. S. Max Edelson, *The New Map of Empire: How Britain Imagined America before Independence* (Cambridge, MA: Harvard University Press, 2017), 1–196

15. Gould, *Persistence of Empire*, 109.

16. Alan Taylor, *American Revolutions* (New York: W. W. Norton, 2016), 95–115; Higginbotham, "War and State Formation in Revolutionary America," 56–59; Gould, *The Persistence of Empire*, 109–116; Bunker, *Empire on Edge*, 17–19.

17. "London, February 10," *South-Carolina Gazette*, April 5, 1770.

18. "From the General Advertiser, on Lord Mansfield," *Gazette of the State of South Carolina*, May 5, 1779.

19. Gould, *Persistence of Empire*, 109–118; Nelson, *Royalist Revolution*, 21–22; Taylor, *American Revolutions*, 114–115.

20. Gould, *Persistence of Empire*, 109–118; Robert Middlekauff, *The Glorious Cause: The American Revolution, 1763–1789* (Oxford: Oxford University Press, 1982, 2005), 56–73; Taylor, *American Revolutions*, 94–100.

21. Gould, *Among the Powers of the Earth*, 81–93, 105–106, 123–134; Taylor, *American Revolutions*, 94–100.

22. Gould, *Among the Powers of the Earth*, 81–93, 105–106, 123–134; Taylor, *American Revolutions*, 91–94.

23. "Boston, March 20," *Virginia Gazette*, April 7, 1775.

24. John Barker, *The British in Boston, Being the Diary of Lieutenant John Barker of the King's Own Regiment from November 15, 1774 to May 31, 1776* (Cambridge, MA: Harvard University Press, 1924), 40.

25. William Bradford to James Madison, July 18, 1775, *The Papers of James Madison*, 1:157–159.

26. George Washington to George William Fairfax, May 31, 1775, *PGW*, Revolutionary War Series, 10:367–68.

27. "Second Petition from Congress to the King, 8 July 1775," *PTJ*, 1:219–223.

28. In *The Royalist Revolution*, Eric Nelson argues that colonists sought a return to the absolute monarchy of the sixteenth and early seventeenth centuries. This claim ignores the colonists' deep devotion to a Protestant monarchy and the constitutional requirement for the king to convene regular legislative sessions. They just wanted their legislatures to stand on equal footing with Parliament. Colonists' ire at the king's ministers reflected their belief that the king should be responsible for policy and that the ministers had corrupted him. Nelson, *The Royalist Revolution*, 4–22.

29. Pauline Maier, *American Scripture* (New York: Alfred A. Knopf, 1997), 25.

30. *Boston News-Letter*, August 14, 1760, in McConville, *King's Three Faces*, 251, 253.

31. John Adams to John Thomas, November 13, 1775, *The Adams Papers*, Papers of John Adams, 3:293–294.

32. George Washington to the Chiefs of the Passamaquoddy Indians, December 24, 1776, *PGW*, Revolutionary War Series, 7:433–434.

33. Brigadier General William Heath to George Washington, October 21, 1775, *PGW*, Revolutionary War Series, 2:215–216n; Gould, *Persistence of Empire*, 109–134; "Baltimore, August 7," *Pennsylvania Gazette*, August 15, 1781.

34. For a few examples of these communications, see "Address from the New York Provincial Congress, 26 June 1775"; Massachusetts Committee of Safety to George Washington, July 6, 1775; Beverly Committee of Correspondence to George Washington, December 11, 1775, *PGW*, Revolutionary War Series, 1:40–41, 68–69, 2:530–531.

35. Benjamin Franklin to Samuel Cooper, March 21, 1776, *The Papers of Benjamin Franklin*, ed. William B. Willcox (New Haven, CT: Yale University Press, 1982), 22:387–388.

36. Enclosure: Poem by Phillis Wheatley, October 26, 1775, and George Washington to Phillis Wheatley, February 28, 1776, *PGW*, Revolutionary War Series, 2:242–244, 3:387.

37. George Washington to the States, June 8, 1783, *Founders Online*, National Archives, Early Access document, http://founders.archives.gov /documents/Washington/99-01-02-11404, accessed August 10, 2017; Knott, *Sensibility and the American Revolution*, 1–4.

38. Joanne Freeman, *Affairs of Honor: National Politics in the New Republic* (New Haven, CT: Yale University Press, 2001), xix.

39. George William Van Cleve, *We Have Not a Government: The Articles of Confederation and the Road to the Constitution* (Chicago: University of Chicago Press, 2017), 102–132; Edmund Cody Burnett, *The Continental Congress* (New York: W. W. Norton & Company, 1964), 613–653.

40. Van Cleve, *We Have Not a Government*, 74–101, 214–244; Burnett, *Continental Congress*, 613–653; Tom Cutterham, *Gentlemen Revolutionaries: Power and Justice in the New American Republic* (Princeton, NJ: Princeton University Press, 2017), 123–142.

41. Van Cleve, *We Have Not a Government*, 133–187; Merrill Jensen, *The Articles of Confederation* (Madison: University of Wisconsin Press, 1966), 198–224; Burnett, *Continental Congress*, 613–653.

42. John Adams to William Stephens Smith, December 26, 1787, Founders Online, National Archives, Early Access document, http://founders .archives.gov/documents/Adams/99-02-02-0298, accessed August 15, 2017.

43. Jack N. Rakove, *A Politician Thinking: The Creative Mind of James Madison* (Norman: University of Oklahoma Press, 2017), 66; Gordon S. Wood, *The Creation of the American Republic, 1776–1787* (Chapel Hill: University of North Carolina Press, 1969), 66, 92, 123.

44. John Jay to George Washington, March 16, 1786, *PGW*, Confederation Series, 3:601–602.

45. Van Cleve, *We Have Not a Government,* 245–278; Burnett, *Continental Congress,* 654–668; Cutterham, *Gentlemen Revolutionaries,* 143–147.

46. George Washington to James Madison, November 18, 1786, and December 16, 1786, *PGW,* Confederation Series, 4:382–383, 457–459.

47. George Washington David Humphreys, December 26, 1786, *PGW,* Confederation Series, 4:477–81.

48. George Washington to Henry Knox, February 3, 1787; George Washington to James Madison, March 31, 1787; George Washington to Henry Knox, April 2, 1787, *PGW,* Confederation Series, 5:7–9, 114–117, 119–121; Van Cleve, *We Have Not a Government,* 245–278; Pauline Maier, *Ratification: The People Debate the Constitution, 1787–1788* (New York: Simon & Schuster, 2010), 1–29.

49. George Washington to Henry Knox, April 27, 1787, *PGW,* Confederation Series, 5:157–159.

50. [May 1787], *Diaries,* 5:147–164; Van Cleve, *We Have Not a Government,* 245–278; Maier, *Ratification,* 1–29.

51. Rhode Island refused to send delegates to the Federal Constitutional Convention in Philadelphia.

52. This was how many Americans viewed the relationship between the king's council and the king. In reality, George III agreed with the measures passed by Parliament and eagerly pursued war against the colonies.

53. US Const., Art. I, Sec. 6.

54. US Const., Art. II, Sec. 1.

55. Prakash, *Imperial from the Beginning,* 37–40, 48–53; Christopher Collier and James Lincoln Collier, *Decision in Philadelphia: The Constitutional Convention of 1787* (New York: Ballantine Books, 1986), 274–311; David O. Stewart, *The Summer of 1787: The Men Who Invented the Constitution* (New York: Simon & Schuster, 2007), 151–162, 207–217.

56. James Madison, *Journal of the Federal Convention,* ed. E. H. Scott (Chicago: Scott, Foresman and Co., 1898), 1:101.

57. Madison, *Journal*, 2:684.

58. *The Records of the Federal Convention of 1787*, ed. Max Farrand (New Haven, CT: Yale University Press, 1911), 203; Edward J. Larson, *The Return of George Washington: United the States, 1783–1789* (New York: HarperCollins, 2014), 140–142; Collier and Collier, *Decision in Philadelphia*, 274–278; Thomas E. Cronin, "On the Origins and Invention of the Presidency," *Presidential Studies Quarterly* 17, no. 2 (Spring 1987): 230–231.

59. "The Virginia Resolutions, 29 May 1787, Charles Pinckney's Plan, 29 May 1787," *DHRC*, 1:243–247; Mary Sarah Bilder, *Madison's Hand: Revising the Constitutional Convention* (Cambridge, MA: Harvard University Press, 2015), 59, 71–74, 84, 119; R. Gordon Hoxie, "The Presidency in the Constitutional Convention," *Presidential Studies Quarterly* 15, no. 1 (Winter 1985): 27–28; R. Gordon Hoxie, "The Cabinet in the American Presidency, 1789–1984," *Presidential Studies Quarterly* 14, no. 2 (Spring 1984): 209–210.

60. Bilder, *Madison's Hand*, 59, 71–74, 84, 119; Prakash, *Imperial from the Beginning*, 39–42.

61. James Madison, *Notes of Debates in the Federal Convention of 1787* (New York: W. W. Norton & Company, Inc., 1966), 596–601. No notes exist to document the proceedings of the Committee of Postponed Matters. On September 7, Gouverneur Morris rejected an amendment to include a council and cites the committee's deliberations on the issue. Morris served on the Committee of Postponed Matters but not on the Committee of Detail, so he must have been referencing the Committee of Postponed Matters meetings that took place from August 6 to August 31. Larson, *Return of George Washington*, 161–167; Bilder, *Madison's Hand*, 144–145; Hoxie, "The President in the Constitutional Convention," 29–30.

62. Madison, *Notes of Debates*, 596–601; Bilder, *Madison's Hand*, 226.

63. US Const., Art. 2, Sec. 2, cl. 1–2.

64. [James Iredell], "Marcus II," February 20–March 19, 1780, *Norfolk and Portsmouth Journal*, in *The Debate on the Constitution*, ed. Bernard Bailyn

(New York: Library of America, 1993), 1:371–378; Prakash, *Imperial from the Beginning,* 39–42.

65. US Const., Art. 2, Sec. 2, cl. 1–2.

66. Collier and Collier, *Decision in Philadelphia,* 293–311; Hoxie, "The Cabinet in the American Presidency," 212.

67. "June 1787," *Diaries,* 5:164–172; Larson, *Return of George Washington,* 137–139, 140; Stewart, *Summer of 1787,* 30–45.

68. Van Cleve, *We Have Not a Government,* 248–275; Maier, *Ratification,* 3–26.

69. *The Documentary History of the Ratification of the Constitution Digital Edition,* ed. John P. Kaminski, Gaspare J. Saladino, Richard Leffler, Charles H. Schoenleber, and Margaret A. Hogan (Charlottesville: University of Virginia Press, 2009), http://rotunda.upress.virginia.edu/founders/RNCN -02-02-02-0003-0003, accessed August 11, 2017; Maier, *Ratification,* 45–48, 57, 118–119, 235, 280–281, 286, 308, 371, 392, 416, 417.

70. "Federal Farmer: An Additional Number of Letters to the Republican," Letter VIII, January 3, 1788, *New York Journal,* May 2, 1788, in *DHRC,* 8:324.

71. "Americanus II," December 19, 1787, *Virginia Independent Chronicle* in *DHRC,* 8:244–246; Maier, *Ratification,* 45–48, 57, 118–119, 235, 280–281, 286, 308, 371, 392, 416, 417.

72. "Marcus II," *DHRC,* 16:243–246.

73. Alexander Hamilton, *The Federalist Papers: No. 70,* Avalon Project, Yale Law School, http://avalon.law.yale.edu/18th_century/fed70.asp.

74. George Washington to Benjamin Lincoln, January 31, 1788, *PGW,* Confederation Series, 6:73–75.

75. Larson, *Return of George Washington,* 177–233; Adrienne M. Harrison. *A Powerful Mind: The Self-Education of George Washington* (Lincoln: University of Nebraska Press, 2015), 151–158.

76. The George Washington Financial Papers Project, Ledger B, 228, 244, http://financial.gwpapers.org/?q=content/ledger-b-1772-1793-pg244,

accessed August 15, 2017; Inventory and Appraisement of the Estate of Genl. George Washington Deceased, entered 20 August 1810, http:// chnm.gmu.edu/probateinventory/document.php?estateID=323.

77. David Humphreys, *Life of General Washington,* ed. Rosemarie Zagarri (Athens: University of Georgia Press, 2006), 44.

78. George Washington to Benjamin Lincoln, January 31, 1788, *PGW,* Confederation Series, 6:73–75.

79. George Washington, "March 1, 1788," *Diaries,* 5:281; Larson, *Return of George Washington,* 177–233; Harrison, *Powerful Mind,* 151–158.

80. George Washington to Benjamin Harrison, September 24, 1787, *PGW,* Confederation Series, 5:339. Washington sent similar letters to Patrick Henry, Thomas Nelson, and Thomas Jefferson.

81. George Washington to David Stuart, October 17, 1787, *PGW,* Confederation Series, 5:379–380.

82. George Washington to David Stuart, November 5, 1787, *PGW,* Confederation Series, 5:411–413; Larson, *Return of George Washington,* 201–233; Harrison, *Powerful Mind,* 151–158.

83. John Jay, "Address to the People of N.Y.," *Pamphlets on the Constitution of the United States, Published during Its Discussion by the People, 1787–1788,* ed. Paul Leicester Ford (Brooklyn, NY, 1888), 4–19; George Washington to John Jay, May 15, 1788, *PGW,* Confederation Series, 6:275–276.

84. John Jay "Address to the People of N.Y.," 4–19; George Washington to John Jay, May 15, 1788, *PGW,* Confederation Series, 6:275–276; Larson, *Return of George Washington,* 201–233; Harrison, *A Powerful Mind,* 151–158.

85. George Washington to Charles Cotesworth Pinckney, June 28, 1788, *PGW,* Confederation Series, 6:360–62.

86. *Annals of Congress,* 1st Cong., 1st Sess., 17.

87. George Washington to John Langdon, April 14, 1789, *PGW,* Presidential Series, 2:54.

88. Knowing that he would have to return to public life, Washington had asked Henry Knox to find him a high-quality American homespun suit that he could wear to his inauguration. George Washington to Henry Knox, March 2, 1789, *PGW*, Presidential Series, 1:353–354.

89. "President-Elect George Washington's Journey to the Inauguration," George Washington's Mount Vernon, http://www.mountvernon.org /george-washington/the-first-president/inauguration; Larson, *Return of George Washington*, 283–287; Kathleen Bartoloni-Tuazon, *For Fear of an Elective King: George Washington and the Presidential Title Controversy of 1789* (Ithaca, NY: Cornell University Press, 2014), 50–56.

4 · The Early Years

1. George Washington to Henry Knox, April 1, 1789, *PGW*, Presidential Series, 2:2–3.

2. George Washington to Catharine Sawbridge Macaulay Graham, January 9, 1790, *PGW*, Presidential Series, 4:551–554.

3. Joanne Freeman, *Affairs of Honor: National Politics in the New Republic* (New Haven, CT: Yale University Press, 2001).

4. Freeman, *Affairs of Honor*, 7.

5. Mark G. Schmeller, *Invisible Sovereign: Imagining Public Opinion from the Revolution to the Reconstruction* (Baltimore: Johns Hopkins University Press, 2016), 22–53.

6. George Washington to David Stuart, July 26, 1789, *PGW*, Presidential Series, 3:321–327.

7. David Stuart to George Washington, July 14, 1789, and George Washington to David Stuart, July 26, 1789, *PGW*, Presidential Series, 3:198–204, 321–327.

8. Freeman, *Affairs of Honor*, 120–125.

9. Freeman, *Affairs of Honor*, 121.

10. Cassandra A. Good, *Founding Friendships: Friendships between Men and Women in the Early Republic* (Oxford: Oxford University Press, 2015), 108–112.

11. William Maclay, *The Diary of William Maclay,* ed. Kenneth R. Bowling and Helen E. Veit (Baltimore: Johns Hopkins University Press, 1988), xvi; Freeman, *Affairs of Honor,* 16–18.

12. George Washington, "[May 1787]," *Diaries,* 5:147–164; David O. Stewart, *The Summer of 1787: The Men Who Invented the Constitution* (New York: Simon & Schuster, 2007), 82–84.

13. Samuel K. Fore, "John Fitzgerald," *Digital Encyclopedia of George Washington,* http://www.mountvernon.org/digital-encyclopedia/article/john -fitzgerald.

14. Alexander Hamilton to William Bingham, October 10, 1789, *PAH,* 5:432–433.

15. "Enclosure: [Questions Concerning the Navigation of the Several States], [15 October 1789]," *PAH,* 5:447.

16. "Treasury Department Circular to the Collectors of the Customs, 15 October 1789," *PAH,* 5:446–447.

17. Alexander Hamilton to William Bingham, October 10, 1789, *PAH,* 5:432–433.

18. "Treasury Department Circular to the Collectors of the Customs, 17 May 1790," *PAH,* 6:418.

19. Gautham Rao, *National Duties: Custom Houses and the Making of the American State* (Chicago: University of Chicago Press, 2016), 76–81.

20. "Treasury Department Circular to the Collectors of the Customs, 18 December 1790," *PAH,* 7:368–370.

21. Rao, *National Duties,* 76–81.

22. "Treasury Department Circular to the Collectors of the Customs, 18 December 1789," *PAH,* 6:18–19.

23. James Madison to Thomas Jefferson, June 2, 1780, *PTJ,* 3:411–412.

24. In 1796, the *Aurora* published a report of cabinet deliberations that took place in April 1793. Jefferson rushed to assure Washington that he had nothing to do with the leak, indicating that he understood cabinet deliberations were to remain secret. Thomas Jefferson to George Washington, June 19, 1796, Founders Online, National Archives, Early Access Document: https://founders.archives.gov/documents/Washington/99-01-02-00633.

25. James Madison to Thomas Jefferson, March 19, 1787, *The Papers of James Madison,* 9:317–322; Mary Sarah Bilder, *Madison's Hand: Revising the Constitutional Convention* (Cambridge, MA: Harvard University Press, 2015), 202–203; Jack N. Rakove, *A Politician Thinking: The Creative Mind of James Madison* (Norman: University of Oklahoma Press, 2017), 11, 33–34, 126.

26. James Madison to Thomas Jefferson, February 14, 1790, *The Papers of James Madison,* 13:41.

27. Harlow Giles Unger, *The Last Founding Father: James Monroe and a Nation's Call to Greatness* (Philadelphia: Da Capo Press, 2009), 36–41, 53, 64–65, 70.

28. James Monroe to Thomas Jefferson, October 16, 1792, *PTJ,* 24:489–490.

29. James Monroe to Thomas Jefferson, September 7, 1794, *PTJ,* 28:145–148.

30. George Washington Financial Papers Project, Ledger B, 1772–1793, 159, http://financial.gwpapers.org/?q=content/ledger-b-1772-1793-pg159, accessed August 15, 2017.

31. Edward G. Lengel, *First Entrepreneur: How George Washington Built His—and the Nation's—Prosperity* (Philadelphia: Da Capo Press, 2016), 205–206, 240; Edward J. Larson, *The Return of George Washington: United the States, 1783–1789* (New York: HarperCollins, 2015), 59–61.

32. George Washington to John Fitzgerald and George Gilpin, January 27, 1789, *PGW,* Presidential Series, 1:257–259.

33. George Gilpin to George Washington, September 2, 1789, *PGW,* Presidential Series, 3:593–596.

34. For examples of advice from Hamilton and Jay, see Alexander Hamilton to George Washington, March 28, 1796, *PAH,* 20:83–85; John Jay to George Washington, March 6, 1795, *PGW,* Presidential Series, 17:618–627.

35. George Washington to Edmund Pendleton, September 23, 1793, *PGW,* Presidential Series, 14:124–126.

36. Harrison, *A Powerful Mind,* 13, 125, 136–137, 143, 155–157, 167.

37. George Washington to William Barton, September 7, 1788, *PGW,* Confederation Series, 6:501–503.

38. George Washington to William Barton, September 7, 1788, *PGW,* Confederation Series, 6:501–503.

39. Both Washington and the American public distinguished between private gatherings and public events. No one criticized Washington for privately socializing with his old war colleagues, but the organization received significant backlash.

40. Tom Cutterham, *Gentlemen Revolutionaries: Power and Justice in the New American Republic* (Princeton: Princeton University Press, 2017), 22–29.

41. Larson, *The Return of George Washington,* 85, 110.

42. William Barton to George Washington, August 28, 1788, and George Washington to William Barton, September 7, 1788, *PGW,* Confederation Series, 6:476–478, 501–503.

43. Kathleen Bartoloni-Tuazon, *For Fear of an Elective King: George Washington and the Presidential Title Controversy of 1789* (Ithaca, NY: Cornell University Press, 2014), 1–6.

44. Maclay, *The Diary of William Maclay,* 39–40.

45. Edmund Randolph to James Madison, September 26, 1789, *The Papers of James Madison,* 12:421; *New York Daily Gazette,* July 16, 1789.

46. George Washington to Davis Stuart, July 26, 1789, *PGW,* Presidential Series, 3:321–327.

47. George Washington to John Adams, May 10, 1789, and George Washington to John Jay, May 11, 1789, *PGW,* Presidential Series, 2:245–250,

270; Alexander Hamilton to George Washington, May 5, 1789, *PAH*, 5:335–337.

48. George Washington Parke Custis, *Recollections and Private Memoirs of Washington*, ed. John Benson Lossing (New York: Derby & Jackson, 1860), 429–430; Abigail Smith Adams to Mary Smith Cranch, July 3, 1798, Founders Online, National Archives, Early Access document, http://founders.archives.gov/documents/Adams/99-03-02-0127, accessed December 10, 2017; David Waldstreicher, *In the Midst of Perpetual Fetes: The Making of American Nationalism, 1776–1820* (Chapel Hill: University of North Carolina Press, 1992), 44, 112.

49. Richard Norton Smith, *Patriarch: George Washington and the New American Nation* (Boston: Houghton Mifflin Company, 1993), 27–29.

50. Amy Hudson Henderson, "Furnishing the Republican Court: Building and Decorating Philadelphia Homes, 1790–1800," Ph.D. diss., University of Delaware, 2008, 66–77.

51. David Shields, Fredricka Teute, and Catherine Allgor have detailed how President John Adams and First Lady Abigail Adams retained the Washingtons' social practices. Jefferson abolished the levees. Instead, he hosted weekly dinners for congressmen and dignitaries (men only), occasional large gatherings to honor the arrival of a foreign minister, and open houses twice a year. The Madisons created a middle ground between Jefferson and Washington. Madison didn't host levees, but Dolley hosted regular large gatherings for men and women. Catherine Allgor, *Parlor Politics: In Which the Ladies of Washington Help Build a City and Government* (Charlottesville: University Press of Virginia, 2000); David S. Shields and Fredrika J. Teute, "The Republican Court and the Historiography of a Women's Domain in the Public Sphere," *Journal of the Early Republic* 35 (Summer 2015): 170–171.

52. Smith, *Patriarch*, 27–29.

53. "January 1790," *Diaries*, 6:1–25.

54. S. W. Jackman, "A Young Englishman Reports on the New Nation: Edward Thornton to James Bland Burges, 1791–1793," *William and Mary Quarterly* 18, no. 1 (January 1961): 85–86, 110–111.

55. Smith, *Patriarch*, 88.

56. Abigail Adams to Mary Smith Cranch, July 12, 1789, *The Adams Papers*, Adams Family Correspondence, 8:388–391; Margaret M. O'Dwer, "A French Diplomat's View of Congress, 1790," *William and Mary Quarterly* 21, no. 3 (July 1964): 434–435; Freeman, *Affairs of Honor*, 40–45.

57. George Washington to David Stuart, June 15, 1790, *PGW*, Presidential Series, 5:523–528.

58. George Washington to John Jay, November 30, 1789, *PGW*, Presidential Series, 4:340–341.

59. "November 1789," *Diaries of George Washington*, 5:488–502; Smith, *Patriarch*, 38–39, 190–191.

60. Smith, *Patriarch*, 87–107; Waldstreicher, *In the Midst of Perpetual Fetes*, 177–124.

61. George Washington to John Hancock, October 22, 1789, *PGW*, Presidential Series, 4:214.

62. George Washington to John Hancock, October 22, 1789, *PGW*, Presidential Series, 4:214; T. H. Breen, *George Washington's Journey* (New York: Simon & Schuster, 2016), 70–72.

63. George Washington, "October 1789," *Diaries*, 5:448–488.

64. Smith, *Patriarch*, 87–107; Waldstreicher, *In the Midst of Perpetual Fetes*, 177–124.

65. Breen, *George Washington's Journey*, 74.

66. George Washington, "April 1791," *Diaries*, 6:107–125.

67. Smith, *Patriarch*, 87–107; Waldstreicher, *In the Midst of Perpetual Fetes*, 177–124.

68. George Washington, "April 1791," *Diaries*, 6:107–125.

69. Smith, *Patriarch*, 87–107; Waldstreicher, *In the Midst of Perpetual Fetes*, 177–124.

70. "Legislative Acts / Legislative Proceedings," *City Gazette or the Daily Advertiser*, May 14, 1791.

71. For Randolph's appointment to aide-de-camp, see "General Orders, 15 August 1775," *PGW*, Revolutionary War Series, 1:309–311. For an example of the openness with which Washington wrote to Hamilton, see George Washington to Alexander Hamilton, April 22, 1783, *PAH*, 3:334–337. Washington demonstrated his trust for Knox by nominating him to serve as a commissioner to negotiate with the British over prisoners of war and the settling of war claims. George Washington William Heath, September 23, 1782, Founders Online, National Archives, http://founders.archives.gov/documents/Washington/99-01-02-09566.

72. For an example of Washington and Jefferson's wartime correspondence, see George Washington to Thomas Jefferson, September 13, 1779, *PGW*, Revolutionary War Series, 22:413–414.

73. "October 1789," *Diaries*, 5:448–488.

74. Gordon S. Wood, *The Creation of the American Republic, 1776–1787* (Chapel Hill: University of North Carolina Press, 1969), 430–432, 487–491. Although the second party was founded as the Democratic-Republican Party, Thomas Jefferson, his contemporaries, and historians more frequently refer to the party as the Republicans or the Jeffersonian Republicans. For the sake of brevity and consistency, I will employ "Republicans" from this point forward to use the same terminology as the source material. This party should not be confused with the Republican Party that emerged in the 1850s, nor the Republican Party of the twenty-first century.

75. Bartoloni-Tuazon, *For Fear of an Elective King*, 1–8.

76. Christopher Collier and James Lincoln Collier, *Decision in Philadelphia: The Constitutional Convention of 1787* (New York: Ballantine Books, 1986), 243–246.

77. Richard M. Ketchum, *Saratoga: Turning Point of America's Revolutionary War* (New York: Henry Holt and Company, 1997), 265.

78. For a more detailed account of Washington's visit, revisit the introduction of the book.

79. Maclay, *The Diary of William Maclay*, 128.

80. Fergus M. Bordewich, *The First Congress: How James Madison, George Washington, ad a Group of Extraordinary Men Invented the Government* (New York: Simon & Schuster Paperbacks, 2016), 133–135.

81. Maclay, *The Diary of William Maclay*, 128–130.

82. Maclay, *The Diary of William Maclay*, 182.

83. Maclay, *The Diary of William Maclay*, 130–131.

84. Bartoloni-Tuazon, *For Fear of an Elected King*, 8–10, 142–151.

85. James Madison to George Washington, January 1, 1785; James Madison to George Washington, December 7, 1786; James Madison to George Washington, October 28, 1787, *PGW*, Confederation Series, 2:248–250; 4:448–450; 5:391–393; James Madison to George Washington, January 4, 1790, *PGW*, Presidential Series, 4:536–537; Larson, *The Return of George Washington*, 86–93; Stuart Leibiger, *Founding Friendship: George Washington, James Madison, and the Creation of the American Republic* (Charlottesville: University of Virginia Press, 1999), 58–65.

86. George Washington, "March 1785," *Diaries*, 4:96–111; James Madison to George Washington, December 24, 1786, *PGW*, Confederation Series, 4:474–476; George Washington to James Madison, May 5, 1789, *PGW*, Presidential Series, 2:216–217.

87. Bordewich, *The First Congress*, 190–191; Rakove, *A Politician Thinking*, 156–159, 164.

88. Thomas Jefferson, "Jefferson's Conversation with Washington, 10 July 1792," *PGW*, Presidential Series, 10:535–537; Stuart Leibiger, "Founding Friendship: The George Washington–James Madison Collaboration and the Creation of the American Republic," Ph.D. diss., University of North Carolina at Chapel Hill, 1995, 272–274, 305–334, 382–389.

89. "Convention Debates and Proceedings, 5 July 17888," *DHRC Digital Edition,* http://rotunda.upress.virginia.edu/founders/RNCN-02-22-02-0002-0019-0001, accessed February 19, 2016; Robert R. Livingston, "Annotation of the Constitution, 17 June–26 July 1788," *DHRC Digital Edition,* http://rotunda.upress.virginia.edu/founders/RNCN-02-23-03-0002-0003, accessed February 19, 2016.

90. "Debates, 12 December 1787," *DHRC,* 2:597–598; Stewart Jay, *Most Humble Servants: The Advisory Role of Early Judges* (New Haven, CT: Yale University Press, 1997), 8–50.

91. George Washington to John Jay, December 13, 1778, *PGW*, Revolutionary War Series, 18:404–406.

92. George Washington to John Jay, May 18, 1786, *PGW*, Confederation Series, 4:55–56.

93. George Washington to John Jay, May 15, 1788, *PGW*, Confederation Series, 6:275–276.

94. George Washington to the United States Senate, September 24, 1789, *PGW*, Presidential Series, 4:75–80.

95. Jay continued as the interim secretary for foreign affairs until the Federal Congress created the State Department on July 27, 1789. George Washington to John Jay, June 8, 1789, *PGW*, Presidential Series, 2:455.

96. George Washington to John Jay, May 11, 1789, *PGW*, Presidential Series, 2:270.

97. George Washington to John Jay, June 13, 1790, *PGW*, Presidential Series, 5:517; Jay, *Most Humble Servants,* 86–99.

98. Alexander Hamilton to John Jay, April 9, 1793, and John Jay to Alexander Hamilton, April 11, 1793, *PAH*, 14:299–300, 307–308.

99. Jay, *Most Humble Servants*, 99–103.

100. Cabinet Opinion on Foreign Vessels and Consulting the Supreme Court, July 12, 1793; The Supreme Court Justices to George Washington, July 20, 1793; Supreme Court Justices to George Washington, August 8, 1793, *PGW*, Presidential Series, 13:214–216, 256–257, 392–393.

101. George Washington to John Jay, April 15, 1794, *PGW*, Presidential Series, 15:596.

102. George Washington to the Cabinet, April 18, 1793, *PGW*, Presidential Series, 12:452–454.

5 · The Cabinet Emerges

1. Washington's military perspective led him to pursue policies that expanded presidential authority. Recently, Saikrishna Bangalore Prakash has argued that the Constitution created expansive power in the executive branch. Washington certainly interpreted the Constitution this way and used his own experience to boost the powers written down in Article II. Prakash, *Imperial from the Beginning: The Constitution of the Original Executive* (New Haven, CT: Yale University Press, 2015).

2. George Washington to Henry Knox, May 9, 1789, *PGW*, Presidential Series, 2:239.

3. George Washington to John Jay, June 8, 1789, *PGW*, Presidential Series, 2:455.

4. Thomas Jefferson, "Circular to the Heads of the Departments, 6 November 1801," *PTJ*, 35:576–578.

5. Bernard C. Steiner, *The Life and Correspondence of James McHenry, Secretary of War under Washington and Adams* (Cleveland: Burrows Brothers Company, 1907), 27n.

6. Jefferson, "Circular to the Heads of the Departments, 6 November 1801," *PTJ*, 35:576–578.

7. Henry Knox to George Washington, January 20, 1790, and George Washington to the United States Senate and House of Representatives, January 21, 1790, *PGW*, Presidential Series, 5:24–25, 32; Mark Puls, *Henry Knox: Visionary General of the American Revolution* (New York: Palgrave Macmillan, 2008), 205–208.

8. Alexander Hamilton to George Washington, September 3, 1790, *PAH*, 7:22–23.

9. George Washington to Alexander Hamilton, Thomas Jefferson, and Henry Knox, April 4, 1791, *PAH*, 8:242–243; T. H. Breen, *George Washington's Journey* (New York: Simon & Schuster, 2016), 214–217.

10. William Short to Alexander Hamilton, December 2, 1790, *PAH*, 7:175–187.

11. Alexander Hamilton to George Washington, April 14, 1791, *PAH*, 8:288–289.

12. George Washington to Alexander Hamilton, May 7, 1791, *PAH*, 8:330.

13. George Washington to Thomas Jefferson, November 25, 1791, *PGW*, Presidential Series, 9:231–232; Thomas Jefferson to George Washington, November 26, 1791, *PTJ*, 22:344–346.

14. Thomas Jefferson to George Washington, November 26, 1791, *PTJ*, 22:344–346n.

15. Henry Knox to George Washington, December 26, 1791, and George Washington to Thomas Jefferson, December 27, 1791, *PGW*, Presidential Series, 9:313–323; 332–333; Colin G. Calloway, *The Indian World of George Washington: The First President, the First Americans, and the Birth of the Nation* (Oxford: Oxford University Press, 2018), 378–396.

16. Had this bill passed, many states in the Northeast would have received additional representatives at the expense of many states in the South and West. Understandably, many southerners opposed this idea. Henry

Knox to George Washington, April 3, 1792; Alexander Hamilton to George Washington, April 4, 1792; Thomas Jefferson to George Washington, April 4, 1792; Edmund Randolph to George Washington, April 4, 1792, *PGW*, Presidential Series. 10:196–211.

17. "The First Presidential Veto, 3–5 April 1792, Editorial Note," *PGW*, Presidential Series, 10:195–196.

18. George Washington to the United States House of Representatives, April 5, 1792, *PGW*, Presidential Series, 10:213–214n.

19. Thomas Jefferson to George Washington, October 29, 1792, *PGW*, Presidential Series, 11:282–284.

20. "Notes of Cabinet Meeting on the Southern Indians and Spain, 31 October 1792," *PTJ*, 24:547–550.

21. George Washington, "Diary entry: 7 May 1790," *Diaries*, 6:75–76.

22. William Maclay, *The Diary of William Maclay*, ed. Kenneth R. Bowling and Helen E. Veit (Baltimore: Johns Hopkins University Press, 1988), 301; Francis D. Cogliano, *Emperor of Liberty: Thomas Jefferson's Foreign Policy* (New Haven, CT: Yale University Press, 2014), 77–79.

23. George Washington to the United States Senate, June 4, 1790, *PGW*, Presidential Series, 5:473–476n.

24. George Washington to the United States Senate, June 4, 1790, *PGW*, Presidential Series, 5:473–476; Cogliano, *Emperor of Liberty*, 77–79.

25. US Const., Art. II, Sect. 2, cl. 2.

26. "Conversation with Thomas Jefferson," March 23, 1790, *PGW*, Presidential Series, 5:270–272; George Washington, "March 26," *Diaries*, 6:54.

27. Thomas Jefferson to George Washington, April 24, 1790, *PGW*, Presidential Series, 5:342–346.

28. Washington, "April 27, 1790," *Diaries*, 6:68.

29. Joseph Gales, *The Debates and Proceedings in the Congress of the United States* (Washington, DC: Gales and Seaton, 1834–1856), 2:1602.

30. For scholarship on the Republican Court and gendered spaces, see Catherine Allgor, *Parlor Politics: In Which the Ladies of Washington Help Build a City and Government* (Charlottesville: University Press of Virginia, 2000); David S. Shields and Fredrika J. Teute, "The Republican Court and the Historiography of a Women's Domain in the Public Sphere," *Journal of the Early Republic* 35 (Summer 2015): 170–171; Amy Hudson Henderson, "Furnishing the Republican Court: Building and Decorating Philadelphia Homes, 1790–1800," Ph.D. diss., University of Delaware, 2008), 66–77.

31. Washington, "May 7, 1790," *Diaries*, 6:75.

32. Maclay, *The Diary of William Maclay*, 275.

33. *Senate Journal*, 1st Cong., 2nd sess., May 31, 1790, 147–148; *Journal of the Second Session of the Senate of the United States of America, 1789–1793* (Washington, DC: Gales & Seaton, 1820), 1:145; Maclay, *The Diary of William Maclay*, 275, 301.

34. Washington, "June 30, 1790," *Diaries*, 6:78–79.

35. George Washington to the United States Senate, June 4, 1790, *PGW*, Presidential Series, 5:473–476n.; *Journals of the Continental Congress*, 26:144.

36. Thomas Jefferson, "Memoranda of Consultations with the President [March 11–April 9, 1792]," *PTJ*, 23:258–265; Calloway, *The Indian World of George Washington*, 378–396.

37. Thomas Jefferson, "Memoranda of Consultations with the President [March 11–April 9, 1792]," *PTJ*, 23:258–265; Calloway, *The Indian World of George Washington*, 378–396.

38. *Journal of the House of Representatives of the United States* (Washington, DC: Gales & Seaton, 1826–), 1:561.

39. Jeffrey L. Pasley, *The Tyranny of Printers: Newspaper Politics in the Early American Republic* (Charlottesville: University of Virginia Press, 2001), 61.

40. "First Draft: First Report on the Further Provision Necessary for Establishing Public Credit [December 13, 1790]," *PAH*, 7:210–225; *House Journal*, 1st Cong. 2nd sess., January 9, 1790, 136.

41. "Final Version of the Second Report on the Further Provision Necessary for Establishing Public Credit (Report on a National Bank), 13 December 1790," *PAH*, 7:305–342; Marie Sauer Lambremont, "Rep. James Jackson of Georgia and the Establishment of the Southern States' Rights Tradition in Congress," in *Inventing Congress: Origins and Establishment of the First Federal Congress*, ed. Kenneth R. Bowling and Donald R. Kennon (Athens: Ohio University Press, 1999), 194–195; Janet A. Riesman, "Money, Credit, and Federalist Political Economy," in *Beyond Confederation: Origins of the Constitution and American National Identity*, ed. Richard Beeman, Stephen Botein, and Edward C. Carter II (Chapel Hill: University of North Carolina Press, 1987), 128–161.

42. [A Citizen], "A Review of the Revenue System in Thirteen Letters," *Independent Gazetteer*, August 6, 1794.

43. Maclay, "June 18, 1790," *The Diary of William Maclay*, 297.

44. Rachel Hope Cleves, *The Reign of Terror in America: Visions of Violence from Anti-Jacobinism to Antislavery* (Cambridge: Cambridge University Press, 2009), 58–103.

45. "Notes of a Conversation with George Washington on French Affairs, 27 December 1792," *PTJ*, 24:793–94. "Thomas Jefferson's Notes on a Conversation with Washington, 7 February 1793," *PGW*, Presidential Series, 12:105–108.

46. Alexander Hamilton, "Amicus [September 11, 1792]," *PAH*, 12:354–357.

47. Alexander Hamilton, "Amicus [September 11, 1792]," *PAH*, 12:354–357; Jeffrey L. Pasley, *The First Presidential Contest: 1796 and the Founding of American Democracy* (Lawrence: University Press of Kansas, 2013), 52–57; Richard Buel Jr., *Securing the Revolution: Ideology in American Politics, 1789–1815* (Ithaca, NY: Cornell University Press, 1972), 8–27.

48. Henry Lee to James Madison, January 8, 1792, *The Papers of James Madison*, 14:183–185.

49. Thomas Jefferson to James Monroe, April 24, 1794, *PTJ*, 28:55–56.

50. James Madison to James Monroe, September 29, 1796, *The Papers of James Madison*, 16:403–405.

51. [Notes for an Oration at Braintree, Spring 1772], *The Adams Papers, Diary and Autobiography of John Adams*, 2:56–61.

52. *Annals of Congress*, 1st Cong., 1st Sess., 635–638.

53. "Chapter XII: An Act to Establish the Treasury Department," *Public Statutes at Large of the United States of America, 1789–1873*, ed. Richard Peters (Boston: Charles C. Little and James Brown, 1845), 1:65–66.

54. George Washington to Alexander Hamilton, October 27, 1799, *PAH*, 23:573–574.

55. Thomas Jefferson to James Madison, August 3, 1793, and August 18, 1793, *The Papers of James Madison*, 15:50–51, 60–61.

56. "Notes on Alexander Hamilton's Report on Foreign Loans, [after January 4, 1793]," *PTJ*, 25:20–23.

57. "Editorial Note: Jefferson and the Giles Resolutions," *PTJ*, 25:280–292.

58. "Editorial Note: Jefferson and the Giles Resolutions," *PTJ*, 25:280–292; "II. William Branch Giles's Resolutions on the Secretary of the Treasury [February 27, 1793]," *PTJ*, 25:294–296.

59. "Fair Play," *National Gazette*, 24 July 1793; "Editorial Note: Jefferson and the Giles Resolutions," *PTJ*, 25:280–292.

60. For just a few examples, see Thomas Jefferson to George Mason, February 4, 1791; Thomas Jefferson to Robert R. Livingston, February 7, 1791; Thomas Jefferson to Henry Innes, March 13, 1791; Thomas Jefferson to Edward Rutledge, August 25, 1791, *PTJ*, 19:241–242, 542–543, 22:74.

61. Thomas Jefferson to Philip Freneau, February 28, 1791, *PTJ*, 19:351; Thomas Jefferson to James Madison, July 21, 1791, *PTJ*, 20:657–658; John Ferling, *Jefferson and Hamilton: The Rivalry That Forged a Nation* (New York: Bloomsbury Press, 2013), 223; Pasley, *The First Presidential Contest*, 52–57.

62. "I. Jefferson's Journal of the Tour [May 21–June 10, 1791]," *PTJ*, 20:453–45; Robert Troup to Alexander Hamilton, June 15, 1791, *PAH*, 8:478–479; Ferling, *Jefferson and Hamilton*, 222–223.

63. "Thomas Jefferson's Notes on a Conversation with Washington, 7 February 1793," *PGW*, Presidential Series, 12:105–108.

64. "Notes of a Conversation with George Washington, 6 August 1793," *PTJ*, 26:627–630.

65. Alexander Hamilton to Edward Carrington, May 26, 1792, *PAH*, 11:426–445; "Catullus No. III (29 September 1792)," *PAH*, 12:498–506.

66. Thomas Jefferson to George Washington, September 9, 1792, and "Thomas Jefferson's Notes on a Conversation with Washington, 7 February 1793," *PGW*, Presidential Series, 11:96–106, 12:105–108; "Notes of a Conversation with George Washington, 6 August 1793," *PTJ*, 26:627–630.

67. Thomas Jefferson, *The Complete Anas of Thomas Jefferson*, ed. Franklin B. Sawvel (New York: Round Table Press, 1903), 163.

68. James Madison to Thomas Jefferson, June 19, 1793, *The Papers of James Madison*, 15:33–34.

69. Jefferson, *Anas*, 51–53.

70. Jefferson, *Anas*, 90–93.

71. Jefferson, *Anas*, 26, 91.

72. Jefferson, *Anas*, 36–39; Joanne Freeman, *Affairs of Honor: National Politics in the New Republic* (New Haven, CT: Yale University Press, 2001), 62–104.

73. Jefferson, *Anas*, 26.

74. Freeman, *Affairs of Honor*, 62–104.

75. Beckwith recorded the conversation with Hamilton and enclosed a copy in a letter to Lord William Grenville, the British foreign secretary, on August 26, 1791.

76. "Conversation with George Beckwith, 12 August [1791]," *PAH*, 9:29–30.

77. Ferling, *Jefferson and Hamilton*, 233–235.

78. "Conversation with George Beckwith [July 15, 1790]," *PAH*, 6:497–498.

79. Alexander Hamilton, "An American No. II [August 11, 1792]," *PAH*, 12:188–193.

80. Alexander Hamilton, "An American No. I [August 4, 1792]"; "An American No. II [August 11, 1792]," *PAH*, 12:157–164, 188–193.

81. Alexander Hamilton, "Civis [September 5, 1792]"; "Catullus No. I [September 15, 1792]"; "Tully No. I [August 23, 1794]"; "The Defence No. III [July 29, 1795]," *PAH* 12:320–327, 379–385, 17:132–135, 18:513–523.

6 · A Foreign Challenge

1. George Washington to Thomas Jefferson, April 12, 1793, *PGW*, Presidential Series, 12:448–449. For the May 1787 trip, see "May 1787," *Diaries*, 5:147–164. For the April 1789 trip, see "President-Elect George Washington's Journey to the Inauguration," George Washington's Mount Vernon, http://www.mountvernon.org/george-washington/the-first-president/inauguration, accessed December 14, 2017. For the November 1790 trip, see George Washington to Tobias Lear, November 23, 1790, *PGW*, Presidential Series, 6:689–690. For the July 1795 trip, see "July 1795," *Diaries*, 6:204–205. See also T. H. Breen, *George Washington's Journey* (New York: Simon & Schuster, 2016), 148, 168–250.

2. George Washington to Elizabeth Willing Powel, March 26, 1797, Ladies Association of the Union, Mount Vernon, VA.

3. Alexander Hamilton to George Washington, April 5, 1793; George Washington to Alexander Hamilton, April 12, 1793; George Washington to Thomas Jefferson, April 12, 1793; George Washington to the Cabinet, April 18, 1793, *PGW*, Presidential Series, 12:412–413, 447–448, 452–453.

4. "The President's House in Philadelphia," Independence Hall Association, http://www.ushistory.org/presidentshouse/plans/pmhb/phi.htm; Stephen Decatur, *Private Affairs of George Washington: From the Records*

and Accounts of Tobias Lear (Boston: Houghton Mifflin Company, 1933), 170; George Washington to Clement Biddle, August 21, 1797, *PGW*, Retirement Series, 1:311–312.

5. Thomas Jefferson, *The Complete Anas of Thomas Jefferson*, ed. Franklin B. Sawvel (New York: Round Table Press, 1903), 118–119.

6. George Washington to Thomas Jefferson, April 12, 1793, *PGW*, Presidential Series, 12:448–449.

7. Alexander Hamilton to John Jay, April 9, 1793, *PAH*, 14:297–299; George Washington to the Cabinet, April 18, 1793, *PGW*, Presidential Series, 12:452–454.

8. "Neutrality Proclamation, 22 April 1793," *PGW*, Presidential Series, 12:472–474.

9. John Jay to Alexander Hamilton, April 11, 1793, *PAH*, 14:307–308; "Cabinet Opinion on Washington's Questions on Neutrality and the Alliance with France (19 April 1793)," *PTJ*, 25:570–571n.

10. Stanley Elkins and Eric McKitrick, *The Age of Federalism* (New York: Oxford University Press, 1993), 338–339.

11. "Neutrality Proclamation, 22 April 1793," *PGW*, Presidential Series, 12:472–474; Thomas Jefferson to James Madison, June 23, 1793, and August 11, 1793, *PJM*, 15:37–38, 54–56.

12. Alexander Hamilton to John Jay, April 9, 1793, *PAH*, 14:297–299.

13. George Washington to the Cabinet, April 18, 1793, *PGW*, Presidential Series, 12:452–453; Thomas Jefferson, "Minutes of a Cabinet Meeting," April 19, 1793, *PGW*, Presidential Series, 12:459; Elkins and McKitrick, *Age of Federalism*, 339–341.

14. Vincent Cronin, *Louis and Antoinette* (New York: William Morrow & Company, Inc., 1975); Henry Edgeworth in J. M. Thompson, *English Witnesses of the French Revolution* (Oxford: B. Blackwell, 1938).

15. "Cabinet Meeting. Opinion on a Proclamation of Neutrality and on Receiving the French Minister [April 19, 1793]," *PAH*, 14:328–329.

16. "Minutes of a Cabinet Meeting, 19 April 1793" and "Neutrality Proclamation, 22 April 1793," *PGW*, Presidential Series, 12:459, 472–473.

17. Abigail Adams to John Adams, December 4, 1792, *The Adams Papers*, Adams Family Correspondence, 9:333–334; Rachel Hope Cleves, *The Reign of Terror in America* (Cambridge: Cambridge University Press, 2009).

18. Thomas Jefferson to George Washington, April 28, 1793; Alexander Hamilton and Henry Knox to George Washington, May 2, 1793; Edmund Randolph to George Washington, May 6, 1793, *PGW*, Presidential Series, 12:487–488, 504, 534–547.

19. Edmund Randolph to George Washington, May 6, 1793, *PGW*, Presidential Series, 12:534–548.

20. Elkins and McKitrick, *Age of Federalism*, 68–73, 77–79, 339–341.

21. "Thomas Jefferson's Notes on a Cabinet Meeting, 6 May 1793," *PGW*, Presidential Series, 12:529–530.

22. "The Franco-American Treaty of Amity and Commerce, 6 February 1778," *The Papers of Benjamin Franklin*, ed. William B. Willcox (New Haven, CT: Yale University Press, 1986), 25:595–626; "IV. Opinion on the Treaties with France, 28 April 1793," *PTJ*, 25:608–619; Carol Berkin, *A Sovereign People: The Crises of the 1790s and the Birth of American Nationalism* (New York: Basic Books, 2017), 96–97.

23. Berkin, *A Sovereign People*, 92.

24. Berkin, *A Sovereign People*, 92; David Waldstreicher, *In the Midst of Perpetual Fetes: The Making of American Nationalism, 1776–1820* (Chapel Hill: University of North Carolina Press, 1992), 130–136.

25. *Correspondence of Clark and Genet, Selections from the Draper Collection in the Possession of the State Historical Society of Wisconsin, to Elucidate the Proposed French Expedition under George Roger Clark against Louisiana in the Years 1793–1794* (Washington, DC: Government Printing Office, 1897), 967–971; Berkin, *A Sovereign People*, 130.

26. Elkins and McKitrick, *Age of Federalism*, 342–343.

27. Berkin, *A Sovereign People*, 92.

28. Elkins and McKitrick, *Age of Federalism*, 341–342; Waldstreicher, *In the Midst of Perpetual Fetes*, 130–136.

29. Jürgen Heideking, Geneviève Fabre, and Kai Dreisbach, eds., *Celebrating Ethnicity and Nation: American Festive Culture from the Revolution to the Early Twentieth Century* (New York: Berghahn Books, 2001), 64.

30. "Memorial from George Hammond, 2 May 1793," *PTJ*, 25:637–640.

31. Stewart Jay, *Most Humble Servants: The Advisory Role of Early Judges* (New Haven, CT: Yale University Press, 1997), 126–128, 130, 138–143.

32. Jay, *Most Humble Servants*, 125–127.

33. "Opinion on the Restoration of Prizes, 16 May 1793" and "Notes on the *Citoyen Genet* and Its Prizes, 20 May 1793," *PTJ*, 26:50–52n, 71–73.

34. "Memorial from Edmond Charles Genet, 27 May 1793," *PTJ*, 26:130–131; Jay, *Most Humble Servants*, 126–128, 130, 138–143.

35. Elkins and McKitrick, *Age of Federalism*, 345–348.

36. Thomas Jefferson to Edmond Charles Genet, June 5, 1793, *PTJ*, 26:195–197.

37. John Ferling, *Almost a Miracle: The American Victory in the War of Independence* (Oxford: Oxford University Press, 2007), 278; Don Higginbotham, *The War of American Independence* (New York: Macmillan Press, 1971), 212.

38. Arthur Lefkowitz, *George Washington's Indispensable Men* (New York: Stackpole Books, 2003), 24, 50, 145–147.

39. George Washington to Patrick Henry, March 28, 1778, *PGW*, Revolutionary War Series, 14:336–337; Lefkowitz, *George Washington's Indispensable Men*, 145–147. The Conway Cabal was a group of senior officers who schemed to replace George Washington as commander in chief of the Continental Army in late 1777–early 1778. It is named for Thomas Conway, a French officer, who served as one of the ringleaders. While the cabal probably never posed a significant threat to Washington's

leadership, it served to consolidate support for General Washington in Congress and the majority of the officers in the Continental Army. Higginbotham, *The War of American Independence*, 216–222; Ferling, *Almost a Miracle*, 282–285.

40. "Enclosure: Thomas Jefferson's Notes on a Conversation with Edmond Genet, 10 July 1793," *PGW*, Presidential Series, 13:202–207.

41. Berkin, *A Sovereign People*, 118–119.

42. Jay, *Most Humble Servants*, 126–128, 130, 138–143; Elkins and McKitrick, *Age of Federalism*, 344–350.

43. "Enclosure: Thomas Jefferson's Notes on a Conversation with Edmond Genet, 10 July 1793," *PGW*, Presidential Series, 13:202–207.

44. Jefferson, *Anas*, 137–144.

45. "Dissenting Opinion on the *Little Sarah*, 8 July 1793," *PTJ*, 26:449–452; "Cabinet Opinion on the *Little Sarah*, 8 July 1793" and "Enclosure: Thomas Jefferson's Notes on a Conversation with Edmond Genet, 10 July 1793," *PGW*, Presidential Series, 13:180–185, 202–207; Berkin, *A Sovereign People*, 116–120.

46. George Washington to Thomas Jefferson, July 11, 1793, *PGW*, Presidential Series, 13:211–212.

47. Thomas Jefferson to George Washington, July 11, 1793, *PGW*, 13:212–213.

48. "Cabinet Opinion on Foreign Vessels and Consulting the Supreme Court, 12 July 1793," *PGW*, Presidential Series, 13:214–216.

49. "Notes of a Cabinet Meeting on Edmond Charles Genet, 23 July 1793," *PTJ*, 26:553–556.

50. Elkins and McKitrick, *Age of Federalism*, 358–365.

51. The American public had largely supported Genêt and the French cause when he first arrived. It wasn't until Genêt threatened to go above Washington's head, thus disrespecting the president, that public opinion turned on him. For example, "That the citizens, as well as the government of the United States, are grossly insulted by Monsieur

Genet, and his inferior officers"; Columbus, "Addressed to the Printers of the Connect Courant," *Harford Courant*, November 25, 1793, 2.

52. Berkin, *A Sovereign People*, 127.

53. Tobias Lear to Thomas Jefferson, May 14, 1793, *PGW*, 12:572; George Washington to Thomas Jefferson, May 15, 1793, and Thomas Jefferson to William Rawle, May 15, 1793, *PTJ*, 26:40–41, 45.

54. Jay, *Most Humble Servants*, 138.

55. "From a Correspondent," *National Gazette*, August 7, 1793, cited in Jay, *Most Humble Servants*, 140.

56. George Taylor Jr., "Cabinet Opinion on the Rules of Neutrality," August 3, 1793, *PGW*, Presidential Series, 13:325–326.

57. "Cabinet Opinion on the Rules of Neutrality, 3 August 1793," *PGW*, Presidential Series, 13:325–327; Elkins and McKitrick, *Age of Federalism*, 352–253.

58. *Annals of Congress*, 3rd Cong., 1st sess., 757.

59. "Notes of a Conversation with George Washington, 1 October 1792," *PTJ*, 24:433–436.

60. "Thomas Jefferson to Walter Jones, 5 March 1810," *PTJ*, Retirement Series, 2:272–274.

61. George Washington to Thomas Jefferson, July 31, 1793, *PGW*, Presidential Series, 13:309–310.

62. "Notes of Cabinet Meetings on Edmond Charles Genet and the President's Address to Congress [November 18, 1793]," *PTJ*, 27:399–401; Elkins and McKitrick, *Age of Federalism*, 368–373.

63. "Notes of Cabinet Meetings on Edmond Charles Genet and the President's Address to Congress [November 18, 1793]," *PTJ*, 27:399–401.

64. "Notes of a Conversation with George Washington, 1 October 1792," *PTJ*, 24:433–436.

65. The only record of this conversation is the notes kept by Jefferson. As such, it's important to note that his recollection of Washington's words

might not be accurate. His description of his own feelings is perhaps more important here anyway. "Thomas Jefferson's Conversation with Washington, 27 December 1792," *PGW*, Presidential Series, 11:552–55.

66. "Notes of Cabinet Meeting on the President's Address to Congress, 21 November 1793" and George Hammond to Thomas Jefferson, November 22, 1793, *PTJ*, 27:411–413, 418; Elkins and McKitrick, *Age of Federalism*, 376–378.

67. Thomas Jefferson, "Notes of a Cabinet Meeting on the President's Address and Messages to Congress, 28 November 1793," *PTJ*, 27:453–456.

68. Alexander Hamilton to George Washington, September 9, 1792, *PAH*, 12:347–350.

69. "Notes of a Conversation with George Washington, 23 May 1793," *PTJ*, 26:101–102.

70. Elkins and McKitrick, *Age of Federalism*, 358.

71. Thomas Jefferson to James Madison, May 19, 1793, *PTJ*, 26:61–63.

72. James Madison to Thomas Jefferson, June 13, 1793, *The Papers of James Madison*, Congressional Series, 15:28–30.

73. For examples, see "Proposed Rules Concerning Arming and Equipping of Vessels by Belligerents in the Port of the United States, First Version [July 29–30, 1793]," *PAH*, 15:139–141; "Cabinet Opinions on Privateers and Prizes, 5 August 1793," *PTJ*, 26:620–621.

74. "No. III to the President of the United States," *National Gazette*, June 8, 1793, in *America's Historical Newspapers Online Database*, v. II, (64), 254. Elkins and McKitrick, *Age of Federalism*, 356–359.

75. James Madison to Thomas Jefferson, June 19, 1793, *PTJ*, 26:323–324.

76. Jefferson, *Anas*, 40.

77. Oliver Wolcott to Alexander Hamilton, October 20, 1795, and "Explanation [November 11, 1795]," *PAH*, 19:364n, 400–426.

78. "Pacificus No. I [June 29, 1793]," *PAH*, 15:33–43.

79. "Pacificus No. I [June 29, 1793]," *PAH*, 15:33–43; Thomas Jefferson to James Madison, August 3, 1793, *Papers of James Madison*, 15:50–51.

80. "No Jacobin No. I [July 31, 1793]," *PAH*, 15:145–151.

81. Alexander Hamilton, "No Jacobin No. I (31 July 1793)," *PAH*, 15:145–151.

82. "For the Diary," *Daily Advertiser* (New York), August 14, 1793, in Jay, *Most Humble Servants,* 144–148.

83. Joanne Freeman, *Affairs of Honor: National Politics in the New Republic* (New Haven, CT: Yale University Press, 2001), 105–125.

84. *Anti-Slavery Papers of John Jay,* ed. Frank Monaghan (1932), 345, cited in Jay, *Most Humble Servants, 98.*

85. Edward J. Larson, *The Return of George Washington: Uniting the States, 1783–1789* (New York: William Morrow, 2014), 289; Kathleen Bartoloni-Tuazon, *For Fear of an Elective King: George Washington and the Presidential Title Controversy of 1789* (Ithaca, NY: Cornell University Press, 2014), 30–56.

86. George Washington to the United States Senate and House of Representatives, December 5, 1793, *PGW*, Presidential Series, 14:474–477.

87. "Introductory Note: To Rufus King (13 August 1793)," *PAH*, 15:233–239, cited in Jay, *Most Humble Servants,* 147.

88. *The Life and Correspondence of Rufus King,* ed. Charles R. King (New York: G. P. Putnam's Sons, 1894), 478, cited in Elkins and McKitrick, *Age of Federalism,* 372.

89. Washington's thin skin is well documented. For a few examples, see Breen, *George Washington's Journey,* 62; John Ferling, *The Ascent of George Washington: The Hidden Political Genius of an American Icon* (New York: Bloomsbury Press, 2009), 338–340, 347.

90. "Notes of Cabinet Meeting on Edmond Charles Genet, 2 August 1793," *PTJ*, 26:601–603.

91. The literature on the public's perception of Washington is vast. For a few examples, see Breen, *George Washington's Journey,* 31–40; Waldst-

reicher, *In The Midst of Perpetual Fetes,* 117–121; Bartoloni-Tuazon, *For Fear of an Elective King,* 30–56.

92. James Madison to Thomas Jefferson, June 19, 1793, *The Papers of James Madison,* 15:33–34.

93. James D. Tagg, "Benjamin Franklin Bache's Attack on George Washington," *Pennsylvania Magazine of History and Biography* 100, no. 2 (April 1976): 191–230; Jeffrey L. Pasley, *The First Presidential Contest: 1796 and the Founding of American Democracy* (Lawrence: University Press of Kansas, 2013), 140–145.

94. Edmund Pendleton to George Washington, September 11, 1793, and George Washington to Edmund Pendleton, September 23, 1793, *PGW,* Presidential Series, 14:67–71, 124–126.

95. George Washington to the United States Senate and House of Representatives, October 25, 1791, *PGW,* Presidential Series, 9:110–117.

96. "Address to the United States Senate and House of Representatives, 6 November 1792," *PGW,* Presidential Series, 11:342–351.

97. George Washington to the United States Senate and the House of Representatives, December 5, 1793, *PGW,* Presidential Series, 14:474–477.

98. George Washington to Alexander Hamilton, October 29, 1795, *PAH,* 19:355–363.

7 · A Domestic Threat

1. Max Edling, *Hercules in the Cradle: War, Money, and the American State, 1783–1867* (Chicago: University of Chicago Press, 2014), introduction n. 14.

2. Alexander Hamilton to Thomas Mifflin, September 9, 1794, *PAH,* 17:210–211.

3. Washington, *Diaries,* 6:178–179.

4. Carol Berkin, *A Sovereign People: The Crises of the 1790s and the Birth of American Nationalism* (New York: Basic Books, 2017), 15–20.

5. Jeffrey J. Crow, "The Whiskey Rebellion in North Carolina," *North Carolina Historical Review* 66, no. 1 (January 1989): 18–19.

6. Berkin, *A Sovereign People*, 21–23; Mary K. Bonsteel Tachau, "A New Look at the Whiskey Rebellion," *The Whiskey Rebellion: Past and Present Perspectives*, ed. Steven R. Boyd (Westport, CT: Greenwood Press, 1985), 97–118.

7. Mary K. Bonsteel Tachau, "The Whiskey Rebellion in Kentucky: A Forgotten Episode of Civil Disobedience," *Journal of the Early Republic* 2, no. 3 (Autumn 1982): 241–246.

8. William Bradford to George Washington, 14 July 1794, *PGW*, Presidential Series, 16:343–346; Tachau, "The Whiskey Rebellion in Kentucky," 248–249.

9. Richard H. Kohn, "The Washington Administration's Decision to Crush the Whiskey Rebellion," *Journal of American History* 59, no. 3 (December 1972): 569–570.

10. Edmund Randolph to Alexander Hamilton, September 8, 1792, *PAH*, 12:336–340; "Proclamation, 15 September 1792," *PGW*, Presidential Series, 11:122–124; Kohn, "The Washington Administration's Decision to Crush the Whiskey Rebellion," 571; Berkin, *A Sovereign People*, 35–39; Thomas P. Slaughter, *The Whiskey Rebellion: Frontier Epilogue to the American Revolution* (Oxford: Oxford University Press, 1986), 108–124.

11. Slaughter, *The Whiskey Rebellion*, 3.

12. William Hogeland, *The Whiskey Rebellion: George Washington, Alexander Hamilton, and the Frontier Rebels Who Challenged America's Newfound Sovereignty* (New York: Simon & Schuster, 2010), 185–186; Edmund Randolph to George Washington, August 5, 1794, *PGW*, Presidential Series, 16:523–530.

13. Edmund Randolph to George Washington, August 5, 1794, *PGW*, Presidential Series, 514–529.

14. For a few examples, see "Enclosure: Extract of a Letter from Kentucky, 25 January 1794," *PGW*, Presidential Series, 15:291–93. The tax

was so unpopular in Kentucky that Washington could not find anyone to fill the positions required to collect and enforce the tax. Similarly, he received extensive correspondence alerting him to unpopularity of the tax in western regions especially. For an example, see Thomas Mifflin to George Washington, April 18, 1794, *PGW*, Presidential Series, 15:612–614 n. 1.

15. Hogeland, *The Whiskey Rebellion*, 185.

16. William Hogeland, *Autumn of the Black Snake: The Creation of the U.S. Army and the Invasion that Opened the West* (New York: Farrar, Straus, and Giroux, 2017), 340–351.

17. "An Act to provide for calling forth the Militia to execute the laws of the Union, suppress insurrections and repel invasions," May 2, 1792, *Acts of the Second Congress of the United States,* 264, https://www.loc.gov/law/help/statutes-at-large/2nd-congress/c2.pdf, accessed January 26, 2018.

18. "Conference Concerning the Insurrection in Western Pennsylvania [August 2, 1794]," *PAH*, 17:9–14.

19. Edmund Randolph to George Washington, August 5, 1794, *PGW*, Presidential Series, 514–529.

20. Slaughter, *The Whiskey Rebellion*, 192–196; Hogeland, *The Whiskey Rebellion*, 185–189.

21. Thomas Mifflin to George Washington, August 5, 1794, *PGW*, Presidential Series, 16:521–522 n. 1; Alexander Hamilton to George Washington, August 2, 1794; Henry Knox to George Washington, August 4, 1794; Thomas Mifflin to George Washington, August 5, 1794; Edmund Randolph to George Washington, August 5, 1794, *PGW*, Presidential Series, 16:460–463, 467–469, 514–529.

22. Slaughter, *The Whiskey Rebellion*, 192–196; Hogeland, *The Whiskey Rebellion*, 185–189; Berkin, *A Sovereign People*, 50–55.

23. "Conference Concerning the Insurrection in Western Pennsylvania [August 2, 1794]," *PAH*, 17:9–14.

24. Hogeland, *The Whiskey Rebellion*, 185–186; Edmund Randolph to George Washington, August 5, 1794, *PGW*, Presidential Series, 16:523–530.

25. "Conference Concerning the Insurrection in Western Pennsylvania [August 2, 1794]," *PAH*, 17:9–14; Berkin, *A Sovereign People*, 49–52; Hogeland, *The Whiskey Rebellion*, 185–186; Slaughter, *The Whiskey Rebellion*, 196.

26. "Proclamation, 7 August 1794," *PGW*, Presidential Series, 16:531–537.

27. "Proclamation, 7 August 1794," *PGW*, Presidential Series, 16:531–537.

28. Slaughter, *The Whiskey Rebellion*, 196–204; Hogeland, *The Whiskey Rebellion*, 185–206; Berkin, *A Sovereign People*, 59–67; Kohn, "The Washington Administration's Decision to Crush the Whiskey Rebellion," 576–577.

29. Edmund Randolph to James Ross, Jasper Yeates, and William Bradford, August 7, 1794, *General Records of the Department of State*, Domestic Letters, 1784–1906, 7:150–155, National Archives Catalog, https://catalog.archives.gov/id/29719917, accessed January 13, 2018.

30. Alexander Hamilton to George Washington, August 2, 1794; Henry Knox to George Washington, August 4, 1794; Thomas Mifflin to George Washington, August 5, 1794; Edmund Randolph to George Washington, August 5, 1794, *PGW*, Presidential Series, 16:460–463, 467–469, 514–529.

31. Henry Knox to George Washington, August 8, 1794, *PGW*, Presidential Series, 16:539.

32. George Washington to Henry Knox, August 8, 1794, *PGW*, Presidential Series, 16:539–540.

33. Mark Puls, *Henry Knox: Visionary General of the American Revolution* (New York: Palgrave Macmillan, 2008), 220–222.

34. Henry Knox to George Washington, August 8, 1794, *PGW*, Presidential Series, 16:538–539.

35. For examples of department correspondence, see Treasury Department Circular to the Governors of the States, January 14, 1791, *PAH*, 7:426–427; "Circular to the Governors of the States, 1 March 1792," *PTJ*, 27:815; War Department Circular to the Governors of the States, August 18, 1794, *PAH*, 17:107–108; Berkin, *A Sovereign People*, 56–59.

36. Berkin, *A Sovereign People*, 56–59; Hogeland, *The Whiskey Rebellion*, 194–196.

37. Henry Knox to Thomas Mifflin, May 24, 1794, Irvine Papers, XII, 49, cited in Harry M. Tinkcom, "Presque Isle and Pennsylvania Politics, 1794," *Pennsylvania History: A Journal of Mid-Atlantic Studies* 16, no. 2 (April 1949): 100; Kohn, "The Washington Administration's Decision to Crush the Whiskey Rebellion," 572–573; Hogeland, *The Whiskey Rebellion*, 186.

38. "Cabinet Meeting. Opinion on Drafting of Militia by Governor Thomas Mifflin, 24 May 1794," *PAH* 16:426–428.

39. Thomas Mifflin to George Washington, June 14, 1794, *PGW*, Presidential Series, 16:227–233.

40. Henry Knox to Thomas Mifflin, July 21, 1794, Irvine Letters, VI, 751–752, cited in Tinkcom, "Presque Isle and Pennsylvania Politics," 111.

41. Kohn, "The Washington Administration's Decision to Crush the Whiskey Rebellion," 572–573; Hogeland, *The Whiskey Rebellion*, 186; Slaughter, *The Whiskey Rebellion*, 196–204.

42. Kohn, "The Washington Administration's Decision to Crush the Whiskey Rebellion," 575–576.

43. Thomas Mifflin to George Washington, August 5, 1794, *PGW*, Presidential Series, 16:514–519.

44. Thomas Mifflin to George Washington, August 5, 1794, *PGW*, Presidential Series, 16:514–523n.

45. Thomas Mifflin to George Washington, August 5, 1794, *PGW*, Presidential Series, 16:521n; Charles Frederic Hobson, "The Early Career of Edmund Randolph, 1753–1789," Ph.D. diss., Emory University, 1971, 234.

46. Thomas Mifflin to George Washington, August 12, 1794, *PGW*, Presidential Series, 16:553–559.

47. Alexander Hamilton to George Washington, August 15, 1794, *PAH*, 17:96–97; Hogeland, *The Whiskey Rebellion*, 194–195.

48. William Bradford to George Washington, August 17, 1794, *PGW*, Presidential Series, 16:568–571.

49. "Minutes of a Meeting Concerning the Insurrection in Western Pennsylvania, 24 August 1794," and Alexander Hamilton to Henry Lee, August 25, 1794, *PAH*, 17:135–138, 143–146.

50. Alexander Hamilton to Henry Lee, August 25, 1794, *PAH*, 17:142–146.

51. Slaughter, *The Whiskey Rebellion*, 196–197; Hogeland, *The Whiskey Rebellion*, 190–191; Berkin, *A Sovereign People*, 55–56.

52. Thomas Mifflin to George Washington, August 22, 1794, and Alexander Hamilton to George Washington, September 2, 1794, *PGW*, Presidential Series, 16:594–595, 624–631.

53. Alexander Hamilton to George Washington, September 2, 1794, *PGW*, Presidential Series, 16:624–631.

54. Alexander Hamilton to George Washington, August 5, 1794, and August 16, 1794, *PAH*, 17:24–58, 101; Alexander Hamilton to George Washington, August 15, 1794, *PGW*, Presidential Series, 16:564–566.

55. "Treasury Departments August 5, 1794," *Dunlap and Claypoole's American Daily Advertiser* (Philadelphia), August 21, 1794, 2; Hogeland, *The Whiskey Rebellion*, 195–196.

56. "Tully No. I [August 12, 1794]," "Tully No. II [August 26, 1794]," "Tully No. III [August 28, 1794]," *PAH*, 17:132–135, 148–150, 159–161.

57. "Philadelphia, Thursday, September 11," *General Advertiser* (Philadelphia), September 11, 1794, 3.

58. Edmund Randolph to Jasper Yeates, James Ross, and William Bradford, September 29, 1794, General Records of the Department of State, 1763–2002, Domestic Letters, 1784–1906, National Archives, (M-60), 7:313.

59. Edmund Randolph to Jasper Yeates and William Bradford, September 8, 1794, *General Records of the Department of State, 1763–2002*, Domestic Letters, 1784–1906, 7:277; Kohn, "The Washington Administration's Decision to Crush the Whiskey Rebellion," 579–580; Berkin, *A Sovereign People*, 61–71; Hogeland, *The Whiskey Rebellion*, 196–206.

60. Thomas Mifflin to George Washington, September 12, 1794, *PGW*, Presidential Series, 16:673–674.

61. Thomas Mifflin to George Washington, August 5, 1794, *PGW*, Presidential Series, 16:521n.

62. Thomas Jefferson to James Monroe, May 5, 1793, *PTJ*, 25:660–663.

63. Thomas Jefferson to James Madison, May 13, 1793, *PTJ*, 26:25–27.

64. Thomas Jefferson to James Monroe, May 5, 1793, *PTJ*, 25:660–663.

65. Hamilton requested Randolph's legal advice on countless issues. For a few examples, see Alexander Hamilton to Edmund Randolph, March 12, 1793, March 20, 1793, and May 10, 1793, *PAH*, 14:196–198, 224–225, 431–432.

66. Alexander Hamilton to Thomas Mifflin, September 9, 1794, *PAH*, 17:210–211.

67. Kohn, "The Washington Administration's Decision to Crush the Whiskey Rebellion," 581–584.

68. George Washington to Henry Knox, September 30, 1794, *PGW*, Presidential Series, 16:744.

69. Puls, *Henry Knox*, 220–222.

70. Washington, *Diaries*, 6:178–179.

71. "October [1794]," *Diaries*, 6:179–198.

72. "Notes on the March from September 30, until October 29, 1794," in Samuel Hazard et al., eds., *Pennsylvania Archives* (Philadelphia and Harrisburg, 1852–1949), 2d ser., 4:361, cited in "October [1794]," *Diaries*, 6: 179–198.

73. "October [1794]," *Diaries*, 6:179–198.

74. Hogeland, *The Whiskey Rebellion*, 237–238.

75. Hogeland, *The Whiskey Rebellion*, 238.

76. Hogeland, *The Whiskey Rebellion*, 224; Berkin, *A Sovereign People*, 75–80.

77. Alexander Hamilton to the President and the Directors of the Bank of the United States, August 21, 1794, *PAH*, 17:119–120.

78. Alexander Hamilton to George Gale, August 27, 1794, *PAH*, 17:150–152.

79. Slaughter, *The Whiskey Rebellion*, 224.

80. Scholarship is a bit more divided. Slaughter, *The Whiskey Rebellion*, and Hogeland, *The Whiskey Rebellion*, both characterize the military response to the rebellion as unnecessary and the product of Hamilton's overzealous desire to enforce tax collection and fulfill his military fantasies. Washington biographers, including Kohn, Ron Chernow, Richard Norton Smith, James Thomas Flexner, and John Ferling, offer a more positive assessment of the administration's handling of the rebellion. Based on the evidence, I think there is no doubt Hamilton was eager to use military force, but that doesn't mean it was the wrong course of action. In fact, establishing precedent that the federal government would enforce tax collection was critical to the financial future of the nation.

81. William Bradford to George Washington, October 17, 1794, *PGW*, Presidential Series, 17, 76–80.

82. Terry Bouton, *Taming Democracy: "The People," the Founders, and the Troubled Ending of the American Revolution* (Oxford: Oxford University Press, 2007), 241–242.

83. Hogeland, *The Whiskey Rebellion*, 215–216.

84. Thomas Jefferson to James Madison, October 30, 1794, *PTJ*, 28:182–183.

85. Thomas Jefferson to James Madison, December 28, 1794, *The Papers of James Madison*, 15:426–429.

8 · A Cabinet in Crisis

1. Fulwar Skipwith to the Secretary of State, March 7, 1794, American State Papers, Foreign Relations, I: 429.

2. Edmund Randolph to George Washington, March 2, 1794, *PGW*, Presidential Series, 15:310–316; Jerald A. Combs, *The Jay Treaty: Political Battleground of the Founding Fathers* (Berkeley: University of California Press, 1970), 120–122, 142–146; Stanley Elkins and Eric McKitrick, *The Age of Federalism* (New York: Oxford University Press, 1993), 377–392; Richard Buel Jr., *Securing the Revolution: Ideology in American Politics, 1789–1815* (Ithaca, NY: Cornell University Press, 1972), 54–56.

3. Brigadier General E.A. Cruikshank, ed. *The Correspondence of Lieut. Governor John Graves Simcoe, with Allied Documents Relating to His Administration of the Government of Upper Canada* (Toronto: Toronto Ontario Historical Society, 1923), 2:148–149.

4. George Clinton to George Washington, March 20, 1794, *PGW*, Presidential Series, 15:417–419.

5. Combs, *The Jay Treaty*, 94–104; Elkins and McKitrick, *The Age of Federalism*, 392–394; Buel, *Securing the Revolution*, 54–56.

6. George Washington to John Jay, April 15, 1794, *PGW*, Presidential Series, 15:596.

7. George Washington to the United States Senate, April 16, 1794, *PGW*, Presidential Series, 15:608–609; Combs, *The Jay Treaty*, 120–27, 142–47.

8. John Jay to George Washington, June 23, 1794, *PGW*, Presidential Series, 16:264–266.

9. *American State Papers,* Foreign Relations, 1:472–474; Todd Estes, *The Jay Treaty Debate, Public Opinion, and the Evolution of American Political Culture* (Amherst: University of Massachusetts Press, 2008), 24–29 n. 11; Elkins and McKitrick, *The Age of Federalism,* 395–403; Combs, *The Jay Treaty,* 142–152.

10. John Jay to Alexander Hamilton, July 18–August 5, 1794, *PAH,* 16:608–610.

11. Combs, *The Jay Treaty,* 148–152; Elkins and McKitrick, *Age of Federalism,* 406–414.

12. John Trumbull, *The Autobiography of Colonel John Trumbull,* ed. Theodore Sizer (New Haven, CT: Yale University Press, 1953), 181; Elkins and McKitrick, *Age of Federalism,* 406–414; Combs, *The Jay Treaty,* 142–152.

13. John Jay to George Washington, September 13, 1794, *PGW,* Presidential Series, 16:676–680; Elkins and McKitrick, *Age of Federalism,* 403–406.

14. John Jay to George Washington, November 19, 1794, *PGW,* Presidential Series, 17:173–175.

15. John Jay to Edmund Randolph, November 10, 1794, *American State Papers,* Foreign Relations, 1:503.

16. James Madison to Thomas Jefferson, August 6, 1795, *PTJ,* 28:432–434.

17. Thomas Jefferson to James Monroe, March 2, 1796, *PTJ,* 29:4–6.

18. Estes, *The Jay Treaty Debate,* 71–103.

19. *Treaty of Amity, Commerce, and Navigation between His Britannic Majesty, and the United States of America, Conditionally Ratified,* 2nd ed. (Philadelphia: Lang & Ustick for Mathew Carey, 1795). Combs, *The Jay Treaty,* 150–157; Buel, *Securing the Revolution,* 56–68.

20. George Washington to Thomas Johnson, August 24, 1795, and George Washington to Charles Cotesworth Pinckney, August 24, 1795, *PGW,* Presidential Series, 18:590–592; George Washington to Patrick Henry, October 9, 1795; George Washington Alexander Hamilton, October 29,

1795; George Washington to the US Senate, December 9, 1795, *PGW,* Presidential Series, 19:36–37, 93–99, 237–238.

21. George Washington Alexander Hamilton, August 9, 1798, *PGW,* Retirement Series, 2:500–502; Leonard D. White, *The Federalists: A Study in Administrative History, 1789–1801* (New York: The Free Press, 1948), 123–125, 147, 154.

22. Edmund Randolph to George Washington, March 2, 1795, *PGW,* Presidential Series, 17:606–607; George Washington to John Adams, March 3, 1795, *The Adams Papers,* Early Access Document, http://founders.archives .gov/documents/Adams/99-02-02-1652.

23. Edmund Randolph to George Washington, April 26, 1795, *PGW,* Presidential Series, 18:90–95.

24. James Madison to James Monroe, March 11, 1795, *PJM,* 15:487–488.

25. Edmund Randolph to John Adams, April 2, 1795, Founders Online, National Archives, http://founders.archives.gov/documents/Adams/99-02 -02-1661.

26. James Madison to James Monroe, December 20, 1795, *PJM,* 16:168–171.

27. *Annals of Congress,* Senate, 4th Congress, 4th Session, 855–856.

28. *Annals of Congress,* Senate, 4th Congress, 4th Session, 859–860; Estes, *The Jay Treaty Debate,* 29–34.

29. Hunter Miller, ed., *Treaties and Other International Acts of the United States of America* (Washington, DC: Government Printing Office, 1931), 2, http://avalon.law.yale.edu/18th_century/jay.asp#art12, accessed February 18, 2018.

30. *Annals of Congress,* Senate, 4th Congress, 4th Session, 861–862.

31. *Annals of Congress,* Senate, 4th Congress, 4th Session, 863–864; Amanda C. Demmer, "Trick or Constitutional Treaty?: The Jay Treaty and the Quarrel over the Diplomatic Separation of Powers," *Journal of the Early Republic* 35, no. 4 (Winter 2015): 586–592; Joseph Charles, "The Jay Treaty: Origins of the American Party System," *William and Mary Quarterly* 12, no. 4 (October 1955): 594–596.

32. *Annals of Congress*, Senate, 4th Congress, 4th Session, 867–868; Demmer, "Trick or Constitutional Treaty?," 586–592; Charles, "The Jay Treaty," 594–596.

33. Edmund Randolph to Rufus King, July 6, 1795, in *The Life and Correspondence of Rufus King*, ed. Charles R. King (New York: G.P. Putnam's sons, 1894–1900), 2:15; Estes, *The Jay Treaty Debate*, 34.

34. Demmer, "Trick or Constitutional Treaty?," 586–592; Charles, "The Jay Treaty," 594–596.

35. Edmund Randolph to George Washington, June 25, 1795, *PGW*, Presidential Series, 18:258–260.

36. "Notes from Edmund Randolph, 24 June 1795," *PGW*, Presidential Series 18:254–257.

37. Oliver Wolcott Jr. to George Washington, June 30, 1795, *PGW*, Presidential Series, 18:276–277; Buel, *Securing the Revolution*, 68–71; Combs, *The Jay Treaty*, 161–165.

38. William Bradford to Alexander Hamilton, July 2, 1795, *PAH*, 18:393–397; Oliver Wolcott Jr. to George Washington, June 30, 1795, *PGW*, Presidential Series, 18:276–277.

39. Edmund Randolph to George Washington, July 12, 1795, *PGW*, Presidential Series, 18:312–326; Combs, *The Jay Treaty*, 165–166.

40. George Washington to Alexander Hamilton, July 7, 1795, *PGW*, Presidential Series, 18:294–295 n. 3.

41. "Minutes of Conference with Count Wedel of Denmark, April 23, 1795," Dropmore Papers, Historical Manuscripts Commission, National Archives, 3:59; Combs, *The Jay Treaty*, 164.

42. George Hammond to Lord Grenville, April 3, 1795, Records of the British Foreign Office, The National Archives, Great Britain, 5:9; Josiah T. Newcomb, "New Light on Jay's Treaty," *American Journal of International Law* 28, no. 4 (October 1934): 685–692; Combs, *The Jay Treaty*, 161–165.

43. Edmund Randolph to George Washington, July 12, 1795, *PGW*, Presidential Series, 18:312–326; Combs, *The Jay Treaty,* 165–166.

44. Edmund Randolph, *Vindication of Edmund Randolph* (Richmond: Charles H. Wynne, 1855), 21–23; Edmund Randolph to George Washington, June 29, 1795, *PGW*, Presidential Series, 18:272–274; Combs, *The Jay Treaty,* 165–167.

45. Edmund Randolph to George Washington, February 19, 1794, *PGW*, Presidential Series, 15:252–253.

46. Alexander Hamilton to Rufus King, June 11, 1795, *PAH*, 18:370–373.

47. George Washington to Alexander Hamilton, July 3, 1795, *PAH*, 18:398–400; John Ferling, *Jefferson and Hamilton: The Rivalry That Forged a Nation* (New York: Bloomsbury Press, 2013), 272–277; Stephen F. Knott and Tony Williams, *Washington and Hamilton: The Alliance That Forged America* (New York: Sourcebooks, 2015), 202–206.

48. George Washington to Alexander Hamilton, July 13, 1795, *PAH*, 18:461–464 n 7; Ferling, *Jefferson and Hamilton,* 272–277; Knott and Williams, *Washington and Hamilton,* 202–206.

49. George Washington to Alexander Hamilton, July 14, 1795, *PGW*, Presidential Series, 18:340–341.

50. George Washington to Alexander Hamilton, July 14, 1795, *PGW*, Presidential Series, 18:340–341.

51. George Washington to Alexander Hamilton, July 29, 1795, *PAH*, 18:524–526.

52. George Washington Alexander Hamilton, July 3, 1795, *PAH*, 18:398–400.

53. George Washington to Alexander Hamilton, August 31, 1795, *PAH*, 19:204–207; Ferling, *Jefferson and Hamilton,* 272–277; Knott and Williams, *Washington and Hamilton,* 202–206.

54. Boston Citizens to George Washington, July 13, 1795, *PGW*, Presidential Series, 18:327–332. Demmer, "Trick of Constitutional Treaty?," 592–593.

55. George Washington to Boston Selectmen, July 28, 1795, *PGW*, Presidential Series, 18:441–443. Over the next several weeks, citizen organizations from several states sent Washington similar applications. Washington used his letter to the Boston Selectmen as a template to send similar replies to each group.

56. Oliver Wolcott Jr. to John Marshall, June 9, 1806, *Memoirs of the Administrations of Washington and John Adams,* ed. George Gibbs (New York: W. Van Norden, 1846), 241–246; Demmer, "Trick of Constitutional Treaty?," 592–593.

57. Timothy Pickering to George Washington, July 31, 1795, *PGW*, Presidential Series, 18:481–483 n. 3.

58. George Washington to Oliver Wolcott Jr. and Timothy Pickering, August 12–18, 1795, *PGW*, Presidential Series, 18:538–541; Irving Brant, "Edmund Randolph, Not Guilty!," *William and Mary Quarterly* 7, no. 2 (April 1950): 179–198; Charles, "The Jay Treaty: The Origins of the American Party System," 597–598; Combs, *The Jay Treaty,* 165–169.

59. George Washington to Oliver Wolcott Jr. and Timothy Pickering, August 12–18, 1795, *PGW*, Presidential Series, 18:538–541; Brant, "Edmund Randolph, Not Guilty!," 179–198.

60. Edmund Randolph to George Washington, *PGW*, Presidential Series, 16:523–530; Mary K. Bonsteel Tachau, "George Washington and the Reputation of Edmund Randolph," *Journal of American History* 73, no. 1 (June 1986): 18–34.

61. "Conference Concerning the Insurrection in Western Pennsylvania [August 2, 1794]," *PAH,* 17:9–14.

62. Tachau, "George Washington and the Reputation of Edmund Randolph," 18–24.

63. Combs, *The Jay Treaty,* 167; Tachau, "George Washington and the Reputation of Edmund Randolph," 18–25.

64. For just a few examples, see Edmund Randolph to George Washington, July 24, 1795, July 25, 1795, and July 29, 1795, *PGW*, Presidential Series, 18:414–415, 419–421, 466–468.

65. Timothy Pickering to George Washington, July 31, 1795, *PGW*, Presidential Series, 18:481–483; Combs, *The Jay Treaty*, 165–170; Tachau, "George Washington and the Reputation of Edmund Randolph," 25–26; Brant, "Edmund Randolph, Not Guilty!," 185.

66. George Washington to Burgess Ball, September 25, 1794, *PGW*, Presidential Series, 16:722–724; Tachau, "George Washington and the Reputation of Edmund Randolph," 24–25.

67. Brant, "Edmund Randolph, Not Guilty!," 180.

68. Jefferson, *The Complete Anas of Thomas Jefferson*, 165; Brant, "Edmund Randolph, Not Guilty!," 180–181.

69. Oliver Wolcott, Jr. to Alexander Hamilton, July 30, 1795, *PAH*, 18:526–532; Tachau, "George Washington and the Reputation of Edmund Randolph," 24–25.

70. Tachau, "George Washington and the Reputation of Edmund Randolph," 28–30; Brant, "Edmund Randolph, Not Guilty!," 185.

71. "Notes of Cabinet Meeting on Edmond Charles Genet, 2 August 1793," *PTJ*, 26:601–603.

72. Jefferson Thomas Jefferson, *The Complete Anas of Thomas Jefferson*, ed. Franklin B. Sawvel (New York: Round Table Press, 1903), 90–91.

73. Tachau, "George Washington and the Reputation of Edmund Randolph," 25–28.

74. George Washington to Catharine Sawbridge Macaulay Graham, January 9, 1790, *PGW*, Presidential Series, 4:551–554.

75. George Washington to Oliver Wolcott Jr. and Timothy Pickering, August 12–18, 1795, *PGW*, Presidential Series, 18:538–541; Combs, *The Jay Treaty*, 165–170; Brant, "Edmund Randolph, Not Guilty!," 181–186.

76. Randolph, *Vindication of Edmund Randolph*, 21.

77. Combs, *The Jay Treaty,* 166–168.

78. Edmund Randolph to George Washington, August 19, 1795, *PGW,* Presidential Series, 18:563–565; Brant, "Edmund Randolph, Not Guilty!," 185–186.

79. Edmund Randolph to George Washington, August 19, 1795, *PGW,* Presidential Series, 18:563–565.

80. George Washington Edmund Randolph, August 20, 1795, and August 22, 1795, *PGW,* Presidential Series, 18:571–572, 579; Brant, "Edmund Randolph, Not Guilty!," 181–186.

81. Joanne Freeman, *Affairs of Honor: National Politics in the New Republic* (New Haven, CT: Yale University Press, 2001), 66.

82. "Germantown, Sept. 15, 1795," *Philadelphia Gazette and Universal Daily Advertiser,* September 19, 1795, 3; Brant, "Edmund Randolph, Not Guilty!," 187–188.

83. Edmund Randolph to George Washington, September 21, 1795, and George Washington to Edmund Randolph, September 27, 1795, *PGW,* Presidential Series, 18:720–721, 741; Combs, *The Jay Treaty,* 165–170; Tachau, "George Washington and the Reputation of Edmund Randolph," 30–31.

84. George Washington to Edmund Randolph, October 21, 1795, George Washington Papers, Library of Congress, Series 4, General Correspondence, 2018:https://www.loc.gov/item/mgw439722, accessed February 11.

85. Randolph, *Vindication of Edmund Randolph.*

86. Thomas Jefferson to William Branch Giles, December 31, 1795, *PTJ,* 28:565–567.

87. Abigail Adams to John Adams, January 3, 1796, *The Adams Papers,* Adams Family Correspondence, 11:120–122; Combs, *The Jay Treaty,* 165–170.

88. Brant, "Edmund Randolph, Not Guilty!," 188–189; Tachau, "George Washington and the Reputation of Edmund Randolph," 31–33.

89. Brant, "Edmund Randolph, Not Guilty!," 197–198; Tachau, "George Washington and the Reputation of Edmund Randolph," 33–34.

90. Octavius Pickering, *The Life of Timothy Pickering* (Boston: Little, Brown, and Company, 1867–1873), 3:188–190; Oliver Wolcott Jr. to John Marshall, June 9, 1806, in *Memoirs of the Administrations of Washington and Adams,* 244–245.

91. Alexander Hamilton to Oliver Wolcott Jr., August 10, 1795, *PAH,* 19:111–113; Combs, *The Jay Treaty,* 165–170; Estes, *The Jay Treaty Debate,* 96–97.

92. "Introductory Note: To George Washington [March 7, 1796]," *PAH,* 20:64–68.

93. Estes, *The Jay Treaty Debate,* 96–126, 130–136.

94. Estes, *The Jay Treaty Debate,* 140–143; Demmer, "Trick of Constitutional Treaty?," 595–596; Charles, "The Jay Treaty: Origins of the American Party System," 599–605.

95. *Annals of Congress,* 4th Cong., 1st Sess., 400–401.

96. James Madison to Thomas Jefferson, March 6, 1796, *PJM,* 16:246–248.

97. *Annals of Congress,* 4th Cong., 1st Sess., 759; Charles, "The Jay Treaty: Origins of the American Party System," 599–605; Combs, *The Jay Treaty,* 176–188; Elkins and McKitrick, *Age of Federalism,* 416–436, 444–449; Estes, *The Jay Treaty Debate,* 154–181.

98. "Introductory Note: To George Washington [March 7, 1796]," *PAH,* 20:64–68.

99. Alexander Hamilton to George Washington, *PAH,* 20:68–69.

100. Washington to the Secretaries of State, Treasury, War, and the Attorney General, 25 March 1796, George Washington Papers, Series 2, Letterbooks 1754–1799, http://www.loc.gov/resource/mgw2.030.

101. James McHenry to George Washington, March 26, 1796; Oliver Wolcott Jr. to George Washington, March 26, 1796; Timothy Pickering to George Washington, March 29, 1796, *PGW,* Presidential Series, 19:627–629.

102. Charles Lee to George Washington, March 26, 1796, *PGW,* Presidential Series, 19:592–597.

103. George Washington to the United States House of Representatives, March 30, 1796, *PGW,* Presidential Series, 19:635–639.

104. George Washington to the United States House of Representatives, March 30, 1796, *PGW,* Presidential Series, 19:635–639; Estes, *The Jay Treaty Debate,* 154–181.

105. George Washington to Alexander Hamilton, March 31, 1796, *PAH,* 20:103–105.

106. *Annals of Congress,* 4th Congress, 1st Session, 1291–1292; "Introductory Note: To George Washington [March 7, 1796]," *PAH,* 20:64–68; Charles, "The Jay Treaty: Origins of the American Party System," 599–605; Combs, *The Jay Treaty,* 176–188; Elkins and McKitrick, *Age of Federalism,* 416–436, 444–449; Estes, *The Jay Treaty Debate,* 154–181.

Epilogue

1. George Washington, "Farewell Address," September 17, 1796, Library of Congress, George Washington Papers, Series 2, Letterbooks 1754–1799, 24; John Ferling. *The Ascent of George Washington: The Hidden Political Genius of an American Icon* (New York: Bloomsbury Press, 2010), 351–367.

2. Benjamin Rush to Dr. James Currie, July 26, 1796, Benjamin Rush Papers, American Philosophical Society.

3. John Adams to United States Congress, December 3, 1799, Founders Online, National Archives, http://founders.archives.gov/documents /Adams/99-02-02-4063; Oliver Wolcott Jr. to John Adams, November 18, 1799, Founders Online, National Archives, http://founders.archives .gov/documents/Adams/99-02-02-4050; Timothy Pickering to John Adams, November 20, 1799, Founders Online, National Archives, http:// founders.archives.gov/documents/Adams/99-02-02-4051.

4. John Adams to United States Congress, November 22, 1800, Founders Online, National Archives, http://founders.archives.gov/documents /Adams/99-02-02-4691; Charles Lee to John Adams, November 12, 1800, Founders Online, National Archives, http://founders.archives .gov/documents/Adams/99-02-024681; Oliver Wolcott Jr. to John Adams, November 11, 1800, Founders Online, National Archives, http:// founders.archives.gov/documents/Adams/99-02-02-4680.

5. Noble E. Cunningham Jr., *The Process of Government under Jefferson* (Princeton, NJ: Princeton University Press, 1978), 74–75; "XII. Robert Smith's Remarks on the Draft Message, [on or before November 21, 1801]," and "XIII. Fair Copy, First Annual Message [by November 27, 1801]," *PTJ*, 35:638–650; Dumas Malone, *Jefferson the President, First Term, 1801–1805* (Boston: Little, Brown, and Company, 1970), 96–100.

6. John Adams to Abigail Adams, November 28, 1798, Massachusetts Historical Society, http://www.masshist.org/digitaladams/archive/popup ?id=L17981128ja&page=L17981128ja_2.

7. Thomas Jefferson to Albert Gallatin, June 3, 1801, *PTJ*, 34:242; Malone, *Jefferson the President, First Term*, 50–66; Cunningham, *The Process of Government under Jefferson*, 60–71.

8. John Adams to Timothy Pickering, March 14, 1797, Founders Online, National Archives, http://founders.archives.gov/documents/Adams/99 -02-02-1893.

9. Notes on Pinckney Case, March 19, 1797, Founders Online, National Archives, http://founders.archives.gov/documents/Adams/99-02-02-1895.

10. Questions about French Grounds for Dissatisfaction, April 5, 1797, Founders Online, National Archives, http://founders.archives.gov /documents/Adams/99-02-02-1924.

11. Oliver Wolcott Jr. to John Adams, April 21, 1797, Founders Online, National Archives, http://founders.archives.gov/documents/Adams/99-02 -02-1944; To John Adams from James McHenry, April 29, 1797, Founders

Online, National Archives, http://founders.archives.gov/documents /Adams/99-02-02-1950.

12. Timothy Pickering to John Adams, May 1, 1797, Founders Online, National Archives, http://founders.archives.gov/documents/Adams/99 -02-02-1954.

13. Thomas Jefferson to Heads of Departments, *PTJ*, 39:241.

14. Thomas Jefferson to Senate, January 11, 1803, *PTJ*, 39:312–13.

15. Thomas Jefferson to the Senate, March 5, 1801, *PTJ*, 33:188–189; Malone, *Jefferson the President, First Term*, 50–66; Cunningham, *The Process of Government under Jefferson*, 60–71.

16. Malone, *Jefferson the President, First Term*, 50–66; Cunningham, *The Process of Government under Jefferson*, 60–71.

17. John Adams to Elbridge Gerry, February 13, 1797, Founders Online, National Archives, http://founders.archives.gov/documents/Adams /99-02-02-1855.

18. John Adams to Abigail Adams, March 17, 1797, Founders Online, National Archives, http://founders.archives.gov/documents/Adams/99 -01-02-1351.

19. Oliver Wolcott Jr. to Alexander Hamilton, July 7, 1800, and September 3, 1800, *PAH*, 25:15–17; Stanley Elkins and Eric McKitrick, *The Age of Federalism* (New York: Oxford University Press, 1993), 596–662; Gordon S. Wood, *Empire of Liberty: A History of the Early Republic, 1789–1815* (Oxford: Oxford University Press, 2009), 239–275.

20. John Adams to United States Senate, February 10, 1799, Founders Online, National Archives, http://founders.archives.gov/documents/Adams/99-02 -02-3332; Carol Berkin, *A Sovereign People: The Crises of the 1790s and the Birth of American Nationalism* (New York: Basic Books, 2017), 193–199; Elkins and McKitrick, *The Age of Federalism*, 617–662.

21. Alexander Hamilton to George Washington, October 21, 1799, *PAH*, 23:544–547 n. 2; Elkins and McKitrick, *The Age of Federalism*, 617–662.

22. Alexander Hamilton to George Washington, October 21, 1799, *PAH*, 23:544–547 n. 2; Elkins and McKitrick, *The Age of Federalism,* 617–662.

23. Thomas Jefferson to Walter Jones, March 5, 1810, *PTJ*, Retirement Series, 2:272–274.

24. Notes on a Cabinet Meeting, May 15, 1801, *PTJ*, 34:114–115.

25. Robert Smith to W. C. Nicholas, January 9, 1807, in Leonard White, *The Jeffersonians: A Study in Administrative History, 1801–1829* (New York: Macmillan Company, 1951), 100; Malone, *Jefferson the President, First Term,* 50–66; Cunningham, *The Process of Government under Jefferson,* 60–71.

26. Caesar A. Rodney to Thomas Rodney, July 1, 1807, in Cunningham, *The Process of Government under Jefferson,* 56–57; Malone, *Jefferson the President, First Term,* 50–66; Cunningham, *The Process of Government under Jefferson,* 60–71.

Acknowledgments

MAYBE THERE ARE historians who can produce books without relying on the help of countless other scholars, but I've yet to meet one and I'm certainly not the first. My debts are so extensive that I will be repaying them for decades to come. Any acknowledgment of this book must start with Alan Taylor. Thank you for teaching me to write, eschewing jargon, allowing me to take my own path, and giving me a second chance when I needed it. Thank you for never lowering your standards, endlessly line-editing my work, and expecting ambition. Finally, thank you for encouraging me to work on a project that I loved and still love all these years later. I hope you are proud of this work.

I have been blessed with the guidance of a stable of wonderful, generous mentors. Graduate school can be a rough process under the best of circumstances, and I'm grateful for the support, both fiscally and emotionally, of the UC Davis History Department. Special thanks need to go to Ari Kelman for never sugarcoating anything and always treating me with bluntness and fairness. Eric Rauchway wrote me countless letters of support, read early drafts, and provided honest and constructive feedback. Going above and beyond, he always did so promptly and way before the deadline loomed—which, as anyone knows, is a huge gift.

So many wonderful "friend-tors" have blessed my career. Liz Covart has been a wonderful friend, mentor, fellow lover of dogs, and public history entrepreneur inspiration. She has been constantly generous with her time, connections, and knowledge. Gautham Rao welcomed me into the ranks of institutional historians when I was truly an impostor and has provided kindness, guidance, and comradery since. Joanne Freeman forgave my very late request and agreed to read my work, even as Hamilton was overtaking her schedule. Since then, she has served as an excellent model for how to write political history and write it well and with enthusiasm.

I have received the support of a number of institutions that made this project possible. I appreciate the Society of Cincinnati, the Robert H. Smith International Center for Jefferson Studies, and the Fred W. Wilson National Library for the Study of George Washington for believing in my work and encouraging my research. Special thanks to Tasha Stanton, Gaye Wilson, Christa Dierksheide, and Andrew O'Shaughnessy for including me in the family at ICJS. The Washington Library was my beloved home for six highly productive and enriching months. Michele Lee (now at the Folger Library) and Neal Millikan (now at the Massachusetts Historical Society) answered six months of random questions with patience and grace. Mary Jongema handled every crisis with serenity and encouraged me to share way too many dog photographs. Doug Bradburn led the library staff with excitement and passion for scholarship and public history. Thank you for promoting my work and including me in ongoing projects. Many of my close friends, co-panelists, and colleagues have come from my fellowship—it is truly the gift that keeps on giving.

It takes a village to raise a new scholar, and I've been fortunate to benefit from the knowledge and expertise of many established historians. These scholars were under no obligation to help me, but took time from their busy schedules because they are excellent and generous individuals. Johann Neem helped me understand historiography when I simply couldn't grasp what was being asked of me. He also graciously served as a reader of the book and offered encouragement and really helpful constructive feedback. While the second reader of this book has elected to remain anonymous, I'd like to thank them for their thorough, constructive feedback and rigorous approach to reviewing the manuscript. They went above and beyond. David Silverman answered my questions about graduate school with kindness and a healthy dose of reality back when a Ph.D. was a far-off dream. Tyler Anbinder was my first history mentor and is one of the kindest people I've ever met. Thank you for overseeing my first major history paper, providing me with history work when I was lost, and always being a trusted confidant.

I've met a number of extraordinary scholars during my time as a fellow at various institutions. Through her support, Karin Wulf has demonstrated that political history has a place in Vast Early America, which has been a real gift. Denver Brunsman is the most generous human I've ever met and has single-handedly provided me with some of the most fun experiences of my professional career. Rosie Zagarri has commented on more papers and panels than I can count—always with great attention to detail and constructive feedback, but also enthusiasm for my work. Many other fellows, students, and co-panelists have become lifelong friends as well. They provided companionship, inspiration, guidance, and support when needed. I would like to especially recognize Katlyn Carter, Erin Holmes, John Fea, Mary Mendoza, Lauren Duval, Kate Brown, Amy Hudson Henderson,

Elizabeth Grennan Browning, Melissa Gismondi, Shira Lurie, Alexi Garrett, Jonathan Gienapp, and Brandon Layton. As I prepared to submit my manuscript, Jim Ambuske read the entire thing and gave me helpful and hilarious feedback for no reason other than that he is an excellent chap.

My time as a postdoctoral fellow at the Center for President History at Southern Methodist University brought this book to life. Jeff Engel and Brian Franklin hosted a manuscript workshop for my book. The experience was painful, but the book is much better for it and the deadline was a powerful motivating force. They also read the book (multiple times) and supported my many revisions. Carol Berkin and Jack Rakove served as outside readers. They absolutely tore it apart and the book needed it. I hope they will see how much I brought their advice into the book. While at CPH, my fellow fellow and officemate, Blake, provided the best emotional support. He endured rants, swearing, and many salty moods. He always made me laugh and forgave my outbursts. Whitney Stewart and Ben Wright—you are my Dallas family. I'm so glad you are in my life. The CPH community is a lovely one, and I would be remiss if I didn't also thank Lizzie Ingleson, Kate Carte, and Edward Countryman for their comradery, advice, and encouragement.

My current colleagues at the White House Historical Association have cheered me on during the final stretches of revisions and editing. I am grateful for their shared excitement for the book and the opportunity to produce public history with them. It is wonderful to work in a place that values your scholarship.

I must thank Harvard University Press and my editor, Kathleen McDermott, for believing in this project and publishing the book. Kathleen immediately understood my vision for the book and has encouraged all of my lofty goals, for which I'm truly grateful. Thanks so much to Isabelle Lewis for creating the beautiful maps and for accommodating my rather last-minute request.

My family deserves my deepest thanks. My siblings patiently waited for me to wade through graduate school and forgave my frequent absences. They also gently poked fun when I carried around a library of books, and they brought necessary levity to my life. They have cheered me on as I worked through this book and shared it widely. I am grateful for such a wonderful support system. My grandparents prioritized education for their daughters long before it was the norm and established a family tradition accordingly. My parents deserve countless appreciation for their investment in my education, support during endless years of school, and for being my biggest fans from day one. Thank you for always believing (and proclaiming to anyone who would listen) that I was capable of pursuing all my dreams.

Finally, my own little family. Anyone who knows me knows that I'm obsessed with my dog, John Quincy Dog Adams. While I'm sure he'd prefer snacks or hikes in lieu of thanks, this book would not exist without him. It's impossible to get through a day without laughing when Quincy is around; he gave me structure, love, snuggles, and the occasional ego check when I needed it. He is my heart dog.

There are no words to adequately thank Jake, my editor in chief. You knew I was supposed to write this book and pursue this career long before I did—and as a result have lived with the General and the cabinet for many, *many* years. Thank you for reading every chapter of this book, for sending me across the country, for moving to crazy places with me, for always, *always* supporting my ambitions, and for reminding me that in life and scholarship, there are two options: keep cutting or get the shovel. Most of all, thank you for believing that I could tell the General's story, even when I wasn't so sure. I am forever grateful.

Index